W9-AMX-710

CULTURAL SECRETS AS NARRATIVE FORM

Storytelling in Nineteenth-Century America

Margaret Reid

The Ohio State University Press
Columbus

Library of Congress Cataloging-in-Publication Data

Reid, Margaret (Margaret K.)
Cultural secrets as narrative form : storytelling in nineteenth-century America / Margaret Reid.
p. cm.
Includes bibliographical references (p.) and index.
ISBN 0-8142-0947-5 (hardcover : alk. paper) — ISBN 0-8142-5118-8 (pbk. : alk. paper) —
ISBN 0-8142-9038-8 (CD-ROM) 1. American fiction—19th century—History and criticism.   2. Historical fiction, American—History and criticism. 3. Literature and
history—United States-History—19th century. 4. Storytelling—United States-History—19th
century. 5. Hawthorne, Nathaniel, 1804-1864. Scarlet letter. 6. Cooper, James Fenimore,
1789–1851. Spy. 7. Wister, Owen, 1860-1938. Virginian. 8. Culture in literature. 9. Narration
(Rhetoric) I. Title.
PS374.H5 R45 2004
813'.309358—dc22

                    2003023639

Cover design by Dan O'Dair.
Type set in Adobe Caslon.
Printed by Thomson-Shore Inc.

9   8   7   6   5   4   3   2   1

for my parents,
James D. Reid
and
Anne Donohue Reid

and in memory of their parents,
Agnes Carmody Donohue
Gerald Donohue
Katherine O'Leary Reid
Richard Reid

For here were God knew how many citizens, deliberately choosing not to communicate. . . . It was not an act of treason, nor possibly even of defiance. But it was a calculated withdrawal, from
the life of the Republic, from its machinery. . . . [T]his withdrawal was their own, unpublicized, private. Since they could not
have withdrawn into a vacuum (could they?) there had to exist
the separate, silent, unsuspected world.

—Thomas Pynchon, *The Crying of Lot 49*

CONTENTS

ACKNOWLEDGMENTS

I AM so happy to have the chance to offer my gratitude to those who have provided so many kindnesses to me. My deepest thanks are reflected in the dedication of this book to my parents, James D. Reid and Anne D. Reid; I thank them both for their boundless love and support and for the fact that they are remarkable individuals whom I deeply admire. I thank my brothers, too: Jim for his generous enthusiasm, and Jerry for being the finest friend I can imagine.

This book never could have come to be without the exceptional generosity, patience, and kindness beyond measure of Sacvan Bercovitch; to him I offer tremendous and particular gratitude.

During the course of this project, I have met extraordinary friends; of these I am especially grateful to Susan Mizruchi, Amelia Zurcher, Clifton Spargo, and George Justice. Their engagements with my work and comments on my writing—along with their pervasive qualities of intelligence, understanding, and humor—have kept me afloat during difficult times. I am grateful as well to Wai Chee Dimock, Philip Fisher, Christine Krueger, Albert Rivero, and Helen Vendler for years of encouragement, support, and advice. For their countless acts of generosity woven into our nearly lifelong friendships, I thank Kimberly Browne Martin, Dana Deubert, and Sandra Berardo. For lively discussions, friendship and support during the challenging years of graduate school, I am grateful to Allison Pingree and Debbie Lopez. Thank you, too, to Robert Cording, Philip Devlin, and Patrick Ireland, who provided me with crucial time and encouragement before the years of graduate study. In addition, I am happy to be able to thank those members of a new generation who have brought me much happiness during the years in which this book was written. In order of appearance: Sascha; Cassandra, Anthony and Luke; Story and Will; Claire and Catherine; and James Elijah.

Finally, I thank Heather Lee Miller, Karie Kirkpatrick, and the rest of the editorial staff of The Ohio State University Press for their support of this project, their patience, and their expertise.

INTRODUCTION
The Storyteller in American National
Romance

THREE immediately popular and long influential American historical romances, James Fenimore Cooper's *The Spy: A Tale of the Neutral Ground* (1821), Nathaniel Hawthorne's *The Scarlet Letter* (1850), and Owen Wister's *The Virginian: A Horseman of the Plains* (1902), share a certain narrative poetics: In the form and language of their narratives, these three texts represent nineteenth-century American culture by interweaving known and planned communal self-definitions (from celebrations of independence and cohesion to belief in manifest destiny) with fragmentary images of unremembered, even secret, historical moments. Layered with elements of romantic design and cultural mystery—layered so densely, in fact, that these symbolic polarities at times may be confused with one another—these novels are expressions of particular cultural moments sharing an impulse toward memory. Within these texts, memory is figured as the temporal and spatial codification of a passing time self-consciously lived as the end of an era. Building the monuments of national independence, America in 1821 was learning of the mortality of the revolutionary generation while also sensing the lasting power of that set of political events. Cooper's writings bear out his interest in this complex shift in cultural understanding.[1] Particularly in *The Spy*, Cooper offers an experiment in memory that points to both the closure of an age and the exhilaration of hope, even as accompanied by anxiety. Hawthorne (we know) wrote *The Scarlet Letter* with an anxious eye toward rising antebellum tensions;[2] his twin revivals of Puritanism and revolution as key historical themes place him at a somewhat different point (from Cooper) in the codification of memory. His work questions—for a breaking or broken nation—the efficacy of the fundamental, if now remote, paradigms through which his culture had been defined to date. Like Cooper in 1821, Owen Wister at the turn of the century writes a novel that is part of his contemporary culture's industry of monuments. From dime novels to the Buffalo Bill shows, Wister's United States eagerly consumed images designed to signal both celebration and nostalgia in the passing of the frontier. Each with some measure of celebration, these three authors put to work familiar gestures of closure, but not without surprisingly close attention to an anatomy of its costs.

The following chapters pursue the specifics of these cases in depth. These three major texts are products of similar moments, moments when the culture from which each emerged was suspended between the ability to receive and the ability to articulate newly updated and urgently needed stories of communal identity.[3] Each text, that is, suggests an understanding of itself as an expression of a world at a moment of transition. These are cultural moments imagined and predicted to be significant not only to their contemporary audiences but also to future generations. What characterizes each historical moment studied here is a sudden sense of times and places falling with more than ordinary speed into remoteness.

First, this argument is situated in the nationalism of the early nineteenth century, among the constructed memories of the revolutionary era at a time when so many of its major actors died; then I turn to the antebellum period, the challenges to that young nationalism in the name of homegrown ideological conflict. Finally, with Wister, the argument focuses on the reassessment of nationalism after the Civil War and expansionism, bolstered by a new mythos of the frontier West. As a whole, this book proposes that, by looking at the particular cases of these crucial moments in the first century of American fiction, we find among the layering of texts a revealing pattern. This emerging model for American cultural self-definition is rooted in a paradoxical dynamic between narrative designs and unspoken secrets.[4] Specifically, these secrets—while still unspoken—are textually rendered as moments from history that linger, without context, in present consciousness. In this silent but extraordinarily powerful sense, narrative designs and secret histories have combined in these landmark texts of American historical fiction to generate stories so deeply rooted in cultural consciousness that they may function as archetypes.[5]

The evolution of these archetypal stories begins with the persistence of those irreducible fragments or traces of past experience, unerased by even the most determined of narrative designs. Such historical fragments are carried into present consciousness, meeting with it necessarily (at first) in moments of silent reception. Once recognized (even if in this silence), these fragments continue to be surprisingly resistant to present understanding. In this encounter there emerges a profound epistemological crisis both for the particular cultural moment into which such fragments arrive and for later readers as well. For the immediate (contemporaneous) audience, this crisis offers two choices: the choice to remain in silence, turning from the unknown, or to accept such ambiguity and thus to move into a process of interpretation of uncertain depth and breadth, in search of stories to explain the mystery at hand; these texts mandate the latter response. Similarly, later readers may receive the moment of this crisis by reversion to familiar answers[6] or, again, by an acceptance of the open-endedness of interpretation; again, a full reading of these texts makes the latter response compulsory. For both early and later audiences, the outlines of these central archetypal American stories lie between that crisis and these interpretive responses.[7] The archetype formed in this suspended state of *betweenness* derives its raw (represented as fragmentary) subject matter from the words surrounding it and finds the shape of its particular incarnation as it emerges into a field of silences, an altogether different dimension of human expression.

Placing this pattern in the context of these crucial moments in the development of nineteenth-century American self-consciousness, specifically within the growth of literary nationalism,[8] this book moves from Cooper (by many estimations, the country's first successful—not to mention best-selling—novelist) to Hawthorne (a figure of centrality in his own literary world as well as in virtually all assessments of U.S. literary history), and finally to Wister (the presumed inventor of the Western). These three examples offer connections suggestive of one sweeping tradition of American self-definition. In turn, the connections among the three texts suggest a trajectory of narrative method, indicative of recurrent techniques used at the height of America's adoption of the historical romance as a vehicle to imagine national identity—techniques common within the canonical tradition to which all three authors belong. However, the identification of such a pattern is meant neither to ignore countless intervening moments lying along this historical path nor to deny the presence of other compelling traditions. These remain, then, first and foremost, examples—primarily sites of depth rather than breadth.

My argument proceeds through attention to the peculiar narrative poetics inherent to the representation of the indecipherable life of Cooper's Spy, the Scarlet Letter, discarded in the dusty corner of the custom house attic, and the elusive, impersonal agency that provides Wister's West a power long lost from American symbolic thought by the time he animates it in his turn-of-the-century hero. I hope this study will provide an anatomy of the imaginative layering between agency and language in the process of accumulating cultural archetypes, myths, and legends.

This project necessarily works from traces. Part of my argument is that the images these traces suggest—images so central to national iconography (an understanding of revolution embodied in the Spy, Hester Pyrnne's manifest knowledge of divisions within her culture, and the Virginian's experiential awareness of the changing West)—never gain more than fragmentary narrative life in the texts themselves. In fact, it is precisely because they are (and necessarily must remain) in exile from a context that would supply ready meaning to them that these historical traces grow (between and among the narrative designs employed to frame them) into stories with almost mythic power. In these examples from the American tradition of historical fiction, such fragments of the past escape or otherwise resist the designs of romance. And yet, here they become the single most powerful tool in the writer's ability to link remote history to present culture: They become archetypal imaginings shaped among patterns of narrative silence, the failures of language.

The ways in which readers may fill out—reimagine—these traces are temporally bound, determined by the functions of language within immediate history. But the transtemporal life of these imaginings is not so limited; these traces and the silences enveloping them eventuate in archetypal stories which may be reclassified as secrets.[9] Thus those moments of cultural transition that give rise to each of these texts are recast most effectually not in plot or character, but in these secrets. Those cultural transitions, then, are indicated metonymically, in the formal patterns of expression that reveal the limits of the symbolic vocabulary, as it exists at the level of plot romance. From among these silences comes a critique of the resolutions of romance. And this critique speaks to ongoing patterns involved in establishing the common texts of cultural knowledge, putting at issue questions of historiography and agency, communal and individual.

THE FORM OF THE PROBLEM

History is vulnerable to the narrative tricks by which both personal and communal memory operate, and it is a critical commonplace to note that the subjectivity of memory restructures history, whether by intention, misfortune, or chance. This process is inevitably distorting, but it is also liberating and even necessary: Borges's "Funes the Memorious" lies incapacitated by a memory so thorough and compelling that remembered time is equal to, or greater than, lived time; the filters of memory—indeed our failures to remember—are all that we have to free us from that fate.[10] There is a certain predictability in the transformations that history undergoes as it enters larger cultural narratives. Less predictable are the shifts in the designs of those ongoing narratives at the points of reception—points of entry as residual fragments of disorderly histories rupture established patterns. One effect, I argue, is that as these fragments enter memory, long-hidden stories of past experience may be reanimated. In the matrices formed by the crossings of transmission and reception, latent patterns are newly outlined. Tales and events that did not fit the evolving shape of historical memory may be glimpsed, whether minimally or more deeply, though the mediating lens of contemporary culture always remains. The accumulation in this lens of a palimpsest, newly inscribed at every reading, demonstrates that in this way, narrative designs, long known for their powers to manipulate history, are shaped by the histories they may be said to subsume. In Hans Blumenberg's terms, "mythicization does not make historical facts and identities disappear so much as it makes them become one, and be consumed, in the typical and the figural."[11] My argument is that a similar process is at work in the historical romances that are at the center of this book. These texts attend to the process of national "mythicization" by taking several of the culture's most sacred subjects as their bases, and in this process, these texts demonstrate both that the secrets of history are never gone and that the designs of narrative never fail absolutely; those designs simultaneously obscure and reveal the ambiguities of each historical legacy.

Layered with popular imaginings, the rhetoric of high art, and the experiences of history, the three novels studied here are thus built upon two codes of cultural expression, first on their apparent separation and then by their persistent bond. As I have been suggesting, these codes may be defined as (1) narrative design, a consciously devised system of meaning, most concretely associated with plot and its resolutions, including those generically associated with the romance; and (2) secret histories, eluding representation in speech or action, meanings not readily transmissible through the operations of referential language.[12]

This second level of expression is related closely to Walter Benjamin's notion of a "storyteller's story."[13] From Plato through the present day, literary theory has recognized the difference between the means and subject of representation. With a power greater than that of narrative design, Benjamin's story marks a form of expression in which the gap between means and subject is—in defiance of all of our expectations—somehow eclipsed or suspended. In the texts studied here, that gap is never suspended fully, yet it partakes in degree of the phenomenon Benjamin explores. Here the gaps between means and subject speak not of the separation between signifier and signified but rather of their peculiar bond in which history and language are fused. In these texts, secret histories eluding narrative representation are fostered and protected in the very matrices of the romance form.

I imagine this alternative layer of cultural self-expression as the product of those crafted conditions of silence—that is to say, outlined by the borders of the very secrets that the codified narratives of national identity refuse to include. This narrative poetics allows for a theoretical space within particularly aesthetic language that might be figured as an imaginative (and temporal) distance between raw experience and narrative record. In these spaces are stories with distinctly temporal dimensions—including process, motion, and growth—as opposed to their framing narratives of reconciliation and ordered design.[14] They exist just beyond the frontier of cultural expression, and there they have the capacity to embody the outer (and the innermost) limits of the meaning of America, up to and including the present moment, the imaginary reconfiguration of that moment, and the new horizon, precisely as it appears to the present moment's eye. The space of the storyteller's story is, then, a field of silence, secrecy, and multivalent power.[15]

This argument enters into a long-running critical discussion of the defining attributes of the genre of the historical romance, including especially the role of Walter Scott.[16] In these analyses of genre, most critics have attended first to what they have seen as the often uncomfortable juxtaposition of past and present in the making and reading of historical fiction.[17] It would be difficult to list all of the definitions and genealogies that have been offered for this genre.[18] Critics agree, however, that this is a richly international tradition that marks its innovations in form through literary representations of historical moments, designed to create something of a living past, as Scott was able to do, in "giv[ing] living human embodiment to historical-social types. . . . [N]ever before had this kind of portrayal been consciously set at the center of the representation of reality."[19] In particular, critical attention has been focused on the model of the hero in Scott's fiction, the "mediocre hero," as Lukács calls him, in contradistinction to the "world-historical man" of Hegelian theory.[20] Among the innovations supplied by the *Waverly*-hero, critics have been particularly interested in studying the interplay of character and context.[21] These textual moments provide among the sharpest contrasts to other kinds of literary-historical writings, such as those of Bulwer-Lytton, one of Scott's more outspoken detractors, who emphasized the quantity and accuracy of historical data in his narratives as a measure of their success.[22]

In his foundational Marxist analysis, Georg Lukács has made a strong argument for an almost precise moment of the emergence of historical fiction as it came to be known in the nineteenth century; he sees the form emerge at the time of "Napoleon's collapse." Lukács's study places Scott as the exemplar of a new mode of historical consciousness that lifted representation of character and context out of the "mere costumery" of earlier confluences of history and fiction.[23] The historical novel as Scott created it, Lukács argues, is the product of revolutionary social forces (specifically in France), in which "the national idea [became] the property of the broadest masses."[24] It is not within the scope of this study to offer a new argument for the genealogy of the historical romance, but two points should be made for clarification. First, I accept Lukács's pinpointing of the emergence of the form in a general sense; his work helps me theorize the roles of revolution and nationalism in the development of American literature. However, the historical romance, in my argument, is less the property of "the broadest masses" than an image—perhaps illusory—of the promised link between the nation's population and its political establishment. I claim that the cultural function of the nineteenth-century American historical romance works in the service of an ideological mainstream more than in the service of any alternative subculture.[25] Second, I argue that in each nation, the achievement of the high literary form of the historical romance is shaped not only by the richness of international dialogue but also, very distinctly, by local traditions, including the folk tale.[26]

In addition to genealogical arguments, the seemingly simple task of assigning a label to what I have been referring to (interchangeably) as historical romance or historical fiction has been a point of controversy. Many critics have insisted upon the distinction between these categories, commonly citing long-standing conventions of romance (stock situations and characters, for example) as generic markers.[27] Part of my argument, however, is that the texts included in this study are decidedly hybrid in form, and so I take my cue from George Dekker and others, who have objected to the sharp delineation "between novel and romance" insofar as they existed in the nineteenth century in particular; I work from Dekker's premise that to call "a novel a 'historical romance' is therefore to direct attention to its extraordinarily rich, mixed, and even contradictory or oxymoronic character."[28] In this tradition it will not be surprising to see this mixed genre exercise has both didactic and patriotic functions as well as potentially subversive ones as it draws audiences closer to the history it represents and then ultimately resists full identification with that historical moment's corollary ideological principles.

One of the early commentators on (and practitioners of) historical fiction, the Italian writer Alessandro Manzoni, wondered that the historical novel ever succeeded at all (though he agreed that it did); his concern was its formal dissonance, which he felt left readers utterly without ground for satisfying interpretation, placing them instead in a decidedly uncomfortable space of suspension between acceptance and doubt as they received the tale.[29] In a sense I agree: The layering of fiction and history together, I argue, increases rather than decreases the narrative spaces of uncertainty. However, this infusion of further mystery into the representation of history does not necessarily have to become a means of increasing the culture's distance from historical consciousness. It may be that precisely this vacillation proves deeply productive of cultural imaginings;[30] surely that is what is suggested by the counterintuitive combination of radical plot discontinuities with exceptional cultural popularity, to which the three texts this project analyzes bear witness. This is not to say that all known aesthetic flaws in historical romance must eventually be recast as strengths; rather I suggest that the characteristic of narrative dissonance, in particular circumstances and at particular times, has functioned as an alternative aesthetic in which historical consciousness and imaginative richness may be knit together as complementary rather than oppositional and in which, despite all conventional understanding, it is not the element of fiction but of historical experience—the fragmentary story—that carries with it the weight of distortion and mystery.

It is true, however, that the emphasis on hybridity risks obscuring one strong legacy of the criticism of historical literature, the argument that a literary frame to historical events is a curative attempt, a move toward filling in the gaps in historical certainty.[31] Indeed it is clear that, at some level, the conventional plot of the romance in such texts is a code set up to transform and so to resolve the disruptions of culture.[32] But within the examples at hand, plot—as it interacts with its historical subjects in Cooper, Hawthorne, and Wister—does something more. We expect (and find) that the romance has certain capacities to redirect the energies of disorder and secrecy toward order and design. Beyond this, however, the romance, in Cooper, Hawthorne, and Wister, *condenses* cultural memory within its layers, endowing those memories with an extraordinary and concentrated power as they enter a larger frame of cultural knowledge.[33] As the romance preserves and transmits more than the designs of its resolution, it gives expression to that second powerful cultural voice, containing its own secrets and repressions. As the subjects of this book's attention suggest, this second voice can be woven within the official romance of popular classics that address central cultural shifts. There, because it is thus both pervasive and concealed, it may be said to create a textual interplay wherein a nationalistic literature addresses itself in the unarticulated alternatives, the silent stories, contained within these romances of national identity.

A vivid figure for such a space as imagined within the tradition of the American historical romance is the attic of Hawthorne's old Salem Custom House, harboring a story long ago lived but not yet told.[34] Gordon Hutner notes Hawthorne's propensity for secrecy—particularly for exploring "the effect of secrecy as an animating, ineluctable condition for his fictions"[35]—and indeed, it is America's secret, and the culture's imagined harboring of Hester's secret, that animates *The Scarlet Letter*. Once found in that attic, Hawthorne's scarlet *A* compels storytelling in a complicated and troublesome way: It is an artifact of cultural history, but it has not found a place in a museum or library; it is an emblem of personal experience, but it has not survived within any familiar context, as, for example, a family heirloom. Instead, the place of the *A* in the Custom House attic suggests that—as an artifact—it hovers just at the outer reaches of the narrator's interpretive responsibility. At once too hot to hold and too oblique to read, the scarlet *A* is an aggressively material fragment of history that must be understood in its inadequate present context as the trace of something more. The predicament Hawthorne's narrator faces as he picks up the Scarlet Letter is the unique predicament inhering in the field of vision both central to and silent within the narrator's created textual space. From Benjamin, then, I call the agent of this space the American storyteller, whose task it becomes first to transmit a story into a context at once stiflingly familiar and perilously foreign and then to find (whether through recognition or construction) places in communal memory that can accommodate not only the historical fragment, but also its remote context, its story.

By all measures, a storyteller's story represents a certain disturbance of narrative regularity. Story exists within the narrative as a vision or belief distinct from plot design and inheres in the consciousness of a character marginalized from the world of plot while privileged (because immersed) in the knowledge of the inner workings of the fiction's historical world. The storyteller, then, is a character to whom many things happen in the present tense of the fiction, but who is, for all of this, relatively undetermined by such events and whose voice and vision remain obscured within narrative expression, linked most essentially to an inaccessible time. Thus a story in this sense is a testament to the persistence of those meanings that can never be articulated, to the insufficiency of selective memory, and (implicitly) to the imagination's dependence upon the whole of history. Likewise, a storyteller in this sense stands in direct contrast to a narrator who obsessively plots a design (as Faulkner's Thomas Sutpen does, a map to make whole the fragments of a broken life); the storyteller has direct access to a vision that permeates the culture while remaining inexpressible without referent or mediation.

Because it exists beyond linguistic representation, the story remains a secret, defying traditional limitations inherent in representation. Nonetheless, the story does not stand as absolute alterity against the designs of romance, either. Instead, the story is a product of the narrative that it may seem to (and does) oppose. As narrative records the designs of particular moments within the culture, an unedited (because untold) repository stores the discarded images. From this unedited space of memory (which is not unlike the mind of Borges's Funes), only particular images will emerge, even in their silent and then fragmentary form; these images are those that become recurrently useful to the cultural imagination. Thus both the place of this repository in cultural consciousness and the persistence of particular images together create an imaginative space for the new language emergent *within* the romance, the language of the story. Although the present study is limited to particular examples, part of my hypothesis is that this repository—collectively speaking, and moving beyond the bounds of the cases set forth here—creates a dynamic structure within a large mainstream tradition of American romance and in doing so serves as a type of fulfillment of the plan for a national language, an alternative mode of expression.

I take the term "national language" from Noah Webster's *Dissertations on the English Language* (1789), which both in date and in spirit coincides with the inception of this narrative experiment; here a national language is a means of collective expression designed to unite and affirm a political and social community, a public language inviting and even compelling participation. Webster's appeal for a "new" language, Federal English, was entwined consistently and deeply with the evolution of an American literary tradition. As for Webster, so in the model of cultural storytelling I am presenting, the strength of this American language is a product of its newness, its distinction from inheritance (including the mechanics of plot, largely derived from continental and British historical romance), and its fusion with the experiential record of the country. By locating a conjunction of design and language—cultural unity and the imagination—within the particular political, literary, and linguistic context of Webster's project, I suggest that the narrative model studied here establishes a legacy of similar concerns.[36]

Certainly the establishment of any self-consciously new culture brings about an immediate need for a language that will fit both present and projected patterns of experience, and Webster's Federalist perspective is one among many to express this broad concern. In his celebratory *American Primer*, Walt Whitman emphasizes the futurity of language's promise, its ability to shadow forth meanings for which the world is not yet ready: "I put many things on record that you will not understand at first—perhaps not in a year—but they must be (are to be) understood."[37] Before the new language becomes a fixed system, there are multiple possibilities for the definitions of social forms and cultural roles, and these definitions will be not only reflective, but also in some measure determinative. The case of postrevolutionary America bears additional complications, and for Cooper, Hawthorne, and Wister the role of the American historical romance is forged in this complexity. As early as 1789, in his *Dissertations,* Webster argues pragmatically for the importance of usage as opposed to rule in the establishment of an American grammar. By 1828—in his preface to the first edition of his *Dictionary*—he goes further, arguing not only that differences between American and British uses of the English language are based on customary usage but also that they grow out of national ideas and principles themselves: "Language is the expression of ideas; and if the people of one country cannot preserve an identity of ideas, they cannot retain an identity of language."[38] Thus it is that those objects and ideas that are not (or would not be) changed in form or function in the Atlantic crossing remain stable in the English language, and yet those concepts considered foreign to British practice, particularly those pertaining to American political and social abstractions, would require not only new vocabulary and grammar, but also—particularly—new stories in which to unfold the fullness of their meaning. The English language in America, then, becomes a system with balanced, oppositional, functions dependent upon one another. As language functions in established communities, English in postrevolutionary America disseminates some conformity of understood meaning; it is this stability that marks the formal properties of narrative romance. As language functions in its earliest emergence in community, though, American English also carries tremendous potential for free speculation, promising a future of almost limitless change in consensually defined meanings; such promise of change links American English to the layer of narrative expression here associated with the American storyteller.

With these framing concerns, this project explores the shaping powers of carefully crafted conditions of silence and finds in them another layer of storytelling, a layer at once alternative to, and yet still generative of, codified narratives of national emergence. Following from Webster's theories on language, it is no surprise that among the key functions of this second layer of storytelling is the expression of cultural anxieties about language itself, its narrative powers, and its limits in the task of cultural self-definition.

NARRATIVE FORM AND HISTORICAL CONTEXT

The storyteller's vision,[39] of course, would provide no cultural function if it were only receptive, trapped in a moment of inarticulate wonder or fright. It finds its cultural function by offering glimpses from a darker, more complicated world, a realm beyond pure hope: In such particular settings of cultural transition, these romances convey in their confusion a vision of urgency, of a time when history faces the familiar symbols of its culture and sees nothing of itself in the reflection. As a narrative construct, the storyteller reacts to this radical disjunction by offering an alternative, a world not reflective of the known but of something at least as important to cultural consciousness. The storyteller's world is one of history, symbol, and metonymy—but now newly defined through the promise of full (though deferred and unspoken) transmission. In order to perform the work of culture, the storyteller does not revise but instead fully absorbs all angles of vision. No purified version of the culture's foundation can replace the facts of its historical experience and still generate the American story. The immediacy of these experiences makes them sacred to the culture and, paradoxically, that immediacy is what the storyteller promises to restore to communal consciousness.

Thus the storyteller—with the story itself—has an ambiguous relation to narrative, being both necessary and threatening to the continuity of culture. The storyteller adds temporal complexity to the imaginative act of retrospection, helping to theorize the relationship between memory and projective cultural imaginings. Narrative conveys the known text of cultural mythology and so may include any established model for self-knowledge—for example, the ideals remembered from the revolutionary past. Requiring understanding and planning for their articulation, narrative designs suggest an essentially retrospective mode of vision.[40] By definition the secret histories within these designs are already encoded, though within a narrative frame not yet ready to acknowledge them.[41] So in this book's examples, there is never a moment when narrative exists alone; the story generated as a countervoice is present from the start of the retrospective imagining. This fundamental paradox is a reminder that the revelation of the story may not be easy or benign, but that in any case it will be disquietingly relevant. In *The Crying of Lot 49*, Thomas Pynchon's central character, Oedipa Maas, wonders about the "Tristero," the seemingly omnipresent and subversive communication system that provides a postmodern figure for the American story:

Would its smile, then, be coy, and would it flirt away harmlessly backstage, say goodnight with a Bourbon Street bow and leave her in place? Or would it instead, the dance ended, come back down the runway, its luminous stare locked to Oedipa's, smile gone malign and pitiless; bend to her alone among the desolate rows of seats and begin to speak words she never wanted to hear?[42]

Like the Tristero, both enticing and threatening in its assumed role as potential truth teller, the American stories imagined through the narrative forms of the three romances studied here always seem to be lurking rather ominously *and* promisingly close to the surface of things. Like Pynchon's Oedipa, the storytellers in (and the readers of) Cooper, Hawthorne, and Wister find themselves amid an ocean of historical clues without assurance of revelation.

If we imagine the romance's formal properties to play the role of the director of the stage play onto which the Tristero makes its appearance in Oedipa's imagination in the passage just quoted, the conflicts of power between narrative and story may become clearer. In the scene described we assume the conventions of theater, where the director may at one level have determinative control over the performance, but only with the consent of the players. If in Pynchon's vision, the Tristero is an actor with an equal ability to defer to or to defy the script and stage directions, so too is the story an imaginative space over which its framing narrative has only illusory control. In this sense the narrative is relegated to the status of a narrowly utopian mode of language working as a defensive impulse toward abstract order, a design to protect the culture from "words [it] never wanted to hear." This level of abstract narration seeks to present an orderly world, but its methods prove insufficient, even damaging, to that ideal.

To encode history's secrets within cultural consciousness, language must work both historically and imaginatively, never presenting a finished world. Only in the submerged development of the alternative story (generated in the constant interaction of the secret and the design containing it) can language unite subject and representation, history and imagination. The innately defensive designs of narrative, then, generate and encode an alternative system of meaning, and that alternative provides—within each of the romances studied here—a new cultural story beyond the romance of history. In each text the new cultural story is figured as a mystery, shaped by the *potential* revelations that might be given through the vision and language of one key consciousness, if only the narrative would allow the full emergence of that perspective.[43]

When it does emerge, the storyteller's story—even unrealized— prompts a reconception of cultural self-definition.[44] For example, despite its elusiveness as a fixed image, the America that Cooper's Spy clearly would have known is far more complicated than either the domestic romance or the revolutionary ideals that design the narrative. The Spy's America includes both of these worlds, as he moves in and out of them, but it also includes whatever lies between them—the hidden threats, the secrets, the possibility of the imminent destruction of either ideal. Thus it is surprising that the same cultural consciousness that designs the orderly narrative may benefit from this more powerful form of language. Obsolete dreams, ineffective abstractions, mistakes of the culture: All of these may be infused with the story, America itself, as it has been imagined *and* lived. This infusion brings with it the possible fulfillment of both promise and threat, of both symbolic national identity and historical self-knowledge: At one extreme is the static ideal, a purified past and present, at the cost of a life in time; at the other extreme is the negation of symbolic value, a bare acceptance of life void of imaginative reconfiguration. Only as two inextricable components of one sustained cultural language can these forms of self-knowledge foster cultural identity without paralysis or destruction.

With the strong recurring pattern of this symbolic method, American literature—even its most mainstream components—is ensured moments, at least, of sharp awareness of alternative realities, an awareness that one layer of discourse challenges yet still sustains the next. Moreover, within these narrative designs, structural divisions—the isolations of codes of consciousness—warn about the sacrifices of this awareness, the price of living and seeing the culture as a storyteller must. When the storyteller, like Cooper's Spy or Hawthorne's Hester, dies, the dangers of such consciousness are transfigured: While some dangers are resolved in the death of their agent, the inheritance these characters then leave is quite different, as it becomes—potentially—the cultural privilege of a transmissible promise left to the community. Death clearly denies the agency of language from one subject—thus creating yet another remove, or layer, that must ultimately lie in between experience and narrative. Yet it also enables the authority of countless different—but not necessarily less powerful—agents of language *about* that subject. This proliferation of tales is the storyteller's private, perhaps quite reluctant, inheritance left to the social world.[45]

In this model, though, the storyteller is a creature whose knowledge has an agency transcending its original context: This is to say, a storyteller may fail to communicate, or a story may never find a storyteller, yet there will be a legacy still, even if that legacy is only the knowledge of an intangible loss, the final alienation of cultural mystery from narrative design. This is the emptiness that Pynchon's novel explores. The Tristero has not found a storyteller in Oedipa; Oedipa ends the story as she began, hardly overwhelmed with knowledge. Nevertheless, the novel has demonstrated that there is a space—a "vacuum," as Pynchon terms it. Into that space, unable to imagine nothingness, character and reader alike infer—perhaps even infuse—the existence of "the separate, silent, unsuspected world," the idea of an abstraction—not a human being—but an abstraction with an agency of its own, which must be responsible for the manifest "withdrawal from the life of the Republic," and the all-too-clear weakness of the known world of narrative.

In short, this project centers on cases in which the consummate agent, the storyteller, is associated with silence rather than with revelation, and this silent agency finally proves to be the fundamental source of power for a certain kind of transmission of story. It is of course not a transmission without loss, but still it is a transmission of the unspoken into a form more easily told and retold. By preserving historical secrets and still soliciting belief in that unrevealed story by way of uncovering its persistent and fragmentary life in the novel's present consciousness, the culture has shaped narrative silence into yet another layer of expression, a deeply, even archetypally, powerful layer, which indeed may function as the foundation of a new—because more richly layered—cultural story. Through an analysis of this process, this book aims to contribute to work on the material and theoretical problems of the roles of experience, language, and secrecy in cultural self-definition.

CULTURAL SECRECY IN THE FIRST CENTURY OF AMERICAN ROMANCE

Each of the three major texts studied here—in differing degrees and combinations—enjoyed some prompt and sustained popularity from literary critics and the reading public at large. In fact, each is remembered today as a landmark in American literary history. Their fictional-historical worlds, in different ways, are just at the limits of their contemporary culture's knowledge and understanding. They record scenes too old for reliable memory, too new to fit into familiar patterns of nostalgia. Each of the three novels represents a crisis in American self-consciousness through a figurative use of the struggle for justice; the American story thus becomes, metaphorically, an arena of competing narratives over which troubling ideals of authority preside, with apparently random power.[46] Because the cultural secret, or the story, remains shrouded in silence while the surrounding knowable worlds of narrative crumble, it may appear to be a curative alternative, a *truth* within a web of lies. Indeed, for as long as they remain less than fully unmasked, secrets invite just such faith;[47] in this way, within my argument, the secret's call to belief allows the story to *function* as a truth ironically precisely through its silent indeterminacy.

The storyteller, then, whose province is that realm of cultural secrecy, invites interpretation as a prophet of sorts by representing a particular knowledge of mystery and gaining strength from that silent undercurrent to the text. The Spy, Hester Prynne, and the Virginian are associated with powers of language peculiar in their world. In order for us to accept that the plots of these novels unfold as they do, we must assume that these characters know more than they tell. Thus by contrast these storytellers point to the linguistic incapacity of their communities. Each in a different way, these characters escape from the confines of design set up by the structure of romance and the narrator's interest. Cooper's novel provides an example of the active creation of such a textual strategy. Hawthorne's novel addresses the complexities of sustaining it, beyond the reliable but outworn tools of nostalgia or progressive historiography. Finally, in Wister's novel, the strategy recoils upon itself, as the deliberate creation of a mythic American mystery ironically drains that mystery of its intrigue. Cooper's Spy derives his particular historical knowledge in the dark forests of the Neutral Ground; Hawthorne's Hester nurtures her untold story on the outskirts of Puritan Boston. But when Wister's Virginian travels beyond the narrative eye, he falls mysteriously and perilously close to death. Seeking too much control, a mastery over the now distinctly separate realm of history's secrets, the cowboy thus loses his capacities as an American storyteller, and he must leave the realm of story, now free (or doomed) to seek peace in the romance.

All of this suggests development in the narrative mode addressed here, as it is incarnated from Cooper onward. In its early forms this formal model is identifiable through certain literalizations of the idea of narrative silence: For instance, there is no place for the Spy in what Cooper calls the "visible space" of the narrative world, and this makes sense.[48] Despite being the focus of the narrative, he is a spy, and so his mere existence is a radical intrusion on an orderly system—even if that orderly system is figured here as the system of war. As the manifest existence of such intrusion, the Spy bears witness to the existence of a second, necessarily abstract (because unknown), world. The sacrifice of his life may be read (on one level, at least) as martyrdom, but though his own life ends, there remains the haunting presence of the world to which his life bore witness, figured particularly in the random, frequent, and cruel moments of violence that are scattered with surprising frequency over the romance.

Later examples remind us that not all storytellers face (or even seem to face) their silent exile, their sacrifice of subjectivity to the cause of a cultural consciousness, with the humble devotion of a patriotic government agent. Some are merely human, and their frailties are all too clear as they fail to break free from an elaborate linguistic trap. They may be characters who want love, as Hawthorne's Hester does, or an escape to a new history, as Wister's cowboy does. In these cases the demands placed on the storytellers may have effects that are more profoundly compromising, even tragic, at least to the storytellers and perhaps to their culture as well. Nevertheless, even with the shift toward ever more costly forms of heroism, the narrative designs encoding the life of the storyteller remain strong. In fact the narrative desire to map an orderly world apparently only gains strength from the disquieting vision of an inconsistent world, a world where martyrdom may not be much more than death. Narrative designs work harder each time these challenges arise, and those competing codes—the narrative maps and the untold stories they cover—still suppress and generate the emergent story.

The Spy, martyred to his country's revolution; Hester, drained of passion, "a living sermon against sin"; the Virginian, a cowboy-turned-capitalist, husband, and father: In their one-dimensional forms, these central characters promise a certain reliable iconic value to the developing system of symbolic thought throughout nineteenth-century America, images celebratory of national achievement and cautionary about the futility of defiance. Those primary symbolic functions, however, work only because they have been textually predetermined to be misappropriations of complex identities. In each case the power of the icon rests in those fragments of identity that escape symbolic representation; these icons wield imaginative power precisely to the degree that they resist interpretation, turning their culture back upon itself, to question the workings of its developing cultural stories.

This is first a relation that the respective authors and their texts have with the cultures into which they write, but it is also a compact with an unknown future of readers sharing certain mythic expectations. Public interpretation—and the storyteller's resistance to it—provide the means of studying some of the complex ties between human agency and language. The agent and language cannot be linked directly; in the development of cultural stories, it is necessary to build layers between experience and its narratives, just as in the reading of such narratives, it becomes necessary to do the archeological work of finding those layers, searching the palimpsests within each text, and in so doing, discovering surprising links as well as predictable distances.[49] That necessity, and an anatomy of its workings, are topics of central concern in this book. Within the texts studied, those layers must make some dramatic, if not impossible, connections:

These narrative layers, I argue, link the Spy's world of meaningless violence with the patriotism his martyred body suggests; Hester's life of passion with the penance inscribed by the *A;* and the Virginian's ventures
beyond the reaches of the law with the evolution of civilization in the
American West. These examples provide models of a mode of reading that
offers a new fullness to the interconnections of aesthetic and historical
concerns; I hope the connections will suggest, if not a dominant tradition,
at least a recurrent strategy of representation in nineteenth-century America worthy of sustained attention.

The first section of the book begins with a study of the designs of popular romance in two widely circulated and well-known tales of the revolutionary experience in New York—the mysterious and violent death of Jane
McCrea, a loyalist sympathizer, and the colonial army's execution of John
André, a British spy. Through an analysis of divergent accounts in newspapers, pamphlets, histories, and dramas and of the emergence of their stories in historical romance, I argue that the cultural work of these tales
includes not only the creation of symbolic forms to be used in a new
national story, but also the representation of a persistent voice of history
that will not allow for new beginnings or self-constructed origins. This
*un*reconciled dimension of the legends—the losses inexplicable within the
teleological design of nationhood—becomes the deepest resource for
Cooper's construction of historical memory in *The Spy.* What is at stake
for Cooper and his surrounding culture in these stories is the possibility of
reconceiving the American revolution as less the consensual product of
public documents or the collective producer of the shared understanding
of monuments, than at once the product and producer of conflicting and
often personal energies. I argue that these unreconciled losses are refigured
as historical secrets.

To explore themes of revolution from the perspective of a nation on the
brink of Civil War rather than a nation immersed in its first age of monu-
mental memory, I turn my attention to Nathaniel Hawthorne, another
central figure in the American canon, influential in his own day and continuously counted as a classic American author. In this second section of
the book I focus less on the thematic and formal establishment of this
secret dimension of history emergent from the relations between disorderly experience and patterned story and pursue instead its particular
workings within the competing historiographies of *The Scarlet Letter.*

This analysis begins with a reading of Hawthorne's "Gray Champion"
(1835), a tale in which this (secret, silent) form of American history is
embodied in one mysterious human figure who returns from a particularly
complicated past. The New England tradition behind this tale of an exiled

regicide judge, living secretly somewhere outside of the known community and well beyond the natural span of human life, evolves to connect the story's present day to several of the most unsettling episodes in early American history: In effect, the Gray Champion's life story links the Puritan revolution and regicide, the New England witchcraft crisis, King Philip's War, and the American revolution. As Hawthorne reemploys them, these seventeenth-century contexts are recast as nineteenth-century tales; through these age-old legends with strong cultural currency in the antebellum years, these contexts become central to *The Scarlet Letter.*

Hawthorne's participation in the development of this legend, so particularly well suited to the narrative concerns of secret history, thus begins in his early writings and, I argue, culminates in *The Scarlet Letter,* a novel built upon a richly ambiguous theory of history's secrets. By way of return to the legend, then, the ambiguous historiography of the novel reaches toward another (surprisingly material) layer of meaning. Writing at a volatile intersection among the (often politically diverse) historical theories influential in his culture, from Clarendon's long-established story of Puritanism to contemporary nationalist and progressivist visions such as George Bancroft's, the crisis of Hawthorne's world is historiography itself, the pursuit of a story of national founding and continuity that might withstand the growing pressures of civil unrest. Hawthorne interrogates these models, showing the role of history within cultural consciousness to be both less predictable than a cyclical model would suggest and more relentless than the progressivist understanding of linear models can explain. His figure of history is trapped between worlds and so causes surprising shifts that challenge either mode of thought; in *The Scarlet Letter* as in his short stories, the most potent forms of history may be imagined as material artifacts, including the person-made-artifact in the figure of the mythic "Gray Champion": an exile who secretly returns to (and then insistently lingers near) a community not yet ready to accommodate his reintegration.

Moments of founding and threats to continuity invite imaginative acts of closure, and these characterize the studied texts of Cooper and Hawthorne respectively. A new context for closure surrounds the subject of the third section of this book. This final major section of the book charts the process by which the West enters cultural memory as (in Owen Wister's words) "the true America" and argues that this symbolic configuration—made possible only after the closing of the frontier—signifies an irrecoverable shift in narrative method. A literary counterpart to Frederick Jackson Turner's frontier thesis, Wister's best-seller was enshrined almost immediately as the prototypical Western novel, the work that invented the cowboy hero. Certainly there is something remarkable in the way Wister weaves a romance of American unity from known threads of discord—sectional differences, vigilante justice, conflicts of gender and class—and even a century later, critics continue to note the masterful design by which the author allows his central character to succeed according to both eastern and western values. Yet this is more than the evolution of one hero's adaptation: This narrative pattern indicates the definitive cultural shift that effectively marks experimentation with, and finally an end to, the narrative strategy I analyze in this book.

Just as there was a popular embrace of Turner's thesis, so also are Wister's characters drawn to clear and final explanations. Overwhelmed by a desire for stability, even closure, within a map of America's historical imagination, Wister's characters—and his America—evaluate the costs of such closure and then acquiesce to them. At stake here is something that does not sound like a loss or sacrifice until it is reconsidered within the narrative model established by the earlier romances: To be the hero of twentieth-century America, the Virginian must evolve specifically in his consciousness of his own will and agency. The leap to self-consciousness leaves this hero divorced from the primal world before expression and locks him within the modern human condition, fully a function of the nationalist paradigm. Here the Virginian must live only in visible spaces rather than crossing borders into the silences of his world.

For Hawthorne the past—as it encounters the present—splinters on contact with the culture, forcibly embedding fragments of itself within the fabric of everyday life and so irrevocably changing lived experience while remaining unknown in its original form. For Wister, though, even these fragments are remote, apparently buried beneath the newly efficient machinery of national memory. The Spy and Hester Prynne each die as guardians of stories of mythic origins, both feared and treasured as cultural secrets. The Virginian's end is different; his narrative development insists that he leave behind his connections to such primary experience. Rather than leaving his potential storyteller as the bearer of knowledge from an older world of cultural mystery, Wister radically changes his hero, taking from him his historical knowledge as necessary payment for his heroism. From his first figural identity as the silent, enigmatic symbol of a culture at war with itself to establish a story of nationhood, the Virginian becomes a model of conformity and accommodation, with the struggle cast aside, backward into the now closed nineteenth century.[50] As should be clear by now, the cowboy's absorption into romance cannot dispel the secrets and mysteries of which he was once a privileged if isolated part; he no longer has access to them, but they remain in the text as figures that haunt an apparently reconciled world.

In the strict sense of the term, perhaps, a cultural archetype cannot exist: It may be that there is no symbol or pattern in cultural consciousness that precedes and shapes the lives of people in history. In America, however, certain stories have grown so deeply rooted in the culture that they may function at least as archetypes. Those stories emerge in different texts and at different moments; this book offers three that have come to be central to American literary imaginings. These stories are irreducible images, "outline[s]," to borrow Michael Taussig's terminology, of "the spectral radiance of the unsaid."[51] Such stories grow from historical fragments and their traces—the residue of past experience most resistant to present understanding, and particularly so much more resistant than it may first appear. The life of Cooper's Spy, the Scarlet Letter in the Custom House attic, and Owen Wister's West: All are figurations of a national story we cannot know with immediacy. Within their literary frames, they are in exile from any context that would supply ready meaning to them, and we come to know them as stories.

These stories with the power to function as archetypes are the unarticulated alternatives, the cultural secrets, sustained within our romances of national identity. They attest to anxieties about the development of a nation's literature and consciousness: Foremost among these is the fear that the story of America is not as clear and grand as Faulkner's Jason Compson—whose extraordinary degree of *belief* fully associates him with narrative design and so precludes his status as an American storyteller—describes: "[W]e see dimly people . . . possessing heroic proportions, performing their acts of simple passion and simple violence, impervious to time and inexplicable." Instead, maybe the connection of narrative design (and the belief in order that sustains it) is as tentative as language itself, which Quentin Compson, *Absalom, Absalom*'s oddly refigured modern storyteller, recognizes as a "meager and fragile thread . . . by which the little surface corners and edges of men's secret and solitary lives may be joined for an instant now and then before sinking back into the darkness."[52] What remains haunting, then, in texts where the secret history is so decidedly remote, is the very enduring fact of these stories, whose existence we glimpse but whose plots we never master.

It would be satisfying if the task of this book could be one of recovery—the reanimation of the lost stories glimpsed in the matrices of national romance. However, perhaps the foundational characteristic of these stories is their remoteness from narrative. With close attention to aesthetic layering, we can see more deeply the historical, and vice versa, but (even if we would wish to) we can never disentangle the layers themselves. Thus it becomes possible in each particular context to work toward an understanding of what is at stake in the attention to such layering, but never to find a pure or hidden truth within.[53] In *The Political Unconscious,* Fredric Jameson argues,

> [B]y definition the cultural monuments and masterworks that have survived tend necessarily to perpetuate a single voice in this class dialogue, the voice of a hegemonic class, [and thus] they cannot be properly assigned their relational place in a dialogical system without the restoration or artificial reconstruction of the voice to which they were initially opposed, a voice for the most part stifled and reduced to silence, marginalized, its own utterances scattered to the winds, or reappropriated in their turn by the hegemonic culture.[54]

This book begins to reanimate that dialogical system—though with an acknowledgment of the impossibility of the full restoration of lost stories and still *without* recourse to an artificial reconstruction of their suppressed voices. While to say that immediate accounts of raw experience never quite reach expression in the texts of cultural self-definition is simply to acknowledge the mediations and distortions inherent in language and memory, it is a quite different task to shift the terms of inquiry, having conceded the ideological forces through which a culture overtly shapes its stories. From here we might look for those historical moments apparently lost and then find them among those official narratives of culture, working as persistent and powerful operatives within the mainstream cultural imagination. To the extent that this project succeeds, we may now see the persistence of voices of discontent, chaos, and mystery within—indeed as part of—the voice remembered and recorded by certain richly paradoxically cultural narratives. We will never learn their secrets fully, but we may see how the existence of their secrets has ineluctably shaped what we say and know about foundational moments in American literary history.

PART ONE

⎯⎯⎯ ⚲ ⎯⎯⎯

Imagining Cultural Origins in James Fenimore Cooper's *The Spy*

Anyone who cannot come to terms with his life while he is alive needs one hand to ward off a little his despair over his fate—he has little success in this—but with his other hand he can note down what he sees among the ruins, for he sees different (and more) things than do the others; after all, dead as he is in his own lifetime, he is the real survivor.

—Franz Kafka, *Diaries,* October 19, 1921

1

<center>~~~</center>

STORYTELLING ON THE
NEUTRAL GROUND

I N James Fenimore Cooper's 1821 novel, *The Spy*, life on the "neutral ground" of revolutionary New York must be negotiated in the volatile regions between unfulfilled plans and unplanned experiences. At some unspecified time before the main action of the romance begins, Cooper's Spy has been tried and condemned to die by the American Army he secretly serves; within this frame each of the Spy's words and actions have heightened urgency, and he lives fully suspended in a zone of stolen time. At every level dissonant histories haunt Cooper's characters and their narrative world. From the contested progress of the sentimental and military plots, to the private history of the Spy, and finally to the textually and historically uncharted regions of America, stories of experience—past, present, and future—struggle against one another on contentious fields, remaining out of the reach of the patterned reconciliation of romance. Though the narrative clearly invokes certain stable designs of romance, the Spy's precarious existence—at times essential to, but then suddenly far beyond, these generic markers—is a haunting reminder of the ultimate weakness of all such structures. His condition magnifies the social disorder that shapes the plot, and, most significantly, his circumstances emphasize the contingencies of telling a story of life still in process—indeed of life (both personal and communal) inexorably bound to motion and change.

By turning imaginative attention away from the comfort of design and toward the immediacy and danger of lived experience, Cooper dramatically revises cultural notions of the self-consciously planned and orderly identity of America; these notions had informed the founders' writings and had been echoed during the decades that followed. Looking back to those founding years in 1842, one reviewer wrote of the popular sense that the United States of America had been "spoken into existence" as a nation.[1]

3

During the revolution and in the first decades of independence, they demonstrated over and again their deep belief in the power of language to assert control and effect change.[2] Recent criticism—including Michael Warner's study of letters in eighteenth-century-America's public sphere, Christopher Looby's attention to the spoken "linguisticality of the nation," and Jay Fleigelman's analysis of the "elocutionary revolution"—has opened for discussion the many strategies by which the founding generations depended upon a sense of themselves as a people of letters;[3] my argument enters into this context. Trusting themselves to be witnessing their own mythic history, the founders felt more than ordinary pressures to keep record of their experiences; their documents tell us that they felt that they were writing their own story of destiny, that they believed in what they wrote and so understood themselves to be living what they believed.

From the close of the Revolution up until Cooper's own time, however, even the leaders of the United States conceded the attendant anxieties within their project: Beyond an existence on paper, the new nation "was in no small degree experimental."[4] From any perspective, narrating culture in the new nation would involve much more than the institution of order through the written (or spoken) word; to tell a story of America would mean continuously accounting for an open-ended sequence of events and assimilating the knowledge and patterns established through experience and lived history. The strategies of cultural storytelling emergent between the time of the Declaration of Independence and the establishment of a native tradition of historical romance in America address this need directly; they offer significant innovations within a culture filled with deliberate attempts to understand its self-created origins. I argue that Cooper's novel works within conditions of storytelling in which a cultural imagination developed precisely through representations of strangely dis-ordered stories of American identity, stories that gained their substance from the often harsh ambiguities of lived experience and found no ade-quate set of cultural expectations by which they might be assimilated into communal knowledge.[5]

In this chapter I explore layers of expression that helped shape this way of imagining communal identity in early America. I argue that pop-ular legends of the revolutionary war both translated the familiar into American terms and established new imaginative forms in which to cast an American story. Several decades later these same processes then inform the development of American historical fiction. Although certainly there are legends with rather direct ideological applicability to the national cause, it is a striking fact that in several of the most popular legends of the Revolution, America demonstrated a remarkable imaginative capacity to transform characters and actions at odds with the culture's emphasis on the ideals of colonial independence into symbols that would work directly for the culture, precisely *for* those ideals and their related terms.

In this process of symbolic transformation, however, a new need emerged to find some imaginative place for the residual dangers latent in these stories. A common technique in the historical romance is the recasting of national dissent into a drama of conciliation, and so too in America, those residual dangers latent in the legends are recast in fictional structures and then resolved by the mechanisms of romance—including inherited narrative styles as well as peculiarly American figures. Cooper's novel, too, is informed by these developing methods of cultural storytelling, but further, *The Spy* is an evaluation of the very methods it employs and so marks experimentation beyond the bounds of what can be explained by genre. In the end Cooper provides a newly complicated model of language and history in American storytelling.

In *The Spy* the style of figural and symbolic representation that had emerged from revolutionary legends is critiqued for its limits. Though these legends had served to open some of the ambiguities of revolutionary experience, they did so only to resolve those ambiguities in communally celebrated romances. For Cooper it is ultimately impossible to transform such complex private life experiences into communal consciousness; thus his novel challenges the very basis of the cultural function of revolutionary legend. Cooper's Spy works entirely for his culture, to the exclusion of all private concerns; he needs no symbolic transfiguration, only historical recognition—that is, a transformation ironically within his own time and culture. But for Cooper, the story of America will not be one of the transformative powers of language, the deterministic shaping of experience through the designs, words, and figures of romance. Instead it will be the record of the dynamics created through the inextricable entanglement of the ideological (cultural process) and the resistant (the mysteries of agency within the subjective imagination) and through the inaccessibility of the only potential space of mediation between these terms—the immediate historical knowledge requisite to the linking of experiential history with the symbolic imagination.

Certain conditions of cultural imagining had changed significantly through the rhetoric and expectations of the revolution, but the project of telling an American story was not new to Cooper's early republican culture; it was not even new to the revolutionary generation preceding his own. By 1820, though, the task seemed somehow more urgent and more complicated than ever before. In a situation of precarious international peace following the war of 1812 and of shifting boundaries west and south with the rapid acquisition of territories and the "threatening aspect" of "the Missouri question,"[6] the United States of Cooper's early career made manifest its need for a common story of origins through an unprecedented outpouring of self-consciously constructed "American" images that remembered the Revolution. Orations and commemorative poems marked the passing of legendary founders, now recognized with reverence earlier reserved for "the great personages of distant lands, or of remote history";[7] works of art, including John Trumbull's paintings for the Capitol rotunda, depicted scenes of the Revolution that were designed "to preserve and diffuse the memory of the noblest series of actions which have ever presented themselves in the history of man";[8] monuments were built for the formal consecration of battlegrounds; and countless soldiers and civilians, hastily buried during active fighting, were disinterred and moved to more decorous graves:[9] As all of these examples suggest, the impulse of the 1820s was to gather history into a cultural imagination through appeals to personal memory and to define America publicly through the intricate complexities of private experience and knowledge.

Cooper's reviewers hailed *The Spy* within exactly this context. With a panorama of American character types from the loyal black servant and the comic Irish barmaid to the pedantic doctor and the mysterious dark lady, the novel remembers the strength of the Revolutionary community as the product of its unique, even idiosyncratic, variety; reviewers were quick to praise Cooper as "the first to people the realms of the interior of the country with creatures of imagination."[10] The lack of a national literature had been lamented since the nation announced its own beginning, but in *The Spy,* a relieved reading public found that Cooper successfully provided the cultural imagination with a visible space of the American landscape, proving to the satisfaction of most reviewers that "our country opens to the adventurous novel-writer a wide, untrodden field, replete with new matter." For this, they were certain, Cooper would enjoy "the future glory of having struck into a new path—of having opened a mine of exhaustless wealth—[because] in a word, he has laid the foundations of American romance."[11] Inscribing America's "untrodden field" with a romance of revolutionary history, *The Spy* might well be expected to provide a description of foundations that would serve as the first stage in the invention of a new national story.[12]

The emergent interest in the form of the historical romance in America during these years apparently offered yet another mode of reconciliation for communal memory. Within the romance form, cultural nationalists had every reason to hope that a writer might reconcile the facts of history with the imperatives of a newly national historical imagination. As Hawthorne later wrote, in the "moonlight medium . . . most suitable for a romance writer," an author might find "a neutral territory, somewhere between the real world and fairy-land, where the Actual and the Imaginary may meet, and each imbue itself with the nature of the other."[13] However, it was part, too, of the very nature of the romance to heighten uncertainty. For Cooper, the "mine of exhaustless wealth" that was America was also a place of darkness, disorder, and secrets never to be brought to light. "[I]t is to be an American novel professedly," Cooper wrote of *The Spy* in 1820, but still its vision is peculiarly impaired with regard to both the land and the experiences of early America.[14]

With little room for the Spy himself and so with no inside perspective on the Revolution,[15] Cooper's novel presents the problem of a narrative space that appears uncomfortably limiting for the vast subject of national origins. However, when reviewers issued *The Spy* "high praise"—especially for its representation of "the history, the character, and the varied face of our country"—they were not simply mistaken.[16] In fact it is the very inadequacy of the narrator's voice—and what might be called the intrusion of the Spy's character into a tale of harmonious process—that together produce an alternative story within the book, and there reviewers indeed could find "witness [to] the long struggle," the "rapine and bloodshed," of national origins.[17] Obscured by (and never reconciled to) the language of plot, this second narrative level is the Spy's story: It is an unspoken knowledge of inaccessible visions; there, Cooper insists—only to be sketched in shadow or outline, never to be revealed to the point of exhaustion—resides the mythic story of the hidden origins of a new culture.

In Cooper's text the ambiguities of history—not the elements of romance—generate the most potent dimensions of the mystical neutral territory; his neutral ground is the battlefield on which plans and experiences contend with one another, and neutrality is a precarious and finally deceptive label for a dynamic field of fiercely partisan, violent, and antagonistic forces—both military and narrative.[18] It is the cultural memory of unreconciled moments in history and not the romantic imagination that stirs on this ground between the real and the imagined; it is the story of lived experience that is at stake in those moonlight minglings, perpetually suspended within a gap in the defined world of narrative and entirely distinct from the predictable form of the romance. These gaps function not as enchanted spaces both magical and real but as the contested grounds ambiguously bridging the dual processes of memory and invention at work in the 1820s.

Certainly remembering origins (if possible at all) is a task different from inventing them; yet silently, perhaps even unconsciously, the distinction would be rendered invisible throughout much of Cooper's culture. In *The Spy,* however, Cooper acknowledges that these belated tales of cultural origins would necessarily be complicated by knowledge and history that predated their formulation, and memory would continue to trouble national narrative. In these very complications Cooper finds a method and process of storytelling that works precisely by emphasizing the limits of its own reach. *The Spy's* great contribution thus lies in its dynamic representation of that narrative strategy entailed in cultural storytelling, a simultaneous dependence on memory and invention, paradoxically fortified by an insistence on uncertainty, a refusal to conflate them into one imaginative structure. In *The Spy,* "the Actual and the Imaginary" do not mingle harmlessly but struggle without resolution to promote their respective, and conflicting, stories of experience.

Cooper's narrator is less a director than a player in this process, as he attends primarily to the ordinary matters of romance: In the plot are the traditional locales of reconciliation, both marital and martial.[19] A domestic plot centers on the Whartons, a family divided in their actual opinions on the war but protected by a carefully designed air of neutrality; a military plot offers a cursory view of the struggles and hardships of the colonial troops. Focal points in the narrative are marked by the intersection of these plots with one another, until the false climax, where "our heroine" (as she is called repeatedly), Frances Wharton, consents to marriage with her one true love, the young American officer Dunwoodie. Their union marks the reconciliation of the two plot lines with one another—in effect promising a victory for America—and so in narrative terms it transforms the symbolic identity of the new nation out of the limiting singular framework of either the Old World domestic romance or the ideals of revolutionary patriotism, and into some synthetic bond of the best of old and new.[20]

Throughout much of *The Spy,* the two plots depend upon their common narrative center, the comfortable home of the Wharton family. Characters and action from both the military and domestic worlds circulate within and around the house, which provides an apparently peaceful, romantic version of the "neutral ground," embodying both the relative tranquility and the latent tension of Revolutionary New York. Within the domestic frame, neutrality is represented in a set of compromises: The family opens their doors to travelers, but with a balance of suspicion; the two sisters, Frances and Sarah, air their opposing national loyalties, but without danger or disaffection; the head of the household assumes a studied distance from the war, for the protection of his land and home. As a focal point within the narrative, this house does not offer an image of Revolutionary ideals—courage and conviction—but of moderate stability and dependable sustenance. It is neutrality in the form of a safety zone where all paths cross, precariously suspended above conflict.

Both the domestic and the military plots prove to be unstable, dangerous, and at best easily threatened. In this sentimental form the neutral territory of romance—the province of Cooper's narrator—is a fragile and transient structure. It seems to offer a temporary source of comfort and protection; yet, Cooper emphasizes, the peace of the Wharton's home depends on deception or at least on the suppression of known answers to essential questions of identity.[21] Toward marriage and the home—indeed, toward all forms of reconciliation—the progress of the story thus directs the threats of time, knowledge, and experience. With nearly a third of the novel left to go, the Wharton's home—this carefully defined narrative space of "peaceful contentment and security"—is obliterated, in a symbolically balanced attack by both old and new world forces.[22] In one brief chapter the structure of the house is engulfed in flames by fortune-seeking marauders from the colonial ranks, and simultaneously the domestic ideals it embodies (love, marriage, family, loyalty) are destroyed in the revelation of Sarah's bigamist suitor, the British officer, Colonel Wellmere. The neutral ground of the home has proven neither safe nor strong, and finally, nothing more remains than the "blackened" "walls of the cottage," "dreary memorials" (294) left by the ravages of British and American alike.

The Spy had found no rest within this home—and in fact has no place within any part of the romance plot—yet he alone can salvage life (though nothing else) from the symbol of all that excludes him: He alone can pull Sarah ("the lovely maniac" [306], rendered senseless from the shattering of her world) out of the fire's range; in his sole exclusion from this space of false security, the Spy acquires his unique power to cross through the borderlands of his world. In the figure of his central character, this American Spy, Cooper thus places not a monument to heroism but rather all that eludes memorial representation—all that lies outside of community knowledge, all that therefore cannot be narrated in the inherited language of culture. Here, silent and unexplained, is everything from a man's surprise movement behind a tree to military secrets; all of the mysteries of the American forest, including contact with its native people; strategies of escape and survival; the privacy of the subjective imagination, its personal history of family and loss. Only the Spy—potentially—could bear witness to two of the great tragedies of the plot, George Washington's failures to see beyond military necessity and the Spy's own fully lost life story; without his voice, readers must find these images only in fragments. Suffering isolation and misunderstanding not only from other characters but also at the hands of the narrator, the Spy finds fictional life through the gaps and silences among the interstices of plot.

In the act of saving Sarah from the fire, the Spy manifests a force of action and experience that can exist only outside of the bounds of the deceptive world of structure. No sooner does he appear on the scene, a "spectre" in the smoke, than he flees back into the obscurity from which he came. In this scene Cooper's narrative suggests the existence of two distinct worlds, the knowable (though now ruined) domestic and military space of Revolutionary New York (a neutral ground of promised reconciliation and safety) and the Spy's world (the neutral ground of the book's title, a ground of shifting borders among fiction, history, and subjective memory), which is yet unknown. Although the first of these worlds is clearly vulnerable, it is a model of identity that is concrete and accessible; it can be conveyed in narrative form. Nonetheless, the novel emphasizes, the story of the second world is decidedly elusive (at least in part because it is still in process) and in this way stands as a figure for the dynamics of the emergent cultural imagination in Cooper's America.

The Spy is the living form of the new nation's alternative story. As a master of escape and disguise, he so fully eludes the perceptions of his community that his own life and identity remain almost entirely untold. He is considered to be eccentric and resistant to being "known" by his community, and he is the source of anxiety to his neighbors, who are uncomfortable with trademark idiosyncrasies such as his unique vision of the dark forests as "friendly" (139) and his unwillingness to speak socially. Cooper makes it clear that the Spy's experiences encompass much more than the daily trade of a peddler. He moves as if "without mortal motion," appearing even ghostly to others: "[B]lows and powder cannot injure him," other characters assume, perhaps because he "has already been in the grave" (311). As a result, without exception, the other characters in his world relegate the Spy's identity to an abstract mode. Whether "he was like the winds in the Good Book—no one could tell whence he came or whither he went" (322)—or whether he "had dealings with the dark one" (147), the Spy is agreed to be other than human. He is at once "hunted like a beast of the forest" (138), seen as a "ball of black," a "dark object . . . hovering in the skirt of the wood" (311)—and he is a "spirit" "beyond the reach of [military] sentence" (244, 240).

The Spy's power comes at the relentless price of personal loss, however, and ironically not even Cooper's narrator seems willing or able to save him from the isolation of an inscrutable identity. The narrative constructs an image of this martyr to the revolutionary cause in terms less appropriate to a political hero than to one of Aristotle's gods or beasts, that creature permanently beyond both the ability and the desire to live within the human association of the state.[23] Through the complicity of his social world—as he is forced to exist beyond the perceptions of both his fellow characters and the narrator—the Spy emerges into another role, a figure of the problem of cultural storytelling.

Precisely because he is not just another character in a new American tale, he comes to life in a world more ambiguous than that of the transplanted traditional historical romance. A significant part of the cultural work of legends of the American Revolution focused on enfolding a broad spectrum of lives within the terms of national martyrdom; this was a process of finding an American vocabulary that might render historical ambiguity a serviceable function within the symbolic imagination. In Cooper's text, however, from start to finish, the Spy escapes exactly this sort of inclusion. He is the only one to know the secret life of an emerging nation's patriotic heroism; at home within a darkness that never receives narrative representation, the Spy recasts the terms of American martyrdom within an irreconcilable dilemma: There is no known symbolic system that will reveal and explain the difficulties of the historical life he embodies. In *The Spy*, then, it becomes the very function of historical life to establish a new story, a new relation between language and history's symbols.[24]

In an image from the narrator's concluding description of the Whartons' house fire and the Spy's mysterious appearance on the scene, the intense light reaches just far enough to establish definitively the boundaries of narrative vision: "The bright light from the flames reached a great distance around [the ruins, and] . . . the gaunt form of the peddler had glided over the visible space, and plunged into the darkness beyond" (292). Up until this episode the narrative impulse has been focused and clear: The novel carefully establishes the "visible space" of home and family, love and marriage, even sickness and death; it is a concrete, knowable image of early America. But with both the structure and the ideals of this world in flames, it becomes increasingly clear that the products of the narrator's vision have been limited, fragile, and too easily assailed by British and American alike. It also becomes clear that surrounding the limited and vulnerable "visible space" (and producing the tensions that permeate it) is a potent "darkness beyond": uncharted and undomesticated regions, not only of the land but also of the American historical imagination. This "darkness" comes to represent an insistent ambiguity within the early republic's story of culture: Through experiments in language and imagination, America—in the production of narrative and other arts addressing questions of national origins—was engaged in a long and remarkable struggle to place the events of its revolution into communal memory. Broadly considered, this was a process of negotiation between the volatile experiences of history and the functions of symbols within an emerging culture. It is a drama that begins with the imaginative creation of an American cast.

2

———— ✤ ————

THE CREATION OF AMERICAN
MARTYRS

Mark this: You must be annalist & Biographer, as well as Aid de
Camp, of George Washington, & the Historiographer of the
American War! . . . God only knows, how it may terminate. But
however that may be, it Will be a most interesting story.
—Hugh Knox to Alexander Hamilton, April 31, 1777

I F from one perspective Cooper's readers were living in a new age of
monuments and memory, in another sense they lived among the ripe
ambiguities of silence. Writing to Thomas Jefferson in 1815, John Adams
asked, "Who shall write the history of the American revolution? Who can
write it? Who will ever be able to write it?" Jefferson's answer echoed the
same fears: "Nobody ever will be able to write it, except merely it's [*sic*]
external facts."[1]

With those facts past and memory unreliable and indistinct, many ora-
tors across the country sought to remedy these signs of "the forgetfulness
of man" each Fourth of July by avoiding the presumed ambiguity of legend
and invoking instead the principles of independence.[2] These ritual events,
however, could do little to recapture the experience of the war. In 1823
James Davis Knowles told his Washington audience, "It is unnecessary, on
this occasion, to dwell on the history of our revolution. . . . [W]hen we are
reproached that the story of our revolution has not yet been fitly told, we
may reply, that the record is in our hearts." Not only might the imagination distort the meaning of the war through legends, but maybe, he suggested, not even the "historian's pen" was the appropriate tool for
conveying the collective memory of national origins.[3] Adams repeatedly
claimed that the Revolution had taken place most essentially in "the minds
and hearts of the people," so there, perhaps, its history would stay as well.[4]

This is not to deny the abundance of voices in the early republic eager
to speak about the recent war, but the project of telling an American experience had been framed with an array of complications that neither public

documents nor broad narrative silence could address. "[M]onuments and statues decay," Joseph Sprague told his Salem listeners a month after Adams and Jefferson had died in 1826, "and in the revolutions of time, history itself becomes obscure and lost."[5] Throughout Cooper's America, there was a felt burden of preserving and expressing cultural memory apart from the ravages of time. To a certain extent it was a product of revolutionary optimism, which had infused American expression with a concentrated anxiety. There had been high expectations for bringing about the birth of a new nation, but behind these hopes were the pressures of establishing foundations and the deep fear of failure. In 1776 Thomas Paine exhorted the colonists, "we have it in our power to begin the world over again."[6]

Through the decades that followed, America was figured as even more than Paine's newly begun world: In a chorus of what John P. McWilliams has termed "oratorical self-justification," Independence Day speakers characterized the new nation as "the sun . . . burst[ing] the cloud of time," "a star of the first magnitude," "a satellite of the first order," and even a "new constellation."[7] It all seemed to have happened so suddenly, almost as if (as one orator put it) "a magician's wand . . . by its mystic influence struck into existence a mighty nation."[8] Near the end of his life, Thomas Jefferson specifically linked that belief in a new beginning to a spirit of optimism in cultural narration. He recalled the Revolution's extraordinary opportunity for the renewal of the promises of language and the boundless possibilities for cultural storytelling. "[O]ur Revolution," he wrote, "commenced on . . . favorable ground. It presented us an album on which we were free to write what we pleased."[9] For better or for worse, each story that was recorded in this context would have more than ordinary power, and each event that occurred would be imagined to indelibly mark the seemingly empty page of a new national story.

Built into the very design of independent America, then, was a peculiar sensitivity to the powers and dangers of language, particularly language used in the service of narrating a story of communal identity. In the events of the recent war, the new nation had a political history, and in the founding documents, a set of beliefs clearly had been framed; the task facing America, then, was "to find a middle term,"[10] a cultural imagination to link history and belief. Within this atmosphere of tension and excitement, the language of American self-definition expressed a remarkable creative urgency.[11] Now, in the newly self-conscious program of national storytelling, there were formative shifts in imaginative expression, shifts designed to elucidate an American identity precisely by addressing some of the most peculiarly confusing components of cultural experience. Since the symbolic rhetoric of independence provided the design for American beliefs, the war for independence, by necessity, would provide the figures to function within it. Here in the experience of the war was the newly empowered vocabulary that would be used in the American story. Here the cultural imagination would recognize certain familiar plots of romance and tragedy, but here also entirely new plots would unfold on American ground. Through the evolution of popular legends of the Revolution, America would gain a *figural* vocabulary for its own stories.

Histories, poems, plays, songs, and fiction remembered the Revolution not only by invoking its principles for continued American freedom but also by focusing on specific incidents that, for various reasons, appealed to the forming cultural imagination. In fact, from the start, popular images of the American revolution assumed no easy uniformity of sentiment; rather, from the first years of the war and well into the nineteenth century, many of the most pervasive legends of the Revolution remarkably focused on disorderly, irreconcilable experiences of the war. This interest and the process by which such strangely captivating images enter into and function within the story of culture dominate Cooper's novel; *The Spy* maps a panorama of people and places shaping American experience, but more telling still, it resonates with the idiosyncratic powers of native legends that had been stirring in the culture long before public efforts toward installing official interpretations of the war could begin.

Many of the most popular war legends evolved into strong national symbols and yet had their only foundations in the cultural notions of absence and loss growing out of separation from England. In part, the paradox of these legends is an imaginative response to the shifting goals of American identity. Historians have established that the colonies had no plan to enact a "*national* revolution," and the vast majority of those involved "never meant to repudiate English culture but rather to embrace and fulfill it."[12] Yet as the early republic sought a myth of origins, it did so from within the perspective that they—like their model societies from the ancient world—had experienced a revolution in which "the great succession of centuries [was] born afresh."[13] Despite the original intent, then, the early republic was left to record a story not only of community but also of a nation's founding era.[14]

By necessity this story would be shaped by certain new conditions of imagining; as a modern form, the nation had none of the traditional apparatus of ancient mythology. Benedict Anderson's model of the nation as an "imagined community" helps illustrate the new cultural conditions with which modern mythology would contend. Anderson has argued that "the very possibility of imagining a nation" came about only as "three fundamental cultural conceptions, all of great antiquity, lost their axiomatic grip" on the human mind: (1) "the idea that a particular script-language offered privileged access to ontological truth, precisely because it was an insepara- ble part of that truth"; (2) "the belief that society was naturally organized around high centers . . . and ruled by some form of cosmological dispensa- tion"; and (3) the "conception of temporality in which cosmology and his- tory were indistinguishable, the origins of the world and of men essentially identical."[15]

The forms in which popular legend emerged in the Federalist and early republican years demonstrate that the Revolution irrevocably denied such conceptions of faith and order. Stories of the war emphasized instead the failures of language to convey truth and the radical disorganization and unpredictability of life in the colonies during these years; such stories drew attention to the fact that the America emergent from the Revolution was not the world begun again, but a human community to be sustained by all kinds of acts of the imagination.[16] Just as the modern nation realized its own inception and promise of power, then, it also recognized its ruptured relation to the secure structures of belief that had sustained the colonies from their earliest forms as religious communities. Conversely, at its moment of the deepest loss of potency, cultural language in the nation was reminded of its earlier, almost sacred, function to the community. Accord- ingly, sacred language would be renewed,[17] now based ironically on nega- tive forms of imagining: a recognition of the limits of language and of the disorder of social structure, a deep cultural need to provide a story of ori- gins—a new context for discerning the meanings of the events of everyday life—for a community ruptured in time and space from ancient patterns of history and cosmology.

In these new modern conditions of culture, the sacredness of language depends not on a presumed allegorical relation to ontological truth but on its capacity to record the indeterminacy of life and belief. In America, nowhere is this clearer than in the remarkable paradoxes of representation at work in popular legends of the Revolution. While much national rhetoric celebrated an image of national unity, as Christopher Looby's analysis reminds us, such images were appealed to as problems and chal- lenges rather than accomplishments.[18] Certainly some events began in contention and yet as stories could be raised quickly to a level of shared communal sentiment: From the 1764 stamp crisis, for example, American writers gleaned methods of representing "a prospect of oppression, bound- less in extent and endless in duration"—a prospect that would generate justified resistance and inspire "the tongues and pens of the well informed citizens" to "kindl[e] the latent sparks of patriotism."[19] Similarly, despite its general taint of mob activity, the Boston massacre was remembered as a clear and decisive turning point, a moment when "the people . . . determined no longer to submit to the insolence of military power."[20]

Stories of events that took place within the years of active fighting often proved more complicated to tell and to interpret; still, in the decades following the Revolution, legends of its heroes would find ways to grow, as most major figures died without falling into public scandal and as partisan causes struggled to find their own principles rooted in the revered War for Independence.[21] An abiding "fear of power," when invested in any one individual, gave the newly independent United States "an inherent antagonism" to endowing its leaders with mythic dimensions, but for heroes who died early, this was less vigorously resisted.[22] Many of the earliest writers inclined to exemplary biographies were happy to extol figures whose contribution, in the end, might be considered comparatively minor. General Joseph Warren, for example, killed at Bunker Hill, was a favorite subject of narrative attention; he was remembered as the very image of "unfading glory," "the purest patriotism," and "the most undaunted bravery," though he died so early in the conflict that he had not yet abandoned his aims for "coalition with the Mother Country."[23] In the same spirit, in the flurry of imitations following Cooper's first success with historical romance, some novelists returned to the literary precision and clarity of crises easily known and since resolved, as Lydia Maria Child does in her 1825 domestic romance, *The Rebels*, a story framed by the Stamp Act and insistent on distinguishing between representations of patriotic fervor and the dangers of chaos emergent in acts of mob violence.

The historical imagination in *The Spy*, however, thrives on a quite different America and engages directly with the problems of language in the story of the modern nation. For Cooper's America, strength is generated in the imprecision of abundance and variety. In the complications of radical uncertainty issuing from that newly American range of characters and settings, in the private history and knowledge of the Spy, in the mysterious and disguised George Washington, in the disappointed love and resulting madness of Sarah Wharton, and in the lawless chaos (personal, domestic, and military) of the neutral ground, Cooper figures the story of American origins as the story of experience, experience as it exposes the limits of cultural language and challenges the known patterns of community. In this way Cooper's vision of America's founding era builds upon the strongest imaginative traditions of his culture.

Indeed, among the most telling clues to an index of the storytelling imagination in early America is the fact that—in the two generations between the end of the war and the establishment of a native tradition of historical romance—no heroic figure or successful battle, no legend that justified resistance through appeals to patriotism or sketches of villainy, could match the pervasive power of and interest in the separate tragic fates of two young British sympathizers, one an accomplished officer and one a civilian woman. Major John André and Miss Jane McCrea may be the two most mysterious ghosts left by the war, if not in their personal histories, at least in their imaginative lives within the American cultural imagination.[24]

The evolution of their legends and the symbolic roles they play exemplify the interpretive capacities of their social world; their stories are evidence of cultural negotiations with hidden history, expressions of an emergent communal identity through figures of irreconcilable ambiguity and events of irreclaimable loss.[25] Both André, Benedict Arnold's British liaison, and McCrea, who chose her Tory lover over all social principles, were killed among ambiguous circumstances on the heavily contested grounds of the Hudson River Valley. Both of their stories were immediate sensations not only throughout the colonies and Britain but into Europe as well; yet both were essentially Loyalist sympathizers whose chance misfortune left them tragic but incidental human casualties of war.

As the British General Henry Clinton's agent chosen to receive Arnold's West Point intelligence, André was captured "within our lines" (as George Washington apparently reported to the trial committee) returning by land to the British encampment at New York. He had taken on "an assumed character," was dressed "in a disguised habit, with a pass under a feigned name," and carried Arnold's notes "concealed upon him."[26] He was hung as a spy on October 2, 1780. Even during the ten-day interval between his capture and his death, André began to take hold of the public's sentimental imagination. Pleas for mercy came from all sides, with rapid, impassioned intensity, and in his last days, André's own words and actions fueled the high "romantic interest" that, as Washington Irving later wrote, "was thrown around his memory."[27]

There are no last words or records of noble suffering to attend Jane McCrea's memory, nor was anyone there to plead for her life and her honor. Interest in her story too, however, was immediate, pervasive, and sustained well into the nineteenth century. With little evidence or knowledge, countless writers retold the story of the young girl, who, hoping to meet with her fiancé, the British officer David Jones, was instead brutally murdered in the forests near Fort Edward, New York, late in July of 1777.

These are the types of legends that had been stirring most powerfully in the years leading up to the development of the historical romance in Cooper's America, and in their ambiguity and terror, no less than in their capacity for romance, they are the imaginative nourishment of *The Spy*.

The persistent interest in the deeply ambiguous legends of John André and Jane McCrea throughout the nineteenth century attests to the early and sustained cultural workings of these challenges to American storytelling, to a historical imagination focused on the renegotiation of the boundaries of communal knowledge based especially on the experiences of lived history. From their earliest appearances in literary and historical texts, the legends of André and McCrea spoke not only to the tragic private losses inflicted by the motion of the emergent culture but also to the sheer power of private, unknowable histories in the shaping process itself. André's image haunted American forests to suggest the frightening permeability of boundaries and the tremendous authority latent in privately held military secrets. His image later came to invoke the losses inherent in cultural independence and questions regarding America's future relations with Europe. In her death, Jane McCrea warned of the dangers of British seduction and the savagery of the American wilderness; she later became an emblem of the threats to home, family, and community unleashed through the energies of the Revolution and believed to be all too rampant in the young republic. Both legends highlight the ultimate limits of civil control; both represent fragmented life histories, stories of knowledge and experience irrevocably lost yet endlessly productive of cultural imaginings.

Fears of revolutionary violence done to the domestic and civil orders had not been resolved by independence. Despite colonial victory, many writers recalled that the war "relentlessly tore asunder" the "thousand ties of affection" by which family and community life long had been sustained.[28] Even in the political realm, it had taken no time at all for voices to emerge claiming that "the enchanting sound of Liberty" had somehow fallen prey to an "infection"; "the weakness and inefficiency of the existing Government," Timothy Dwight lamented in 1801, had ironically "been fashioned in the wild moments of enthusiasm, and founded on visionary ideas of patriotism, [and yet] became also a new and most distressing source of universal perplexity."[29] Inextricably fusing the best and worst of America, these anxieties, broadly considered, generated a need for cultural symbols that would work toward utopia by drawing symbols from the "still valid past" and claiming them as "ambiguously fit for the future." Such symbols thus defy the limits of time, history, and representation, while anchoring the imagination to these categories. In so doing they transform the "cultural surplus" of past and present anxiety into a mechanism of the new national imagination and its anticipations of future cultural forms.[30]

By mid-century the artist Horatio Greenough would write to William Cullen Bryant, "I wish to erect a monument which shall record on the same spot—the treason of Arnold—the capture and death of André and the fate of Capt'n N. Hale. I believe this idea may take a form exceedingly significant of our system, highly expressive of our democratic ethics—& a caution to egotistical intrigue."[31] That monument—a spiraling cultural story of disorder, danger, and the optimism of national pride—would never be constructed, but as a shape toward which the American historical imagination was tending in the nineteenth century, it might be figured first in the circulating stories of two of the most ambiguous martyrs of the revolution and then (quite differently) in the narrative dynamics of *The Spy*.

THE MASSACRED BRIDE

In the summer of 1777 Loyalists were advancing with success under the command of Howe in the south and Burgoyne in the north. Driving colonists from Canada and the lake regions, Burgoyne's northern campaign aimed to control the crucial Hudson River valley; this would open British communication between posts in New York and Canada and thereby sever New England from the other colonies. Ticonderoga had fallen easily to the British, and with Albany only seventy miles away, Burgoyne seemed destined for unprecedented conquest. But by midautumn, a series of reversals so shocking had occurred that Burgoyne and his troops had surrendered at Saratoga, while France began the process of forging an alliance with independent America. "Tho' our affairs, for some days past, have worn a dark and gloomy aspect," Washington had predicted to Major General Philip Schuyler on July 22, "I yet look forward to a fortunate and happy change. I trust General Burgoyne's Army will meet, sooner or later an effectual check, and . . . the success he has had, will precipitate his ruin." These were "critical" times, Washington emphasized, "big with important events."[32] It is no accident that this crucial turning point in the war provided the culture with one of its most popular legends, yet it remains a surprise that—of all of the happenings in New York during those few months—the one event to capture the public imagination most passionately was the random death of a young woman who was purportedly in love with a British officer.

The story of Jane McCrea's death "was told throughout the continent with the rapidity of lightning."[33] "In the history of the Revolutionary War," one writer later remembered, "perhaps no single incident is recorded which, at the time of its occurrence, created more intense sympathy;" "by every fireside, in public assemblies, in the national councils, it was told and re-told"; "it spread still farther, through France, Germany, Italy, and over all the nations of Europe that recognized the rules of civilized warfare."[34]

It even issued in the first book-length narrative to focus completely on an American incident, Michel René Hilliard's *Miss McCrea: A Novel of the American Revolution* (1784).[35] With every retelling, the story seemed to change. The certainties of the case are few, but a consensus suggests that the McCrea family was divided in loyalties. Jane's father had died, and Jane was living with her brother's family (colonial sympathizers) outside of Fort Edward as Burgoyne's troops approached from the north. At the time of Jane's death, most citizens of the area (including her family) had removed to safer ground in Albany—why she stayed behind, how, by whom, and under what circumstances she was killed—all of these questions were subjects of conjecture and fertile grounds for romance.

Only a month after the mysterious murder, the American general Horatio Gates announced that Jane had died at the hands of a band of Iroquois employed by Burgoyne, and in his letter of remonstrance to the British commander, he cast Jane to play an exalted symbolic role: "[T]he miserable fate of Miss McCrea was particularly aggravated by her being dressed to meet her promised husband; but [instead] she met her murderers employed by you."[36] It proved to be a brilliant strategy. Everyone who heard the tale—from the editor of London's *Annual Register* to readers of Patriot newspapers—abhorred such a savage violation of innocence. The British press "loudly condemned and reprobated" such policies of war that seemed to forget that this was essentially "a civil contest." If their "own government . . . could call [on] such auxiliaries" as the accused Indians, perhaps the public had been deceived—perhaps British policy had not been, "as they said, . . . to subdue but to exterminate, a people whom they affected to consider, and pretended to reclaim as subjects."[37] The metaphor was strengthened for the British by a common belief that Jane's father had been loyal to the crown.

Patriot presses circulated the story at once: It "passed through all the papers of the continent, and, . . . being retouched by the hand of more than one master, excited a peculiar degree of sensibility."[38] By 1847 George Lippard looked back to "the simple History of David Jones and [Jane] M'Crea" as the answer to all complaints "of the destitution of Legend, Poetry, [and] Romance" in America: "[T]ell me, did you ever read a tradition of England, or France, or Italy, or Spain, or any land under the Heavens, that might, in point of awful tragedy, compare [to this event]?"[39] Lippard's version has a long pretext in the American storytelling imagination, from Gates's letter through the transformative lenses of countless narrative and poetic renderings.

To Gates's inflammatory imagery of the massacred bride, Burgoyne responded with great indignation; he was "struck with horror" by the action, and he "positively denied" the American account.[40] Gates's letter, Burgoyne insisted, was the product of the "rhapsodies of fiction and calumny"—and so it almost certainly was, but seemingly nothing could halt the generative power of the tale's fragmented facts.[41] Little was certain about Jane's death, but in that very uncertainty were the most legible of civil terrors; the sharp polarities that were invoked made possible seemingly endless variations and embellishments. Whether the home where Jane was staying had been invaded or not; whether Officer Jones sent for Jane, intending to meet and marry her or not; whether Jane was mistakenly killed in a struggle between two Indian chiefs or not—she remained a violated ideal: the home life as set against wilderness and wartime savagery; love as set against death; innocence as set against violence.

These are the symbolic terms of most accounts of Jane's death. The players in the drama are two bands of Indians, Jane, Officer Jones, and British and colonial troops; the roles they play shift dramatically but still within certain bounds. Accounts of the Indians' collective role range from one of honor and good intention (they may have conveyed a letter from Jones and offered Jane safe passage to the British encampment) to full-scale violence (they may have killed her with a hatchet, taking her scalp to the British camp to taunt her lover). For his part, too, Jones could be played as either tragic hero or treacherous villain; he may have sent Jane a letter insisting that she remain safely in the house and promising to come for her, and after her death he may have deserted the war or died of grief. Or he may have seduced her and later been hoping to escape her affections as she sought him at his camp.

The role of the other British soldiers was also amply detailed by Patriot presses: The Pennsylvania *Evening Post* propagated the image of Jane "scalped . . . in the sight of those very men who are continually preaching up their tender mercies and the forbearance of their more than Christian King"; "the brutal scene," the paper reported on August 12, 1777, "was transacted by four Indians, under the cover of 300 British regulars, drawn up at a small distance." Further, that appalling act had been made into a torturous spectacle for "an advanced party of Americans" held at bay by the British.[42] In one of the most significant variations of the legend, however, Jane is killed not by Indians or even in the presence of the British, but mistakenly by the fire of pursuing American troops. Whether kidnapped or accompanying the Indians voluntarily, in this version she is seen leaving the settlement in their company, and the Americans shoot intending to save her.[43]

Despite the flexibility of the legend of Jane McCrea, particular possible interpretations remain unspoken. There would be no sustained interest in condemning Major André as a duplicitous Royalist scheming the down-fall of Patriot ideals, and so too Jane McCrea's memory curiously avoids two of the darkest patriotic possibilities. On the one hand, her own morals might have been questioned: What was she doing—an unmarried woman in the forests of America, apart from her family, traveling to her British lover's military camp? Second, the legend claims that either Indians (in savagery) or Americans (in a tragic accident of war) killed Jane: Why had no legend emerged to place the deadly weapon in the hands of one of those many complicitous British?

Even without acquiescence to the easy allegorical answers these ques-tions imply, it remained clear that the many and varied threats to civil order in America's forests were somehow instigated by the British and demanded a response from the colonies. While the London press may have seized upon the image with the fear that it represented a British policy of colonial extermination, the American imagination seemed to ignore this most propagandistic interpretation. Instead, the reigning metaphor—which indefinitely extended the imaginative play of the story—was that of a British policy of seduction. Whether the terms of seduction were love and the promise of marriage or simply an insidious exploitation, the prey was innocence and the consequences were dire.[44]

Like many romances that followed, Jane's story openly evoked fears that as "the tide of public indignation was rising higher and higher," "the current of domestic happiness" lost strength in proportion.[45] The dramatic function of her legend was to play out exactly this dynamic and to recast these two structures of community into a pattern of resolute interdepen-dence. In its cast of an innocent girl and a British seducer, Jane's story was familiar to American audiences conditioned by the eighteenth-century European sensibilities of Pierre Marivaux and Samuel Richardson. The seduction plot took American form in the 1790s with popular novels such as Susanna Rowson's *Charlotte Temple* (1791; Philadelphia, 1794), Hannah Webster Foster's *The Coquette* (1797), and the anonymous *Amelia, or the Faithless Briton* (1798).

Certainly it was not the novelty of Jane's story that gave it such a potent cultural function, but rather its very familiarity made possible particular structural changes in the American story. Traditionally stories of this sort set domestic happiness as a separate ideal, against the progress of war. In the story of Amelia, for example, a soldier nursed back to health by a young girl and her father "conceive[s] the infamous project of violating the purity and tranquility of [that same] family," and the author explains further that "the success of the contending forces was alternately fatal to the peace and order of domestic life": "[T]he objects of policy or ambition are . . . accomplished at the expence of private ease and prosperity; while the triumph of arms, like the funeral festivity of a savage tribe, serves to announce some recent calamity—the waste of property, or the fall of families."[46] What was new in Jane's story, then, was the concerted effort to unify the ideals of domestic happiness and colonial victory.

To Jane's America, the notion of colonial independence was at best new, and like the legend of her ill-fated life in the wilds, it suggested the very same dangers of self-imposed vulnerability. Once Jane had been claimed as an American symbol, it became possible not only to dismantle the Loyalist metaphor of the ungrateful child rebelling against the mother country, but also to recast the very entrance of British troops onto the American continent as an act of rape. In Hilliard's *Miss McCrea* this metaphor is clear in the manner of Captain Belton, the character in the role of David Jones. Here, this British officer moves beyond seduction, as he writes from London to proclaim his love to Jane with striking aggression: "I am returning under the banners of General Burgoyne to conquer your country and you in order to possess you forever."[47] Through these terms, the enormous symbolic capacities of this essentially private story of love and death expanded to address the relative attractions and dangers of a new national identity. All confusion aside, the legend taught that Jane's seduction by a British officer eventuated in her death. Further, the American cultural imagination was seduced in turn by the romantic story of an ill-fated Tory love affair.

Jane's story was so uncertain because it was truly her own, not planned, witnessed, or authorized. Perhaps it was so appealing to the romantic imagination because it was a story of the strength of private feelings to the exclusion of social concerns. But as the American imagination made the story its own, the dangers of this most intense subjectivity were obviated in remarkably pointed interpretive reversals. In the developing American tradition, it became popular to suggest a design behind the killing and to cite "authorities" for the truth of a particular version; in both cases, the attempt was to bring the private life story fully into the public realm. However, among the cited authorities, the only possible witness, Jane's neighbor Mrs. McNeil, was invoked for contradictory stories.[48] Other presumed experts ranged from Jane's distant nephew to Samuel Standish, whose authority is based solely on the reputation of his own lineage (he was the "ancestor in a direct line" of Miles Standish, "the famous military leader of the first Pilgrims at Plymouth").[49] The result was a story shaped by and for communal life but empowered strictly through the inviolable secrecy of its subject.

Early public versions of the legend assumed that the murderer's hand was that of an Indian, and though the British themselves were not accused of lawless murder, Burgoyne's policies were imaginatively reshaped in order to provide a fitting contextual design.[50] Just over a month before the incident, on June 21, 1777, Burgoyne had given a public speech to his employed Iroquois in which he attempted to forbid excessive violence. He outlined "the vast differences between a war waged against an entire nation, 'and the present, in which the faithful were intermixed with rebels, and traitors with friends.' "[51] Though the text of the speech was extensively read and known, analyses of its content and effects ranged widely. James Thacher recalled that "Burgoyne's manifesto" actually caused "innocent persons [to be] made victims of savage barbarity, by means of the toma-hawk and scalping," and later Patriot historians agreed.[52] The "employment of hordes of wild and inhuman savages" was "the most base feature of Bur-goyne's plan," and it was no surprise that "those hell-hounds of cruelty" would kill the innocent Jane; in fact, they argued, her death was "the legit-imate fruit of such a policy as that of Burgoyne."[53]

Posited as part of a larger narrative in the American versions, the event had not only a pretext in Burgoyne's June speech but also an unfolding series of results—most immediately in the reversal of fortunes for the two armies that summer in New York. With both cause and effects traced into the public realm, the developing legend drew the incident away from the terms of privacy and into the widest arena of the growth of national strength. Once the war was over, the ultimate failure of Burgoyne's north-ern campaign appeared to have been an essential turning point; his own letters confirmed that import as well.[54] A standard patriotic refrain thus claimed that "the blood of this unfortunate girl . . . was not shed in vain. Armies sprang up from it. Her name passed as a note of alarm, along the banks of the Hudson: it was a rallying word among the Green Mountains of Vermont."[55]

This young woman with no expressed commitment to America—and more than likely deeply tied to the Loyalist cause—became a martyr to the "renaissance of patriotism, a reawakening of the public spirit, an arousing of the lion-heart in a dominant population, with the ultimate result of the birth of a new nation"; from her grave grew "the flowers and blossoms of progress."[56] Hers was the most timely "sacrifice to the drooping spirit of Liberty."[57] This sacrifice issued on one side in reinspired patriotism and on the other, in lost support for Burgoyne—including defections of some of his Indian troops, now monitored with a harshly watchful eye. Perhaps most significantly, the legends recalled, this event changed the military map of largely ambivalent New York, for "the murder of Miss McCrea resounded throughout the land."[58] In response to the news of the incident, many of the uncommitted "flew to arms [with the Americans] to defend their families and firesides."[59] Though they would have to leave behind "their shrieking wives and children," it became clear through the legend that the colonial soldiers could fulfill their domestic duties *only* by rushing to the aid of Jane's memory, "haste[ning] to the glorious field, where LIBERTY, heaven-born goddess, was to be bought for blood."[60] No longer believing in the safety of neutrality, colonists in the New York area were seized by an "immediate concern."[61] A "general conviction [spread] that a vigorous determined opposition was the only alternative for the preservation of their property, their children and their wives. . . . An army [to preserve civil and domestic peace] was speedily poured forth from the woods and mountains."[62]

Jane McCrea's death, wrote David Ramsay, thus stood as the ultimate and pointed rebuke to Loyalist claims of the violated filial bond inherent in colonial revolution and so was the strongest possible antidote to objections that the Revolutionary cause stood against domestic tranquility and happiness. In military terms it was an "almost irrelevant happening."[63] However, the American cultural imagination had quickly transformed "chance into destiny."[64] In turn, the bounded symbolic polarities that this death evoked gave the legend a shaping role in the evolving cultural imagination. In many ways the story came to be a central text in "a cleverly manipulated and highly successful Patriot propaganda campaign."[65]

However, insofar as the terms of the event provided America with a different vocabulary for its experience and its story, there was something substantially more than a propaganda war at stake. The extraordinary power accorded to this single private tragedy supplied a resonant life of personal experience and romance to a cause that so many civilians in America had feared was only an empty "myth of liberty," even an impediment to all chivalric ideals of love and honor;[66] it did so moreover without representing the costs of American military strength as the loss of American family life. In these terms the legend of Jane McCrea was a symbolic construction that countered any deep sense of American loss precisely by recognizing these fears and making their resolution dependent upon devotion to the national cause; all of these interpretive reversals were contained within the highly charged figure of one lost (British) life.

A COUNTRY IN RUINS

Early in the war the stance of neutrality had been a means of preserving those treasures said to be desecrated in the death of Jane McCrea—family, home, and property. By 1777, in both the cultural imagination and in lived experience, the meaning of neutrality had begun to shift, or rather, it began to take on paradoxical meanings where it had earlier signified the very absence of meaning. Where neutrality was preserved after this incident, the threats lurking around and within that position would be all the more evident. In fact, as the war continued, neutrality came to suggest not peace or safety but latent danger. Investigating the living conditions of uncommitted residents in this region, the Congress of 1777 concluded that a "general face of waste and devastation" had "spread over a rich and once well cultivated and well inhabited country."[67]

Those decimated homes and families were not only fearful but also feared, for their capacity to harbor people and intelligence aiding the British cause. Acts of law regarding the neutrals were debated, passed, and revised in New York between 1777 and 1778; commissions were appointed to "detect and defeat . . . all Conspiracies which may be formed in this state against the liberties of *America*." Silent neutrals were brought before panels to swear patriotism; they were generally regarded as persons with "poverty of spirit and an undue attachment to property," dangerously unknowable and perhaps "ungratefully and insidiously . . . by artful misrepresentations and a subtle dissemination of doctrines[,] fears[,] and apprehensions [not only] false in themselves and injurious to the American cause, [but also] seduc[ing] certain weak minded persons" to Loyalist ends; in short, the neutrals were widely perceived to be "evil" in "example" and "practice," "acting a part so unmanly and ignominious."[68]

While the neutral property holders seemed quietly subversive to the ideals of the Patriot cause, the neutral ground itself seemed to come alive with a character of its own that was indiscriminately dangerous. As one historian recalled it,

> the Neutral Ground . . . was infested by two gangs of marauders, the off-spring of civil commotion, respectively denominated Cow-boys and Skinners. . . . [Inhabitants] were exposed to the depredations of both parties, . . . often actually plundered, and always liable to . . . calamity. They feared everybody whom they saw, and loved nobody. . . . Fear was, apparently, the only passion by which they were animated. The power of volition seemed to have deserted them. . . . Their houses . . . were . . . scenes of desolation. . . . The world was motionless and silent.[69]

Draining the people of all forms of expression, from speech to volition to movement, the neutral ground ironically seemed to be the place of the most intense fervor of revolution, a place where passions had spun madly beyond cognition or control, seemingly beyond the agency of individuals.

In 1777 even Robert R. Livingston—who had been a member of the committee to prepare the Declaration and later would serve as secretary of foreign affairs—described this sense of life in his home state of New York. Even though he was one of the guiding hands of the cause, he too felt that he was "swimming with a stream it is impossible to stem," yielding "to the Torrent" and abandoning all reservations about the war in the best possible effort to help "direct its course."[70]

Fully infused with the spirit of war, the Hudson River Valley no longer provided peace or protection. By late in 1780 the neutral ground was by all accounts a place of misery rather than of cowardly hidden privilege. James Thacher's *Military Journal* recalls the "abandoned . . . farms" with "rotting fruit in the orchards"; the "rich and fertile" country had been deserted as Tories escaped to New York and Patriots ventured to still more remote interior lands. "[T]he privileges which their neutrality ought to secure them," wrote Thacher, are negated by "the ravages and insults of infamous banditti": "[I]t now has the marks of a country in ruins."[71]

The latent violence of the neutral ground threatened passing soldiers of both armies. Like the residents of the area, these soldiers faced very real dangers of vigilante killings or even simply mob robbery—with death in the name of no cause at all. In March of 1781 Thacher wrote again of widespread fear of the "Cowboys" and "Skinners" on the neutral ground: "This is to be considered a very hazardous situation; it requires the utmost vigilance to guard against a surprise."[72] This was bipartisan violence, and its horrors prompted participants of any ideological cast to recognize an essential difference between political ideals and the terrorist acts spawned on either side.

On July 4, 1781, the New York publisher James Rivington—perhaps the most notorious and powerful civilian Loyalist on the continent—lambasted American leadership for the abhorrent conditions of life along the banks of the Hudson River. Only a small number of New Yorkers, he said, were patriots; those "consist only of such as despair of escaping the vengeance of their countrymen," and (he continued) in the madness of that despair, they "abandon themselves to all the cruelty of cowardice." He argued that the root cause of the "miserable condition[s]" there was not the marauding of both sides, but a deeply conceived fear of the secrets hidden in the region, which was at once the coveted prize of both armies and a resistant, ideologically unchartable, terrain: "Alive to suspicion, the general consideration [of Americans] is about spies and harborers of spies, and in the extremity of their terrors, the slightest preparations pass with the tyrants in office for demonstrable proof."[73] No longer did the neutrals affront both armies only by their comfort and property but now also by their invisible powers, the knowledge they may easily have absorbed simply through their presence on a tract of land resounding with the hushed tones of military secrets and the unspoken horrors of private tragedy.

It was on this neutral ground—just over three years after the death of Jane McCrea—that Major John André assumed the living form of devastating secrecy. This time, as legends would tell, not an innocent girl but the sacred trust of a virtuous cause would be violated. When André emerged from the woods, becoming visible to American forces, there could be no doubt of his fate. Like a specter that comes only in a dream, André had to be eradicated at that moment and in that world, or else he and the silent secrets he (for a moment) embodied would surely return in another guise. André's story did not offer the sentiments of love gone wrong; it was instead the haunting tale of a Loyalist officer who had carried within his boot papers capable of shattering the possibilities of independence. The legend proved seductive even so: The effusion of love and praise for André from the American imagination seemed utterly unguarded.

THE GENTLEMAN SPY

"Buoy'd above the terror of death, by the consciousness of a life devoted to honorable pursuits," Major André wrote from captivity to General Washington, requesting to die the honorable death of a soldier rather than the ignominious death of a spy.[74] At his trial too, André had spoken to redeem his honor. Denying the motive of "apprehension for [his own] safety," André stated that he hoped "to secure [him]self from an imputation of having assumed a mean character, for treacherous purposes or self-interest." He rightly believed that his "condition in life" and "the principles that actuated [him]" would evoke the esteem of his American captors, and he knew that he could produce letters to prove that he had been only "involuntarily an imposter."[75]

Though André's words would not save his life, they enshrined a virtuous portrait of his character. Both Patriot and Loyalist presses quickly circulated the trial documents, laced with partisan commentary. Even his captors esteemed his rank and cultural sophistication; to popular audiences it seemed an unfortunate irony that a man of such nobility should be captured by mercenaries, the Cowboys who roamed the neutral ground. The American troops who held André came to believe that he had "refused to be carried within the American posts" only to find that "the promise made him by Arnold was not observed." Accordingly, they treated him well during the days of his captivity, but in the end insisted that the laws of war dictated his death.

After all (as both the colonial forces and later American historians emphasized), the loss of West Point could have literalized—through military and political consequences—the deeply internal wound that the colonials had suffered in the defection of the prominent American general, Benedict Arnold. "No position in America could afford the British greater advantages," wrote Thacher in his *Military Journal*. West Point "commands the whole extent of country on the Hudson from New York to Canada, and secures a communication between the eastern and southern states."[76] The *Pennsylvania Packet* conveyed the gravity of the incident by reporting it in an extract from General Nathanael Greene's formal military orders: "TREASON of the Blackest Dye was yesterday discovered. General Arnold, . . . lost to every sentiment of honor, of public and private obligation, was about to deliver up [West Point] into the hands of the enemy. Such an event must have given the American cause a deadly wound if not a fatal stab." And so it seemed that the only way that the utter dissolution of the colonial cause had been prevented was in the chance detection of the event, which doomed André but also proved "that the liberties of America are the object of divine protection." In this context the colonial leaders hoped that André's execution—though regrettable, since (as even the newspapers reported) he was "one of the most eminent officers and polite men in the British Army"—would offer resounding proof that the forces for independence "are not to be deterred by great menace" and that they are "determined to extirpate [their] enemies one by one, until peace shall be restored."[77]

The West Point crisis focused both critical and reverential attention on the ethics of colonial principles and on both the integrity and humanity of its leaders. "In every officer," Frances Wright recalled, there was—potentially—"another Arnold."[78] All actions would be suspect now, but none more so than the decision to hang André as a spy. From a British perspective Richard Lamb argued that at André's trial, Generals Greene and Lafayette "thirsted for the blood of the unfortunate victim whom fate had put in their power."[79] But most of the controversy involved the role of the Commanding General Washington. When "the news of André's arrest and Arnold's treason fell like a thunderbolt upon the public ear," historians recalled, "all hearts turned for relief to the wisdom of Washington."[80] Correspondingly, later ages turned to his image as they retold and interpreted the event. As the legend developed, it became emphatically necessary from the American perspective to establish both reluctance and control in Washington's decision. With "the interests of his country at stake," wrote

Patriot historians, Washington must have seen that "private feelings"—his own, as well as André's—"must be sacrificed."[81]

Indeed, David Ramsay and others would emphasize the cultural loss in paeans that echoed André's own words: Stating and restating that his life was "stained with no action that gave [him] remorse," André fashioned himself not only as a cultivated man of the arts but also as a man of deep moral values.[82] Patriot historians believed him, and without self-conscious irony, they praised "his fidelity, . . . his high ideas of candor, and his abhorrence of duplicity".[83] The mission had been discovered, they claimed, because of that simple honesty which betrayed André to his captors. The earliest Loyalist pamphlets on the subject had made the same claims, and they explicitly contrasted André's image to that of their villain, George Washington, whose character, they argued, would now be "fixed [with] an indelible stain . . .—a stain which no time can efface." He would be remembered forever as "the unrelenting MURDERER of Major André."[84] It was part of the cultural work of the American legend to efface that stain without assault on André's purity.[85]

Washington had not met directly with André during his captivity, nor did he respond to (much less grant) André's last request for an honorable soldier's death; from these events Loyalists would infer the callousness of a man motivated by policy alone. Washington's silence, however, provided American legends with alternative possibilities: They imagined their commander—so deeply distraught as to understand the need for isolation and meditation, in the throes of a crisis both personal and military—still successfully enduring, steeling himself against the ineffable tragedy of war. "Washington's hand," Patriot writers contended, "could scarcely command his pen, when signing the warrant for the execution of Major André."[86] The fine character of the British officer had "melted [Washington's] angel soul."[87] This proved at once his compassion and its ultimate (safe) subordination to his reason and principles.[88]

Had André not been so personally and symbolically appealing, the story of the event would have been simple. In military terms the Americans could say that the net effect of the West Point plot was a clear colonial victory: With the loss of both André and Arnold, the British "exchang[ed] one of their best officers for the worst man in the American army."[89] André, however, had quickly ascended to be "a shining model of all that was excellent."[90] He was a model gentleman and suitor, as Alexander Hamilton noted, when he wrote to his fiancée, Elizabeth Schuyler, "I wished myself possessed of André's accomplishments for your sake."[91] He seemed to have all that America lacked, in his "industrious cultivation" of an "elegant taste for literature and the fine arts."[92] Thus his death was perceived not simply as a loss to Britain, but also as an indication of cultural sacrifice, an encoded fear of the inevitable losses that would attend American independence. The passing of two generations between the execution and the emergence of the historical romance in America did nothing to appease the controversy. Richard Snowden's "scripture style" *History* expressed a sentiment common not only to American historians but also to novelists, poets, and dramatists in 1823: "Even the scribe, at this late hour, hath caught the soft contagion; and is not ashamed to acknowledge, that the fate of *André*, entered deep into his soul."[93]

As the event passed into American legend, it maintained an ambiguity of tone, celebration mixed with caution. The loss of André became an emblem of "the fatal fruit of [Arnold's] treachery."[94] Writers of Cooper's era were caught by a sense that "there is a moral that breathes from the tale."[95] Only in the immediate sense had both Arnold and America escaped the consequences of the plot; the legend of André taught that each "midnight negotiation . . . carried on in darkness among the trees"[96] had costs and effects for both personal and cultural history. At the time of Arnold's treason, David Ramsay writes, the American army was in a particularly "distressed state" that promoted deep fears of "the contagious nature of treachery." And so it was that this one plot could suggest to the American forces a "boundless field of possible contingencies"—including rumors of other high-ranking traitors.[97] Perhaps more importantly, however, the tale of André revealed a broad fear of the hidden corners of subjectivity, its alarming power to resist or even betray the nascent civil order, and the fundamental inadequacy of modes of communication (both personal and military) to neutralize such power.

By 1798 William Dunlap's *André* would already display many of the cultural anxieties that the legend had begun to serve. The perspective of Dunlap's play is conciliatory and patriotic: Here André is clearly a sentimental hero, yet he remorsefully acknowledges his wrongs; the central conflict is thus cast as the insoluble human division between reason and passion, and accordingly the play gives no stage time to evil but only to the problems of ignorance and misunderstanding. As the play opens, George Washington is alone and silent, "wrapt in meditation deep" as he plans "the welfare of our war-worn land," while his officers find themselves "assail'd" by "many strange tales and monstrous rumors" of an incident of high-level treason.[98] As knowledge of the case comes to light, Washington—after the obligatory sentimental hesitation—insists on the necessity of André's death. Within the drama this execution is necessary to uphold the order of all human life—"to stem the flood of ills, which else . . . would pour uncheck'd upon the sickening world, sweeping away all trace of civil life"

(WD, 33). Nevertheless, this order comes at the high cost of immediate social distress. Fears of retaliatory killings prompt one American officer's wife to "kneel [and pray], till André, pardoned, ensures to [her] a husband [and to her children] a father" (WD, 36). Later, André's beloved Honora ends in madness as she cries that André's death will be "murder of the blackest dye" (WD, 60)—the language of her despair echoing Greene's announcement of the treason and thus equating Washington's decision with the villainy of Arnold's betrayal itself.

From Shays' Rebellion to the XYZ affair, serious threats to domestic and international order had been launched during the Federalist era, and to those threats, too, Presidents Washington and Adams had been firm in their resolve.[99] However, with the father of the country retired to private life and a new century on the horizon, Dunlap's America again faced uncertain dangers. Dunlap's play attests to fears of these divisive energies and—through the symbolic terms of the legend—expands the issues to include considerations of the place of America's new national culture in the larger world.

Two of the play's characters are at least as interested in their own theories of cultural development as they are in the fate of André. Seward, a low-ranking American soldier, seizes every opportunity to muse on the happy prospects of American isolation: It would be "heaven," he imagines, if "midway between" the "sever'd worlds" of America and the other continents, "barriers, all impassable to man" could stand, preventing any contact "till either side had lost all memory of the other" (WD, 23). However, M'Donald, an American officer and the embodiment of reason, insistently envisions America as a repository for all that is best in natural and human creation. Waves from the Atlantic Ocean "bathe" "Columbia's shores," while they "chafe" and erode the European and African continents (WD, 23). America seems a "new world," "a resting spot for man, if he can stand firm in his place while Europe howls around him" (WD, 11), and in these winds and waves, he believes, the best of the Old World will find its way to American soil. Only those with "ignorance curst," M'Donald insists, would disdain the treasures of "enriching commerce" and "blest science" that may be acquired from "Europe's knowledge" (WD, 24).

M'Donald never names André as one of those Old World treasures, destined for rest in America, but certainly within the context of the play, the *legend* of the incident is one such gift to American culture. Replacing the chaotic swirl of the "strange tales" and "monstrous rumors" of treason opening the play is M'Donald's vision of a true American legend of reason and virtue—a vision expounded in the closing monologue: The sadness and dismay of the moment of André's death, along with the sentimental cult of personality attending it, will be transformed by "the children of Columbia" into an understanding of the past and fortitude for the future. "In times to come," M'Donald predicts, America's children who "lisp the tale" will be dissuaded from the truth by "no foreign force, no European influence"; "the tongue of eloquence" will not be "awe[d] . . . to silence," and the story will be so fully and universally known that there will be no possibility of "misstat[ing]" the honorable American response to this early crisis of character.

From the frantic, disorderly imagination of the Revolutionary years, the enlightened reason will read the story of America's virtue: This is the resolution of Dunlap's play, framed as it is by the fearsome rumors of the opening scene and the confident synthesis of M'Donald's closing speech. Despite its formulaic quality, the resolution offers a powerful image of transformations in the cultural imagination. The play's innovation is the record of a brief interval of time during which the living André and the legend André coexisted; thus Dunlap dramatizes the entry of historical romance into the cultural imagination. In M'Donald's vision America achieves a strength that cannot be endangered by the world at large; this identity evolves out of an imagination focused on the sorting and careful use of the best raw materials to arrive on Columbia's shores. Sorting, in the case of Major André, necessitates execution, the obliteration of threat, while careful use entails the preservation of the residual imaginative power derived from his life, which in turn would provide the sustenance of the American storytelling imagination.

In Dunlap's drama, André's story works metonymically to illustrate the dynamics of the communal imagination within a new culture deeply unsure of the parameters of its identity. In raising the stakes of *André* to include both the lived history of the event and the beginnings of the cultural history of the legend, Dunlap emphasizes that in America both life history and imagined history are created from—and made powerful by—their enactment of the uncertainty of boundaries. André's mission and capture had been, literally, all about boundaries—the "dark and secret machinations" that seemingly pervade only the ambiguous Neutral Ground (WD, 6); the unknowable edges of this darkness through which one can pass unaware into enemy territory; the essential power—extending to life itself—of these borders, even if (or perhaps because) they are simply products of communal imaginings. So too was the legend of André about renegotiating boundaries within the emerging stories of American community. In this sense the residual power of the story had its haunting effects, including the measurable anxiety attending virtually all sympathetic portraits of André in early-nineteenth-century America. Facing death "with unfaltering nerve and steady eye," André's composure—as it was recorded in words and paintings alike—seemed an almost eerie reproach to his captors, and in his tie to Arnold, he was a reminder, too, of the possibility of threats from within Patriot lines and so of the impossibility of full, ideological control.[100]

꙰

Compiling a set of forgotten tales about the war, the New York editor Oliver Bunce mused on the near loss of Nathan Hale's memory and the persistence of André's: "There is something more than natural in this, if philosophy could find it out."[101] A few lonely voices lamented the fact that "so much mawkish sentiment has been expended" on André while Patriot spies were too often forgotten.[102] Hannah Adams and Jedidiah Morse complained that, despite an almost universal love for André, historians of the Revolution had left Nathan Hale "unnoticed, . . . it is scarcely known that such a character existed."[103] As Bruce Rosenberg notes, however, "[m]ost of the nation felt that, compared to André, Hale was a spear carrier."[104] In fact America's preference for the legend of André was part of a cultural reflex essential to nourishing a new story for a nation coming to understand itself (in James Thacher's words) as "a country in ruins." In this expansive (and troubling) form, the developing cultural story of America became an agent of mediation between the violent and disordered experience of lived history and the highest ideals of the romantic imagination. It was not that the legends would justify the history, nor that history would avenge the legends—though both are implied dimensions of the cultural work to be done. More importantly, the legends and the history would seduce and resist one another to the end, both in the utter incapacity of the culture to absorb or even to bring to light all of its secrets into a finished public identity and in the insistent refusal of the subjective imagination to surrender its knowledge and passions.

The legends worked—empowered a national imagination and found sustenance in community life—because they were stories of the very life of paradox, its appeal and its dangers. Though in some clear sense, Jane McCrea and John André belonged to the British cause, in their deaths they became creative agents of the American cultural imagination. When the spoils of the war were divided, America had no claim to possess these two martyrs, and for precisely this reason they became, potentially (and then actually), among the most vital symbols of culture. Utterly resistant to full appropriation, these two legends would carry with them a preserved dynamic potential; outside of both the security and the restrictions of known cultural patterns, these stories had tremendous capacities for symbolic representation, yet for the same reason they remained in a volatile relationship to the culture. In the emerging process of storytelling in America, the deaths of Jane McCrea and John André contributed enormous shaping powers that Cooper incorporates and substantially revises in *The Spy*. Very much in the tradition of these two legends, the tale of the Spy depends essentially on the unsolved tension among his possible identities—the idealized, the feared, the rumored, and the experiential; in each case, this tension speaks for the deeply disordered experiences of American origins, transmuted into figures for the (often dangerous and always alluring) power of cultural secrecy.

3

FROM REVOLUTIONARY LEGEND TO HISTORICAL ROMANCE

I n response to the problem of actively producing a symbolic America, the legends surrounding John André and Jane McCrea had stirred common sympathies in order to uncover and then contain disorder within their richly symbolic figures. The historical romance, on the other hand, assumed the presence of such disorder, often taking as its very subject the discordant relation among various possible cultural identities. Like the legends about André and McCrea, these stories were saturated with anxieties about the new nation's relationship to the private sphere and about the costs of establishing an independent way of life. But the romance was a more confident form of cultural expression. In fact, the more discordant the narrative, the greater the potential power of the romance: As confusions of plot and action were regularly dispelled by conventions of marriage or military glory, early American historical fiction—like so many British and continental texts in the same tradition—affirmed the power of narrative to display (in both theme and structure) the dangers of its world while still maintaining order.[1]

Texts in this tradition fused the divergent spirits of mythic optimism from high anxiety, as these twin forces dominated the cultural imagination during the Federalist and early republican years. In the preface to his romance of the War of 1812, *The Champions of Freedom* (1816), Samuel Woodworth defines the reconciliation of possible communal identities as both the matter and the method of the American historical romance. The object of his novel, he writes, is to mediate between the inevitable discontinuities of cultural experience: "to soften the rough notes of the bugle by the gentler tones of the lyre—to mingle the flowers of fancy with the laurels of victory—and to shift the scene occasionally from the hostile camp to the mansion of love. . . . To this end, many private events have been interwoven with the thread of public history."[2] To an anxious audience surely it must have seemed appropriate for the communal imagination to find a literary mirror in the flexibility and powers of reconciliation suggested by the neutral ground between public and private stories in the romance.

In this way the romance form served within the imagination as a new figure of the Revolution's contentious battlefields, ground for experiments and improvisations in communal identity. When the Revolution came to a close, orations continued to proclaim that in the newly formed republic, each citizen still had a battle to fight—an extensive tract of undefined space on which to write the story of America. Within the early republic this was first and foremost an imagined space of language and definition. As Henry Cumings put it, the end of the war marked the commencement of a struggle for self-definition and control: "Every patriot . . . has now an extensive field opened before him," he proclaimed in 1783, and if each citizen fulfills "all moral, social, and civil obligations," collectively they would "secure . . . all the blessings of society on earth," claim "vast tracts of uncultivated land," and "change this world into a sort of paradise."[3] In some real sense the romance signified a continuation of the long war for self-definition. Now, however, in this safely circumscribed realm of language, America was offered something of a new revolution. The spoils this time would include all of the raw material of undefined symbol and belief.

The growth of the early American novel had been meeting hostility, especially from those to whom political or social position had taught the powers of language. Acutely conscious of the cultural authority of words, they also recognized the dangerously permeable bounds of literary and historical discourse.[4] But even Thomas Jefferson, who distrusted "the inordinate passion prevalent for novels," conceded that historical fiction promised something other than the usual literary "poison."[5] In addition, Rufus Choate's famous proposal for remembering America through "a Series of Romances like the Waverly Novels" emphasized that "such works . . . would possess a very high historical value." They would be "not substitutes for history, but supplements to it," containing, as he said, "gleanings, if you please, of what the licensed reapers have, intentionally or unintentionally, let fall from their hands."[6] In Choate's essay and before, the recovery of these matters was presumed to be the recovery of knowledge that would be both powerful and welcome in the creation and maintenance of the self-created story of a strong nation, and—if successful—the historical romance in the United States offered to prove that "time-worn castles and gloomy dungeons" held no more "romantic interest" than "the war of the Revolution."[7]

Newly forming literary and historical societies strongly supported that unique interest in American subjects, and they turned their attention toward improving methods of recording. Such organizations were among the voices emphasizing that a vigorous new language must develop to tell the American story. With the Revolution, America had an event that it wished to remember and preserve; the mandate now was to sustain the life of the event, not simply to embalm it. The goals of both literature and history, Jeremy Belknap explained at the opening of the Massachusetts Historical Society, should be *"active,* not *passive,"* and guardians of those forms of language must "not . . . lie waiting like a bed of oysters, for the tide (of communication) to flow in . . . but to *seek* and find, to *preserve* and *communicate,* literary intelligence, especially in the historical way."[8] Through its chosen subjects, the historical romance would preserve national history. Through divergences built into its form, it would attempt to communicate new meanings for America, the experiences *between* the genre's official fields of inquiry, "the hostile camp" and "the mansion of love." It was in this spirit that the historical romance—above all other known means of expression in America—seemed to be a form capable of addressing some of the deepest anxieties of self-expression that plagued the Federalist and early republican years. In the effort to "preserve *and* communicate" the story of American origins at once, however, the historical romance would find itself strongly dependent on the forms of mystery not easily claimed by any imagined design. In their sentimental plots and their often inadequate or costly resolutions, these romances often recalled the mysteries invoked by legends such as those of André and McCrea, thus reopening the residual dangers within the stories. Most strikingly, the romances demanded attention to the subtext of those legends, the frightening, even hostile, images of the American land.

The land had deep and proven powers in the American cultural imagination—powers bivalent in form. This was the same symbolic land that had the nationalist capabilities of refiguring violently killed Loyalist sympathizers as symbolic American martyrs, as if they had magically cloaked their transformations in the powerful mysteries of the forest; it continued to be a place so resonant with competing potential meanings that it seemed infinitely fertile for the American story. Much of the romance of the land, though, had to do with its dangers. These were acknowledged in fictional and political writings alike. Romances of the Revolution frequently suggested that the "wild times" of national foundation had been shaped by "unseen powers . . . crossing their meshes here around us."[9]

In the political realm, the America of Cooper's time envisioned these threats by focusing on the dangers posed by Indians and by shifting (communal and national) boundaries. President James Monroe first sought to establish security along America's external boundaries: He reiterated—

especially to Russia and Spain—"that the American continents . . . are henceforth not to be considered as subjects for future colonization by any European powers." He assured other leaders that such landings would be considered "dangerous to our peace and safety" and indeed would suggest a revision of the United States' neutral policy in the Spanish Wars. Perhaps more surprisingly, however, he also directed exhaustive efforts to build roads and canals with the expressed purpose of casting out "unseen" terrors along the "inland frontiers."

From Monroe's policies alone it is clear that if the United States at 1820 was concerned with the vulnerabilities of its status as a neutral territory in an "unsettled" world, so too was it concerned with its own interior ruptures that might already exist, internal fissures that would precipitate the disintegration of even the most carefully defended nation. In his second annual message (1818), Monroe argued that independent Indian communities that existed within the claimed United States territories could not continue as such. It had become, in Monroe's words, "indispensable that their independence as communities should cease, and that the control of the United States over them should be complete and undisputed."[10]

The increased attention toward America itself in the romance form clearly suggests the nation's symbolic capacity to embody an untold story far more powerful than the stories that took place within its material space. As these romantic developments emerged, the figural land was far more than setting. The land began to take on almost human qualities in its suffering: Along the Hudson River, "blood of the soldiers mingl[ed] with the flowing brooks,"[11] and "the woods all rang with shrieks and dying groans."[12] In response to the demands of this complicated representation of the land, a series of stock figures became newly necessary in early American fiction. These were characters whose danger and power came from their abilities to hide in, and negotiate through, an undomesticated terrain; their existence was necessary to the cultural imagination, for within this setting—alive with mystery—was the only possible access to America's story.

Countless images suggested that what was harbored within the land was unmediated cultural truth; in revolutionary legends and historical romances, it was the land that had (theoretically) the most complete story to tell. From Woodworth's *Champions of Freedom* (1816) through revolutionary romances of the 1820s such as *Saratoga* (1824) and *Frederick De Algeroy, the Hero of Camden Plains* (1825), the woods are uniformly seductive; violence is the rule of existence, often taking place with an apparent randomness; all forms of knowledge—prophecies of glory and doom alike—are coded among the disorderly landscape, legible only in fragments.

Accordingly, in these texts, narrative order consists of illuminating the truth that is already there, at once instructing and reassuring an interpretive community in their powers to read the world around them. From the start the land was figured in a search for chosen listeners to receive its prophecies. Like the revolutionary martyrs, these figures had a bond with America that they could not find with any human community. They were isolated individuals characterized by mystery and integrity. One of the first to fill the role was the fictionalized George Washington, who proved to be as strong here as he had been in resolving the Arnold/André affair.[13]

Figurally, Washington became the heir and guardian of the land. Further, the "natural" qualities of his appearance and behavior became associated with the ancient mysteries of the Indians and the (quickly passing) relationship they made manifest with their native lands.[14] The most elaborate of the imaginative identifications of Washington with the Indians (and so with the continent) was a tale of an "Indian prophecy," a legend circulated through the early republic in newspapers, fiction, drama, and biographies.[15]

One version of the tale was published in the *United States Gazette* in 1826. In 1770, writes George Washington Parke Custis, while surveying lands along the Ohio to be given to those who had served in the French and Indian War, Washington and his companions were approached by a Great Sachem and taken to share in a banquet. After the meal the Sachem, through an interpreter in Washington's party, recalled a 1754 battle during which his men had repeatedly tried to kill Washington. But, he remembers, "a power far mightier than we, shielded him from harm. He can not die in battle. . . . [I] speak in the voice of prophecy. Listen! *The Great Spirit* protects that man and guides his destinies—*he will become the chief of nations, and a people yet unborn, will hail him as the founder of a mighty empire!*"[16] Through that promise, spoken (as it is said to be) by a native leader whose "influence extend[ed] to the waters of the great lakes and to the far blue mountains," the figure of George Washington is given a consecration that could be found nowhere else.

Within the tradition of the vast symbolic capacities of the American forests in the developing cultural imagination, it must have seemed especially appropriate that Washington should learn of the glorious destiny awaiting himself and his nation as he surveyed an unmapped interior territory. Here revelation and the work of culture fuse, each lending credence to the other, and—through the symbol of America—uniting symbolic and historical process. Many public commemorations of the Revolution sought to portray the spirit of the war as a cohesive force, moving within the continent ("the mighty energy of the whole mass . . . [and] the momentous heaving of the troubled ocean . . . [were] propelled onward by the lashing of its own waters, and by the . . . irresistible impulse of deep seated passion and power").[17] From the martyr's legends to the emerging myth of Washington, however, it is clear that stories of individual lives and events linked to cultural foundations could not stake the claim of conciliation so easily. Instead it was a major function of the legends within the culture to establish—through their symbolic method—a pervasive reach to the fragmentary manifestations of this spirit.[18]

COOPER'S USE OF THE LEGENDS

Although the emergence of John André and Jane McCrea as symbols of American martyrdom is in retrospect an extraordinary paradox, their assimilation into the new national story allows for new possibilities for cultural storytelling, in particular for the creation of an identity in process. If the essential meanings of the lives and deaths of these mythic martyrs could receive strong narrative shaping, still—even in their stories—the matter of America grew only more ambiguous through the multiple retellings. In part, this was the direct result of the inaccessibility of subjective vision within the legends: Both stories suggested that the interior of America had finally been seen, only to be taken to the grave as an unrevealed secret. It may have been unclear exactly how or why Jane McCrea died or what John André had intended by crossing American lines on his return from West Point. Without a doubt, however, their legends claimed, both figures entered the forests innocent and emerged so fully violated that their only possible end was death.

In these legends, then, the reconciliation of disorderly experiences within the frame of national martyrdom was attended by a paradoxically increased complexity within the symbol of America, so that out of this process the image of American identity was increasingly characterized by ambiguity and confusion. This is an inheritance claimed in the historical romance and addressed through figurations such as the ghost of Washington, preternaturally wise hermits, and, of course, Cooper's Spy. In *The Spy*, Cooper too replays the familiar conflicts among levels of language, experience, and knowledge in the cultural imagination; in doing so, he echoes Woodworth's novel, using structural division and a liminal hero to play upon the expectations of resolution. In both the social and the political sphere, it would seem that the disorder of the novel's neutral ground tends toward reconciliation; it is, after all, upon a familiar symbolic landscape that a common set of literary mechanisms—the figure of Washington, the sentimental romance, and the mysterious hermit spy—negotiate their struggles.

While invoking this same set of clues for reading a mysterious world, Cooper insists that at all levels, what these clues offer is no more than a false promise. In *The Spy*, as the narrator looks on, the land will not reveal its many stories: It is "rough," "dark," and—to the eye of the romantic narrator—it is even "barren" (299, 392). To this narrator and to the worlds of order and romance for which he speaks, the woods of America are dangerous not just for what is on the surface, but also for what lies beneath. They harbor a story he cannot see or tell, and it is a story that threatens the very reconciliation on which his authority rests. Rather than decoding this wilderness, then, Cooper's romance must acknowledge it as unreadable. By refusing to enter into the dark forests of the neutral ground, Cooper's narrator remains safe from the violent fates of Jane McCrea and John André; the resulting limitations in this narrative vision echo the residual ambiguity of these legends, reinscribing the mysteries of the American past that lie at the very center of the novel.[19]

In his inherited tradition of revolutionary legends, Cooper found the cultural construction of a "charismatic origin" from which a host of stories might proceed. In telling these stories, the mythic qualities of the receding past had to be reinvested in the culture in order for the American story to empower itself through the processes of transmission.[20] Searching for a national literature, William Ellery Channing complained that America's problem in expression was that words had fallen as "disjointed and dead . . . [as] inert materials." The power to animate them, he argued, "comes from the soul."[21] Cooper's revisions of American storytelling are part of this larger revaluation of cultural expression, a concern not only with subject matter but also with the methods and processes of imparting the American story to new generations. More particularly, Cooper's vision of these methods focuses on the complicated and necessary costs of investing human understanding in the experiences rather than the designs of history.

To this end Cooper returned to the ambiguous legends of experiential history that grew from the Revolution. Throughout America, not only had the tales of André and McCrea sustained their general resonance, but in the months surrounding *The Spy*'s publication late in 1821, New York was conspicuously active in reconsidering these particular histories and reconstructing memories of their lives. In the fall of 1821, John André's body was disinterred from the place of his execution and moved to Westminster Abbey;[22] six months later Jane McCrea, too, was moved from her wilderness grave to a ceremoniously marked tomb near her home community.

Cooper's return to these stories did not simply further the iconography they had already come to represent; this he only loosely invokes, as he focuses instead on excavating what he can of the prehistory of the legends, their initial status as events.

While quite a few historical romances in the United States had refigured these legends as ways of investigating the threatening qualities of the American wilderness, in the end most of them recast the legends in order to demonstrate their own methods for emphatically guarding against the dangers of history. By subordinating the mysteries of subjective experience to the mechanisms of romance, they still bore witness to the extraordinary symbolic powers of the martyrs within the cultural imagination. Cooper, though, insistently privileges the story of history above the narrative of reconciliation. Insofar as he invokes the legends, he does so at once to challenge their symbolic claims and to continue the storyteller's investigation of the imaginative gulf opened and unresolved by the legends, the America of a new cultural symbology.

During the main action of the novel, Cooper's temporal frame begins with anticipations of Burgoyne's northern campaign (in which Jane McCrea's death had played such a tremendous symbolic role), and—with little room for visionary speculation—the frame (preceding an epilogue scene that I discuss later) closes in the text's historical present, the immediate aftermath of the treason of Benedict Arnold and the execution of John André. In addition, within the plot the two legends are quite distinctly replayed in the ruin of Sarah Wharton, upon the knowledge of her British lover's betrayal, and in Henry Wharton, captured as a spy as he, assuming a disguise, crosses into the neutral ground on a visit home from the British Army. In each case, however, Cooper's version of the potentially symbolic figure becomes instead a bungling, awkward, and even comical character; the heroics of the stories are reserved for parallel characters—Frances Wharton and the Spy—strong figures whose experience, behavior, and skills all bear inverse relations to the misguided (and often absolutely incompetent) actions of Sarah and Henry.

Sarah's first words in the narrative are in praise of General Burgoyne and his northern campaign of 1777 (42)—the very campaign surrounding Jane McCrea's tragedy. Echoing the expansive tradition that had marked the British officer David Jones as "a liar and a deceiver" who lured Jane into danger,[23] Cooper betroths Sarah to an intended bigamist, Colonel Wellmere of the British Army (certainly his name is no accident and simply more proof of Sarah's inability to read the clearest of texts). As the couple discusses the war, Cooper laces their words with irony:

[T]he Colonel and Sarah [were] seated on a sofa, engaged in one of their combats of the eyes, aided by no little flow of small talk, . . . when the gentleman suddenly exclaimed—

"How gay the army under General Burgoyne will make the city, Miss Wharton!"

"Oh! how pleasant it must be," said the thoughtless Sarah in reply; "I am told there are many charming women with that army; as you say, it will make us all life and gaiety." (51)

A narrative gap (54) then eclipses the actual time of Jane's death and the reversal of Burgoyne's fortunes. As the action shifts three years ahead, however, still Sarah embodies a version of Jane starkly focused on exactly the terms of her life that went unnarrated in legend. Most romances allowed Jane's image into their stories precisely to obviate a recurrence of the tragedy. For example, the "enthusiastic and high-minded" heroine of *Saratoga,* Catherine Courtland, remembers "the frightful deed" of "the murder of the lovely and unfortunate Miss McRea" while she imprudently wanders alone in the woods; "she shuddered, as if she actually beheld the perpetrator of the cruel act before her."[24] In this novel the cultural symbol works its proper conservative function, and Catherine is recalled to caution. Sarah, in contrast, seems oblivious to this moral tale, and though her terrain is the parlor rather than the woods, she is in no less danger. Too easily flattered and excessively trusting, Sarah meets her downfall in her tendency to take "all the idle vaporings of her danglers to be truths" (50).

Embodying the inverse side of Jane's legend, Frances Wharton does enter "the darkness and dreary nature" of the forest, but not with the questionable motive of pursuing a lover.[25] Instead, Frances is "impelled by the generous wish of saving her brother" (378) from the unjustified accusations of espionage. Her motion in the woods "seem[s] to bid defiance to all impediments," and she travels through the very terrain on which she has seen the Spy. She considers the dangers to her person and to her reputation, but remembering that she is nearest to an American camp, she feels "but little apprehension": "They were her countrymen, and she knew her sex would be respected by the Eastern militia who composed this body. . . . Outrages of any description were seldom committed by the really American soldiery; but the maid recoiled with exquisite delicacy from even the appearance of humiliation" (376). Though Frances avoids the errors of both her sister and Jane McCrea, she still sustains little force as a center for narrative attention. Representing the narrator's ideal of a "heroine" (377) and uniting the disparate plots, Frances, her good deeds, and her marriage stand for an orderly alternative to Jane's legend.[26]

However, the ultimate failure of the alternative imagined through Frances becomes clear through the troubled form of narrative closure that her actions invoke. It is romantic closure, yet it is barbaric in its techniques. In the domestic sphere it demands the spurious deaths of several characters, including that of the lovesick Isabella, whose passion for Major Dunwoodie becomes a fatal flaw within the narrative logic. In fact, the weakness of the domestic structure is magnified through the novel's failure to imagine the security of married life; no such relationship is allowed during the course of action, with Sarah's narrow escape of a bigamist marriage representing the deepest affront to such order. Some spouses may be presumed to have been displaced by war, but many more, the narrative records, have been lost to tragic deaths or simply never found. Like the genteel Sarah, several lower-class characters, including the housekeeper Katy Haynes and the barmaid Betty Flanagan, meet only disappointment in their consuming searches for love and marriage.[27] The one happy marriage in the book, the climax of the formal romance pattern, is fraught with its own demons from start to finish: Not only does the union of Frances and Dunwoodie mandate that Isabella must die, but before the closing scene of the novel, Frances herself is dead.

Sarah was fated to disaster through her blindness to the lessons of history; yet Frances's solution offers little to address that problem. Though at opposite ends of a spectrum, both Sarah and Frances seek the safety of an orderly social world, and it is Frances's strength that she is willing to work toward that order. In the end, however, Cooper's narrative suggests that these have been misguided energies. The solutions that Frances's actions promote provide at best a temporary (and false) sense of equilibrium but no advances in knowledge.[28] Despite several contacts with Washington, Frances never sees through his disguise, and even her best efforts at saving her brother must be superseded by the Spy's covert activity. Each of Cooper's subplots suggests that the maintenance of order is premised on deception, and the cumulative power of this reiteration makes the strength of the rewritten order of Frances's world deeply suspect. Like the Wharton's home—a temporary, comfortable space within a chaotic world—all symbols of peace and contentment borrow heavily on compromising terms.

If Henry Wharton could have maintained his disguise, he would have been free to continue his visit home from the British army. Because George Washington assumes an alternative identity that does not reveal his real knowledge or power, he spares the families he visits any substantial reason for fear. If Colonel Wellmere could have suppressed word of his wife in England, Sarah Wharton would have been married to the man she loved. For all of the different implications of these tricks—ranging from loyalty to betrayal—each case presents disguise, even deception, as the necessary means to obviating the most rigorous challenges of experience and knowledge.

Cooper forces a parallel between Henry Wharton and André, but again the result is a pervasive irony rather than an invocation of a resonant cultural symbol. Henry's first concern on arriving home in his ill-fitting disguise is the possibility that, in the atmosphere of heightened tension following André's execution, he might suffer a similar fate (54).[29] Indeed, a similar charge is eventually made against Henry; a trial ensues, and the death penalty is imposed. But the facts of Henry's life—even the facts of his story—have virtually no relation to André's except in the realm of utter misinterpretation. Henry is not a spy; his lack of knowledge and skill rather than his covert powers entrap him in these charges. Further, once Washington publicly approves the execution order for Henry, the effect of that decision is quickly reversed by an escape plot that the Spy orchestrates, with Washington only as his necessary consultant. This is not the world of high heroic action and firm resolve that André's legend illustrates. Instead, each stable element of André's story is cast aside and subordinated to the inexplicable operatives of history. As a result of the trial, Henry emerges not as any sort of cultural symbol but in his truest identity as a pawn moved by historical forces he will never understand. Washington's identity too becomes strangely complicated by his incomprehensible entanglement with the mysterious forces of war on the neutral ground.

THE GENERAL AND THE SPY

Both disguised, "solitary traveler[s]" (35), characterized by "impenetrable reserve" (57), Washington and the Spy are at times indistinguishable from one another.[30] In this novel, however, it is the Spy and not Washington who is "ubiquitous" on the land, performing saving roles wherever he is needed.[31] This historical efficacy is linked directly to the Spy's inversion of the plots of the legends within the text. When he saves Sarah from the fire, for example, the Spy succeeds exactly where Jane McCrea's lover had failed: He is present at the site of danger, and he is capable of thwarting its powers.[32] He even succeeds in overturning the tragic execution order that alone provides any real evidence of Henry's tenuous identification with André. Neither Sarah nor Henry becomes an American symbol; they do not even become American sympathizers. The Spy's activity on the margins of these two failed legends suggests a different rewriting of the American story. Frances seeks to reverse the disorder of her world and to reconstruct it into a new narrative of stability, but the Spy's experiences show that—for him—this possibility must be dismissed. In place of that impossible desire, both Burgoyne's campaign and André's execution become the central matters of deepest interest to the Spy (323), and yet whatever his visions of the story of either event might be, they would have little to do with the cultural symbology that had grown out of their legends.

The Spy's radically new narrative promise comes from these particular images of the paradox of vision without voice; as a character type, he would have been familiar to Cooper's audience. Throughout the romance tradition were many hermits and spies who moved "from one place to another, . . . meeting with sundry accidents," teaching them far more than the settled American could know.[33] The ambiguities encoded in their liminal visions offer an otherwise unavailable critique of the new nation. Most of the hermit spies in American fiction were constructed as figures deeply entwined in the history and causes of the United States, but varying methods of distancing were necessary to allow for their unique visions.

William Wirt employs a British spy, for example, to write of America's lack of "that sacred *amor patriae* which filled Greece and Rome with patriots, heroes, and scholars." Ignoring American historiographical traditions, this spy looks not at the founding age of the Revolution (nor even of Puritanism) but at geology as he speculates on a story of the origins of the land.[34] In *Frederick de Algeroy* (1825), the real hero proves to be not the noble soldier named in the title, but a hermit who lives "surrounded by an extensive and spacious forest, so thickly interwoven as to be impervious to the searching eye." His isolation connotes both wisdom and sorrow and prompts the "general consideration" of "various and legendary tales concerning [his] reason."[35] Lacking clear roles within the known culture, these characters—like Cooper's Spy—were imagined to have potential powers beyond even those of officers and leaders.

Like the resolutions of familiar romance plots or the almost divine appearance of George Washington, who dispels narrative chaos in *The Champions of Freedom,* the hermit spies of American historical fiction promised their communities revelations of the mysteries of their world. The same promise is strongly suggested in the figure of Cooper's Spy. Harry B. Henderson argues that the Spy "redeems the anarchy of revolution by symbolizing the principle of nationalism," replacing all that is disturbing in early America "by reference to a national Ideal."[36] Nowhere in the text is a national ideal visualized, however. The frame of *The Spy*— moving as it does from the Americans' sudden favorable reversal with Burgoyne's defeat to the cataclysmic reversal of the Arnold/André affair—instead portrays a nation in crisis, without access to adequate sustaining ideals. In this context the Spy and his story come to embody not an abstract principle or value but a process of constructing a communal imagination from the materials of history, a mandate for the culture to sort from its emerging traditions a revised understanding of the relations between symbolic memory and the experiences of lived history.

The Spy thus enacts a paradox within the cultural imagination: Cooper invokes the methods of storytelling most potent in his culture, only to highlight within them not their powers to resolve history into narrative but the peculiar imaginative effects of the mysteries most resistant to that shaping process. For whatever celebration of American independence Cooper's chosen theme suggests, it is also clear from the formal structure of the novel that within this fictional frame the new nation is *not* created in the "broad daylight" imagined to surround modern foundations.[37] The patriotic glow of the revolutionary spirit is not even enough to illuminate the central subject of the novel, the Spy and his clandestine forest travels. In this way *The Spy* thematically invites the reader back into the culture's founding moments, issuing a call—as his most influential reviewer put it—to follow a newly American hero into "dreary and dangerous solitudes; [to] follow him through the perils and difficulties he surmounts, and [to] witness the long struggle of civilization, encroaching on the dominion of barbarism." As he uses the Spy to absorb the story of experience that the narrative never records, Cooper promises that this is a character who has the potential to be the storyteller no one else in his world can ever be. Structurally, however, this promise is revoked: The language of memory shaping the record of Cooper's narrative eye emphatically *denies* the reader a vision of the hero in his "solitudes" and "perils," providing *no one* but the isolated Spy to "witness the long struggle" of national birth.[38] In the final irony of the text, the structure of the novel ensures the silence of the Spy's voice—the only possible source of a new language of cultural foundation that exists within Cooper's fictional world.

4

REMEMBERING THE REVOLUTION
IN *THE SPY*

I am mortified to death—having just received (what I had been
so anxiously expecting) a Letter . . . and . . . perceiving it contained an invisible page . . . I assay'd it by the Fire, when to my
inexpressible vexation, I found that the paper, having by some
accident got damp on the way, had spread the solution in such a
manner as to make the writing all one indistinguishable Blott.
            —Major Odell to John André, May 31, 1779

I N *The Spy,* the American cultural imagination partakes of both the language of unspoken memory and the language of planned and articulated foundations, building on these toward a story of American experience. As the novel defines it, that imagination is the source of cohesion
around which the culture circulates. The submerged development of the
Spy's character and actions throughout the book provides a figure for the
evolution of the imagination he represents: Like the Spy, the cultural
imagination in Cooper's terms protects the promise of an American story,
directs communal consciousness toward the acceptance of experiential history, and yet abandons any demand for the immediate and full revelation
of the knowledge encoded within. Though harboring cultural secrets, this
is an imagination generated by utopian hopes and fortified by a particularly nineteenth-century American national loyalty. Horace Bushnell
described this loyalty as creating a communal bond "sanctified to be the
matrix of the coming nationality and the Constitution to be":[1] So too
these cultural imaginings of America's future created a story that would
be sacred before it functioned at all, and yet also (paradoxically) one that
must be consecrated only through its workings in history. In *The Spy,*
Cooper develops this notion in opposition to what he represents as the
pervasive impoverishment of other cultural rituals that had been
employed in memorializing the Revolutionary War. Within the novel, a
different American ritual of expression supersedes the failed structure of

familiar imaginative resolution, and the replacement process illuminates a model of the relations between ideology and form in American literature through which the events of history witnessed in life—but not in writing—come to play a central role in the very narratives that most forcefully exclude them.

This becomes evident through the Spy's position within the narrative. The novel explores the position of American memory and imagination with relation to an inaccessible past and an unknown future. Each recognizably patterned cultural story that the novel includes ultimately fails, and so the novel portrays an image of the nation as the product of unknown history and unpredictable experience. Like the symbolic tomb of a nation's Unknown Soldier, Cooper's text encases the elusive nexus between personal and cultural history, conceding without hesitation the irreclaimable loss of the subjective component of experiential knowledge and leaving that resonant silence to be (in Benedict Anderson's terms) "saturated with ghostly *national* imaginings."[2] *The Spy*, however, has a dimension that is not fully satisfied with this modern image of a community's consensual retrospection: The Spy's job—as he stands on the threshold of a new state—is not only to receive such imaginings, but more specifically, to solicit the will to imagine. It is an act of primordial power, with a visionary's belief in future promise.

In that capacity as the harbinger of a coming age, Cooper's Spy has a familiar role in American literary history. In his classic study, *The American Adam*, R. W. B. Lewis demonstrates the ways in which nineteenth-century American literature searched for ways of representing "a new kind of hero in a new kind of world." Lewis's Adam is "an individual emancipated from history," who "takes his start outside the world, remote or on the verges," and who must "master or be mastered by" his world's "power, its fashions, and its history." In his modern condition of exile from the very world he serves and symbolizes, in the new story he has to tell, in his wandering homelessness, and in his search for a community of understanding, the Spy stands as an American Adam.

His role within the emerging story of American culture, however, includes a central reversal of the Adamic model as well. While the American Adam is a character innocent of historical knowledge and "unconscious of time" who enters a "history laden environment" that he then helps to renew, the Spy is a character deeply laden with history—personal and cultural.[3] He enters a world that has been somehow blinded to the content of its own experiences. In his case, the cultural function of renewal lies not in compensating for the injuries of time and experience through innocence but precisely in bringing about a communal acceptance of historical knowledge while absorbing the disruptions that such knowledge will bring. Carrying with him the historical knowledge necessary for cultural renewal and yet standing alone in a precarious position on the brink of a new age, the Spy lives within the rift between past and future in American culture.

It is telling that the Spy is not a part of the chaotic opening scene of the novel. Amidst "chilling dampness, and increasing violence . . . of the approach of a storm," "darkness," "a thick mist," and an atmosphere in which "[g]reat numbers . . . wore masks," the Spy is "away . . . wandering" (35–37), and no one knows where. His textual absence creates a silence that is, paradoxically, a form of expression, apart from the confusions of plot. The Spy's existence, like his silence, is (by contrast with the represented world) assumed to be saturated with private experience and the utopian project of cultural order, just as, within the novel, the shaping forces of that story come from the deepest internal knowledge and from the static narrative frame. Interdependent and unresolved, the Spy and the novel's plot, along with their attendant layers of expression, serve as voices of American language that—through their dynamic resistance as much as through their own limited achievements—encode the story of a culture in process. It is the space between these levels of expression, the field of their interactions, that the narrative silence in *The Spy* records and that (Cooper suggests) is both the most promising and the most dangerous ground for the development of the cultural imagination.

THE SPY'S OWN STORY

Narrative silence in *The Spy* becomes a language unto itself—a language never received by, but still shaping and shaped by, the narrative structure. Cooper emphasizes the incongruity between experiential history and the realm of the romance as a means of illustrating the separation between these levels of cultural language. Nowhere are the limitations of romance more evident than in the novel's fruitless struggle to bring the silence of the central character's experience into the language of narration. The silence of the Spy's knowledge long precedes his actual death: Both in life and in death, the Spy embodies a force and a vision irreconcilable to plot or pattern, and both his isolation and his cultural power are most clearly marked by the limits of narrative language. When the Spy is surrounded by "conversation . . . on the ordinary transactions of life, his air is abstracted and restless" (60); he finds that language in its ordinary descriptive function is no avenue to power or knowledge. Accordingly, on issues of personal experience, passion, and devotion ("of the war, and of his father") the Spy "seldom" speaks; when he finally meets the disguised George Washington, it is with an appropriately "silent bow" (60).[4]

Living a life fraught with moments of an even sublime danger, the Spy feels the inheritance of memory; it is as if the silence and the dangers help him to listen—not only to the soldiers and their plans—but also to the land itself and each symbolic claim upon it. The Spy's disengagement from social language, along with the narrator's distracted attentions toward the reconciliation of visible plots, combine in the novel not only to expose the representational limits of the narrative voice within available forms of language but also to associate the Spy with that distinctly potent silence, one so potent as to be imagined as a language bound closely with the deepest knowledge of history.[5]

For all of the Spy's promise, there is an attending frustration left to those (within and outside of the text) who must interpret him because his promise depends upon an elusiveness that prevents settled understanding and stable knowledge. Although this "neutral ground" of character and history is a field of competing forces of language and consciousness for which no single voice can provide adequate reconciliation, Cooper's narrator still directs all efforts toward that language of mastery. Like many of his characters, this narrator proceeds according to a single design of comfort, order, and stability. Furthermore, like Sarah Wharton, who is driven mad by the knowledge of betrayal, this narrator demonstrates no capacity to confront that which will not fit neatly within a preconceived system. Though in spirit the narrative consciousness shares the desires of the colonial "civil authority [that] thought it incumbent to examine narrowly into [the Spy's] mode of life" (59), it is exactly this narrowness that prevents substantive knowledge: "[G]lances at him were uncertain and fleeting. The intermediate time no eye would penetrate" (146). The Spy's travels through history and experience thus take him "where no man" (including the narrator) "will dare to follow" (372). He lives among "the imperfect culture of the Neutral Ground," in a lawless borderland. Here, among "rough and unequal hillocks" and "the barren sterility of the precipices" (399), the Spy's knowledge and motion are hidden by "the obscurity of the night" (137). In terms of his experiential knowledge of the Revolution, the language of storytelling, and the cultural imagination, the Spy's world is predicated explicitly on the powerful existence of something beyond the narrator's articulated romance, essential to the causes and events of that world, and yet beyond the acknowledged patterns of culture.

Whether the narrator is aware of it or not, the Spy's story is the real matter of Cooper's book. The ironies abound here, as the Spy—even before his complicated military service begins—is virtually invisible to his culture, an impoverished man, "but little noticed and but little known" (58). However, his life enacts a story of the submerged disorder of national origins—including but not limited to the victimization of the weak, the arousal of the most self-serving instincts, betrayals, poor decisions, and needless violence. Even this disorder, though, is necessary to the culture; like all myths of origins, it cannot be replaced, not even with an easier tale of harmony or reconciliation. "One of the misfortunes of a nation," Cooper wrote in his 1843 preface to *Wyandotté*, "is to hear little besides its own praises." There, in the last of his novels of the Revolution, Cooper would issue a warning to his American audience: "[A]lthough the American revolution was probably as just an effort as was ever made by a people to resist the first inroads of oppression, the cause had its evil aspects, as well as all other human struggles. . . . [T]here is a danger of overlooking truth, in a pseudo patriotism. Nothing is really patriotic, however, that is not strictly true and just."[6] Everything about *The Spy* suggests that the dangers facing America in 1821 are even more grave: In this earlier novel, the issue at stake for the communal imagination is not simply an established ritual of patriotism but the process of sorting the earliest memories on the way to establishing the very essence of cultural identity. Neither heroic nor pure, these are the life experiences left out of cultural classifications. As a frequent interruption to the narrator's dual plots, the Spy is a persistent reminder that even if these plots contain (as they quite nearly do) all of the essential action of *The Spy*, they hardly touch upon its story.

As George Washington's most trusted secret agent, the Spy is the novel's namesake, presumably the main character, and the *only* agent of meaningful change in his community, yet his actions rarely cross the borders into the narrative vision. Making only brief and ambiguous appearances in the knowable spaces of his culture, the Spy might be anyone; his personal history is sealed. In fact, all aspects of the Spy's identity, and the secrets he must know, are locked deeply beneath the level of the narrative plots in a space entirely apart from the acknowledged patterns of his world.[7] Thus the subject of the novel struggles for survival not only among the violence of the fictional world but also within a narrative framework that plainly cannot accommodate his story. Both within Cooper's narrative structure and among the emerging traditions of American romance, then, the Spy is an anomalous figure.

The Spy's ambiguity, however, functions primarily as a critique of perception: The Spy remains enigmatic only (or exactly) insofar as both his culture and even the narrative form that surround him have no adequate language for the reconciliation of his life and the expression of his story.

The emergence of the Spy's story comes instead as the social world presented in the novel—made up of the dual plots between which the Spy exists—proves to be easily challenged and quickly proven vulnerable. A vivid example of this is the Spy's improvisational decision as he is chased by the colonial officer, Captain Lawton, to dive to the ground and trip the officer's galloping horse: "[B]oth steed and rider came, together, violently to the earth," and the officer calls out for a " 'bone-setter . . . to examine the state of [his] ribs' " (139–40). Expecting that the Spy would either fight or flee, Captain Lawton becomes the easy victim of his inflexible imagination, making the simplest opposition devastating. Like Captain Lawton, the narrator (and reader too) rides quickly along familiar paths; it is the extraordinary distraction—even the radical intrusion—of the Spy across these paths that utterly alters perspective and expectation.

Similarly, when the Spy speaks in the text, he is most often unheeded, as when he arrives at the Locusts to warn of the impending fire (275).[8] Ironically, within most of the plot, only the gossip-hungry Katy Haynes does the Spy "'partial justice' " (201), and this because of her financially driven romantic designs on him. Reflections on Katy's desires and on what may be the Spy's own authentic love of money thus offer among the few— and slight—insights into the Spy's character; he becomes, then, strongly associated with the idea of acquiring cultural currency, literal and figurative.[9] By remaining isolated from traditional familial and social bonds, the Spy succeeds at this; he devotes himself entirely to his overtly political culture and submerges his personal experiences within this communal role. Thus within the fictional frame, the Spy's actions demonstrate his quiet belief that the apparent deviance of the role he plays is local and time-bound—that his actions (despite his culture's failure to understand them) will serve well in the present crisis, and that he, in a new role (or at least free of the restricting misinterpretations of his wartime identity), will be able to reassimilate into the changed society that he will have done so much to establish. One of the improved features of the new social order thus should be a larger narrative framework, expanded boundaries of knowledge, which would permit the ritual integration of a once-exiled figure.

If indeed this were the case, then the Spy's temporary sacrifices would serve well within the familiar terms of cultural ritual.[10] Traveling the forests to learn the higher cultural wisdom of revolutionary secrets, for a time the Spy necessarily would be "structurally, if not physically, 'invisible'" according to his society's categories of knowledge; he would be hidden beneath the concrete and fixed details of his social world, or in textual terms, submerged beneath narrative representation, awaiting an invitation to exchange some of these powers of wisdom for social re-aggregation.[11] Within both the Spy's fictional world and the language of the text, however, no such exchange is possible. In life and in death, the Spy maintains both his invisibility (with its narrative form, silence) and his powerful relationship toward his emergent culture.

Rather than leaving a community and then returning, the Spy—consistently, actively—is engaged in the actual production of culture, the rewriting of ritual, experience, and knowledge. In his paradoxical condition of exile to the most fertile borderlands of his world (historical, experiential, and imaginative), the Spy is in constant motion, as if his life experiences were etching the signs and symbols of a new language for a new story along the changing frontier.[12] In just one of many scenes of disguise and escape, the Spy's borderland existence demands his social death and sustains his mortal life:

> He knew that by bringing himself in a line with his pursuers and the wood, his form would be lost to the sight. This he soon effected, and he was straining every nerve to gain the wood itself, when several horsemen rode by him but a short distance on his left, and cut him off from his place of refuge. The peddler had thrown himself on the ground as they came near him, and was in this manner passed unseen. But delay now became too dangerous for him to remain in that position. He accordingly rose, and, still keeping in the shadow of the wood, along the skirts of which he heard voices crying to each other to be watchful, he ran with incredible speed in a parallel line. (138)

Rarely able to stop moving, at times inside and then suddenly beyond the borders of both social and narrative space, the Spy has neither a "place of refuge" nor a fully composed identity. Thus within the fixed structures of knowable worlds, the Spy has no voice, no means of self-expression; he is left within the liminal mode of perception in a moment of mysterious revelations requiring full immediacy of response (as figured here in his constant motion), and so implicitly denying the possibility of a retrospective description or report. Because he is unable to move far enough from the forest to be able to tell his community what he knows, the Spy finds his peculiar form of liminality no easy state to escape.

The remarkable absence of reaggregation in the life story of the Spy implicates his culture specifically in a failure to acknowledge those stories that defy the definitions and classifications of accepted historical knowledge. While the boundaries of this knowledge are ambiguous, in Cooper's text and throughout many texts of the early republic, they are boundaries notably excluding the lived history of cultural origins, the experiences preceding symbolic formulations. In the Spy's silence, however, Cooper reopens that field of language to suggest an extraordinary range of possible results for the new revolution in storytelling that might grow from a philosophy of experience and lived history. The Spy's silence is not just a matter of textual absence. It is a matter of labyrinthine structural forces—both cultural and narrative—directing the imagination toward a certain set of questions shaping the interpretations of the events of national origins. The inadequacies among these interpretations then suggest that secrecy, subversion, and lost or inaccessible knowledge are all laced among the familiarities of cultural reassurance; in this way, the limits of all such known patterns of life and narration are illuminated through the form of narrative silence. Suspended between the remembered and the forgotten, the Spy plays with equal importance at each end of the imagination. The Spy—as the American story making up his subjective vision—embodies process, motion, and growth; he exists at the frontier of signification. The unmapped distance between the subject of interpretation—the Spy himself, and America, too—and the language of orderly, confident representation—the narrator's world—becomes the most expansive form of the "neutral ground" of the book's subtitle.

In this formal rather than thematic sense, *The Spy* is most forcefully an inaugural expression of developments within the American cultural imagination. Like the cognitive impossibility of knowing a full experiential history of America's cultural origins, the Spy—in relation to his narrative's epistemological frame—permeates his world and yet (or, and so) still has no recognized place within its consciousness. As Walter Benjamin has written, while a story remains untold, the potential storyteller's identity is inseparable from the essence of the story; in this model is a partial accounting for the Spy's unrelieved isolation. He is story waiting to become storyteller; he has all of the potential accorded to both. While Cooper's narrator sets out to design, control, and explain a world apart—from the safety of codified memory—a true storyteller, Benjamin writes, "will let the wick of his life be consumed completely by the gentle flame of his story."[13] With knowledge that extends beyond the power of his own culture's language—and then framed within an imaginative structure still (in 1821) unable to sort contradictions fully—the Spy's voice and identity indeed remain inseparable. As a storyteller, then, he can transmit his life and his knowledge only by maintaining his fidelity to a program of cultural secrecy.

THE PROBLEM OF RECONCILIATION

The Spy's only structure of community had been based on a relationship of deep understanding, sustained, Cooper suggests, by a private language perhaps formed in the closed secret of his family's tragic past; as such, it no longer promises (if it ever did) an escape or retreat from the surrounding culture. Instead it is a form of communication that the public realm has proven unable to read or accommodate. There are secrets written just beyond the threshold of narrative understanding that would perhaps illuminate the bond between the Spy and his father, the "tie . . . of no ordinary kind" (151) within the "sacred offices of filial love" (155). These are not private stories for a retreat of the imagination, but instead they have functioned as the generative force of belief shaping the Spy's actions throughout time. To Cooper's culture, there is something newly modern in this way of living and imagining. As Hans Blumenberg has written, a new style of "self-assertion" in history first becomes possible, even necessary, when "the vanishing point" of "human hope" is no longer clearly placed "beyond the world," when the processes of history and experience replace the visionary belief in providence and cosmological order.

Perhaps because he has lost his bearings with the loss of his family, the Spy, Cooper makes clear, cannot believe in order, only in history. The Spy's dilemma is that he lives within this modern consciousness—the conditions, as Benedict Anderson has argued, for the emergence of the nation—while his interpretive community does not. For most of Cooper's characters, life history has surprisingly little to do with predicting future experience; gender, ethnicity, and class have less than their ordinary powers as they are lost amidst a host of escapes and disguises on the lawless neutral ground. For the Spy, however, Cooper makes it clear that the precise circumstances of his identity formatively shape the range, if not the intensity, of his anticipations as he encounters his culture. For the Spy as for no other character, the "historical situation" of his life—shaped especially by his isolation and his poverty—is acknowledged to be the determining factor in his negotiations with the surrounding world. Nothing less immediate than the Spy's life, his familial history, and now his national devotion, "determine the horizon of possible experiences and their interpretation"; his own circumstantial knowledge thus embodies "the 'a priori' of the world's significance" for him.[14] Superstitions and symbols dominate communal interpretation in the novel, but only historical necessity and experiential knowledge dictate the Spy's actions and beliefs.

The Spy is left to make these negotiations with history and his world alone because the alternative frame of horizons and the potential agent of his assimilation—the narrative itself—fails. Certainly throughout the novel, the Spy has gained cultural currency—both literal and figurative. Within Cooper's framework, however, the Spy has neither asked for social acceptance nor turned from his world; thus he has become inexplicable within the language of his culture. By maintaining a silent guard over his secrets, the Spy has both served his culture and resisted its coding. This is an ambiguous and costly freedom, and the price the Spy has paid is clearly evident in the ways in which the language of his world refuses to include him. In this way both his unrelieved isolation and his exclusion from all patterns of language begin simply at the level of character interaction but then extend to the very form of the novel. In only one episode does the buried history of the Spy's life approach the narrative surface; it is a telling moment not simply in its firm establishment of the Spy's isolation but also in the narrator's clear refusal to enter into the dynamics of that powerful realm of secrets.

To Katy Haynes, the housekeeper, the Spy and his father are surrounded by an impenetrable and mysterious sadness. She has overheard enough to know that years ago "a fire had reduced them from competence to poverty, and at the same time diminished the number of their family to two" (58). However, through the Spy's "awful warning," Katy had then learned that "there were bounds [of knowledge] beyond which she was not to pass" (59); her quest for the Birch family history is easily thwarted, and gossip or speculation serve her purpose.

Years later, though, Katy by chance has access to the story she desires, and this time there are no imposed bounds. On legitimate business she opens the family bible to look for a will, but—as if drawn back to that mystery of origins—her eyes fall immediately to the family record. She begins to "read . . . with great deliberation" from the very first page written "with the labors of a pen"; she finds the catalogue of births interrupted by a passage relating the secret tragedy both she and the reader have long waited to learn. Promising to help explain the melancholy and mystery of the Spy, the scene elicits every romantic expectation; it even evokes patterned resolutions such as the transformation of Major André's story from "monstrous rumors" into a legend of American honor in William Dunlap's play. Perhaps, it seems, the Spy will finally assume for his community and his readers a life story based on some words beyond idle chatter.

However, just as Katy begins to read the sentence recording the "*awful day* [when] *the judgment of an offended God lighted on* [the Birch family's] *house*," she "instinctively close[s] the book" (150), frightened, she believes, by a ghost.[15] With this perverse closure Cooper forever seals inquiry into the Spy's personal past, allowing his narrator only a brief commentary, no more informative than those words Katy had overheard some time ago: "[H]ad Katy but read a few lines further in the record, she would have seen the sad tale of their misfortunes. At one blow, competence and kindred had been swept from them, and from that day to the present hour, persecution and distress had followed their wandering steps" (151). In Katy, this failure to read is an expected moment of carelessness and haste. In the narrative replication of her blindness (including this "explanation"), however, the narrator makes a significant and complex gesture—the refusal to know—thus exposing the limits of his vision in the very attempt at omniscience.

Through the ignorance of his housekeeper and his neighbors, the Spy loses all chances for private domestic happiness, and within the novel, this loss is a figure for the even higher costs of failing patterns of interpretation, too weak to understand or explain the secrets of history. Nowhere are the dynamics of this secrecy more in evidence than in Cooper's complicated representation of George Washington as America's historical father. In Samuel Woodworth's *Champions of Freedom*, the natural processes of time and maturity take the young hero beyond his own father's care, but just when he feels most bereft of support, the "allegorical" father, the "Spirit of Washington," provides an invitation to new levels of knowledge and understanding through the comfort of wisdom and kindness. In mythic terms Woodworth's romance argues that the familial bond is thus continued—even strengthened—through a symbolic system invulnerable to the ordinary limits of experience, the inevitable distances of time and space. In the Spy's (ultimately impossible) transition from the ties of kin to the ties of community, however, the exchange he makes by sacrificing his personal life for a cultural role is exposed for an essential incongruity: The attempted transition is framed within the stark representation of an impoverished culture unable to supersede or even to replicate the bonds of private loyalty.

Of all of the characters on the neutral ground, the Spy had found only his father would understand him. After each of his "secret marches of danger" he would return to the "consolation" of his father's "blessings and his praise" (201). In words never recorded in the narrative, the Spy had told stories of his journeys to his father, and in doing so he had found compensation for his utter isolation from the larger community. Within the symbolic vocabulary of the narrative, the process of the Revolution has rendered the Spy's father weak: Although he alone has access to the immediate story of the true experiences of time and history that his son's life represents, this knowledge makes him only more vulnerable to history's own powers for destruction. Living in the "single inhabited building" on "the ground on which [the novel's] action [is] fought" (145), the Spy's father inevitably falls victim to plunder, disease, and finally death. But to his son—who longs to retreat from the crippling falseness of his imputed symbolic roles (god, beast, enemy, in uncanny simultaneity)—the elder Mr. Birch retains a particular strength; he is a repository of historical understanding, a deep source of human recognition.

Thus when his father dies, the Spy waits with high expectations to meet with George Washington, the second father he has served. Perhaps here the symbolic and personal roles will fuse, now freeing the Spy's locked history by means of cultural assimilation. This is a recognition scene explicitly set to counterbalance the earlier loss of the true father; it promises also to reverse the comic failure of Mr. Wharton to recognize his son in the opening scene (43). Earlier in the novel the Spy looks forward to this moment; swallowing the identifying note that would set him free from his captors, he had reminded himself of the rewards to come. When one of the American soldiers threatened the Spy by saying, " 'even the justice of Washington condemns you,' " the Spy had replied "in a manner that startled" his captors: " 'Washington can see beyond the hollow views of pretended patriots. Has he not risked his all on the cast of the die? If a gallows is ready for me, was there not one for him also? No—no—no, Washington would never say, 'Lead him to a gallows' " (221). Here the Spy's denial of possible betrayal, as well his "trembl[ing]" and evident fear, suggest both the strength of his desire for recognition and his fear that it will never come.

So it must be read as a great disappointment but not a surprise, when Cooper's Washington claims the restraints of civil order in his deeply limited recognition of the Spy's duties. Here, the Revolution is nearly over; the Spy has remained faithful to the cause (even to the brink of death) by suppressing all essential facts of his identity. He comes—as he once came to his father—to alleviate his isolation, to collect the justice due his memory. This time, however, the father's recognition leads only to further isolation. There is no social parallel to the rewards of familial intimacy; Washington offers the Spy neither the laurels of cultural heroism nor even the public restoration of good character:

> [A]t length the officer arose and, opening a desk that was laid upon the table near which he sat, took from it a small and apparently heavy bag.
>
> "Harvey Birch," he said, turning to the stranger, "the time has arrived when our connection must cease; henceforth and forever we must be strangers."

The peddler dropped the folds of the greatcoat that concealed his features and gazed for a moment wildly at the face of the speaker; and then,
dropping his head upon his bosom, said meekly—
"If it is Your Excellency's pleasure." (422)

The Spy, the faithful son of liberty, refuses the monetary reward and simply reaffirms his commitment; "conceal[ing]" his face again, he is apparently willing to see his life devoured by the secrets he carries, to watch the
affirmation of his name on Washington's lips once again turn him into a
"stranger."[16] As Washington explains it, a cultural imperative now formally
relegates the Spy's personal story to silence; for the present stability and the
future good of America, "it is necessary" that the gaps in perception and
knowledge sustained throughout the text be reconciled only through his
"fidelity" to the maintenance of an untold story (422–24).

In her 1822 review of *The Spy*, Sarah Hale had objected to "the manner in which Gen. Washington" is portrayed in the novel by suggesting
that "too great a violence [is done] to our veneration of this immortal man"
when he is represented only in actions and situations that equally would
suit "an inferior agency."[17] Nonetheless, she admits that the dangers of
assumed familiarity with one of history's heroes—as a mechanism of fiction—can at times facilitate an aesthetically pleasing resolution. Writing
fully within the vocabulary of expectations shaping the early American
historical romance, she praises the recognition scene between Washington
and the Spy for its reconciliation of secrets and promises. In Cooper's portrayal of American loyalty, she finds not loss or ambiguity but a fully satisfying reward, an adequate blend of realism and magical revelation, and a
just conclusion to the story:

[T]he war [draws] nearly to a close, [and] Harvey Birch has an interview
with Washington, whom we now discover to have been the dignified and
efficient *Harper*. Such is the consummate skill with which the part of the
Spy is sustained, that we now learn with surprise that he has been,
throughout, the confidential agent of the great father of his country—
and firmly devoted to the interests of America. Under every vicissitude
he had been sincere and constant, vigilant and formidable. He is offered
gold as a compensation for his services, which he rejects, but receives
with gratitude, a frank testimony to his merits, although he is told that
he must remain perhaps, for ever, under public reprobation, as his con-
nexion with the commander in chief, cannot be avowed.

With this scene, Hale writes, "the work might very satisfactorily have concluded." Hale's appreciation of the final meeting between Washington and the Spy obscures the fact that the narrative simply does not resolve itself into harmony at this or any other point. In fact, by the time they meet, the Spy's role and even the identity of Harper have long been clear to readers, and Washington's "frank testimony to [the Spy's] merits" ("to me, and to me only of all the world, you seem to have acted with a strong attachment to the liberties of America" [422]) is as much a formal command, a life sentence to silence, as it is a reward. After his father's death, the Spy is left to find "all places . . . now alike, and all faces equally strange" (201). In his relationship with Washington, the Spy finds only further alienation, a social death suggesting the ironic inversion of the security and comfort of a father's care. In their meeting Washington's first words to the Spy are not of recognition but of the necessary cessation of a dialogue that—in terms of narrative representation—has never even begun. As if the voice of this founding father truly might have the power to mute all revelation, personal and historical, the Spy can only stare in disbelief and then acquiesce. He leaves as he has entered, "unheard by the officer" (422), understanding that Washington and a fragile idea of America have just condemned him "to descend into the grave, branded as a foe to liberty" (424).

If, as Hale claimed, this is the reconciliation scene of "so fair a specimen of native talent," then it has taken a surprisingly antagonistic form.[18] These paradoxical conditions for the convergence of narrative energy provide an image of a deep ambiguity running throughout the narrative: the persistent opposition between the expectations of romance and the events of history, extending well beyond the lives and actions of the characters. In every instance, plans and disguises on the neutral ground—plans to convey or to receive information, to give or to accept a reward—work only in the service of deception, to be challenged ultimately by the crosscurrents of experience, the changes mandated by time and history. Through these tensions the novel critiques a system of cultural interpretation in which symbols have a scarcely legible connection to the life histories they represent. Opened through the structured silence of the Spy's story is a space for a new model of interpretation: There the American imagination would be most threatened with the loss of its ideal forms, but *only* there might the possibility of renewal still exist.

MARTYRDOM OR DEATH

It takes death to invite the Spy, story and storyteller, into the realm of traditional language. Even then, however, the revelations available through him are limited. While he is evidence of all that is unseen throughout the book—America's story and America's symbol, now potentially at one—he remains impossible to read fully. He carries an identifying note—Washington's one gift of acknowledgment—and in certain ways, the revelations it contains are both a reproach to the world of narrative and an ironically post facto offer of "arcane knowledge," an original story that might transform that world into the inheritance of a storyteller.[19] After "the fatal lead" of a bullet has burst through the "tin box" that the Spy keeps in the pocket over his heart, the young soldiers who find him indeed learn of his identity. In the box, and somehow divinely protected from the bullet, is a paper that reads:

> *Circumstances of political importance, which involve the lives and fortunes of many, have hitherto kept secret what this paper now reveals. Harvey Birch has for years been a faithful and unrequited servant of his country. Though man does not, may God reward him for his conduct.*
>
> George Washington

In a moment of willful appropriation, the narrator allows that, in death, the Spy is finally "a martyr to [America's] liberties" (432) and thus too finally culturally (and narratively) reaggregated.

Within this perspective, perhaps the Spy's work has succeeded; new possibilities for human understanding seem imminent. Recording a scene within what was once the Spy's dark landscape, the narrator sketches a clearly visionary moment in the lives of the two "favored youth[s]" who appear there, as well as in the life of the nation. As these young American soldiers wander over the past neutral ground of Revolutionary New York, they survey the land as if "for the first time"—though it is now a battlefield again, nearly forty years after independence. Yet, although there are battles still waged there, a new generation sees no dangers, only an embodiment of the "wonder" they feel for "the western world" (427). Significantly, the two men witness the death of the Spy among this paradoxical world of promise and violence; the Spy's sacrifices, Cooper clearly implies, have done much to ensure that his "native land" will be continually "improving with time" (428). Although the Spy is never recognized or rewarded in his own time, Cooper's narrator has certainly suggested from the start that the Spy's life has been one of devoted and patriotic sacrifice and that his death must be the culmination of these revolutionary heroics. From this narrative perspective, when the Spy dies decades after the Revolution, his anonymity is the proof of a lifetime of successful escapes and disguises; his survival into old age is evidence of the lasting victory of his cause, and his finally revealed identity is the ultimate reward—interment into the memory of coming generations.[20]

In fact, here at the close of the narrative and the death of its hero, Cooper allows his narrator to suggest that the Spy achieves a cultural (even a pseudoreligious) apotheosis, a split second of personal fulfillment and an entrance into a realm of eternal memory, of constant and immediate recognition—from the young soldiers who find him and from all who will be inspired by his sacrifice. Without offering rites of return, the Spy's narrative world still sustains a hope that his story, which is his own self, will eventually emerge into the culture, in a sort of delayed reaggregation rite as the story that he lived becomes accepted as origin. For Benjamin, the expression of a true story requires the death of its subject: "[N]ot only a man's knowledge or wisdom, but above all his real life—and this is the stuff that stories are made of—first assumes transmissible form at the moment of his death."[21] So—potentially—it is in *The Spy*, where the lawless, even chaotic, neutral ground harbors the experiences of revolution and the emerging new order, and where (in theory) all of these competing meanings could be resolved by the Spy's knowledge.

However, although the narrator presents the Spy's life and death as a unified sacrifice to the revolutionary cause, Cooper's narrative form revises this notion.[22] He suggests that it is the Spy's *untold* story rather than the familiar tale of his symbolic martyrdom that becomes a symbol of foundational knowledge, knowledge of American cultural origins.[23] While the Spy's identity has finally been revealed, his secrets have not. The note that he bears tells us nothing we did not know, and thus it is only to a limited extent that even death can return him, as story and storyteller, to the realm of traditional language. While to argue that Cooper deliberately stages the Spy's trace identity as a subversive undoing of American identity would be counterintuitive at best, nonetheless the text's effect is to render the Spy a figure of ambiguity, paradoxically evidence of all that was unseen throughout the book.[24] In his death he takes with him the experiential knowledge of the "darkness beyond" (292): the secrets kept by history (and within history), safe beyond the power of language to betray, and the sole property of subjective vision, and quite distinctly beyond authorial reach. As an embodied story, the Spy persists in death, as he did in life, as a principle of disorder and a challenge to community understanding.[25]

Moreover, the perpetual resistance of the narrative frame toward the accommodation (or even acknowledgment) of these challenges is nowhere more evident than in the description of the very moment of the Spy's death. From the narrator's imagery, it would seem that the ambiguities of the Spy are almost reconciled in the familiar image of the martyr; he is at once national hero and individual outcast:[26] "He was lying on his back, with his face exposed to the glaring light of the fusée; his eyes were closed, as if in slumber; his lips, sunken with years, were slightly moved from their natural position, but it seemed more like a smile than a convulsion which caused the change. A soldier's musket lay near him, where it had fallen from his grasp; his hands were both pressed upon his breast . . ." (431).

This narrative attempt to reconcile the ambiguities of plot and character cannot hide the emergent facts within the description, including the fact that the Spy's identity has been "exposed" only by "the glaring light" of his violent death. Even if the text suggests that this is an image of a finally fulfilled obligation to die for the state, any such obligation must be negated in the Spy's radical absence of membership in his community.[27] The time for human recognition has passed, and in the very scene that the narrator sets is another, less glorious, perspective on this death. When he dies on the battlefield a generation after his active duty has ended, the Spy is dying too late to belong to his cause: The Revolution has been won and its martyrs enthroned; worse yet, he has lived to see that the violent social struggle for which he had risked his life (and lost his name) was not so unique after all.[28] Dying so late in the course of the installation of monuments for the Revolution, the Spy's silent end is that much more poignant. Among the random fire of an unidentified battle during the War of 1812, the Spy perhaps dies only a forgotten old man whose hopes for national recognition had "long lain mouldering in the tomb with Washington" (426).

Not without reason, then, did Sarah Hale express her dismay about the novel's (and the character's) end. Disappointed that Cooper did not end his work with the reconciliation scene between George Washington and the Spy, she objected to the "gratuitous" event of the Spy's lonely death in 1814: "This, we are compelled to say, is a lame and impotent conclusion. The work should have terminated with the interview in Gen. Washington's camp, in which the reader might have been led to believe that the faithful agent had been rewarded by a competency in some part of the country, remote from the scene of his services."[29] Even in the optimistic spirit of literary nationalism, Hale cannot accept the narrator's attempt to resolve the Spy's death through an invocation of national martyrdom. What she reads as Cooper's failed final scene, however, is—within the novel's own vocabulary—a paradoxically appropriate end.

Despite the best efforts of his narrator, the Spy and his story suggest the impossibility of a bounded frame of reference for the experiential knowledge that distinguishes his voice from all others in the novel and encodes the life of history within the story of America. His life and his death have told of Washington's weaknesses, including what is presented as an excessive dependence on the enlightenment principle of reason; he has seen and felt the turning of neighbor against neighbor, the high costs of physical and emotional violence, and the many incidental casualties of war. The Spy's life reveals these as fragments of the deepest complexities of the war, and these give us a sense of what is at stake in the new form of cultural storytelling advanced in the novel. These fragments, however, are the mere outlines of what Cooper—through *The Spy*—suggests that his culture must see in the process of enshrining the Revolution as myth of origins.

As a profoundly effective cultural symbol, the Spy is not a presence that character or narrative will contain; in fact, as a definable force, he is possible only after the end of character and the acknowledged bursting of traditional narrative boundaries. The Spy's silence can thus be claimed by America only in its form as a sustained cultural secret. Like a family secret, the cultural secret has the power to absorb and explain all kinds of disorderly results that cannot be attributed to any of the comprehensible designs of life experience. While the topic of this kind of secret is circumscribed within the interpretive community, its powers within the imagination are not. In addition, like all secrets, it has inexhaustible powers to generate stories, stories that circulate around a common center of acknowledged mystery. Building a system of cultural storytelling from the very subjects that functioned effectively only as long as they were preserved in resolutely private form, America developed a communal imagination that cohered around an unspoken center of acknowledged power.

There was something more richly imaginative in this style of narrative order than a simple conspiracy of appropriated life histories. Insofar as the evolving cultural imagination required an unspoken text for its cohesive center, it demonstrated America's need for a system of symbolic language that could revise its stories according to the shifting grounds of experience and knowledge; that secret and unspoken text became the figuration for the actual movement between interpretations and states of being. Only through such imaginative structures would history and the imagination fortify one another; only such a story was worthy of the implications of generative power that myths of cultural origins had throughout the ages. "The history of mankind . . . is full of wonders," John Adams wrote in 1815, "and the greatest wonder of all is, the total destruction of all the monuments and memorials by which we could have formed a correct and impartial judgment of characters and events" (*Works*, ed. C. F. Adams, vol. 10, 157). In his unexplained life and his silent death, the Spy might be just another of Adams's tragic wonders. Nevertheless, in giving a particular form to the haunting questions and paradoxes of the early republic, Cooper's Spy—not as a martyr but as a character who dies with his story untold, and as that formal principle of secrecy within the larger narrative of cultural knowledge—embodies the dynamic potential of uncharted territories, boundary lands, constant motion, and their analogue in language, the unspoken story. Resistant to definition, these forms encode not only the promise but also the dangers to (and from) a new way of life and the revelations of history, whatever they may be.

PART TWO

History's Revolutions in Nathaniel Hawthorne's *The Scarlet Letter*

We have a few old mouth-to-mouth tales; we exhume from old trunks and boxes and drawers letters without salutation or signature, in which men and women who lived once and breathed are now merely initials or nicknames out of some now incomprehensible affection . . . we see dimly people . . . performing their acts of simple passion and simple violence, impervious to time and inexplicable. . . . They are there, yet something is missing; they are like a chemical formula exhumed along with the letters from that forgotten chest, carefully, the paper old and faded and falling to pieces, the writing faded, almost indecipherable, yet meaningful, familiar in shape and sense . . . you bring them together again and again and nothing happens: just the words, the symbols, the shapes themselves, shadowy inscrutable and serene, against that turgid background of a horrible and bloody mischancing of human affairs.

—William Faulkner, *Absalom, Absalom!*

5

THE ARTIFACT IN THE ATTIC

I n "The Custom House," Nathaniel Hawthorne's narrator claims to revive the story of Hester Prynne within what he calls the "neutral territory" of romance, but the historical and imaginative space of both his world and hers may be considered "neutral" only in a profoundly ironic sense of the term.[1] Here as for Cooper's Spy, the emblematic American story is lived and then re-imagined on ground so steeped in history's conflicts, disruptions, and reversals—so contradictory in all of its signs—that it may be presumed pristine only because it is vacant of *legible* meaning.[2] But the novel courts a belief in the possibility—however tenuous—of new beginnings invited by this setting. As his heroine emerges from the dark prison door, Hawthorne floods his text with images of the new—the sunlight, the infant, the just-blooming rose, and—particularly—the letter *A:* All of these images conspire to "transfigure" (55) Hester. The result, Hawthorne writes, is that the "SCARLET LETTER, so fantastically embroidered and illuminated upon her bosom. . . . had the effect of a spell, taking her out of the ordinary relations with humanity, and inclosing her in a sphere by herself" (55).

Both in the novel's fictional Puritan community and in 1850, Hester is brought forth before an audience to embody a new world, a world of meanings not yet spoken (though clearly active, perhaps even dominant) within present culture. In both contexts, Hester's life animates the self-conscious construction of an American story out of particularly American materials—the child, born in the new colony, the rose rooted in its earth, the *A*, designed and woven in the new world and later stored for centuries within the town's space of public record. In the tradition of Noah Webster, an American language promised the words for what the Revolution had claimed by deeds: separate, distinct, and specifically national self-definition. This project necessarily would begin with an examination of already active forms of social discourse along with bold new experiments with their dangers and powers, particularly as they might apply to the early stages of a culture.[3] Like Cooper's Spy, Hester Prynne—another story-teller—is one such experiment. Contemporary reviewers were quick to extol Hawthorne for "found[ing] a new principality of his own" without "dethron[ing] any established prince in literature," and indeed the image is apt:[4] Hawthorne's historical fiction focuses on the revolutionary possibilities of a new story, incorporating an accumulated—rather than obliterated—past.

These revolutionary possibilities—as situated in mid-nineteenth-century America—comprise the context for my reading of *The Scarlet Letter*, and in turn, my understanding of Hawthorne's interests and sympathies owes much to recent scholarly works that have revised our understanding of the political engagements of the canonical authors of the "American Renaissance." Larry Reynolds has argued that "revolutionary struggle stirred at the front of Hawthorne's consciousness as he wrote *The Scarlet Letter*";[5] evidence for this claim abounds in the novel. For Reynolds, this revolutionary consciousness is primarily nourished by Hawthorne's interest in the European revolutions abroad from 1848 to 1849, and I would like to extend this argument by layering this proven concern—Hawthorne's skeptical and even fearful interest in the upheavals in Europe—with a long-established interpretive truism about Hawthorne, that is, his known interest in landmark moments in American colonial and national history.

Jonathan Arac has argued that Hawthorne's life and writings bear witness to his "uncertainty between 'progressive' and 'conservative'" impulses and show that this uncertainty led him to embrace "the contradictory wish of the Democrats in the early 1850s . . . to go ahead into the future without losing control of what they had established: let us call this the tension between motion and regulation."[6] If the colonial Revolution as a story of origins in America had provided the nation with—in Arac's term—"regulation," establishing aspects of cultural life and identity not to be risked, the revolutions of 1848, as Reynolds has shown, offered far too much in the way of "motion": "[T]o a man of Hawthorne's temperament, the violence, the bloodshed, the extended chaos that accompanied the revolutions of 1848–49 were deeply disturbing."[7] For Arac, the space between what has been regulated and what remains in motion, what the nation "fear[ed] to lose" and what it "wish[ed] to gain" is Hawthorne's America of 1850, a "political impasse" in "a structure of conflicting values."[8] Perhaps we might see, then, as one outcome of this tension—one expression of this impasse—Hawthorne's interest in revolution seeking a space less overdetermined than the America of 1776 and less volatile than the Europe of 1848.

Indeed the America of "The Custom House" is one such example. Many critics agree that there Hawthorne displaces both the real violence and the potential glories and tragedies of revolutionary ages when he uses the rhetoric and imagery of revolution in relation to his own removal from the Custom House. In so doing, as Arac points out, Hawthorne returns the word "revolution" to "the etymologically related action of 'rotation' in office."[9] But there is more than a wry parallel here; in "The Custom House," Hawthorne's narrator instructs readers how and why to understand antebellum America as distinctly, if oddly, revolutionary. First the narrator pushes us to consider the chaos that ensues for any party affiliate as a shift in power, however regulated, occurs; this we understand as a subjective sense of mock-heroic disenfranchisement. Despite the narrator's disdain for government work, he concedes, "[t]he moment when a man's head drops off is seldom or never, I am inclined to think, precisely the most agreeable of his life" (44). More broadly, however, "The Custom House" offers a world so rigid, so moribund, that any change—no matter how small—might be imagined most vividly as the overturning of governments and kingdoms. Among this world of idle chatter, with his mind free (or empty) of the distractions of imagination, the narrator finds a peculiar capacity still active: "[I]t lay at my own option to recall whatever was valuable in the past" (28). Much to his own surprise, the very past he envisions evokes revolutions of thought.

Sacvan Bercovitch has shown that "antebellum culture was particularly volatile—in the sense now not of transition but of consolidation: volatility redirected into channels of social growth."[10] In such a world, revolution comes in minute forms; every small shift asks again what will be carried forward and what will be left behind. No time is more dangerous to national narrative than that of consolidation; in such ages, aspects of national experience—not unlike small-time political players—are most easily left behind. At this moment, then, of world revolutions coupled with a strange and tense stasis at home—with the northern call for consolidation, in all of its willful compromises—it is no surprise to find that the very means and subjects of national storytelling would fall into question.

In this atmosphere, too, broadly cultural imaginative desires for consolidation may be seen working at the level of historiography; if George Bancroft is the best known of the historians writing with these goals, he is hardly the only one.[11] In nineteenth-century United States historiography, treatments of previous revolutions—Cromwell's, as well as that of the colonies—were favorite subjects, as if in traditional romance style these progressive histories might effect consolidation in narrative by recasting conflict and thus dispelling it before it might recur of its own accord. The

U.S. Civil War is history's direct response to those efforts at containment, and the rise of tensions before the war adds perhaps the most significant layer to Hawthorne's cultural context. Critics have come to see the Civil War as "the latent context of the American Renaissance," which, in turn, is filled with works that "depend on [a] utopianism . . . that circumvents or submerges actual divisions of time."[12] As I have been arguing throughout this book, the voice of the storyteller most clearly emerges within (as well as against) such determined idealism, and so we find Hester Prynne among this matrix of utopian impulses.

With the rise of regional tensions preceding the Civil War, newly established conceptions of the national, cultural identity of the United States came into question. For antebellum America, early republican rhetorics of an independent nation, unified and expanding, clearly were not only inadequate but actually false as accounts of contemporary historical process; they were, in fact, variations on a theme, a theme, that is, of that "circumvent[ion] or submer[sion]" of the "actual divisions" all too clearly manifest within historical life. In relation to this narrative tradition, the experiences of everyday life threatened to exceed the bounds of national imaginings, perhaps even to overturn the stated meanings of American identity. There are many important ways to understand the complexities of antebellum culture and its crises, and foremost among these will always be the emergent crisis of slavery in mid-nineteenth-century America. Nevertheless, it is not tangential to note that northern liberalism in 1850—in its ambiguities so central to the problem of understanding race in its time—has at its core a crisis of identity, experienced by self-consciously American authors as a crisis of storytelling. This crisis is one built of responses to the European revolutions, to the shifts in party power in the United States, and to the legal and political maneuvering of both North and South. This crisis of national narrative provides the primary context within which I see Hawthorne's fiction working.

For Cooper, particular matters of revolutionary history—the character of leaders, the confusion of causes—were at stake in the narrative silence of *The Spy*. For Hawthorne in *The Scarlet Letter*, Hester's silent story puts at stake the possible belief in the continuity of American cultural history.[13] Gordon Hutner demonstrates the significant pattern of "secrets[, which] so predominate Hawthorne's plots, settings, characters, and style."[14] In this tradition I would like to continue a study of such secrecy now more specifically within the realm of the historical. Within Hester's silence are a variety of matters of dissent—from the most personal to the most socially engaged—all with the potential to challenge a fragile story of continuity. Within her silence, however, are also the possibilities of creating links between seemingly remote ages. Through its experiments in binding language to history, *The Scarlet Letter* enacts an experimental repair of a proto-revolutionary situation, a moment of rupture between history and its known narratives; the romance thus becomes, as Brook Thomas argues, a "civic myth."[15]

To be able to use language in such a way that it cannot be immediately divorced from a living historical voice—from a memory, personal or inherited—is, as I noted earlier in this book, the art of Walter Benjamin's Storyteller. For Benjamin, the late conditions of narrative are such that "no event any longer comes to us without already being shot through with explanation."[16] Hawthorne encounters a similar world, where language is structured with a nationalist rhetoric so superfluous as to be almost deadening, carrying with it certainly nothing to address the emergent sense of the United States as a country divided within and against itself. Under such conditions the language of the nation's story would need careful revitalization if it were to continue as a system of social cohesion. As he addresses it, then, Hawthorne's America is not what so many in the Jacksonian era believed it to be, a "vast new country," yet free of known "boundaries" and "heaving with restless impatience . . . to exemplify new ideas in new forms."[17] It is instead a country vastly burdened with histories and thus filled with dissension. Just as a new national narrative would have to take in the ever-accumulating past even as it wrote a new history, so also in *The Scarlet Letter* Hawthorne gives readers a world focused on the conditions of creating *while inheriting* a story. The Custom House's narrator receives, in that remarkably material form, the inheritance of a story about life in the New World. Interestingly, however, that inheritance includes profound implications about the way stories are told—about how language meets, evades, or denies the experiences of life itself.

When Hester is reanimated from that scrap of cloth and its attendant manuscript left in the Custom House attic, her return to American culture embodies a theory of history's return deeply complicated by both overt and silent connections to more than one revolution.[18] In this sense Hester is a more fully developed image than that of a similar embodiment of history and revolution that Hawthorne introduces in "The Gray Champion" (1835), and perhaps surprisingly she will prove more radical, too. There, with reference to feared Old World Puritan leaders, Hawthorne invokes a legend familiar to nineteenth-century audiences:[19] the legend of the three judges—from the Puritan regicide court—who had escaped into hiding in New England to live out their lives in exile after the Restoration. The story of the regicides in New England is the story of a new culture, able to contain (shelter *and* tame) old world radicalism. As such, it is the story of lives—meanings—wrapped within the fabric of an emergent society and thereby understood in new contexts rather than returned to the site of origin, where they would be bound by purposes understood and acts taken within a no longer coherent context. It is then a story of dissenters who are protected from feeling with immediacy the full ramifications of their dissent because they have come to live within a world that looks past their time-bound political position and choice, seeing in them instead something useful for present cultural purposes. The appeal of such a tale to a country on the brink of civil war is easy to see.

By the middle of the nineteenth century, legends of the regicides and of the Puritan revolution in general—not only as they came to exist in stock fictional form but also as they might be more fully imagined given popular historians' familiarity with colonial texts—had come to suggest not only a pattern of recurrence in history (a prefiguration of the American revolution and later national successes), but also the critical problem of assimilating these recurrences into present consciousness.[20] It is this necessary reintegration that Hester Prynne enacts in her life as a symbol to Puritan Boston. Like the judges, Hester Prynne is overdetermined, so much so that what she represents is newly enfolded in secrecy—a strange condition of excessive solitude and silence that must eventually generate its own story, even its own language.

The *A* that she wears bears witness to her story but more pointedly to her secrecy—her refusal to name her child's father, to reveal her husband's presence, or to record her own knowledge and passion; any such revelation would shatter the very principles of her community. The latent danger and power of Hester's life comes from her silence rather than from her adultery, just as the imaginative power of the regicides comes from their hidden life rather than their known act. In this circuitous acquisition of silent power—associated with the most potent of political crises but offering, too, a route to consolidation—both the regicides and Hester (with her *A*) acquire an authority not only to create, but also to respond to—indeed to palliate—Hawthorne's sense of cultural crisis some two centuries later.

The crises in Hester's (and Hawthorne's) worlds may be imagined as political and moral, but they are first and foremost rooted in language. There we see the rigidity of communal expectations and the failure to yield to the evidence of experience. Hawthorne portrays these social limits within the text's community through the frame provided by two of the town leaders and major players in the action. Dimmesdale, the preacher and unacknowledged father of Pearl, and Chillingworth, the doctor and wronged husband of Hester, are set up in the romance as models of the ways in which language has heretofore both sustained and entrapped the colony.

At one end of the spectrum is Dimmesdale, who is nothing less (and nothing more) than a self-styled symbol. His manipulation of context makes the process of demystifying his character impossible for his congregation, and through a series of well-orchestrated performances, Dimmesdale severs referential language from experiential existence. He can, as Hawthorne notes, confess to being "altogether vile, a viler companion of the vilest, the worst of sinners" (142), only to have his audience "reverence him the more" (143). Dimmesdale's language is on constant display, but it never leads to knowledge.

At the opposite end of the spectrum is Chillingworth. He too keeps meaning inaccessible from his community, denying his very name and identity by "withdraw[ing] his name from the roll of mankind, . . . vanish[ing] out of life as completely as if he indeed lay at the bottom of the ocean" (117). However, he does so not with the distracting flourishes of rhetoric but with the silent, even primal, expressions of rage and joy that Hawthorne places as prior to language itself. Within this paralyzing context, the image of language (though as yet unspoken) that Hester brings to the community has clear radical potential. In both her world and that of her narrator, Hester's letter is much more than the emblem of an unspoken sin. It is an image of language at its most basic, referencing the most primary of experiences, nearly—but not quite—erupting into conscious meaning that will devastate the order offered (indeed forced) by a community bound between the false rhetoric of the preacher and the inarticulate madness of the physician.

It is in this sense that the real power of the *A* within the fiction lies in its positive force. In trying so hard to define Hester, the colony realizes that it cannot make sense of her. By revealing these interpretive inadequacies, Hawthorne identifies Puritan Boston as the dangerous utopia that it is. In terms helpful to specifying the nature of this incarnation of utopia, Hans Blumenberg writes that "in its intensified instances utopia is the sum of negations, when it is focused solely on avoiding contamination by what currently exists and when it culminates in a prohibition against saying anything positively imagined. . . . The utopian prohibition of images demands submission, by refusing to provide stories."[21]

Hester's disapproving society gives her a badge rich with cultural capital. The image will not submit to any one inscribed meaning and so turns on the order of the utopia by generating a myriad of stories, not only as Hester evolves to be known as "Angel" or "Able," but even from the start. Like the haunting laughter echoing in the streets of "My Kinsman, Major Molineux," the *A* in *The Scarlet Letter* is the means of revelations beyond the known language of the community. It is a force conveying an unnamed negative message into a world where such negations of form and knowledge have, as yet, no codified place. With more potential interpretations than places in the culture for those interpretations, the force given to Hester is, by definition, radical.[22]

If we imagine that the maintenance of utopia is the job of the colony's most powerful leaders, it is then no surprise that they choose to mark Hester with a letter that is to stand in for a word, to forestall the generation of language. But as if to remind his fictional magistrates that their act works within only a single, limited context, Hawthorne emphasizes repeatedly the historical life of the image itself, the inevitable birth and persistent materiality of the "positively imagined" essential facts of America's living record. Though given in the impulse of exclusion, the letter, like the laughter in "My Kinsman, Major Molineux," derives a power from the significance of the gesture of giving: Through the giving, the abdication of powers unknown to the giver, new cultural roles evolve that only the recipient can play.[23] In giving her this symbolic object, the town fathers add to Hester's private share of the community's history and knowledge. The *A*, in fact, comes to represent revolutionary possibility and danger in its capacity to transform identity for a world trapped by otherwise static modes of knowing.

In his perusal of Surveyor Pue's antiquarian papers, the narrator of "The Custom House" reports, "a portion of his facts, by and by, did [him] good service in the preparation of the article entitled 'Main Street'" (33). With this in mind, certain distinctive qualities of the scarlet letter as one among these "facts" become particularly apparent. In Hawthorne's story "Main Street" (1849), history is communal, conflicted, and dark. There the narrative moves through several generations of history, providing images primarily of town crisis. Apologizing for the "all too sombre" nature of the visions he presents, the narrator of "Main Street" claims the burden of historical accuracy: "[T]he blame must rest on the sombre spirit of our forefathers, who wove their web of life with hardly a single thread of rose-color or gold."[24] The contrast, then, between the bulk of the inherited materials found in the Custom House attic and the luminescence of the *A* is immediate and profound: "[T]he object that most drew my attention, in the mysterious package, was a certain affair of fine red cloth, much worn and faded. There were traces about it of gold embroidery, which, however, was greatly frayed and defaced. . . . It was the capital letter *A*" (34). Worn by time, this artifact too signifies a story of dark communal conflict, yet it is woven of those rare threads of "rose-color" and "gold"; in the simplest visual sense, the letter announces itself as both representative and novel among the attic's holdings.

As an emblem of history, the letter has an uncanny record of survival indicating some dimension of its exceptional power in the romance by drawing out its explicit connection to American revolutionary history. According to the narrator, the letter survives into his own day only by virtue of an odd accident of history: It is one of very few relics not pillaged in the violent discord of two hundred years of New England's existence. Specifically, the narrator recounts that among the holdings in the Custom House attic, "there is a dearth of records" from all years "prior to the Revolution." He explains that "the earlier documents and archives . . . probably [were] carried off to Halifax, when the King's officials accompanied the British army in its flight from Boston," and he laments what he imagines among the lost, speculating that "going back, perhaps to the days of the Protectorate, those papers must have contained many references to forgotten or remembered men, and to antique customs" (31).

Imagining the king's army robbing New England of its stories because it could not rob the colonies of their future, the patriotic narrator endows the *A* with historical authority derived from both of America's mythic founding eras; it thus becomes both a Puritan and a Revolutionary artifact, thus both foundational and disruptive.[25] Like the exiled judges of legend, the *A* is tied explicitly to the recurrence of crisis. Whether surviving because it was hidden from the king's officials, or whether to English eyes the artifact appeared insignificant, the endurance of the *A* through British raids lends it a little-recognized symbolic authority—that of revolution, concentrated and ready to flower into any of its myriad forms.

As Hester accepts and then decorates her emblem, then, her life animates a revolution in both history and language. She uses her "delicate and imaginative skill . . . of needle-work" (81) to create an American symbol. As she does so, Hester and her symbolic work—including both the letter and her daughter—suggest that in Hawthorne's world she stands as a dangerous and formidable challenge to her culture.[26] If, as Walt Whitman predicted, an American language would emerge out of the stories of its people ("words follow character—nativity, independence, individuality"; "words are a result"[27]), Hester Prynne represents the most radical challenge to American identity, a thorough reconception of communal consciousness. It is then the narrator's task, as he reanimates Hester, to see that she, like the Puritan judges, is allowed her momentary radicalism and then contained as a cultural secret.

Like those judges, Hester will stand for both a devastating break in history and its reintegration into communal knowledge as something entirely different, a mythic vehicle for continuity between her world and that of Hawthorne's readers. All of this will be true, however, only if the narrative can catch up with, even outpace, the flowering interpretations of the letter on Hester's dress, and it is hardly clear that this will be the case. Unlike the judges, then, Hester embarks on a journey fraught with moments in which her extraordinarily material tie to the American story allows (or compels) her to elude the control of the narrative frame surrounding her, including the fictional romance, Hawthorne's own designs, and her reception in culture. Hester is revolutionary: The question remains, is she revolution as prelude to reform and consolidation, or revolution, defiant of all such cultural uses? Placing her in context with her fellow revolutionaries of legend, the regicide judges, may provide an answer.

6

NEW ENGLAND'S REVOLUTION
IN HIDING

For I have observed, that the Devil of Rebellion, doth commonly
turn himself into an Angel of Reformation.
—Letter from Charles I to Charles II, 1648–1649

T HE perfect subject for the generation of the historical imagination
in nineteenth-century America proves to be the founding age of
Puritanism in the New World. Michael Davitt Bell notes that American
romances written between 1820 and 1850 reveal an extraordinary interest
in seventeenth-century New England history.[1] While a previous generation had worked to remember the American revolution as a site of national
origins, Hawthorne and his contemporaries reveal anxieties about the limits of this narrative by turning further back, suggesting an anterior point of
origins, an alternative founding story. A turn back to the colonial era of
New England is, of course, a narrowly focused search for origins, but
Hawthorne was not alone in assuming "that New England's priority in
historical influence lent it primacy in determinations of national identity."[2]

To Hawthorne and his contemporaries, the very remoteness of early
New England history might be useful for purposes of imaginative consolidation, and so through that apparently narrow regionalism the new
national story—potentially—would expand its bounds. In contrast to
Cooper's America of 1821, here there is no longer an active anxiety about
a dying generation of leaders taking sacred memories to the grave, but
rather national storytelling must address a broad sense of far-flung descendants with perilously little to connect them to their forefathers' history.
The task, then, is not to ensure the continuity of memory, but to prove
connectedness, that is, to reimagine fully—to bring back to life—a story
with no tangible threads holding it to the present.

Stories of the founding era risked revealing America's condition of ruptured isolation from that foundation; thus the appeal of the golden age of
Puritanism may have appeared at times less as an image of promise than of

threat. If Puritanism thus came to signify both a belief in connection and a fear of division, it seems fitting that new interest might arise in Old England's Puritan revolution, that aspect of New England's Puritan heritage from which there was greatest distance, thus the least to be lost and the most to be gained, imaginatively.

Critics have noted *The Scarlet Letter's* particular resonance with the Old World Puritan revolution because the major action of the story is set between 1642 and 1649.[3] In England, of course, these are the years of bitter civil strife between Charles I and the Puritan army. In New England these years are remembered for a decidedly mixed set of portents—events seen at the time as great crises, but later as harbingers of consolidation. As crises, these events had been interpreted to be direct results of Old World events: substantial reverse emigration (often to support the Puritan army), the establishment of the New England confederation (a protonationalistic movement), the first execution for witchcraft, and the death of the Massachusetts Bay Colony's legendary leader, John Winthrop.

In their broad folkloric life, the Puritan judges were linked in some way to all of these, and all in turn have resonance within Hawthorne's novel. This is not to say that Hawthorne's primary context is that of the fiction's setting. On the contrary, by reviving alternative stories from the Puritan ages—stories that had proven, through their repetition, to be particularly resonant to antebellum America—Hawthorne examines these inherited stories, finding some connections to his own day as well as some limitations in their capacities to restore imaginative order to nineteenth-century audiences. Thus these seventeenth-century contexts become useful to Hawthorne insofar as they have remained resonant to antebellum audiences; invoking such familiarities, *The Scarlet Letter* explores the sources and the boundaries of their nineteenth-century resonance.

In numerous retellings and several versions lasting well into Hawthorne's day and beyond, tales of the regicide judges focused on their uncanny return at moments of crisis. In their fictional and symbolic lives, the judges' ability to lead the Puritan colonies away from the dangers of the first century of colonization and later repetitions of the same—desertion, witchcraft, failures of cohesion or leadership, and enemy attacks—made them heroes. As the stories go, it is by the hidden care of the colonies that these men—whose lives represent a radicalism never fully embraced by New World Puritans—are saved. In one sense the regicides might seem to be historical figures too overdetermined for an elastic life within cultural mythology; their lives are so fully shaped by one past event. But that past event—the conviction and execution of Charles I—never finds a comfortable place in the cultural consciousness of America, in either the colonial or the early national periods. For that reason, the judges of legend develop a paradoxical relationship to their own history: Their relation to history makes them unknowable rather than familiar, and they are effectively separated from the Old World consequences of their actions.[4]

As characters within American folklore, the regicides are larger than their British context, and so they implicitly transcend blame for their excesses; this becomes possible because, inversely, in the American tales, they are absolutely subordinate to their American context. That is, in colonial and early national legend, the judges are imagined to be restored to potency only within carefully controlled national (or protonational) crises during which their particular powers of radicalism would be deemed necessary rather than dangerous; despite their formidable powers of agency, these men are reborn only to facilitate cultural continuity rather than radical change in the American imagination.[5] The emergent mythology surrounding the judges' symbolic lives deepens with the necessary secrecy of their existence. Hidden in a cave near New Haven and in a basement in Hadley, Massachusetts, traveling only at night or in disguise—and yet always well known to loyal citizens of the colonies—the judges become a perfect symbol of carefully muted rebellion, essential in spirit, but always fortuitously controlled by external ideological constraints.

AMERICA'S CROMWELL

In both England and America, these judges—along with other players in the Puritan revolution—had been favorites in the invention of heroes and martyrs beginning with the publication of *Eikon Basilike,* which inaugurated "the cult of the martyr king" immediately after Charles I's death.[6] Not surprisingly, in America the status of hero or martyr is reserved for those on the Puritan side, although during the Protectorate, New England's relations with Cromwell were hardly enthusiastic. Early American accounts express a cautious uncertainty, easily imagined in light of Cromwell's decidedly ambivalent attitude toward the colonies. As one nineteenth-century historian explains it, "The protector possessed great energy of character; and it was his object to raise both the glory and the terror of the commonwealth. For this purpose, he was disposed to keep the colonies in due subjection."[7] In fact, a petition to Parliament in 1651 from the Massachusetts Bay leaders expresses concern in response to "the parliaments pleasure that [Massachusetts] should take a new patent" from them; the threat of more restrictive patent conditions and other matters led Governor John Endicott and the General Court to say, "These things make us doubt and fear what is intended towards us."[8] Letters between Cromwell and Endicott in 1652 and 1654 reveal more of this relationship. Here Massachusetts first successfully resists being drawn into Cromwell's campaign against the Irish after Cromwell had proposed transplanting the Bay Colony to Ireland to assist in his conquest. In response to Cromwell's further request to raise troops to help against the Dutch in New Netherlands and Jamaica, again the Massachusetts leaders diplomatically reply, "It hathe beene no small comfort to us poor exiles, in these utmost ends of the earth" to see Cromwell rise in power, and yet, they say, they prefer to "forbeare the use of the sword" on his behalf.[9]

Despite these tentative early relations between New World and Old during Cromwell's lifetime, later American interest in Cromwell is strong and sustained through the nineteenth century.[10] Many seem to have agreed with Emerson, who writes of his respect "for the simplicity and energy of . . . evil" in both Cromwell and Napoleon.[11] George Bancroft's *History* (1834–1876) romanticizes Cromwell's ambition and criticizes him only for trying to do too much, too fast. According to Bancroft, "hypocrisy" and "piety" are almost equally blended in Cromwell and his army, but this contradiction is not the cause for their failure.[12] Instead, Bancroft argues that "Nations change their institutions but slowly: to attempt to pass abruptly from feudalism and monarchy to democratic equality was the thought of enthusiasts, who understood neither the history, the character, nor the condition of the country. It was like laying out into new streets a city already crowded with massive structures. The death of the king was the policy of Cromwell, and not the policy of the nation."[13]

According to Bancroft, the "fatal mistake" dooming this historical movement is Cromwell's radicalism, not the revolution itself. Radicalism here may be abstract and ideological at one level, but it is also decidedly concrete, reflected quite clearly through its temporal manifestations.[14] Cromwell's ultimate failure comes because he seeks "immediate emancipation" where "moderation" is the better course, and according to this view Cromwell's achievements are not as great as the age they usher in; "his death was necessarily a signal for new revolutions."[15] "The authority of Cromwell marks but a period of transition. His whole career was an attempt to conciliate a union between his power and permanent public order, and the attempt was always unavailing, from the inherent impossibility growing out of the origin of his power. It was derived from the submission, not from the will of the people."[16] Unable to gain "a concert with the national affections," Bancroft's Cromwell is a man of great power but not of "truth," and it is "truth only that of itself rallies men together."[17]

Cromwell, then, takes his place in American historiography through the nineteenth century as an individual in the most powerful and most restrictive senses of the word.[18] These historians remember neither his ability to garner popular support nor his management of the Puritan army. Despite "profess[ing] himself the servant of Providence, borne along by irresistible necessity," Cromwell "did not connect himself with the revolution, for he put himself above it, and controlled it."[19] As a player in the drama of the Puritan revolution as remembered from afar—in America's nineteenth century—Oliver Cromwell stands apart from the very revolution he leads, leaving him at once untouched by its corruption and/or alienated from its purity of spirit, depending upon historiographical perspective.

This symbolic separation from the war itself paradoxically helps shape American imaginings of Cromwell; taken from the very context that gave him fame, America's Cromwell is at once admired in spirit and considered to be a sort of lost kinsman, one close to them in spirit and yet fatally divided from their colonial venture. Two representative works on the subject of the lost possibilities of Cromwell's possible affiliation with New England are an 1850 lecture by Sherman Canfield to the Young Men's Literary Association of Cleveland and an 1866 pamphlet reviewing evidence of Cromwell's reputed desire to emigrate to New England. John Dean's eleven-page pamphlet, "The Story of the Embarkation of Cromwell and his Friends for New England," announces its purpose as the "bring[ing] together [of] the different accounts" of the legend—in the various authors' own words—in order to survey the evidence behind the one mythic claim that most closely links Cromwell to the colonists:[20]

> [E]migration had become so general, that in April 1637, the King issued a proclamation to restrain the "disorderly transportation of his subjects to the American colonies." It commanded that no license should be given them without a certificate that they had taken the oaths of supremacy and allegiance and conformed to the discipline of the established church. A fleet of eight ships was soon after stopped, which were lying in the Thames and ready to sail. In one of those ships were actually embarked Oliver Cromwell . . . and others who afterwards figured [prominently] under the commonwealth. Charles little suspected, that by his arbitrary measure, he was detaining men destined to overthrow his throne, and to terminate his days by a violent death.[21]

As Dean recounts his sources and their evidence, he shows a strong interest not only in pointing out the foibles of the monarchy, but also in claiming Cromwell for New England as an idealist and an adventurer. Canfield's lecture similarly casts Cromwell in the mold of a typically "American" hero. He sets out to redress the "horrid caricature—drawn by political and ecclesiastical partisans" with what he will consider to be an accurate, even exemplary, portrayal. As a Presbyterian pastor, Canfield's overt social purpose here is to provide in the image of Cromwell an appropriate role model for his audience of young church members. Canfield invokes the legend of Cromwell's intended emigration to demonstrate the sincerity of a man "willing to forsake his country and retire to a wilderness"; he writes much in the spirit of Thomas Carlyle, and he goes on to promote an image of Cromwell's great integrity by citing characteristics common to "our own Washington."[22] Like Washington, Cromwell stands for the "natural state" of justice that precedes the order of a nation.[23]

The lesson in Canfield's lecture is that "men devoted to literature and the fine arts" must recognize the "genius" of the man of action; this recognition is saved for a redeemed world, perhaps the future America: "[A]s resurrection trumpets to tribes and nations spiritually dead, then will mankind begin to render a due tribute to the memory of Oliver Cromwell."[24] American affections for Cromwell all share a complex patriotism as they celebrate their own achievements (and perhaps, implicitly, their own moderation and restraint) in the lost figure of a foreign revolution: "Had Cromwell had his way he would have made the political system of England akin to that of the United States."[25] According to the logic of these accounts, the early American colonies are naturally, wisely, intimidated by this man of action. Now in the nineteenth century, however— with the new nation firmly established—America stands at a safe distance, ready to embrace this symbol of its newly achieved present state, precisely because that symbol is forever mired in his own Old World past. These admiring, even affectionate, American portraits of Cromwell all depend upon the knowledge that he is, culturally speaking, irrecoverable. To Hawthorne's world, Cromwell has come to stand as the emigrant manqué, an agent whose actions prove that, despite disasters in his own land, he heroically served the chosen New England world as prophet.

NEW ENGLAND'S REGICIDES

New England's three regicides are born into legend through their successful act of emigration, and as they emigrate into a secret existence, they too become figural prophets. One historian writes that when Cromwell's cousin, Edward Whalley, and Whalley's son-in-law, William Goffe, arrived in Boston on July 27, 1660, "no such prominent Englishmen had visited New England during its entire Colonial existence."[26] Whalley and Goffe had been high-ranking participants in the Puritan revolution. They were among fifty-nine signers of the execution order for Charles I, and the same ship that carried them to New England also brought confirmation of the Stuart Restoration.[27]

Although Whalley, Goffe, and John Dixwell (who joined the others in New England in 1664) all play important official roles within the Puritan army, they come to represent a kind of link between New England and the Old World revolution that is substantially different from the one Cromwell represents. Predictably, early British accounts of the Protectorate's rise and fall, celebrating the restoration of the monarchy, do little to separate one regicide from another, and they are filled with condemnation of all of the high-ranking revolutionaries with relatively equal vitriol. Such pamphlets accuse not only Cromwell but all of the regicides of being "savage creature[s] in the midst of a Civil People" and of committing violations of biblical proportions:[28]

> [The regicides], not having fear of God before [their] Eyes, and being instigated by the Devil, did Maliciously, Treasonably, and Feloniously . . . Sign and Seal a Warrant for the Execution of His Late Sacred and Serene Majesty.[29]
>
> Next [to] our Saviours Crucifixion, never Sins wore a deeper Dye, than that Horrid Cruelties of these Matchless Regicides. . . . To commit Villany unparallel'd, and bravely to outface Death, is the badge of a desperate Traytor, and an Unhappy Christian . . . as if the Murther of a King, and the Ruine of Church and State were of so slight a consequence, that among birds of his own feather Treason becomes meritorious, and his detestable death a glorious Martyrdom.[30]

Overall, if there is a distinction to be made between Cromwell and his officers, it seems that Cromwell is the less maligned in these Restoration-era pamphlets, most likely (at least in part) because he is no longer a threat, having died before the Restoration. Many of these British texts focus their anxieties on the possible spread of revolution via those who have escaped prosecution ("so many Poisonous Opinions having gone abroad"[31]). Others, however, celebrate their sense of justice by insisting that vengeance will find every accomplice.[32] In their religious hyperbole and political metaphor, all of these early accounts sow the seeds of romance that will later revive these figures abroad and draw them into international legend, while the regicides' own countrymen seem to wish to forget them following their successful escape from Britain.[33]

New England accounts offer chronologies of the regicides' travels in the colonies; these may be established from local and family histories, letters from the regicides preserved among such papers, and Thomas Hutchinson's foundational account in his 1764 *History*.[34] Virtually all sources agree that Whalley and Goffe arrived in the Bay Colony on July 27, 1660.[35] Their ship had left England in May, the same month that the restored King was officially proclaimed.[36] In October of that same year, twenty-nine other regicides were tried and convicted for their crimes in England; by this time, most authorities believe that New England was aware that Whalley and Goffe were wanted by the crown.

Before his death—hoping for an eventual restoration of his family's position—Charles I had written to his son, instructing him: "[S]how the greatness of your mind, rather to conquer your enemies by pardoning than punishing. . . . If God give you success, use it humbly and far from revenge."[37] Charles II did indeed issue offers of pardon for those of his father's judges who would be willing to turn themselves in voluntarily under stated conditions, but Whalley and Goffe had already fled England shortly before that offer of indemnity, which followed the House of Lords' order of arrest.[38] All of those who failed to appear—including, of course, Whalley, Goffe, and Dixwell—were then excluded from the offer of pardon by an act of Parliament.[39] By this time Whalley and Goffe had been enjoying the open hospitality of New England for more than a month.

As pressure on the colonial authorities increased, Whalley and Goffe apparently left Massachusetts Bay on February 26, 1661, arriving in the New Haven Colony by March 7. This initial removal marks the end of their charmed first year as celebrities of sorts in New England, but it marks only the beginnings of their mythic existence. Although their lives would soon become much more difficult, the judges enjoyed safe travel to New Haven, as facilitated by John Davenport. In preparation for their arrival, Davenport delivered a sermon to his congregation, asking the citizens of New Haven to avoid using "the reproachful titles put upon the people of God, whom prophane men call Phanaticks." The lesson, Davenport emphasized, is God's commitment to the chosen people even (or especially) as they suffer in captivity, and the event of this sermon marks the judges' transfiguration into symbol within New England culture:

> Let us . . . own the reproached and persecuted people and cause of Christ
> in suffering times. With-hold not countenance, entertainment, protec-
> tion, from such, if they come to us, from other Countreys, as from France
> or England, or any other place. Be not forgetful to entertain strangers, for
> thereby some have entertained Angels unawares. . . . [P]rovide safe and

comfortable shelter and refreshment for my people, in the heat of prosecution and opposition raised against them, hide the outcasts, betray not him that wandereth.[40]

Davenport's sermon not only sets the tone but actually establishes the vocabulary for many New England memories of the regicides. Their lives—as documented in their own letters and by local legends—were recalled as a mixture of the mundane and the fantastic, and they were immediately embraced by the American imagination (in the words of one Scottish historian) as "men dropped down from heaven."[41]

According to Hutchinson, on March 27, Whalley and Goffe traveled from New Haven to the town of Milford, nearby but to the west, apparently to throw pursuers off track by seeming to head for New Netherlands. They then returned to New Haven to stay for about a month at Davenport's home. On April 28, the official king's order arrived, commanding the capture and return of Whalley and Goffe, and historians have long believed that within ten days the authorities of all of the New England colonies would have known of the order:[42]

> Trusty and well-beloved,—Wee greete you well. Wee being given to understand that Colonell Whalley and Colonell Goffe, who stand here convicted for the execrable murther of our Royall Father, of glorious memory, are lately arrived at New England, where they hope to shroud themselves securely from the justice of our lawes;—Our will and pleasure is, and we do hereby expressly require and command you forthwith upon the receipt of these our letters, to cause both the said persons to be apprehended, and with the first opportunity sent over hither under a readiness and diligence to perform you duty; and so bid you farewell.[43]

Here the regicides' travels would take on a greater sense of urgency. From late April through late August they moved quickly among friends and protectors: From Davenport's house, they moved to the home of William Jones, "said to have been the son of the regicide John Jones," who had recently been executed.[44] In May, a search party led by Thomas Kellond and Thomas Kirke, two merchants who had recently arrived from England and remained zealous supporters of the crown, formed in Boston.[45]

When Kellond and Kirke arrived in the New Haven area, the regicides apparently embarked on one of their more famous adventures. Governors Winthrop (Connecticut) and Leete (New Haven) are credited by early New England historians with delaying the search: The search party reported that the New Haven magistrates in particular were "'obstinate and

pertinacious in their contempt of his Majesty,'" and during this manufac-
tured delay the regicides left Jones's home for a cave near New Haven harbor.[46] Kellond and Kirke were then persuaded to push their search to
Manhattan, and from there they returned, without success, to Boston by
sea. Hutchinson reports that the regicides left the cave at West Rock and
returned to the public space of the New Haven Colony on June 11, 1661,
and in an effort to take pressure off of friends who had concealed them,
they offered themselves to Governor Leete for arrest. When Leete
declined this opportunity to turn them in, the judges returned to West
Rock and stayed there for two more months before leaving for Milford
once again, where they lived for two subsequent years.[47]

Despite the failure of the Kellond and Kirke expedition, British
authorities did not give up their pursuit of the escaped judges, nor did they
forget to punish the colonies for their rather evident complicity. On April
20, 1662, when Charles II granted a charter for Connecticut, he listed no
men of New Haven among the patentees.[48] On June 28 of the same year,
the king again wrote to the authorities in Massachusetts, reiterating the
fact that he had not issued pardons for the escaped judges. In a 1662 letter to his wife, who remained in England, Goffe mentions this atmosphere
of heightened anxieties present on both sides of the Atlantic: "Pray be private and carefull who you trust."[49] In the summer of 1664, when commis-
sioners for the king arrived in New England to attend to various
administrative matters, they listed among their concerns the apprehension
of not only the regicides but also of anyone who had aided them. During
this tense interval, the judges left the home of friends in Milford and again
headed for their cave at West Rock. Around that time, too, legend relates
that the judges were comfortable and contented, enjoying the luxury of
irony while reading British reports that they had been found and killed in
Switzerland.[50] However, all historical evidence shows that they were still
facing substantial dangers. Sources agree that on October 13, 1664, Whalley and Goffe began their night travels to Hadley, a town in western Massachusetts. At Hadley, they stayed at the home of John Russell, and there
John Dixwell joined Whalley and Goffe several months later.[51]

According to all evidence, the regicides saw themselves as a part of a
world about to end rather than at the birth of a nation. Letters to and from
the exiled judges recall their sense of acting in a time "the like hardly
falling out in the memory of man."[52] Goffe writes to his wife in 1674,
"These are dying times, wherein the Lord hath been and is breaking down
what he hath built, and plucking up what he hath planted, and therefore it
is not a time to be seeking great things for ourselves."[53] Particularly while
hiding in Hadley, the judges were apparently eagerly awaiting the fulfill-

ment of their apocalyptic expectations. Hutchinson reports that "they were much disappointed, when the year 1666 had passed without any remarkable event."[54]

Those who sheltered them had also come to expect the end-times, as John Davenport shows in a letter to William Goodwin, a prominent Hadley citizen: "N. England allsoe hath cause to tremble, whose day is repentance & reformation prevent not, for our backsliding, & changing our waies, from the ancient pathes, to comply with Old England, in theire corruptions."[55] The judges often wrote of their concerns about "what may become of poor England, whose sins are grown to a great Heighth."[56] They received with horror news of celebrations of the Restoration, parliamentary acts passed against the Puritans, and even festivities culminating in the vilification of "the effigies of the Protector, Hugh Peters, & others."[57] Throughout their years of exile, they watched for portents of God's wrath—in crop failures, hailstorms, an earthquake, and birthing disasters—while eagerly awaiting the time when such wrath might prove curative, "cutt[ing] asunder the spirit that is in Princes, and be[ing] dreadful to the Kinges of the earth."[58]

While the three regicides lived secretive lives at Hadley, British interest in their capture failed to diminish. But in one letter to Goffe from his wife, she "regoyce[s] to heare that the contry agres so well with [him] & that [he] thryve[s] so well." From such personal letters we see evidence suggesting the regicides' engagement with their outside world. When Mrs. Goffe makes the simple offer of "a perreweg" "by reson of the cold" in New England so that her husband might "in[j]oy more of the Are," her words clearly suggest that the judges are not spending all of their time in confinement.[59] Even so, the lack of historical documentation from those years suggests that they remain most often hidden.

By 1673, however, Dixwell is known to have settled in New Haven under the assumed name of James Davids. There he married and lived under that identity until his death on March 18, 1689. Whalley and Goffe, however, never emerge from hiding into the public sphere. Hutchinson dates Whalley's death in late 1674 or early 1675, and he bases this information on a letter (no longer extant) written by Goffe. Goffe traveled from Hadley to Hartford sometime before September 8, 1676; with this as the last documented sighting of him, neither the date nor the place of his eventual death is known.[60]

Given this information, only Goffe could possibly have been at Hadley during the late summer raids of King Philip's War in 1675. He, then, is at the center of the legend of the Angel of Hadley.[61] And with this, the most famous of the regicide tales, Hutchinson's *History* concludes its discussion of the judges; his sources are ambiguous at best, as he concedes when he writes, "I am loth to omit an anecdote handed down through Governor Leveret's family":

> The town of Hadley was alarmed by the Indians in 1675, in the time of publick worship, and the people were in the utmost confusion. Suddenly, a grave elderly person appeared in the midst of them. In his mien and dress he differed from the rest of the people. He not only encouraged them to defend themselves; but put himself at their head, rallied, instructed and led them on to encounter the enemy, who by this means were repulsed. As suddenly, the deliverer of Hadley disappeared. The people were left in consternation, utterly unable to account for this strange phenomenon. It is not probable, that they were ever able to explain it. If Goffe had been then discovered, it must have come to the knowledge of those persons, who declare by their letters that they never knew what became of him.[62]

Hutchinson's account sets off centuries of elaboration and debate on the accuracy and, more importantly, the imaginative currency of the legend. Eager to support Hutchinson's tale, later historians offer reasons for the mysterious and heroic act: "[H]ad Hadley been taken the discovery of the judges would have been unavoidable";[63] further, they argue "it is utterly inconceivable that this old Commonwealth veteran of many battles could have remained shut up in a secret chamber, when the Indians either approached or attacked Hadley."[64] A look at the progress of the war, as told by Increase Mather immediately afterward, however, may provide insight into less concrete, but at least as compelling, reasons for the birth of the legend as well as some of its particular details.

Though Hutchinson is somewhat ambiguous, Goffe's intervention is most often dated as September 1, 1675. Increase Mather tells of little other than terror for Hadley during that time, and he recalls that a series of bloody episodes proved that "God saw [New England was] not yet fit for Deliverance." In a September 12 letter from John Russell, quoted at length in Mather's text, the colonies indeed sound far from deliverance: "'If the Lord give not some sudden check to these Indians, it is to be feared that most of the Indians in the Countrey will rise.'"[65] Throughout September, Mather reports, the colonists fared badly, losing many men and suffering thefts of their provisions. Specifically, on September 18 "The Indians, whose cruel Habitations are the dark corners of the Earth, lurked in the Swamps, and multitudes of them made a sudden and frightful assault."[66]

Mather's description of this Indian assault is brief but includes a marked emphasis on the Indians' invisibility among the wild landscape and their victory through the element of surprise. In these details the account resonates powerfully with the mythic reversal attributed to the Angel of Hadley, but with a full inversion of victor and vanquished. Certainly it is noteworthy that this legend of colonial victory is born out of days characterized by such bitter colonial defeat. Perhaps in this darkest moment of the war, Hutchinson (or his source) finds images still potent and dangerous despite the eventual colonial victory, or perhaps that eventual victory later seems to merit some greater signifier to account for what really had to be a series of deadly struggles with so many innocent lives lost. In either case, the revision of those images to feature the machinations of a Puritan warrior rather than Indian forces might help dispel colonial anxieties about the land and its leaders, might make the victory more decisive, even portentous. Later New England historians do not acknowledge the ironic parallel between the historical account of the Indians' actions and the legendary account of Goffe's intervention; rather they argue that Mather simply suppressed or omitted the story of Goffe's actions in order to preserve the secrecy of the judge's identity.[67] Perhaps, then, the image of the Angel of Hadley emerges specifically as a curative symbol to rewrite one of New England's darkest moments in King Philip's War. Similarly, as their broader legend grows in America, the escaped regicides undergo nothing less than transfiguration: Indeed it is not too much to say that their cultural function has shifted so dramatically that they fulfill the peculiar prediction of the king whom they condemned, and from "Devil[s] of Rebellion" they have turned into American "Angel[s] of Reformation."[68]

CULTURAL USES OF THE REGICIDE TALE

Ezra Stiles's *History of Three of the Judges of King Charles I* (1794) is still the most extensive treatment of the "fugitive pilgrims," and by providing the generational link between Hutchinson's prerevolutionary account and the mid-nineteenth-century revival of the legend, this is the work that figures most prominently in the establishment of cultural uses of the judges' lives in the American imagination.[69] The highly partisan tone of Stiles's work helps to ensure that the judges will stand out among the American landscape as persecuted exiles rather than as Old World visitors bearing unprecedented political power. His strategy begins with an epigram, a biblical allusion echoing Davenport's sermon:

They wandered about—being destitute, afflicted, tormented—they wandered in deserts, and in mountains, and in dens and caves of the earth.

—Of whom the world was not worthy—

Be not forgetful to entertain strangers: for thereby some have entertained Angels unawares. Heb. xi, xiii

The work is structured as a defense. Stiles argues that he is providing a corrective to the reputation of "infamy" that has surrounded the regicides "for a century and a half," although in America, at least, there does not appear to be any such dominant history. For Stiles's purposes, however, the assumption of generations of misunderstanding provides the symbolic context necessary for his postrevolutionary, early national, account to work in the service of a new cultural truth rather than as Old Puritan propaganda. The spiritual-national quality of that assumed truth is clear in the rhetoric he uses: Stiles writes that the regicides have already begun to experience "resurrection in France, Poland, and America," and he promises further that—with his work—"the memoirs of these suffering exiles" will "hereafter be approved, admired and imitated."[70]

Perhaps to obviate potential criticism of the colonies' complicity with deception, much of Stiles's early narrative focuses on the less complicated relations between New Englanders and the judges in the first year of their arrival, before they are known to be wanted by the crown. Stiles warmly recalls the open welcome provided by John Endicott, John Davenport's hospitality and support in New Haven, the later protection of Goffe's journal in Cotton Mather's library, and, in general, the quickly established esteem of the colonists for the judges.[71] While Stiles concedes that his own view is that "the judges achieved a great and important work, and it was well done," he also notes that there are "those who did not approve of their political conduct," although even these critics (according to Stiles) admire the judges "for their professions of piety, and their grave deportment." He reports in detail that there are "stories . . . scattered and circulating all over New England to this day" of those who sheltered the judges, gave them food, and risked their lives for them. Thus New England's later tacit agreement to shelter the judges from British law becomes an issue of local communal loyalty as well as a demonstration of early, protonational, independence. The tie between spiritual and national identity, furthermore, is clear again when Stiles insists that much of New England looked upon the possible execution of the judges as "the slaying of the witnesses."[72]

While historically the age of the judges would have seemed remote to

Stiles's audience, his work ensures that mythically they will belong to a new configuration of time, the national future of a great democracy. As emblems of exile and persecution, the judges in Stiles's account *must* herald the coming of fulfillment, and he grounds this spiritual claim in history by suggesting that their image leads a new political revolution even after their struggle against the monarchy has been lost: "All Europe is ripening with celerity for a great revolution; the æra is commencing of a general revolution. The amelioration of human society must and will take place. It will be a conflict between kings and their subjects. This War of Kings, like that of Gog and Magog, will be terrible." Stiles argues further that this large-scale social change—the "natural course of events" after "established systems arrive at a certain height of corruption"—will "abundantly repay all the blood and treasure expended in the glorious contest with tyranny, from 1641 to 1660, inclusive of the twenty or thirty regicides who were ingloriously sacrificed at the Restoration."[73] Writing in the wake of the successes of the American revolution, Stiles suggests that such spirit was born in America at least in part due to the regicides' years of residence and that now similar success will spread abroad.

Writers of Hawthorne's time make the same immediate ironic shift as they resituate the significance of the lives of the judges from past to future. Although upon arrival in New England they may have appeared to be mere relics of a lost cause—"the forlorn hope of civil and religious liberty for the English race,"[74] the progress of legend ensures that they are quickly disassociated from England's failed revolution and recast quite specifically as omens of future glory, a glory that Hawthorne and his contemporaries see reflected first in the everyday life of the colonies, two centuries before their own time:

> Except in New England, royalty was now alone in favor. . . . The democratic revolution had been an entire failure, but that, with all its faults, its wildness, and its extravagance, it set in motion the valuable ideas of popular liberty which the experience of happier ages was to devise ways of introducing into the political life of the nation. We still presently see that the excessive loyalty of the moment, too precipitate in the restoration, doomed the country to an arduous struggle, and the necessity of a new revolution.[75]

Both the escaped regicides and those executed for their crimes in London, George Bancroft writes, herald "a better world . . . opening to receive them."[76] As living symbols, then, Whalley, Goffe, and Dixwell evade absolute identification with the excesses of the past from the very first moment they are refashioned by colonial experience from hunters into the hunted—from the very moment, that is, that they become not English but American.

Indeed, by the middle of the nineteenth century, the escaped judges stand unambiguously as a favorite historical and imaginative topic in New England, and, more specifically, use of their legend plays a strangely purifying role in the reconsideration of antebellum America's Puritan origins. Speaking at the bicentennial celebration of the town of Hadley, Frederic D. Huntington tells his audience that a major part of the region's historical interest lies with "the true romance of the regicides," and as evidenced in the events of the day, apparently many others in the town agree. The preface to Huntington's text recalls that a masque competes with the regular procession in the bicentennial's opening festivities: "[A]n episode not laid down in the programme, occurred. It was no less than an attack from a party of Indians. . . . The troops gave way as if badly frightened" until a second group of colonials, "marshaled by an old continental, with white hair and queue, representing Goffe, came to the rescue."

Throughout the text of his speech Huntington is torn between representing aspects of "romance" and aspects of "history" for his town's recollection. He generally objects to "superstition[,] that mournful and destructive form of moral hallucination," yet he cites the "two very different causes" of Hadley's colonial fame as "English politics, and man's universal passion for the marvelous." Huntington finds no reason to doubt the legend of the Angel of Hadley, and he finds all of the regicides' legendary status to be well deserved: "[T]he public service which exiled them and made them prisoners hidden from men for a few short years, lifted them up into the sight of after ages, and gave them an imperishable fame before the world."

As he makes the proud claim of having "the blood of the regicides" in his veins, Huntington even lays claim to his authority by producing a relic of sorts, a tooth (he claims) from the disinterred remains of one of the judges.[77] Holding this out toward the audience, Huntington laments the loss of all else proving their earthly existence, and he wishes aloud that he had the dust of their bones to "keep it as a Christian talisman in the village Pastor's study, as long as Christ has a minister here to preach the Gospel that is deliverance to the captive, and the opening of prison-doors to the bound!"[78]

In hiding for so much of their time in New England, the regicides feed imagined legends well because of the inherent mystery of their lives, from the basic facts of the quotidian to the complex truths of their now shrouded personal history.[79] In one sense their lives are overdetermined, fully shaped by one past event. But because that event has no comfortable place in their adopted culture's present consciousness, the past they embody is a matter only for whispers and (often fearful) speculation. Their relation to history, then, makes them unknown rather than familiar. The paradox of their definitively mysterious character is nicely illustrated in one of the common rumors that circulates about them in nineteenth-century America, a tale laced with dramatic irony. As an explanation for one of the judges' removals from New Haven toward Hadley, this story is offered:

> The incident which caused them to leave the cave [at West Rock, near New Haven harbor] was this: the mountain being a haunt for wild animals, one night as the judges lay in bed, a panther or catamount putting his head into the aperture of the cave, blazed his eyeballs in such a frightful manner upon them as greatly terrified them. One of them took to his heels and fled down to Sperry's house [the home of a family that had provided them with food] for safety. Considering the situation too dangerous to remain any longer, they quitted it.[80]

Clearly, in American imaginings, these are not the savage, bloodthirsty revolutionaries—men of blind rage, action, and ambition—that early British accounts describe. Stripped of their combative military qualities, the regicides' situation in New England as it is reimagined in the nineteenth century is reminiscent of the particular moment of mythic purity associated with the first generation of New World settlers, suffering in quiet exile, with barely shelter or known context. The threatening fanaticism of their reputation fades for audiences among the image of the familiar horrors of the American wilderness, and the judges become—even more so than Hester Prynne—the most domesticated of revolutionaries.

7

HESTER PRYNNE'S ANCESTRY

> Persons who have wandered, or been expelled, out of the com-
> mon track of things, even were it for a better system, desire noth-
> ing so much as to be led back. They shiver in their loneliness, be
> it on a mountain-top or in a dungeon.
> —Hawthorne, *The House of the Seven Gables*

W HILE James Fenimore Cooper's early republican audiences still
struggled to articulate their historical imaginings, Nathaniel
Hawthorne's audiences of the 1830s, 1840s, and 1850s had been quickly
and well stocked with tributes to history in language and the arts. Like the
Custom House narrator, however, Hawthorne's audiences faced new challenges—what to do with the materials they had, particularly how to
assimilate them into an ongoing national narrative of increasing complexity. Rufus Choate's 1833 oration, "The Importance of Illustrating
New-England History by a Series of Romances like the Waverly Novels,"
demonstrates a shift in cultural interest, past the problem of uncovering
the records of history and on to new understandings of their uses.[1] Bringing together tales of "illustrious achievement, of heroic suffering, of
unwavering faith," the artistic guardians of American history must,
Choate argues, "weav[e] it all into an immortal and noble national literature." The function of such work is to be "telescope, microscope, and
kaleidoscope in one," that is, to see national art beyond, into, and among
varieties of the everyday.[2]

In his address Choate indicates more than just an endorsement of a
newly American literature. He imagines the specific quality of a living
voice, built of an almost spiritual or prophetic language, accessible in and
through particular conditions of New England history:

> The whole history of the Puritans,—of that portion which remained in
> England and plucked Charles from his throne and buried crown and
> mitre beneath the foundations of the Commonwealth, and of that other
> not less noble portion which came out hither from England and founded

a freer, fairer, and more enduring Commonwealth . . . was out of the ordinary course of life; and he who would adequately record their fortunes,
display their peculiarities, and decide upon their pretensions, must, like
the writer of the Pentateuch, put in requisition alternately music, poetry,
eloquence, and history, and speak by turns to the senses, the fancy, and
the reason of the world.[3]

By necessity America—the prototypical modern nation—would develop a
national story that was both old and new, where established forms are
given life with new subjects and an inherited language is revised and newly
regulated for the needs of a new country. For Choate this new national literature depends at once on being an art of the common and the everyday,
though only under the particular conditions in which the "common" is elevated not quite to symbol, but somewhere above its material existence.[4]
The voice capable of effecting such transformation is one that Choate elsewhere associates with "the deliberative eloquence . . . [of] times of revolution," and he claims (borrowing from Milton) the dual purpose of this
voice is the persuasion of audience to "high actions and high passions."[5]
    Within the context of a culture determined to develop its own new
annals of history and legend, there is reflexivity to this argument: Such
persuasions of voice not only incite "high passions," but by doing so they
also revive action and passion into narrative—a new form of narrative,
which, then, as it is recorded and passed on, becomes in itself action and
passion. According to such logic, during the Jacksonian era and soon after,
America's new revolutionary project thus becomes the telling of national
stories, built of the cast and set derived from recent national (and even protonational) dramas.
    While Choate and Hawthorne would have had different political
interests behind their respective desires for a revival of the past, and
Choate—unlike Hawthorne—hoped for no unseemly return to the sins of
the past, the two shared a sense that the key to the success of a new
national literature must begin with the appropriate choice of subject matter. Choate's essay emphasizes that "all the predominant objects of interest
and excitement," including "the wars, revolts, revolutions, and great popular movements" of New England history, provide promising material. He
cites a specific example in the history of King Philip's War: "What do our
historians tell us of that war? and of New England during that war?"
Choate is satisfied that America knows something about the principal
players, has some accounts of when and where hostilities begin and end,
knows of the effects of the war on the colonies, and has some understanding of the causes and intents on both sides.

Within and among these known aspects of history, however, Choate points out that "the poet or the novelist" should be able to find and record for the nation images "so full, so vivid, so true, so instructive, so moving, that they would [en]grave themselves upon the memory, and dwell in the hearts of our whole people forever." These images would be drawn either from "information . . . not contained at all in our popular histories" or from materials that exist in the annals but have not taken form such that they have "fix[ed] the attention of the general reader." The projected endurance of these tales would be based on the archetypal shadows they cast—forward toward the product, a new national literature, and back, outlining the foundations, the "plain, massive, and deep-set, the basement stories of our religious, civil, and literary institutions." The central message of Choate's address is that for lived experience to be transfigured effectively into that desired "immortal, noble national literature," it must have the capacity to revive history as a living drama so direct in its impact on the present generation as to "fix the attention" of the people fully on the very meaning of the nation, to jar them from their perceived distance from the past by putting before them a sort of *tableau vivant,* a spontaneous and collective creation of living memory.[6]

That fixed attention, and within it the jolt toward a creative historical imagination, is exactly the paradoxical condition in which Hawthorne places his Custom House narrator. Throughout Hawthorne's texts, the image of a national story is directly linked to the idea of an American language, and the possibility of an American language is based on the imperative of the recognition of history. Through the at once regulatory and limiting powers of language, such a story would promise, in degrees, some social power of immediate control and conformity as well as the cultural counterpoint to that control—radically latent future promise. Hawthorne's symbolic method entwines these contradictions with one another and grounds them, materially and specifically, in history in its immediate, experiential sense. Though remembered so much as a recorder of his culture's history, in fact much of Hawthorne's historical emphasis begins with complicated considerations of the inevitabilities of flawed memory and the ultimate inaccessibility of the primary experience of past time; these laments stand as early figurations of an expressed need for a new language of culture. His travel notebooks and letters revel in art and architecture that have survived the modern revolutionary spirit, while still he sees the persistence of such material history as perhaps some failure of strength in the course of progress. In these writings there is an anxious lament for the fact that there is no language to stand as a bridge joining the relics of the old with the ethos of progress, thus leaving the past utterly at odds with both present and future.[7]

In Hawthorne's fiction, however, this conflict is recast as ambiguity in tone and is registered in the clear inadequacy of those who forget, coupled with the sleeping danger, only temporarily quieted, of those who are forgotten. In the earliest stories this ambiguity is, allegorically speaking, quite clear. There is first the hostility of "My Kinsman, Major Molineux" (1832)—where only uncomprehending mockery surrounds the tarred and feathered figure of history, as if he were a "dead potentate, mighty no more, but majestic still in his agony."[8] Other early stories further emphasize the culpability of quiet ignorance. "Alice Doane's Appeal" (1835) is set among "a people of the present [who] have no heartfelt interest in the olden time," and "The Gray Champion" (1835) reemerges into a world where he and his heroic age have "passed so utterly from . . . memories" as to be completely unrecognizable.[9]

In slightly later stories such as "Legends of the Province House" (1838), however, as well as in the romances, history is not forgotten, lost, or unrecognized, but it is present in such complicated forms as to elude comprehension. History is masked—literally—in the performance of "Howe's Masquerade" and too in the material manifestation of time that obscures the painting in "Edward Randolph's Portrait." The danger that history might unveil itself—to reveal some form less glorious than the Gray Champion—permeates such tales and gives rise to the consideration of a violent fantasy of forgetfulness, such as that found in *The Liberty Tree*, in a children's sketch on "The Hutchinson Mob." There Hawthorne's play between memory and forgetfulness imagines the violence of the latter through the figure of untold losses to national inheritance: "Then began the work of destruction. . . . The volumes of Hutchinson's library, so precious to a studious man, were torn out of their covers, and the leaves sent flying out of the windows. Manuscripts, containing secrets of our country's history, which are now lost forever, were scattered to the winds."[10] In Hawthorne's fiction, America's story requires some compensation for such losses; an American language—as imagined through the work of *The Scarlet Letter*—emerges as a vehicle capable of restoring and so making transmissible lost stories such as those pillaged from Hutchinson's library.

Among those papers lost in "The Hutchinson Mob" would have been the letters and papers of the regicides in New England. In this event Hawthorne's familiar themes of Puritanism, the American Revolution, and the dangers of mob activity come together to mark a particularly troubling moment in New England history, when a rich storehouse of multilayered, multiply resonant information—British and colonial—may have been lost. This suddenly unavailable narrative stands as an imagined lost bridge between now radically separate ages; it marks a rupture in history that only storytelling, in the work of recovery, can repair.[11]

Not only, then, did the escaped judges stand in the American imagination as harbingers of a better age, but the tale of their lost manuscripts also foregrounds the ways in which New England—especially the New England Puritans—understood the uses of language to be filled with power, a power infused with an extraordinary degree of historiographical self-consciousness.[12] This story of the New England regicides becomes, then, the story of recovered history bearing witness to the power of secrecy. In the hidden care of the colonies, the escaped judges are—in life and particularly in symbol—preserved, even protected. So too Hester's *A* and the manuscript found with it: The former is a token, a material artifact, bearing witness not only to a story but also to secrecy, and the latter is a set of pages giving rise to a tale, but never transcribed (or even read) for themselves. According to legend, both the regicides and the material bases of Hawthorne's narrator's story thus maintain historical authority because of their association with cultural crisis. However, like the Spy in relation to the figures of John André or Jane McCrea, Hester follows the pattern of the regicides and adds something more. Specifically, she becomes more richly associated with revolution even than these regicide judges are.

In the fiction's Puritan context and in the novel's antebellum context, Hester Prynne and the history she embodies bring to a young America the story of a multilayered revolution, reaching within (not beyond) history, through life and symbol. Hester is a revolutionary possibility hidden in the guise of society's scapegoat.[13] Had she been rather more fully integrated into society as the judges are in legend, the power of the scapegoat would be dispelled—crisis would be more neatly erased in consolidation. As I elaborate later, however, she retains that power, and so she is an urgent reminder that rebellion is alive and well. Communicating through an inherited language—one with rules and meanings established long ago—Hawthorne's Puritans, so intent on self-definition, recreate the powerful Adamic moment of language, but in a different way; here, tropes, including metaphors and narrative silences, acquire unique meanings within their new culture where perhaps inherited words would fail.

Hawthorne reimagines this moment of extraordinary creative vitality through the new cultural role that Hester Prynne acquires. Indeed, in *The Scarlet Letter*, rebellion—particularly as revolution—is everywhere, in character, context, and symbol. It dominates every level of language in the romance, from the historically referential images of both the English Puri-

tan and the American colonial revolutions, to theoretical questions surrounding the radical emergence of new meanings. These specters of revolution range from utopian promise to violent dissolution, with the most
powerful of these images shared and traded within the novel among Hester, Pearl, and their symbolic *A*.[14] When Hester accepts and then decorates
her emblem, using her "delicate and imaginative skill . . . of needle-work"
(81) to create a distinctly American symbol, her life recontextualizes these
themes of revolution, questions their meanings for Jacksonian and nineteenth-century America, and offers multivalent rewritings of this most
troubling national inheritance, an inheritance, specifically, of revolution's
bond with secrecy.

In a way, the mob attack on Hutchinson's library foreshadows the
image of history put forward in *The Scarlet Letter*, where—although history is not lost, masked, or assaulted but is instead resolutely, even saturat-
ingly, present—there is a rupture in understanding, a gulf of historical
knowledge that compels the participation of a storyteller. Hester's dual
function (marked sinner and unmarked angel) arises from the particulars
of her historical moment—ironically, especially from the unforeseen
nature of those particulars, and her complex relation to history makes her
Hawthorne's image of an American storyteller.

There in the imagined moral crisis of the Massachusetts Bay community, Hawthorne creates a moment with an import hidden to the characters themselves but in which he later finds that volatile—indeed
revolutionary—transition from one world of language to another. Instead
of imagining this transition as a gulf of forgetfulness, as it is so often figured in the short stories, *The Scarlet Letter* maps that gulf for the first time,
sketching there a series of experiments—figuring the historical in a multitude of ways, from the commonplace to the nearly transcendent—before
finding, in the image of the *A*, the bridge among these. Once this transition has occurred, once the scarlet letter turns from dusty artifact to "gold
[up] on the page" (37), the contradictions inherent in a new American language become symbiotic rather than oppositional; this is the course of cultural storytelling as it evolves in *The Scarlet Letter*.

America's normative state, Hawthorne suggests, is to be forgetful, if
not ignorant, of history. Any character who varies from this paradigm is
immediately set apart as an outsider, whether prophet or deviant. Like the
Gray Champion, these characters are layered with a double secrecy; their
past experiences are unknown and for some reason unknowable, and then,
because of that, their immediate lives, their present existence that follows
whatever had set them apart, too becomes mysterious. Hester Prynne—
first through what her community configures as the unknowability of her

adultery and then through the privacy of her life as an exile—fits this formula precisely. Like Robin Molineux's "kinsman," Hester is vulnerable through her difference, but like the Gray Champion, Hester's life as a figure of unacknowledged history has provided her a time and a space within her culture to shift in the public imagination from fully vulnerable, to mysterious, and finally to powerful, in the prophetic sense.

There is no inscribed limit to her power; her limits, Hawthorne suggests, inhere in nature, in history as time rather than as social practice. Thus like the legend of Whalley, Goffe, and Dixwell, frightened into hiding not by law or government but only by the appearance of a mountain lion at the mouth of their rocky shelter, Hester Prynne may be domesticated not by any magistrate's decree, but only by the broader forces impinging upon her life of solitude and mystery within the not-quite-settled American land.

The centrality of such characters to Hawthorne's historical imagination is perhaps no surprise, given the fact that the elusive qualities of contradiction characterizing the project of a national language—of which such characters are the prophets—more broadly characterize Hawthorne's famously ambiguous theory of romance. Outlined in his prefaces, romance is a decidedly liminal state of existence: It is a "theatre, a little removed from the highway of ordinary travel, where the creatures of [the writer's] brain may play their phantasmagorical antics, without exposing them to too close a comparison with the actual events of real lives," where "the truth of the human heart" is paramount, yet placed within broadly experimental "circumstances . . . of the writer's own choosing or creation."[15] All of this, of course, is given simultaneously its most complex and concise formulation in "The Custom House," "where the Actual and the Imaginary may meet, and each imbue itself with the nature of the other" (38). In these prefaces Hawthorne imagines this new language and the new literature it would create: a language of ambiguous "truth," giving voice to a literature shaped in turn by the formal properties of the romance.

The regicides, as they took imaginative form in the American imagination, are precisely the sort of figures suited to the realm of romance as Hawthorne sketches it.[16] Though clearly liminal, these figures of the historical imagination are, in Hawthorne's rendering, above all authoritative. In "The Gray Champion," the regicide has "a face of antique majesty" and walks with "unbroken dignity" in "a warrior's step"; he wears in every way the "attitude of command."[17] Even for his children's book, *Liberty Tree,* Hawthorne imagined stern authority in these figures of historical knowledge. Writing to his wife Sophia in September of 1841, Hawthorne describes his vision of an illustration that might attend this collection:

"The people may be as rough and wild as thy sweetest fancy can make them;—nevertheless, there must be one or two grave, puritanical figures in the midst. Such an one might sit in the great chair, and be an emblem of that stern, considerate spirit, which brought about the revolution."[18] The authority here—a revolutionary spirit seated centrally in the very image of stability, the "great chair"—is based, paradoxically, on silence and isolation, in marked contrast to the surroundings, lively with "rough and wild" figures.

It is notable just how similar Hester Prynne is to that oddly distant, yet central, figure of authority, if not in her first appearance before the multitude, at least by the time she can pass the taunts of Boston's children without flinching (85), and certainly by the time she appears with the "air" of "a great lady in the land" at Governor Bellingham's home (103). Like a noble Puritan among the mob, Hester, by means of her symbol, "walk[s] securely amid all peril" (161) until her isolation becomes almost material and "[h]er face . . . [is] like a mask; or rather, like the frozen calmness of a dead woman's features" (225), protecting her for the final revelation, when at Dimmesdale's last sermon, she stands "statue-like, at the foot of the scaffold" (242).

In fact, throughout the novel, Hester's silence and her stillness foreshadow her condition in death and, quite specifically, the Marvellian imagery through which Hawthorne pictured it.[19] There is clear irony in the poetic reference; both Hester and Dimmesdale are certainly "unfortunate lover[s]." Perhaps there is something more than irony too, however. Marvell's full couplet—concluding his poem on the violent despair of love—reads: "And [love] in Story only rules, / In a Field *Sable* a Lover *Gules*." As a prophet of sorts, Hester, the narrator makes clear, "rules" her story with the same stern authority with which she conducted herself in Puritan Boston, and perhaps she gained that authority through her isolation, her "delicious Solitude," in which she, like the speaker of Marvell's "The Garden," finds a place of thought "Annihilating all that's made / To a green Thought in a green Shade."[20] Here once again is the image of the revolutionary—the annihilation "of all that's made"—with the recuperative power of a new, larger, and more organic, context; perhaps it is not too much to see the suggestion of such recuperation in the new American story for which Hester Prynne lives and dies. But if so, we see Hester's radicalism fully drained by the story's end, leaving her still a strong cultural function, but not one more potent than that of the regicides. This, I think, we cannot do—at least, not until we consider the final incarnation of Hester's *A*.

8

FROM ARTIFACT TO ARCHETYPE

> Be these things how they might, [she], fair as she looked, was
> plucked up out of a mystery, and had its roots still clinging to her.
> —Hawthorne, *The Marble Faun*

A T the end of *The Scarlet Letter*, the *A* reappears, and through its image Hawthorne reminds readers that the artifacts generating (then framing and containing) his story are inextricably bound in a symbolic vocabulary within which the meanings of revolution have come full circle but without closure, promising to regenerate yet again its own spontaneously variable cycle. When we imagine the gravestone that Hawthorne tells us was carved for Hester and Dimmesdale together, we remember the tattered cloth *A*, still remarkably red after those many years. Here in this final scene, the rediscovery of the letter takes on an eerie, if not sinister, aspect. In this incarnation the letter stands out in sharp relief from the dark historical memory of Puritan Boston. That obliquity of memory, still a part of the Custom House attic in 1850, once again paradoxically enables the inexplicable recurrence of a deeply foreboding sign of primal divisions— images disquietingly relevant in a new way to Hawthorne's antebellum America:

> *On a Field, Sable, The Letter A, Gules:*

So the narrator describes the tombstone that looms over the "old and sunken grave" (262) of Hawthorne's tragic Puritan lovers.

With this final image of the novel—a herald's shield in red and black— Hawthorne raises the banner of revolution one more time. The story begins under the watchful eyes of the federal eagle of colonial revolution and the rippling shadow cast by the national flag flying at the Custom House door. It ends with Andrew Marvell's image of blood and war, now etched as a gravestone to commemorate fallen Puritans far from their British roots. Standing apart from—above—the bodies themselves, the letter (*A*, gules) and its given context (a field, sable) exist so saturated with histories that they continue to generate meaning to the "curious investigator" (262) who may wander through the burial ground and who is the last living presence Hawthorne imagines for us in the novel.

Hawthorne's readers, too, are compelled to reread the image. The marker records its own testimony, its weakness as a shield for the living, insofar as its endurance as an artifact engraved in stone marks an utter contrast to "the dust of the two sleepers" (262) buried below. And, no doubt there is further irony in the fact that it is a heraldic image put to work only as a memorial to the dead. As a monument, this stone's face is more than a testimony to those who have passed; it is, to be sure, the first American coat of arms, designed by history's accidents, for the family of the ever-enigmatic Pearl Prynne.

Despite—or through—the *A*'s dizzying array of meanings, it is clear that this symbol is not transcendent. It is created, maintained, and replicated from within its own material, historical existence and from the interplay of that existence with each interpreter's historically bound imagination. In the abundance of that interplay—which at every turn bears witness to history's power over the imagination—we ironically also see how such historical symbolism might appear transcendent in its seemingly boundless capacity for incarnation. There, in the boundlessness, is its revolutionary quality—the quality of language and meaning as *not* containable, even within the broader bounds of the narrative. However, the *appearance* of transcendence, boundlessness, here is a return to origins—origins of the text, the story, its language. The tombstone—that fragment of language standing outside of Hester's own time—returns the reader to that opening image, the worn yet magnificent *A*, both in its status as historical artifact and as a storyteller's talisman. It remains on the fringes of containment, edging ever toward the new, as we must remember when we recall that this object carried the power to mandate the birth of a historical imagination from even the most unpromising of candidates, the Custom House narrator. In that process the *A* has moved from artifact to archetype, or rather, its role as archetype has been layered onto its role as artifact. As archetype, it speaks to the powers of consolidation; as artifact, it bears witness to the lingering embers of history.

The process allowing for the preservation of the radical within the broader, new, cultural story offered by the romance plays itself out in large part through character interaction. When, through the narrative poetics of his romance, Hawthorne explores the crisis of the symbolic foundations of American language, the layers of storytelling within the romance construct a system of language and irony that first allows (or compels) Hester to regenerate the very conflict her penitential life is designed (by her town leaders) to dispel. Hester and her scarlet *A* are part of a symbolic vocabulary active within a dogmatic religious code as well as a democratic political code; indeed, she and her symbol together embody the enduring conflict that at first is the only connection between these codes.[1]

While Hester's town magistrates understand transgression and punishment in traditional, hierarchal terms, Hester's own experience as the transgressor is creative, innovative, and even obliquely prophetic. Thus, Hawthorne brings forth Hester in all of her contradiction and ambiguity as an example of the productivity of America's crisis in language and storytelling. Hester's complexity specifically mirrors the ambiguous roots of America's linguistic independence and the power of such ambiguity to effect both origin and union for a new modern culture, even a culture, like Hester's or Hawthorne's, divided. Noah Webster's vision of an American language promised an opportunity to examine national rhetoric, revise national self-definition without discarding the known, and be reminded that—especially in the early stages of a culture—the danger and power of language are never so far apart. *The Scarlet Letter* is an experiment in that tradition. In fact, because the romance itself enacts the culture's shift beyond a point of potentially revolutionary impasse, it is one of the most complex assessments of the history of the American language as it develops over the two centuries that separate Hawthorne's political and social world from his fictional setting.

In *The Scarlet Letter* Hawthorne directly addresses the foundations of language, the "story" within the rhetoric of national narrative. Suggesting danger in the "theoretical" nature of both Puritan rhetoric and nineteenth-century American symbology, he makes a progressivist's argument for a new infusion of history into theory. Michael Colacurcio describes the damaging results of "progressive history" as the reduction of "multiplicity to unity, not only in 'explanation' but in 'reality.' What is edited out from the past will not be available soon again."[2] Here we find an echo of "The Custom House" narrator's fears, as he is effectively "edited out" of what he sees as the story of national progress. *The Scarlet Letter's* historiographical progressivism, however, prevents Hawthorne's experiments with language from falling into the traps of reductionism. Through the romance's narrative voice and the ambiguously radical and yet often silenced consciousness of Hester Prynne, the novel provides a complex system of language theory dependent upon irony and, in so doing, establishes as a first priority the task of making available exactly that which progressive historiography had "edited out." Further, these recovered materials function in the service of a revised plan based on oddly familiar progressive sentiments, which in turn are strengthened through their newly appropriated material and knowledge.

From its initial appearance, the *A* itself first asserts revolutionary authority within Hawthorne's text. Clearly that scarlet letter is not only what it first appears. Although the narrator introduces it to us as if he can know it—"It was the capital letter A. By an accurate measurement, each limb proved to be precisely three and one quarter inches in length" (34)— it is immediately clear that what Hawthorne calls the "deep meaning" of the "mystic symbol" is neither clear nor inviting, as it radiates the "burning heat" of a "red-hot iron" (34). At once too hot to hold and too oblique to read, then, the scarlet *A* is an aggressively material fragment of history.

Once found in the attic of the old Salem Custom House, it compels storytelling in a uniquely troublesome way: It is an artifact of cultural history, but it has not found a place in a museum or library; it is an emblem of personal experience, but it has not been protected within any familiar context, as, for example, a family heirloom. Instead, the place of the *A* in the Custom House attic and the vigor of its imaginative assault on the narrator demand that this material fragment be understood in its inadequate present context as the trace of something more—something out of its own temporal sphere. As an artifact, it hovers just at the outer reaches of the narrator's interpretive responsibility. The strangeness of the find ignites the storyteller's imagination, and the story to be told is, at this initial moment, dangerously open ended.

"The authenticity of the outline" (36) is all that the narrator claims to find in Surveyor Pue's attic papers, but the romance springs forth in full, with decidedly little to mark it as the work of the Custom House narrator as we have come to know him. Jarred from his life as a bored bureaucrat— watching over a "dilapidated wharf" (7) in rooms "cobwebbed and dingy" with only "venerable figures" for company, "talking . . . in voices between speech and a snore" (9)—this narrator has been charged with much more than he knows. This story about life in the New World is a story distinctly larger than his own consciousness. Whatever the *A* signifies, that significance is beyond the common vocabulary of the narrative world, and yet it represents only the smallest fragment, the most basic experience, of the world from which it came.

To allow the emergence of this story into the narrator's consciousness and—through that—into cultural knowledge is to unleash a set of unfamiliar (and potent) forces, forces far removed from the narrator's—as well as the reader's—ordinary practices of everyday life. The narrator, then, somewhat unwittingly invites a total reconstruction of his epistemological and historical frames of reference. Reading the meaning of the *A* mandates a radical revision of the culture of Hawthorne's known interpretive world, from the elemental—that is, beginning with the first letter of the alphabet—to the most complex, the secrets of the past, of experiential history, now gone from human consciousness yet still vibrant within that scrap of red cloth. The *A* itself, as a material, historical, and linguistic fragment, overthrows the authority of the narrator ("decapitate[s]" [46] him, in his own terms[3]) and instantly begins to act the part of the revolutionary.

As I have been suggesting, *The Scarlet Letter* offers as a response to this violence the considered attention to the role (at once historical and theoretical) of language in the development of America, even the participation in the making of a national language. For Hawthorne, inheriting British empiricism, surrounded by transcendentalism, descending from Puritanism, and setting out to revitalize history, the manipulation of language into a reenactment of the moment of founding a language for the New World potentially promises the reaffirmation of America in new modern terms.[4] Here (as for Benjamin), storytelling means both preservation and transmission: Secrecy and speech are equal and mutually dependent, without division or impediment between them. Further, from this unlikely union of opposites the theory of national storytelling—first suggested by the coexistent and contradictory religious and political significations of the scarlet *A*—begins to cohere.

Hawthorne's manipulation of levels of language and communication in *The Scarlet Letter* reveals the fact that no character in Puritan Boston has either the ability or the desire to narrate history in its deepest communal sense. Nonetheless, the novel further demonstrates that such a history persists. The narrative voice of the romance, which is at one level a denial or suppression of history, turns on itself to become a vehicle for a kind of spontaneous eruption of the new American story. Only the narrator—and none of the characters—can see "how far removed . . . hidden meaning [is] from revelation, and how close [it can] be brought by the knowledge of this remoteness."[5] The narrator in "Endicott and the Red Cross" defines "the policy" not only of his "ancestors" but also of himself and of the similar narrator in *The Scarlet Letter:* "It was the policy of our ancestors to search out even the most secret sins, and expose them to shame, without fear or favor, in the broadest light of the noonday sun."[6] In *The Scarlet Letter* Hawthorne suggests to his readers that now, with some distance, it may be the time to look back at what that light has exposed, at the bases for community interpretation. Moreover, to create a narrator who can put cultural history into transmissible form, not simply into the form of information or rhetoric, and who can at least attempt "to regain pure language fully formed in the linguistic flux"—is some triumph in itself; beyond that it is also direction and exhortation for the newly reviving program of an American language.[7]

The paradoxical difficulties of storytelling, including the impossible goals of approaching pure language and truth, affect *The Scarlet Letter*'s narrator but do not render him powerless. Because removed from the story by several generations, this narrator is able to speak, to tell the story of a town in the New World: By looking back, he ensures that his words are neither purely rhetorical promise nor simple information. By his own admission, this narrator tends to write from an "autobiographical impulse" (3). He has less to lose, however—and also less to gain—through his storytelling than one of the original players would have had. Instead, the past becomes the present writer's story; his desire is to imagine "that a friend, a kind and apprehensive, though not the closest friend," is listening to his story, so that he "may prate of the circumstances that lie around us, and even of ourself, but still keep the inmost Me behind its veil" (4). As a storyteller he must be more than a man of mere instinct, as is the Custom House inspector, who is tied so closely to his homeland that he has "no power of thought, no depth of feeling, no troublesome sensibilities." In addition, like any authentic storyteller, this narrator wants to be creator and truth teller at once; he realizes that the way to do this is to tell what has never before been told but has long been true:

> Literature, its exertions and objects, were now of little moment in my regard. I cared not, at this period, for books; they were apart from me. Nature,—except it were human nature,—the nature that is developed in earth and sky, was, in one sense, hidden from me; and all the imaginative delight, wherewith it had been spiritualized, passed away out of my mind. A gift, a faculty, if it had not departed, was suspended and inanimate within me. There would have been something sad, unutterably dreary, in all this, had I not been conscious that it lay at my own option to recall whatever was valuable in the past. (25–26)

Thus this narrator "contend[s] for . . . the authenticity of the outline" (33) but openly claims great liberty of invention; this narrative stance, in which the imagined truth of the past stands between and indeed binds literature and nature, is a type of perspective unavailable without a distancing of time and place. Hawthorne, too, is a storyteller at another remove. With the same theory of language, a lens of "suspended and inanimate" consciousness, he represents but does not define Hester Prynne. She in turn becomes the model of the unconscious promise in the evolution of a national vocabulary and language: The various imagined truths of Hester's past life also stand between—and bind—rhetoric and experiential history.

Though the autobiographically inclined narrator sees in retrospect "the true and indestructible value that lay hidden in petty and wearisome incidents and ordinary characters" of his own life, at no given time is he able to "diffuse thought and imagination through the opaque substance of today, and thus to make it a bright transparency" (37). Overt and conscious definition—maybe especially self-definition—eludes the storyteller precisely because it must be saved, condensed instead for future transmissibility: "[T]he page of life that was spread out before me seemed dull and commonplace, only because I had not fathomed its deeper import. A better book than I shall ever write was there . . . only because my brain wanted the insight and my hand the cunning to transcribe it" (37). However, hope matches frustration in the narrator's response: If he can make, in his own mind, "a bright transparency" of his cultural past, then perhaps his own story will be as distinctly present to future readers as the *A* emblem seems to him. Perhaps the novel, like the adorned letter, will be transfigured for future readers; perhaps it will "turn to gold on the page" (37).

The depth of understanding implied in narrator, character, and fictional community in *The Scarlet Letter* bears a direct correlation to facility with language, and while "understanding" suggests social participation in a system of codes, facility is actually dependent upon distance, separation from the congregation, and an ability for nonrhetorical, truthful but creative, leadership. Despite the narrator's claims of distance, even he has difficulty extricating himself from the paradoxical webs binding the spoken and unspoken. He can no more say "adultery" than the town fathers can. It seems that he has inherited some degree of language deficiency—but in its reduced form, this language deficiency ironically also embodies the promise of a "bright[er] transparency" for future narrators of the culture's history.

As the narrative eye passes by a rosebush at the prison door, the narrator can "hardly do otherwise than pluck one of its flowers and present it to the reader" (48); this is a strange and jarring moment—another startling narrative symbol. No longer is the narrator so clearly removed from his story, nor is the reader safely distant. Narrative, tale-teller, and reader are here linked in an unsettling way: It is a gesture that implicates all three in the linguistic game that Hawthorne has begun to play. Interestingly, when the *North American Review* complained that "the master of such a wizard power over language as Mr. Hawthorne manifests" had wasted his talent on such a "revolting subject," it is specifically Hawthorne's most overt symbolism that seems most bothersome: "[F]ine writing [about adultery] seems as inappropriate as fine embroidery [on the scarlet letter]"; "the ugliness of pollution and vice is no more relieved by it than the gloom of prison is by the rose tree at its door."[8]

The rose blossom is in once sense as clear and familiar a symbol as is the *A*—either one can be read through context, tradition, and common intuition. Also like the *A*, however. the blossom is left with free-floating meaning, undefined by the narrator and the characters. Both symbols are too close to the storyteller (who makes a point of describing them tactilely) to be explicated, and similarly both are overly (even aggressively) accessible to the reader. Hawthorne provides in these symbols historical and imaginative links that preserve two opposing halves of their respective symbolic functions. Such connections put demands on the present moment—demands instinctively rejected by visions of history and symbolism that look for the "relief" of "ugliness" and "gloom" by beauty and new life, the cancellation of history through any alternative aesthetic. This narrator refuses such solutions and instead enters into the historical consciousness of New England Puritanism as Hawthorne would have it, even to the extent of recreating the ritual—now in the fulfilled linguistic form of the novel—that placed Hester and her sin before the community.

Through this ritual aspect of his novel, Hawthorne linguistically reenacts a moment of founding. Such a moment is necessarily unspeakable in its original nature but infinitely powerful as well. In order to represent the paradox of the founding moment, Hawthorne cannot have his Puritans give Hester a label reading "Adultery" or "Adulteress." From his own description it seems clear that if the narrator of "The Custom House" had found a cloth label of such specific kind, his historical imagination would have suffered reduction because of the label's specificity: The less concentrated form of language, the word or phrase, could not have cast the same imaginative spell; it would not have represented the "secret" sin. In the *A*, this narrator feels the preternatural power of an unspoken story, the "burning heat" as if of a "red-hot iron" (32). Both he and the seventeenth-century players in Hester's drama feel the danger and the power of that undefined idea—of a symbol as opposed to a label—and both intend to communicate meaning through that symbol.

Nevertheless, the meaning that Hawthorne, the narrator, and the fictional Puritans communicate is not definition; it is instead a sign of the entrance into the process of creating a new cultural language. Hester has suddenly embodied a transgression previously invisible to her community, and first efforts at language can acknowledge only importance, difference, and the need for attention—all indicating an intent to define later, once collective competence is achieved.[9] Like the New England regicides, Hester

Prynne bears the extraordinary potency of the forbidden and the mysterious, but as Hester escapes that first instinct to define (and so to limit), she thus preserves the radical potential so quickly drained from the judges in their almost immediate cultural incorporation as symbolic figures.

In these first efforts toward communication, the town magistrates reveal their inability to differentiate between dangerous and otherwise powerful functions of language. Though she is bearer of their symbol, Hester alone can produce the freedom to think and to function in a nonsymbolic (that is, not *only* symbolic) realm. Her understanding and her use of language are based on—but not restricted to—the primary rational and empirical function of words.[10] In Hester, Locke's "arbitrariness" of the word or sign is counteracted by what emanates from that sign; within Hawthorne's work, the interplay of "sign" and "emanation" produce effective cultural symbolism. Hester is only another powerless Puritan woman destroyed by sin without the (ironic) gift of the imposed, dead letter of the law from the magistrates. With this gift, though, Hester begins to embody some interplay between sign and emanation (as between history and symbol); she thus revives her social order and a dying language—connects them to a future from which they are about to be ruptured—by becoming a living letter, that is, a letter of the emerging law.

As the latent promise of a second age, Hester's *A* is significantly unlike other Puritan forms of linguistic punishment, which were based on the principle of restricting language use.[11] In the language of both the fictional Puritans of Hawthorne's story and the historical Puritans of seventeenth-century New England, there is the consistent expression of a cultural hope—perhaps even a belief—that "they had captured the whole of reality in the texture of a rational language"; "word, thought, and thing were one" in this equation.[12] If language could be culturally monitored, then through organized education, controlled speech and literacy, and the use of only metaphors that would consistently refer to the biblical "Word," known to all, the leaders of the colony might blanket the population with a common morality.[13]

In "Endicott and the Red Cross," where an early figure of Hester Prynne first appears, the "Wanton Gospeller" reflected in Endicott's shield is one of Hawthorne's examples of language used in the service of controlled authority. He is defined, clearly and publicly, so that the community will immediately contextualize any of his "unsanctioned" "interpretations of Holy Writ" as "wanton." [14] Here "definition" ironically depends upon the vagueness necessary to cover a multitude of possible interpretations. This is the trick that escapes those punishing Hester: These Puritans clearly know that, in order to avoid being reductive, one's definitions must not confine in such a way as to be immediately obsolete. Metaphorical and symbolic language, ways of anticipating challenge and feeding imagination, are integral parts of Puritan thought.[15] However, the critique given through *The Scarlet Letter* points out an excessive reliance on the symbolic and the attending danger to the social structure. The conflicts within the romance show that although early America could count on importing rituals—of language, religion, or punishment—the interpretation of these rituals within the new context soon moved beyond predictability. In addition, this lost connection between sign and interpretation had eroded the primary function of ritual—social control—in the colony.

Ironically, the ritual nature of American language remained, though control of the ritual function had failed. In this world so conscious of language, the letter *A* on Hester's dress would stand for two uncreated sentences: the biblical criminal sentence—death by stoning—waived in favor of the letter, and the sentence within the narrative that would name her sin. In these first days of the colony, however, one founded on the belief in a need for a new code of values, there are words for laws, but no words for broken laws. That is to say, there are laws to restrict activity and belief, but no clear understanding of the persistent existence of deviant behavior. In this context there is no way to harness the *positive potential* of deviance.[16] This leaves one simple reason that it seems as though no one within the story (including the narrator) can give even a capsule summary of Hester's sin: The necessary words—with the deviance they signify—have been deeply suppressed within the vocabulary of the colony, just as Hester's life story is so deeply buried under layers of narrative romance. Words within this society have either been tied too closely to actions in an excessively rational way or radically divorced from actions in an immediately symbolic way. In both cases words for sin—or any transgression, for that matter—are comprehensible only within the context of the negative imperative, in this case, the biblical commandment. By negating potential action and by making symbolic meaning explicitly referential, the commandment allows sin no existence of its own. Clearly the punishment of sin remains a ritual in structure, but an empty one—it is a ritual without function, without a defined nemesis.

Although this is a community for which "religion and law were almost identical" (50), they are not quite identical. In Hester's world as Hawthorne draws it, the faith systems of both religion and protonational identity only coexist with—but do not match—a legal system that must address and work within lived history. Nonetheless it is true that both Puritanism specifically and laws generally are essentially reactionary: Both begin in restriction and dissent, thus acknowledging a dangerous power structure beyond themselves. If the conflict between the reactionary culture and the feared alternative identity is simply denied or artificially blanketed with an agreed-upon value system, then culture and power will never fuse into a "positive pattern" of social reality.[17] The narrative poetics of *The Scarlet Letter* suggests a different approach—a way to harness the easy route to self-definition guaranteed to the defensive party with the large-scale "positive pattern" available only to a potent culture that has moved beyond the language of negativity. Hawthorne represents all of this—the power of defense, establishment, conflict, and deviance—in the ironically empowering punishment of the scarlet letter.[18] Like Pearl, this letter has as its "principle of being" the "freedom of a broken law" (134).

In this model, Puritan Boston's town fathers are aware only of the first of language's powers, the ease of defensive self-definition based on contrast or negation. They acknowledge and even emphasize that Hester is different. They do not go back to this first step in communication to seek definition, however. Instead, they would prefer that she simply embody "difference," thereby encouraging the general, vague "conformity" of the rest of the town. Instead of banishing Hester, sending her like a true scapegoat into the wilds and thus acting as if she and her sin are closed off from society, this community chooses not only to keep her with them, but in fact to make her especially noticeable—to give both her and themselves a clear vision of her failing, to give visible form to the absence of a virtue.

As they lead Hester out of prison, the town fathers' one known purpose is to keep this transgression as part of Hester's identity for an unlimited time, whether with the scarlet letter or through the collective memory of her public confession. Working in part with "mercy and tenderness" (63), the magistrates want to help Hester achieve "an open triumph over the evil within [her]" (67). However, at least as strong is the community's motive of self-defense: It is as if these leaders, like Dimmesdale, think that a saturation of the community with the image of sin will be some ritual of purgation. But also like Dimmesdale, these men are manipulating language in such a way that they avoid the very core of its meaning: They suspend the demands of knowledge and transform the stigmatized Hester immediately into a cultural symbol. Depending upon the power of interpretation, but also with no means to control that power, the town magistrates set free a symbol that takes on a life of its own.[19]

Without the sanctioned codification of an explicitly spoken and positively asserted language, the Puritans have trouble controlling the meaning of the *A*. In this context—the tradition of sacrifice—it is significant that Hester is not only branded but also decorated, not only damaged but also adorned. However, the positive force of this punishment is an emblem of paradox, a demonstration that this sign still signifies only an abstract need for differentiation and not a definitive action or value. The absence of the *A* becomes a badge of honor and respectability: To be a member is not to wear an *A*—not to embody what the *A* symbolizes and not to know the experiential meaning of the *A*. Thus the strangeness of the sign, rather than any rational meaning fused with it, is the essence of the shame it conveys. While the terms of Hester's own integration require the active binding of experiential and rational with the symbolic—that is, the abandonment of a belief in definitive meaning as established in one realm or the other—society as a whole is still working too defensively to challenge the symbolic with the historical. In this colony, no affirmative statement of values can come about for those who do not wear the *A* because, as the narrative emphasizes, the entire response has been defensive rather than self-assertive: No purging of sin has occurred, no progress on a doctrine of ethics has been made, and—most specifically—no forward-looking codification of the transgression and punishment has emerged.

LANGUAGE IN HESTER'S WORLD

The promise given into Hester's charge is nowhere more evident than in her first emergence from prison. Walking out of the darkness into light, seen as a different person from the one who entered because she is now a mother and wears an *A*, Hester has been transformed as an image to the community. Nevertheless, instead of that transformation marking an end, it is surrounded with the images of beginnings—the baby, the first letter of the alphabet, the light. The town fathers believe that they can make of Hester what they will—for them that means to make her purely a symbol of sin—but in her historical life and in the empirical life of her fictional character, the important implicit gesture is an assumption that her personal past, including her adultery, is washed away in a ritual gesture of purification. The whole "ceremony," which was meant as a purification rite for the town—a transfiguration of the historical Hester into the symbolic Hester—empowers her not so much because she cares for their forgiveness but because it shows her that she is a presence threatening to her town, one too real to expel and—as yet—too strange to name. Hester thus acquires both the freedom and the burden of fusing her lived experience to a cultural symbol.

Wearing only the single letter, Hester is to flower into the grandest form of Puritan language, a "living sermon against sin" (63). As symbol and as sermon, she is to stand as the embodiment of the negative potential of every resident in her community. Like Dimmesdale's rhetorical assumption of this same role, Hester's involuntary assumption is outside of the realm of common speech. Although in Hester's case there is an assumed understanding of the message she wears and in Dimmesdale's case there is an assumed misunderstanding of the sermons he delivers, the two are connected in their knowledge of the "truth" and their status as perceived symbols. As symbols in the possession of the community, Hester and Dimmesdale are elusive and malleable: They are sacred and they are sinners, angels and humans, prophets and mutes; most importantly, they are the holy sermon whose subject is the unspeakable sin.[20]

The primary importance of one specific obligation—the commitment of the subject's experience and knowledge to the larger community—characterizes Benjamin's Storyteller and also governs the ranks and powers of characters in Hawthorne's world, as evidenced in his (at first apparently schematic) distribution of language abilities in the novel. In order to function most efficaciously as historical symbol, such a figure must allow the imposition of culturally chosen meanings; only Hester fulfills this political role.[21] All of the other characters within the fiction either elude or impede its progress. For example, Dimmesdale is a self-styled symbol. His manipulation of context, his tendency (whether conscious or not) to see to it that his words are inscribed within a situation he knows will be presumed "spiritual," makes the process of demystifying his symbolic character difficult for his congregation. Through an overdetermined rhetorical self-definition, Dimmesdale—like the colony itself—lives as if rational meaning is not only inaccessible but also obsolete. He thus severs his referential metaphors from his historical life.

Similarly—though in a less complex way—Chillingworth expresses himself only in ways that keep meaning at bay from the Puritan community; his primal passions are deeply out of place, and, in the eyes of this community, they are probably better placed among the Indians with whom he has spent recent time in captivity. Within these poles, however, is Hester. There is only the *A*, nothing elaborately rhetorical, nothing mythically prelinguistic; it is the familiar *A* of the hornbook. Whereas Dimmesdale and Chillingworth seem trapped in their respective symbolic modes, Hester is empowered by hers in a perverse sort of way. So simple and so clear, the import of Hester's symbol is thus the more strikingly undefined in speech. Boston's children can speak of her cultural meaning, but without comprehension: They utter "a word that had no distinct purport to their own minds, but was none the less terrible to [Hester]" (85). Thus the importance of Hester's story—its potential to help define the culture's values—coupled with its unspoken mystification, delineates the weaknesses of the emergent American language at mid-century and points to a vision (however remote) of a better way, of a language based upon the whole of experiential life.

Pearl, as part of the generation of children who are the only ones to be able to name—if not to understand—Hester according to her sin, shows a greater freedom with her language and thus implicitly offers a vision of a different future.[22] She is interested in learning meaning and applying it to the familiar people and things of her world; she asks questions that have never before been asked, questions embarrassing to her elders. Nevertheless, although Pearl has the desire absent from the older Puritans, she does not have the distance necessary for revelation. As the "living hieroglyphic" (207), Pearl can set in motion the impulse to speak in her world: She can question, but the answers, the language and stories that she may see latent in the *A*, can emerge only slowly, through a growing distance from New World culture; some of this distance—and its tempting claims to objectivity—the romance's narrator hopes to gain. Pearl, so often defined in criticism as the *A* embodied, is one version of that already-fulfilled living form, that transmissible essence, of Benjamin's theory. As that form, however, she is constrained in another way: She has no way of giving voice to the story that has created and encoded her, and so she too depends to a certain extent on the machinations of narrative.

The historically distanced narrator compensates for—and so implicitly comments on—Boston's inability to make sense of the transgression that Hester has committed. He sees and represents the town fathers' bungling of ritual, their failure to demand a foundation—a primary moment when language is bound to meaning—for the creation of their new cultural symbol; from this evidence, the narrator sees and represents also the ironic purification of Hester, gained only by way of ritual defilement.[23] Even though it is the suppression of story, the denial of conflict, and thus the maintenance of a utopia of sorts that is the job of the town's most powerful members, they are the ones calling for truth to be visible, to come out of the shadows. Hester's reply—a determined secrecy—thus undermines their decision and recoils upon their traditional strategy of the suppression of language: Now the suppression of language has been coopted by the town's outrageous transgressor.[24]

In this way, the shift in power to Hester Prynne begins the narrative's most extraordinary challenge to communal understanding, wherein Hawthorne's formal properties of narrative emphasize over and over the historical properties of the *A* and the irreducibility of this trace that stands for so many material facts of America's living record. The magistrates are not the only offenders in their narrowness of vision: Through these same errors, this blindly utopian project of submitting to the refusal of story-telling, the preacher and the doctor—two other individuals with roles centered on providing for the health and welfare of the community—fail as communicators within both their own social world and the world of the text.

At odds with Hester's cultural role of advancing society through a linguistic fusion of symbol and history is this utopian mode of rhetoric, which we might associate with the romance itself but for Hester's own vivid interruptions of its tone and function. It is a dysfunctional theory of language for which Dimmesdale and Chillingworth provide the frame. Together they fashion a model of the trap of language that both binds and sustains this community's present state: Dimmesdale replaces fundamental statements with rhetoric, and Chillingworth represses every essential fact of language. Both men manipulate their language to suppress their (threateningly transgressive) identities in order that they might blend into Boston, as members essentially the same as everyone else—Chillingworth in his "purposes to live and die unknown" (76), and Dimmesdale, who, because of his position in the community, must say to Hester, "I charge thee to speak out the name of thy fellow-sinner" with such passion that any observer would expect that the "guilty one himself . . . would be drawn forth by an inward and inevitable necessity" (67–68). Purely symbolic communication—including Dimmesdale's celebrated rhetoric and Chillingworth's primal avoidance of the spoken or written word—is a literally empty symbolism. In both cases the substance (or the secret) that gives rise to symbolic language has been fully removed, and what remains is a shell, an outline of a truth once lived. Though overtly supportive of the status quo, such symbolism is all the more dangerous for its persuasiveness; in reality it threatens the culture with nothing less than a loss of foundational knowledge through its denial of the relevance of generative mystery within cultural symbolism.

Chillingworth's refusal to express himself verbally is clear in his defiance of the simplest duty of human language, the dissemination of information in the community. He obscures both of the primary facts of his life related to language, his name and his marriage vow; for all of these overt similarities, Chillingworth stands as a marked contrast to the New England regicides, whose dangerous silence was directed toward the abstraction of monarchical power and never (apparently) toward their own neighbors. Chillingworth, though, choosing to erase his prior self and become instead a "dark miner," waiting for "the soul" of his usurper Dimmesdale to "be dissolved, and flow forth in a dark, but transparent stream, bringing all its mysteries into the daylight" (124), indeed has emptied himself of all substance. "[W]ithout any intrusive egotism" or any "disagreeably prominent characteristics of his own" (124), he is the inverse of Dimmesdale, who has "extended his egotism over the whole expanse of nature" (155) in such a way as to leave the burden of his self-styled identity ironically on those around him. Chillingworth instead surrenders his individuality to the project of invading a consciousness outside of his own, and by doing so he forsakes both the promise and the integrity of his own mind.

Furthermore, what Chillingworth knows is certainly important. But by denying the existence of an active self (the potential storyteller) in favor of preying upon Dimmesdale's soul—by insisting, that is, on being a reader of another man's heart rather than writing the new and unique facts of his own heart—Chillingworth refuses to advance any cultural story. What he thinks and feels would surely be an important element, one that must be gathered into the collective knowledge of the new society as part of their memory of an early instance of a direct challenge to their own laws, their primary social bonds. From his story, the town could learn about whatever is most real, most human, in the consequences of sin as they understand it. If he played the role of King Arthur (for example), he could be wise and just, doomed to sorrow, nevertheless providing a real presence to the abstract notion of the betrayed and so embodying just what the Puritans need to see, the nature and substance of a law transgressed.

Because Chillingworth renders himself incapable of expressing his perceptions, however, he denies to others the possibility of codifying his role within the community; this makes him a failure with regard to his own purposes and to his potential as a productive member of his society. He has denied to this community the language necessary to be able to make sense of experience by refusing to contribute his perceptions—represented here as the first of their kind within the colony—to society's code of norms. Just as the strangeness of Hester's *A* infuses it with power, so too the secrets in Chillingworth's knowledge make his choice of nonparticipation extraordinarily damaging. He withholds the especially important knowledge accessible only in the elusive liminal areas, those places explicitly beyond the known social world that cannot be entered by choice but only by circumstance, historical necessity.[25] Thus, Chillingworth's linguistic failures and denials play a crucial role because of the abnormality that they conceal. So far from playing the prophet, Chillingworth stifles his voice until he exists within an almost prelinguistic state. As he flies into a wild dance of repressed language upon finally seeing the minister's secret pain branded on his chest, Chillingworth's manner of victory celebration is precisely what manifests his failure:

After a brief pause, the physician turned away.

But with what a wild look of wonder, joy, and horror! With what a ghastly rapture, as it were, too mighty to be expressed only by the eye and features, and therefore bursting forth through the whole ugliness of his figure, and making itself even riotously manifest by the extravagant gestures with which he threw up his arms towards the ceiling, and stamped his foot upon the floor! (138)

Consumed by "ghastly rapture," the "extravagant gestures" of the moment have no translation into language. As one who ventures beyond the norm—both in terms of personal consciousness and the fiction's own geography—only to return speechless rather than prophetic, Chillingworth's social failure is commensurate with his personal betrayals.

Hawthorne layers Chillingworth's role with additional irony by describing Chillingworth's methods of uncovering secrets with language and imagery reminiscent of the narrator's description of his own storytelling process. However, the distinction is one of vision. While the reading of the Puritan past that Hawthorne does through his narrator is infused with a belief in progress and a search for foundations, Chillingworth's parallel reading is only backward looking and so must be destructive. Chillingworth is not a reader who advances through the revelation of secrets; he is a voyeur, waiting for the explosive results of a fact that he already knows. His failure is even greater than suggested in the common leech/host image often used to characterize his relationship with Dimmesdale; he is less than a leech because Dimmesdale, the nearly lifeless figurehead, lacks the substance to be a host.

This doctor's revelations about his patient's misery are not achieved through confidence but through silence. Between the poles of rhetoric and gesture and embodied in the complete lack of communication between Dimmesdale and Chillingworth is only a "nameless horror" (156), a "silence, an inarticulate breath" (124)—only this to define a world without a language sufficient to its experience. This absence of name, confession, or confrontation, which characterizes the Chillingworth/Dimmesdale relationship, is a model of the linguistic vacuum within which Hawthorne places Puritan Boston; the bipolar opposition that the two men create represents the range of experiences of language possible before the radical transformation of Hester and her symbol.

With regard to the community's evident need for self-empowerment through new vocabulary and language, Dimmesdale is both a victim and a failure as culpable as Chillingworth. He fails to take responsibility both for his own transgression and his own language; in fact, Dimmesdale actively avoids such responsibility through careful orchestrations and manipulations of circumstance. He speaks in abstractions and chooses contexts that are more theoretical than experiential; that is, he speaks in contexts where words are not expected to bring about ordinary understanding of the present tense (or to make "a bright transparency of to-day"), but rather where they are elevated immediately into symbolic thought. He speaks from the pulpit, and so his confessions are impersonal. There he takes responsibility for the general state of sin, and adultery (as action, or at least as thought) is foremost among the failures that give substance to that general state.

Although implicating himself in that generic state of fallenness, however, Dimmesdale moves no closer to confession of his own specific transgression, of its place in history. If he could leave behind his support system of the pulpit and the crowd—even if he could say the same words, but to an individual in the town, outside of the church context, he would be using language for a different—and more fundamental—purpose: to establish mutual understanding. Though like Hester, Dimmesdale plays a symbolic role largely controlled by the community, he accrues some of his own guilt and responsibility in his attempts to step outside of his own consciousness, to objectify himself as a symbol, and then to manipulate that objectified role. Like Chillingworth, Dimmesdale is given the chance to tell a "true" (that is, experiential) story. Dimmesdale's refusal to take on that role is far more complex than Chillingworth's brute repression, however: Dimmesdale's response is not silence but a careful narrative that, ironically, through the very perfection of its design, becomes as ineffective (for both his culture's needs and ironically his own designs) and as far from revelation as simple denial.

As a preacher for a group of nonseparatist Puritans whose intentions were not schism but reform, Dimmesdale naturally receives the benefits of some inherited respect for his station. The expectations that come with his social role are not easily or quickly abandoned. Even Hawthorne's audience shares some degree of this attitude, and as the *North American Review* points out, it may cause readers to be "cheated" into sympathizing with Dimmesdale if they carry with them the "habitual respect for the sacred order, and . . . faith in religion."[26] However, it is quickly evident that Dimmesdale is perceived as a good speaker because he reinforces comfortable perceptions. In the description of Dimmesdale as "a young clergyman, who had come from one of the great English universities, bringing all the learning of the age into our wild forestland" (66), Hawthorne suggests that this preacher has been met by an uncritical reverence based specifically on Old World principles. Dimmesdale's accomplishments are well suited to the "shelter and concealment" (214) of

England and its universities, perhaps, but ineffectual for pioneer life in "the wilds of New England" (214):

> Notwithstanding his high native gifts and scholar-like attainments, there was an air about this young minister,—an apprehensive, a startled, a half-frightened look,—as of a being who felt himself quite astray and at a loss in the pathway of human existence, and could only be at ease in some seclusion of his own. Therefore, so far as his duties would permit, he trode in the shadowy by-paths, and thus kept himself simple and child-like; coming forth, when occasion was, with a freshness, and fragrance, and dewy purity of thought, which, as many people said, affected them like the speech of an angel. (66)

His "scholar-like attainments" become as empty and artificial as a modern reading of Hawthorne's language makes them sound, now that Dimmesdale is in this "forestland."[27] Similarly, feeling "quite astray and at a loss in the pathway of human existence" is certainly an unfortunate image to put forth to one's followers, particularly at a time when these followers urgently need to cut pathways into a New World. Finally, for his congregation to perceive these manners as "dewy purity of thought" "like the speech of and angel" is an extraordinary leap of faith—clearly no one knows either Dimmesdale's thought or an angel's speech but may at best intuit both; such leaps of faith entirely bypass the primary epistemological necessities of colonial living.[28]

The Dimmesdale his congregation knows is not a man but little more than a cipher (albeit one functioning as a figurehead) into which all community expectations go—at his carefully chosen times and in his manipulated circumstances. Dimmesdale does not conform, and yet his contradictory nature ironically helps perpetuate a static social order. By embodying the antisocial and contextualizing it within accepted parameters, he reinforces an unquestioning embrace of the status quo rather than forcing the expansion of the boundaries of social understanding. With the goals of ordering his perceptions, designing his world, and thus converting history and human truth into lies of social belief, Dimmesdale appears afraid to be the prophet and to lose his life in the process; he is afraid to "let the wick of his life be consumed completely by the gentle flame of his story."[29]

Dimmesdale's communication outside of the pulpit reflects this fear. Much like his community's cultural consciousness, Dimmesdale embodies an unresolved dichotomy, the tortured condition of defense, in which patently experiential knowledge—the individual experience of lived history—is contained (in two senses) within familiar and formulaic language. Clearly Dimmesdale has "lived"—and, compared to his fellow Puritans within the novel's world, perhaps, he has done so with some depth of sensitivity and passion. It may be that these same traits generate the system of rhetorical defense by which he must protect himself—by which he expresses preference for the safety of structure and stasis over the dynamics of cultural process.

Dimmesdale voices specific, true, and dangerous facts, but his mode of expression ensures that these facts are transformed before entering the ears of his congregation; this orchestration is so complete that his extraordinary fear and tremulousness—qualities that push the community to question his nature—are revered, and he is elevated further from history's carnal world into the sphere of spirit: "He had told his hearers that he was . . . a thing of unimaginable iniquity. . . . [T]hey heard it all, and did but reverence him the more. . . . He had spoken the very truth, and transformed it into the veriest falsehood" (143–44). This he does by depending upon a predictable (rather than new) interplay of history and language; he depends upon his context, upon his mastery of that context, and thus, upon the effects of that context on his words.

As Dimmesdale sets up a confession scene filled with portentous distractions, his reliance on a given set of expectations to absolve him from the consequence of his words is clear: He ascends the scaffold in the night, not because he is finally "driven hither by the impulse of . . . Remorse" (148) but because he is attracted by the gothic horror of the setting, sure to account for any frightening events that might occur that night.[30] There is "no peril of discovery" in this context even after a scream escapes from him, because in the town's collective belief, aided by the black of night, such a sound sooner would be thought of as "something frightful in a dream, or [taken] for the noise of witches; whose voices, at that period, were often heard to pass over the settlements or lonely cottages, as they rode with Satan through the air" (149). In this way Dimmesdale's confession has been quite brilliantly (if perhaps unconsciously) orchestrated in such a way that its message will be transformed completely before being codified by the town. Every one of Dimmesdale's actions shows that he seeks inscription within an established story; he rejects the role of truth teller in favor of setting himself within layers of inscription that will protect him from the simplest and most fundamental consequences of word and thought. His reliance on rhetoric, context, and expectation provide him safety but at the cost of any possible cultural potency.

In the aftermath of his adultery, then, it is not surprising that Dimmesdale's mistakes are many and varied yet always related to the intemperate use of language—whether as deception or as radical revelation. His period of transformation just before delivering the Election Day sermon is marked significantly by multiple temptations related to language, suggesting the wearing away of his defenses. He suffers impulses to teach profanity to small children and to speak blasphemously to the elderly and is nearly consumed by these desires. Clearly Dimmesdale's passion allows him to approach a new—even revolutionary—framework for language use.

Ironically, however, his final reversal will only prove his utter entrapment. He cannot free himself from the extremes of language use; he cannot locate the foundations of meaning to his all-too-plentiful words. This failure is clear in the narrator's inability to record those words of his final sermon—directly or symbolically—within the text; those words, it would seem, swim somewhere beyond the historical eye of the narrative. Because of his self-disabling language, Dimmesdale cannot fuse his life in history to its symbolic definition; he has both lived and spoken, but the link between these two acts has been severed.

Dimmesdale's final confession is, then, self-destructive without the potentially redemptive promise of contributing to the developing colony. He makes yet another mistake as he explodes the mystery of his experiences by attempting to define in his forever powerless words that which has much more cultural force than mere information. His efforts at reintegration fail because his personal identity has long since ceased to be his own. He cannot just change it at will any more than Hester can make herself a new life in the Old World; the two of them are in some sense communal property. There is a unique problem with Dimmesdale, however: Both in his language and his social identity he has come to embody an abstract system that demands the *universal* consent and faith of the community. He can change his language and his identity, but he cannot achieve reintegration because—in that change—the universal belief that he had embodied challenges itself from within and crumbles under its failure to maintain the status of an absolute. Multiplicity of interpretation attests to an inherent flaw in the pure ideal—and here, in the figure of Dimmesdale, purity stands as the entire basis for belief.

What Dimmesdale fails to do is to participate actively in the growth of the culture. Though his vision in the Election Day sermon is apparently one of the future, his life is locked in the past, and he has been able to construct no present ground on which to stand and unite these trajectories of time. In the mid-nineteenth century, popular heroes of the Puritan era derived their greatness in large part from their bond to the future and through the present responsibility for leadership that such a bond engendered; they were decidedly not men of the past. Sustaining the traditional model of the Christian hero's necessary submission to divine purpose, a widespread, mainstream, belief in nineteenth-century America suggested that the greatness of such Puritan figures rested in (to use Horace Bushnell's terms) "their unconsciousness"—their selfless dedication and their "secret love" for the advancement of an order, which they might establish but not bring to completion.[31] But Dimmesdale is impatient. Frustrated by years of repressing his story, he leaps beyond what might eventually be the "silent growth of centuries," and in doing so, he once again fails to contribute to his society—now not through deception, but through another mistake of an overdetermined consciousness, the inability to allow for the fulfillment of an ideal by forces beyond subjective consciousness.

Unlike "the story of the scarlet letter[, which] grew into a legend" (261)—gained cohesion, transmissibility, and meaning in Hester's absence—Dimmesdale's story has a far less profound effect on his world. Some in his audience believe him and some do not; the diversity of interpretation mirrors the fragments of the ideal system, which he had perpetuated falsely and then broken necessarily. There is the initial promise that the crowd's response to the sermon—"a strange, deep voice of awe and wonder, which could not as yet find utterance" (257)—might emerge in a "bright transparency" in later ages, but that promise expires with the same excessive speed as has attended Dimmesdale's telling of the story.

After "many days" rather than generations or centuries, "time sufficed for the people to arrange their thoughts in reference" to the meaning of Dimmesdale's sermon (258); little time is necessary when the story bears no great promise, only the fragmentation of belief. As a character who has depended on his society for his (false) identity, Dimmesdale's revelation leaves him without a role. His death is not the patriotic culmination of the truth teller "with high aspirations for the welfare of his race" (130); rather, it is the only end to a Puritan who had made himself unreal (ultimately vulnerable, fragile, and unregenerative) through his denial of his experiential life and his crippling excess of consciousness, achieved through artificial constructions of language and self-serving manipulations of ambiguity.

As opposite poles in a paralyzing trap, Dimmesdale is false rhetoric, with all of its flourishes, and Chillingworth is inarticulate gesture, with all of its passion. Their common problem is a demonstrated inability both to understand language as it emerges from history and to recognize the substantiality of the bond between the poles (and, as men, between them too; in either case, the bond is Hester—the only one who knows both of their secrets as well as her own).[32] By choosing to play the roles that they do, both Dimmesdale and Chillingworth fail to work toward a new code for a New World, a national story in an American language.

HESTER AS STORYTELLER

The strength of this linguistic trap and its enforcement from prominent figures such as the doctor and the preacher make it no surprise that the same frame defines the language relations between Hester and her town. Previous to her transgression, Hester was a member of her society, which at its inception imagined itself as a "Utopia of human virtue." Like all such places, however, this community "invariably recognized it among their earliest practical necessities to allot a portion of the virgin soil as a cemetery, and another portion as the site of a prison" (47). From the start, even the most idealistic settlement will understand death and crime (here perhaps synonymous with sin) as part of the common lot: For idealism to thrive, there must be a simple and clear repository for whatever does not fit. The potential problem, of course, is that such aberrations need not be clear or final; the sin (or the death, in horror stories) may not fundamentally transform the subject.

Then there is a violation that cannot be sealed in a vault, and the whole order of the utopia stands threatened. Before Hester's time, Puritan Boston's static framework for knowledge and language had been tenuously sufficient. As the task of self-definition grew more complex, however, and as history unfolded in unpredictable ways, the community found the weakness in their utopian order: No longer was it clear that sin would be transformative. In fact, Hawthorne suggests that those who continue to insist upon living by the rules of the orderly utopia write themselves out of the progress of history: Of the two who believed in a future world of freer expression and love, only Hester is left.

However, because of the distance necessary to revelation in Hawthorne's model, Hester herself is prophetic by the end only in a limited sense; she is an active but speechless prophet. Just as the *A* is only the smallest step toward a linguistically potent culture, so too is Hester's own life meant only to begin and to set into motion a new and active perception of language and story. With the deaths of Chillingworth and Dimmesdale, the paralyzing bond is broken, and Hester's life itself continues to make the wilderness somehow more domestic, less mysterious: "Her sin, her ignominy, were the roots which she had struck into the soil. It was as if a new birth, with stronger assimilations than the first, had converted the forest-land, still so uncongenial to every other pilgrim and wanderer, into Hester Prynne's wild and dreary, but life-long home" (80). As the only one actively breaking down the barriers to effective language in her society, the only one fusing symbol and meaning, Hester is ironically estranged from the common symbolic frame of reference; she makes her own life as she walks through the "moral wilderness" (199). Even so, as a prophet of sorts, Hester is animated by her historical memory and a complicated, perhaps buried, drive to live her story fully and so to bring it into a future age.

A historical memory and a compelling desire to transmit: These are exactly the two qualities most essential to participation in the establishment of a national language and literature in Jacksonian and antebellum America. While Hawthorne is born into a rhetoric of nationhood, perhaps he too feels a "story" within his memory—something transmissible (paradoxically) because unexplained, something that had never been conveyed as information but that instead permeates "the life of the storyteller, in order to bring it out of him again."[33]

For the storyteller in this formulation, language presents a peculiar problem: It must encode rather than define, transmit but not expend, its story; Hester Prynne is that storyteller. Creating as she goes, Hester is a pioneer who accepts a challenge to make real words, ideas, and all fragments of language that are only empty rhetoric to the others in her society, to infuse lived meaning and historical experience into a cultural symbol. She has no one, however, not even her lover, with whom she can discuss her pioneering; the power of Hester's "magic circle" (246) of language both denies her possible consciousness of personal revelation and secures those revelations for Hawthorne's America. So much of Hester's storytelling is left to later generations.

Hester's reality is palpable. It has the dimensions of both life and symbol, "infant" and "shame." As she emerges from the prison, made a new woman, she accepts that some transformation has taken place and that her perception of the world must likewise change: "Could it be true? She clutched the child so fiercely to her breast, that it sent forth a cry; she turned her eyes downward at the scarlet letter, and even touched it with her finger, to assure herself that the infant and the shame were real. Yes!— these were her realities,—all else had vanished" (59). To say that Hester is empowered by the *A* is not to say that she enjoys this power, that it is desirable in the abstract, or even that she knows exactly what the power is. From even the little Hawthorne tells us about Hester's society, we know that she is not the only person guilty of adultery. To return to her town, however, to live out her life wearing the *A*—that is to accept a role never before taken in that wilderness utopia.

What is more, Hester, with her decorated *A*, can perform a proto-nationalistic function only because of this unique role in which symbol returns to history. According to Hawthorne's own records, not only did his chosen ending to *The Scarlet Letter* send his wife Sophia to bed with an incapacitating headache, but he too could hardly bear to see what he had left for his heroine to do: "When I read the last scene of The Scarlet Letter ... just after writing it—tried to read it, rather, for my voice swelled and heaved, as if I were tossed up and down on an ocean, as it subsided after a storm ... I was in a very nervous state, then, having gone through a great diversity and severity of emotion, for many months past. I think I have never overcome my own adamant [coolness] in any other instance."[34] He had given Hester the burden of living for another age entirely; the sacrifice entailed is overwhelming.

In his description of the American development of the English language, Noah Webster anticipates the role Hawthorne thus gives to Hester: "To cultivate and adorn [the language], is a task reserved for [those] who shall understand the connection between language and logic, and form an adequate idea of the influence which a uniformity of speech may have on national attachments."[35] To place Hester in this role is to see her enduring function as escaping—if only to a limited extent—the frame of containment that Hawthorne's plot seems to wish to force upon her, to see in her, that is, a persistent layer of the radical. Just as the magistrates imposed upon Hester a scarlet letter, which then grew to take on all manner of unexpected meanings, so too does Hawthorne's narrator impose upon her an apparently final sentence, sending her back to dark New England, and yet there—her tombstone assures us—her life will continue to generate among its many meanings at least a few of residual illegibility, a few that is, that will escape expected narratives.[36]

Thus we are reminded that the reading of Hester's life—particularly as a symbol whose meanings reach downward and inward into the private world of love, as well as outward into culture, and upward into moral (and/or transcendental) meanings—makes it compulsory for audiences to return, to reread, and finally to acknowledge the irrecoverable losses of history and memory. The interpreter cannot help but sense distance, even intrusion, as we—with the romance's "curious investigator"—look upon the "dust of the two sleepers" with "one tombstone [carved] for both" (262). Hawthorne's extraordinarily meticulous historiography ensures that, again with the wandering investigator, the text's interpreter stands at a place in history distant from Hester and yet also nowhere near an age that can find itself utterly separate from her.

Hester Prynne and her *A* thus leave us in the most complicated of situations, neither trapped nor free, as we move back and forth between interpretive positions. The romance, Hawthorne makes clear, has not finished the task of imagining. Not only are we turned back to the *A* as we imagine the tombstone, but we should also recall in the end that there is another manuscript to read, another origin to the story of Hester Prynne: "Prying further into the manuscript, I found the record of other doings and sufferings of this singular woman. . . . The original papers, together with the scarlet letter itself,—a most curious relic,—are still in my possession, and shall be freely exhibited to whomsoever, induced by the great interest of the narrative, may desire a sight of them" (35). To return and to reread: That is ever Hawthorne's imperative to us, and in this image of a manuscript outside of the romance itself, we are compelled to acknowledge the layers of storytelling, which make that task endless. In our distance from certainty we will surely envision the ruptures of revolution, but in our insatiable appetite for imaginative interpretation, we continue to enact their repair.

PART THREE

"Traces of a Vanished World" in Owen Wister's *The Virginian*

There is a zone of insecurity in human affairs in which all the dramatic interest lies. The rest belongs to the dead machinery of the stage.

—William James, *The Will to Believe* (1897)

9

ROMANCE AND NOSTALGIA IN
THE VIRGINIAN

T wenty-five years old and depressed to the point of nervous exhaustion, Owen Wister followed his physician's advice and sought rest
with a change of scenery in the summer of 1885. When he left Philadelphia by train, bound for Wyoming, Wister was distraught by both his present circumstances and his prospective future, but the effect of the trip was
immediate and dramatic. Wyoming, he wrote home to his mother, looked
to him "like Genesis," primitive and unspoiled, filled with promises of new
life and adventures.[1]

In a journal entry from that first summer visit, Wister celebrated the
mythic potential of the west, predicting "it won't be a century before the
West is simply the true America, with thought, type, and life of its kind."[2]
Certainly there was something ironic and belated in Wister's prophecy,
especially because he first looked on the landscape only through the prism
of modern industry, the railroad car window. When he emphasized the
west as the land of the future, Wister must have been thinking of something other than the raw symbolic value of the frontier, which by then had
already been saturating America for decades.

Indeed, not only as a traveler but even as an author, Wister was arriving late on the scene of the frontier west. All sections of the continental
American West had been claimed as territories before Wister's birth in
1860, and as Edwin Fussell has written, by that time "the West was no
longer a field of boundless opportunity.... The figurative frontier and the
teleological West were drained of expressive value."[3] Well before Wister's
time, the construction of American self-definition in relation to the frontier was a familiar literary topic, dominating many genres, from Puritan
captivity narratives through travel diaries, emigrant guides, and Cooper's
Leather-Stocking Tales. In these texts and others, the land had been
mapped by contradictions that prompted symbolic thought: American
and European audiences knew the West as a land of freedom and lawless

violence, hardship and potential wealth, savagery and civilization.[4] Though he was young and the scenes were new to him, when Wister first looked on the Western landscape through the window of a transcontinental train, even he must have sensed the interpretive dilemma his generation faced in their engagement with Western mythology.

Wister was not alone, however, in this somewhat anachronistic enthusiasm; his writings were eagerly received in the literary establishment of the East without any label of belatedness. In fact, upon *The Virginian's* publication, the reading public made Wister one of the most popular and influential authors in American literary history. Even now, critics acknowledge that this novel "is the template on which every Western since has been cut"; a century of critical attention has not always agreed on the quality of the novel or on particular approaches to its interpretation, but all attest to the fact that "[t]he most remarkable point about *The Virginian's* influence is how thoroughgoing it has been."[5]

This Wyoming story of the courtship and marriage of a cowboy— complete with a Southern drawl—to a New England schoolteacher— descendant of Revolutionary heroes—became a prototype for a new American story and provided America with a new (if oddly belated) embodiment of a national hero. Traditional Western heroes had intrigued audiences with their isolation, independence, and inscrutability, and the Virginian has all of these traits.[6] Critics throughout the twentieth century have proven the multiplicity of established symbolic roles that Wister's hero can play, beyond even those of Western folklore. Whether seen as a "synthesis of Cooper's opposition of nature and civilization with the gospel of success and progress" or as a fictionalized version of a past American icon—from Andrew Jackson or Theodore Roosevelt back to George Washington or Thomas Jefferson—the Virginian (the character and the novel) has been consistently placed within familiar, well-established contexts of the national imagination.[7]

This chapter begins by surveying the romantic machinery that Wister inherited for the construction of this character, the surrounding cast, and the plot within which all of these figures would act. Here the relationship between the novel and the popular legends underwriting it is somewhat different from that in either of the two previous chapters. First of all, unlike Revolutionary or Puritan legend, Western lore is an industry unto itself; the odd prominence of the legends of Jane McCrea and John André during the Revolutionary years, for instance, does not have a direct parallel here, where at once there are more varieties of circulating stories as well a more immediate sense of the folktale's function as entertainment within broader culture.

As with Cooper's Spy and Hawthorne's Hester Prynne, early critics of *The Virginian* sometimes sought historical models for the central character, but this has not been part of my project in the use of popular legend in either of the two preceding chapters, nor is it here. In those two chapters I show how a particular narrative shape—a set of questions, expectations, and answers—is set up in certain popular tales and then recast—but now with only questions and expectations, not answers—in the form of the historical romance. Here, the materials interact differently, and so the structure of this chapter is different as well.

First (in the second part of this chapter) I provide an overview of the general trends of representation in the legends of the West; this I do not for particularities of narrative shape, but rather to illustrate a broad sense of the romance of frontier history, as emblematized by Western heroes preceding Wister's novel. I then turn to an analysis of the novel (the third part of the chapter) to illustrate the ways in which the novel invokes and yet challenges these narrative bounds. Following this section of the analysis, I argue that the novel, in its late plot developments, returns to the narrow bounds of romance rather than leading readers outward into further historical questions, as Cooper and Hawthorne had done. Thus there is less in the way of specific historical material here, but further attention to a layered reading of Wister's landmark novel as both "storyteller's story" and plot romance.

WISTER'S WEST

While knowing that he had missed the actual years of the "Wild West," still it seems evident from his writings that Wister sought and found glimpses of lingering novelties on his first trip to Wyoming. His return trips to the area were regular, and so it appears that in his experiences traveling west from 1885 on, perhaps Wister imagined that he had lived a condensed version of frontier history.[8] In any case, when he published *The Virginian* in 1902, he crafted it into his own vision of a culminating romance of the frontier. By exaggerating the historical distance between its fictional setting and its cultural context, *The Virginian* assured readers of America's safe remove from the risks of the Wild West. The dangerous allure of the "half-savage romance" was here packaged within a tale of the power of an individual frontiersman's new and evolving virtues.[9]

As a product of the distance Wister constructed between his own world and that of his fiction, a seemingly deliberate and structured nostalgia emerged to characterize readers' relations to the novel. This crafted nostalgia dominates particularly the early portions of the novel, where the perspective of its tenderfoot narrator—a distinctly Eastern consciousness—brings to a new century's readers a growing sense of familiarity and comfort toward the once mysterious, even menacing, Western frontier. That nostalgia remains (though less overtly) entwined with later sections of the novel as well, even as the narrator, as character, becomes much less visible. When reviewers of *The Virginian*—and even Wister himself— spoke of the novel's hero, it was with affection driven by this determined nostalgia, reflective of the troubling knowledge of the vividly recent loss of this rich world: Reviewers lamented that *The Virginian*, as a "final apotheosis of the cowboy," reminded them longingly of a world that was believed to have "almost completely vanished—although it was real enough a quarter of a century ago."[10] Wister encourages exactly this sentiment, as he writes in his preface:

> [The cowboy] will never come again. He rides in his historic yesterday. You will no more see him gallop out of the unchanging silence than you will see Columbus on the unchanging sea come sailing from Palos with his caravels.
>
> And yet the horseman is still so near our day that in some chapters of this book, which were published separately at the close of the nineteenth century, the present tense was used. It is true no longer. . . . Time has flowed faster than my ink. (xlviii)

Clearly this setting is something other than the familiar Old West of tall tales and legends. By placing the romance on the frontier, the historic borderland within which traces of savagery and civilization were long believed to have mingled, Wister enhances that sense of immediate and self-constructing nostalgia, and the force of this imagined distance is further highlighted in the comparison of the cowboy's remoteness to that of Columbus. Here Wister offers a central imaginative shift; with the cowboy as the new Columbus, the West is not future only, but also a site of origins for America. In these ways—as Western hero or as symbol of the nation's future now visualized in its origins—the Virginian as a character exists most powerfully within a romance of nostalgia.

But the backward glance of nostalgia—no matter how carefully and deliberately crafted by the novel's narrative frame—does not prove strong enough to hold as a design enclosing frontier history. Like *The Scarlet Letter* in 1850, Wister's novel speaks to its contemporary culture by evaluating and even challenging the systems of belief it inherits and in doing so exposes established modes of cultural memory as the outmoded machinery they had so quickly become. By playing out expected plots, *The Virginian,* as narrative, enacts a search for a different form of memory. Within this process, the nostalgia deliberately offered as an opening paradigm will be among the first forms of memory to be proven inadequate and in need of revision. Nostalgia is not abandoned as a narrative model, however; it is instead reinvigorated in a new form. Thus the novel becomes a key cultural artifact because it finds new "living options" still viable among the outmoded machineries of the romance, vital methods of historicizing to be excavated from the debris of a century of nationalist storytelling.[11]

This chapter goes on to consider Wister's attempt to animate these new living options as both invocations and critiques of the power of tradition, from Western tall tale to the historical romance of the East. I argue that the narrative form he constructs bespeaks a distinct struggle for a culturally controlled use of character, setting, and other familiar trappings of romance and that the achievement of the novel is ironically the proof that such a struggle for narrative control must eventually fail. With this failure, the novel shows that history, shattered as a monolith, will now cover the land even more visibly, materially, and powerfully, blowing across the plains in dangerous and often unrecognizable fragments.

Ironically it is the Virginian's identity—seemingly mapped with the figurations of previous frontier heroes—that first signals the existence and then persistence of these dangerous and decontextualized fragments of the historical. Oddly and noticeably, the Virginian had always haunted audiences with ambiguity. There was no consensus among Wister's friends about the proper fate for this hero. After seeing the character's early appearance in print in the short story "Balaam and Pedro," a fellow law clerk asked Wister, "Is that man dead, that Virginian?" Wister claimed that he did not know, that he had cast the Virginian there as a minor figure, a bystander to the action who disappears into the forest, perhaps to meet his fate at the hands of Indians. The clerk was more than dissatisfied, declaring to Wister, "If you kill that man, I'll never speak to you again."[12] This threat, Wister recalls, prompted him to revive the character for a novel, and more significantly, it seems that Wister's own attachment to the nameless cowboy grew in kind. He would not kill his cowboy even when so many of his plot's circumstances mark him for death. Henry James objected to the novel's sentimental ending: "Nothing," he wrote to Wister, "should have induced me to unite him to the little Vermont person, or to dedicate him in fact to achieved parentage, prosperity, maturity. . . . I thirst for his blood. I wouldn't have let him live & be happy; I should have made him perish in his flower & in some splendid sombre way."[13]

James's instinctive critique points to the fact that nothing marks this novel as a story bearing witness to the simple solutions of the familiar struggles of romance, and what the law clerk, Wister, and James all share in their response to this character is the sense that he is larger than his context, that he cannot be treated as a pawn in a narrative driven by forces outside of his own character. This is, in large part, a comment focused on the mythic strength of the character Wister created. At the same time, it suggests that the novel in which he has his freest play must be a clear testament to the limits of designed narrative resolutions.

When Wister addresses the question of why the Virginian is never given a name, he writes in the preface to his 1928 edition of the novel, "Who was the Virginian? The answer is—metabolism" (xliii).[14] From that answer alone it is clear just how little this character has in common with the heroes and villains of the Old West. He is the life of change embodied, a process inseparable from the product he creates. Whoever he is, he exists beyond the boundaries of a particular fictional character, and Wister attaches a strong historiographical significance to his life. The Virginian is anything but a frozen icon. Despite the mythic qualities that threaten to seize him, the Virginian absolutely resists being frozen in time—he will not be fixed in death or in dramatic climax, and this marked adaptability in relation to historical process distinguishes Wister's cowboy from the conventional frontier hero of Western lore.

Through this model, beyond experiments in character, Wister's novel presents a theoretical perspective on historical narrative: When the historiographical significance of one life is transmitted (like metabolism) to a new generation, it faces new sets of circumstances, new contexts.[15] Its transmission signifies continuity joined with unpredictable adaptation, an inherited map of the historical imagination, updated to include the boundary shifts and landmarks established by new life histories. Merged with these ideas of biological adaptation, however, Wister's novel conveys a living model of the ways that cultural narratives, no matter how deeply ingrained with pattern, remain vulnerable to the intrusions of history; adaptation, that is, is here directly focused on the ability to negotiate the surprises emergent from an unknown past. In this novel no one character has the sustained ability to live and convey the archetypal mysteries newly assumed by the form of the historical romance, and so these fragments of history acquire an agency of their own, an agency that directly challenges the development of the characters into modern heroes.

In these ways—both explicitly through character and implicitly through form—the novel suggests that the symbolic systems of narrative romance had left inadequate methods for telling a national story by the end of the century. Rather than abandoning those limited symbolic frames, however, Wister's novel leans heavily on those old paradigms once again, and the pressure of the Virginian's myth of identity exposes their common weakness: Wister's novel clearly reveals that, as narrative frames, both nostalgia and progress are similar and deeply intertwined expressions of a manifestly desperate search for order and continuity to overwrite the increasingly present ambiguities of experience.

Whether seeing in the Virginian echoes of Revolutionary patriots, outlaws of the Old West, turn-of-the-century figures such as Buffalo Bill or Roosevelt's frontiersman, readers would slowly discover that the Virginian is only superficially, perhaps even deceptively, familiar.[16] His resemblance to both the founders and early heroes of the Old West first works predictably, overtly, but then paradoxically turns to illustrate important symbolic distinctions through a series of reversals. All of the Virginian's traits that suggest such myths prove themselves to be starkly time-bound, and all in turn cast suspicion on the highly crafted nostalgia that the book announces at its opening.

Perhaps what is most surprising is that even the critique of these myths is time-bound and usurped by the end of the narrative. Like *The Spy* and *The Scarlet Letter, The Virginian* animates historical secrets within its narrative silences. Unlike these earlier texts, however, Wister's novel recuperates the power of design—not in compliance with the early model of nostalgia offered by the text's opening, but rather by a revised design that is no less romantic. In fact, ever since its publication, the novel has troubled readers with its sudden acquiescence to the familiarities of romance. A pattern of problems in form, character, and plot all suggest that if nostalgia is at the heart of this novel, *The Virginian* is an exercise in a decidedly unfamiliar form of that sentiment.

The romance of the frontier is only one layer of Wister's story, and its resolution leaves many questions unanswered, questions turning reader attention not backward but forward. The nostalgia that *The Virginian* had invoked from its beginnings is closely intertwined with nineteenth-century nationalist beliefs in progress, and the interdependence of these ideas is written directly into the central character's narrative life: By the end of the romance, Wister's hero has triumphed according to both Eastern and Western values. Not only is he a renegade cowboy turned into a devoted husband, but he is also a cowboy-turned-capitalist, whose shrewd investment in land rich with coal promises to carry his family comfortably from frontier to industrial-era living. As a survivor in a Darwinian world, he is a virtual machine of national progress, demonstrating continuity with original pioneer strengths and a progressive movement on the scale of economic and social virtues.

In fact, Wister goes to some trouble to extend the plot (somewhat awkwardly) beyond the anticipated showdown between hero and villain, to a telescopic conclusion ensuring the fairy-tale domestication and modernization of the Western hero. Henry James was certainly justified in pointing out that the longevity of Wister's hero is somewhat perverse. The Virginian far outlasts the expected life span of the hero of historical romance, with the final scene of the novel picturing the aged cowboy settled into domesticity and slated "to live a long while" yet (392). However, this seemingly forcible extension of plot appealed to readers.

No doubt much of the novel's overwhelming popularity at the turn of the century was a response to that vision of progress born of nostalgia, the romantic sketch of American incorporation that left to the twentieth century a new order of nationhood—imagined as a product of an economic and regionalist evolution—ascendant on the frontier, superceding the older conflicts of East and West, North and South. In the context of turn-of-the-century America, the nostalgia implied in this model of memory becomes a yearning not simply for lost symbols and forms, but also more broadly for a system of perpetual order. Here, that is, nostalgia for the wild and innocent West was an invitation to return to a world comfortable in its belief in social evolution, a world where change would promise to clarify rather than to disrupt the known patterns of culture. In history, literature, and social science, this myth of unity had become fundamental to the national symbolic identity of the West around the turn of the century.[17]

As Jane Tompkins notes, however, the novel's romance is only one layer of its story.[18] Woven among this highly developed, even strangely paradoxical, machinery of the romance of progress, Wister's nostalgia serves an atypical purpose not only within the plot but also within literary history: The Virginian's adaptability has ensured his survival into another century, but precisely that elastic conformity has drained his character of its primary authority and power. His mythic frontier individualism snares him into the world that his independence demands he should scorn; ironically, the traits of the frontier loner become effective only as mechanisms of definitive control over the ever-narrowing world that we expect the hero to elude and even to disdain. As long as he is contained within such structures, his popularity is easy to explain, and yet his power as cultural icon is limited. Precisely because of his capacity to represent so many sides of American life, the Virginian is trapped within a carefully framed symbolic system that inheres in the very concept of nostalgia: He can neither challenge nor threaten the symbolic vocabulary of his culture because—at so many levels and in so many ways—he so perfectly conforms to it.

Cowboys had been ruling the Wild West in legend and fiction for decades, but Wister's hero pleased audiences with more than the mastery of a type. To the usually static, even timeless, cowboy of folklore, Wister added new dimensions of change and adaptability. Yet in this ability to grow, the Virginian is not simply a survivor, one who escapes or rises above the expected traps of the fictional hero, nor is he a timeless allegory, resolutely standing for any one aspect of his social world. Instead, early in the novel the Virginian makes his primary claim to heroism in his unique ability to negotiate, even control, an increasingly changing world. Surprisingly, while the Virginian is a hero insofar as he controls his world, that ability to control makes the Virginian anything but representative; that is, his unique capacity for control does not lie in the expected realm of the powers of the mythic frontiersman. Through an analysis incorporating a view of Wister's hero, the effect of the hero on narrative structure and its possible readings, and the relevance of such structure to broad changes in social theory at the turn of the century, this chapter argues that the Virginian is a unique "Western" hero because he both stands for and illustrates the limits of evolutionary understandings of history.

In this context, with Frederick Jackson Turner's speech on "The Significance of the Frontier" (1893), Wister's romance stood at the climax of a century-long project to define the changing continent.[19] While Turner's reception at the exposition in Chicago was at best lukewarm, it would not be long before the impact of his theory would be clear. As his thesis seeped into cultural consciousness, it was evident that he had given voice to a tremendously important idea that had been in the air for some time and that—now as the century was ending—had become urgent. In 1919 Turner himself recalled, "the ideas underlying my 'Significance of the Frontier' would have been expressed in some form or other in any case. They were part of the growing American consciousness of itself."[20]

Wister's book is shaped by that same growing consciousness, and it synthesizes that transitional intellectual moment as well—here within a different layer of cultural expression. For both Turner and Wister, the frontier West had at its core a simple and powerful myth of continuity, moving (for instance) from dream through evolution to fulfillment, from the raw West through the real West to the West as symbol, or from the easterner's West through the emigrant's West to the synthesis of America at the turn of the century.[21] What *The Virginian* proves, however, is that even the uncontested triumph of continuity is not without its own losses.

10

~~~

IMAGINED CONTEXTS FOR
FRONTIER HEROES

I N a 1903 essay for *The Outlook,* William R. Lighton articulated a representative perspective on the beginnings of the Old West as recalled in the U.S. popular press at the turn of the twentieth century: "The pioneering of a new land separates men from the conventional institutions of organized society, from constitutions, codes, and creeds, and throws them back upon the native resources of human nature. Naturally, they set up some rude standards of behavior, standards in which fixedness counts for much less than adaptability."[1] Looking at legends of the Old West with this interpretive frame in mind, a surprising, even illogical, contradiction surrounds the prototypical hero: The memory of these rough individualists seems carefully crafted in American folklore so that such stock images of frontier mythology are strangely circumscribed by stark limits on their creative agency to form and direct the culture.

Lighton continues: "The familiar 'bad man' of Western lore was the product, not of wickedness, but of untrammeled freedom. . . . For a time those little differences in manners were regarded as the distinguishing traits of the West, until time showed them to be ephemeral. They were never so much in the ascendant, even when the West was at its wildest."[2] Perhaps these characters were never "ascendant" in established Western authority, but even Lighton's own language concedes the near saturation of these images in the culture. In this imaginative (rather than historical) ascendancy, such characters belonged to the realm of the abstract and so gained their imaginative life from strictly defined symbolic polarities. Despite the "new land" on which they made their lives, they faced exceptionally narrow limits framing their creative agency. America's heroes and heroines of the Old West played within a fixed symbolic system. By the turn of the century, that system would change, and the Virginian's complexity outlines this central symbolic shift; he is by contrast the figure

Lighton's text imagines as the ascendant.

Although Western lore is rich and complex in its traditions, some generalities may be ventured and then explored through attention to several of the best-known figures of the American West. Many older Western hero tales typically grew from historical individuals, with varying amounts of true life history, engaged in stock episodes of cleverness and physical prowess and providing occasional glimpses of their (presumably) true—though hidden—gentility; epic significance was liberally added by journalists, fiction writers, and historians alike.[3] From popular legends, dime novels, histories, and later romances, original heroes of the Old West might be remembered most for their capacity to embody—within a single figure—the best and worst qualities of human behavior imaginable to nineteenth-century America. Billy the Kid, for example, was remembered within weeks of his death by one sourece as "a delicate looking child" with "wonderful energy and remarkable bravery."[4] Another source, on the other hand, described him as "a low down vulgar cut-throat, with probably not one redeeming quality."[5]

Sheriff Pat Garrett, Billy the Kid's executioner, was an ex-outlaw himself, and his conversion to the world of order made him a hero to some, a heartless mercenary to others. In telling the stories of the frontier hero, it quickly became custom to adhere to a symbolic strategy that might somehow contain the western experience by framing it within its deepest contradictions. The hero, like the territory itself, could be alternately dangerous and wonderful, but in either case drawn boldly, every image reaching for the extremes of possibility.[6]

Perhaps the most familiar name among the figures of Western mythology, Billy the Kid actually came from the east, where he was born in 1859 or 1860. He was something of a latecomer when, as a child, he moved with his family to the New Mexico territory. From this minimal sketch of his origins, legends of Billy diverge, but it appears quite certain that he was a fatherless teenager working as a ranch hand just before he became involved in his notorious crimes. His fame grew within the context of one of the important local wars of the time: The Lincoln County War began when the boss of the ranch where Billy worked was killed, and it escalated with subsequent retaliations.[7] By the time he died in 1881, Billy the Kid was national news, and despite the fact that his own executioner was one of the first to shape a narrative about him, countless tales sentimentalized his life and actions.[8]

Indeed, from the start, tales of Billy the Kid's life emphasized a surprising side of his character. The first dime novel to cover Billy's life claimed that when he was first jailed for robbery, the arresting sheriff's wife and daughter freed him from jail, having succumbed to his innocence and charm. As the story is told, it was not only their "feminine weakness" that brought this about, but also their perception of something deeply true, even noble, in Billy's character. In fact, according to this account, Billy's moral demise is tied directly to a tragedy of love gone wrong. This author claims that Billy's love for a Mexican woman of questionable character— and her engagement to another man—prevented him from "settl[ing] down to a quiet life [as] . . . a good citizen." In the madness of unrequited love, Billy—according to the tale—then kills his beloved's fiancé "with a devilish grin on his face" and the "laugh of a demon." From that point onward, Billy is simply no longer human within the tale. He is at once an extraordinary hero of the range war, rewarded with a job as a constable, and he is a merciless killer.

Even with the breadth between these divergent personae, however, Billy never again emerges with the ambiguities of humanity, as a complex figure with conflicting desires. His exaggerated symbolic roles translate easily into superstitions about his life and existence: "The more superstitious regarded him as immortal. Wonderful stories were afloat as to his vanishing into air. . . . He was called a wizard, a spook, a devil, anything that was supernatural and horrible."[9] Later commentaries too echo this theme; in 1926 Eugene Cunningham reports the disappearance of any proof of Billy's death: "Today, so utterly has all trace of the grave vanished, that there are those who say that the Kid has never been killed."[10] Beautiful, young, violent, and lost to this world in the advance of civilization and progress, Billy perfectly embodies what so much of nineteenth-century America saw as the passing ways of the Wild West.

Daniel Boone—a quite different figure from the highly romanticized Billy—is one of the best-known characters representative of the frontier movement referred to as "overland expansion" in Henry Nash Smith's classic account of the West. Boone's life has somewhat less drama and more ambiguity as it is translated—first in John Filson's 1784 frontier biography and then in Daniel Bryan's *Adventures of Daniel Boone* (1813)—into a frontier archetype.[11] Appended to *The Discovery and Settlement of Kentucke,* the Boone narrative was popular in the United States and Europe. It was translated into French for a 1785 printing and also reprinted in London; further, it helped establish conventions that would shape Western tale telling for at least a century.

Filson's text was advertised to be "as accurate a description of our country as . . . can possibly be given."[12] Both in the description of Kentucky and of Boone's life, Filson claimed that he "cautiously endeavoured to avoid every species of falsehood."[13] In this narrative Boone's adventures read

much like the captivity narratives of earlier generations; the most significant change from those earlier texts is that this hero comes to rely on himself rather than on God for deliverance. In Filson's account Boone becomes
"the representative hero of the trans-Appalachian frontier," the first to
"define the tradition of the Western hero."[14] As an articulate woodsman
who prefers nature to society, the image of Daniel Boone resonates with
European primitivism. Whatever the factual links for the Boone legend,
Filson's narrative sketch of his life clearly dominates the tradition that follows.

Filson had gone west to Kentucky to receive land awarded to veterans
of the Revolutionary War. There he taught school and worked in the fur
trade and as a land surveyor until he died, allegedly killed by a member of
a local Indian tribe in October of 1788. Filson's narrative is meant first as
an educational tract but quickly becomes sensational, focusing on Boone
rather than on the western territories. Ironically, according to Filson, Boone
was the only member of an original exploration party who was not killed by
Indians. Purportedly he lived in the wilderness of Kentucky—known by
local tribes as "the Dark and Bloody Ground"—until 1771, when—as a
very old man—he moved to Pennsylvania.[15] Kentucky, Filson writes, is "the
most extraordinary country that the sun enlightens with his celestial
beams."[16] In this context, Filson's account expands into a tale of the divinely
ordained process of settlement originating with Boone, whom he presents
as the self-proclaimed representative of God.[17]

Given Filson's military service with the colonial army and the fact that
Boone reportedly lost at least two sons during the Revolutionary War,
readers might expect more narrative attention to the events surrounding
1776, particularly perhaps as a harbinger of frontier individualism. Actual
battles, however, are mentioned merely in passing, and overall the focus
remains only obliquely related to colonial politics. Like Crèvecoeur's
Farmer James, Filson's Boone seems most pleased at the thought of the
war's end rather than of independence:

> What thanks, what ardent and ceaseless thanks, are due to that all-super-
> intending Providence which has turned a cruel war into peace, brought
> order out of confusion, made the fierce savages placid, and turned away
> their hostile weapons from our country! May the same Almighty Good-
> ness banish the accursed monster, war, from all lands, with her hated
> associates, rapine and insatiable ambition. . . . This account of my adven-
> tures will inform the reader of the most remarkable events of this coun-
> try.—I now live in peace in safety, enjoying the sweets of liberty, and the
> bounties of Providence.[18]

This passage is replete with irony from both historical and mythic points of view. The narrative refuses to clarify whether it is indeed the Revolution or the border skirmishes between Native Americans and frontiersmen that accounts for "the most remarkable events of this country." The determination cannot be made because Boone's narrative voice claims to speak from Pennsylvania in the 1770s, after returning from decades in Kentucky. As potential hero, furthermore, the voice behind this passage clearly credits the divine with whatever peace has been established, though a major point of the Boone tale as a whole is the development of a self-reliant hero.[19]

From these details alone it is clear that the Boone narrative deviates in significant ways from the Wild West tale exemplified by the stories of Billy the Kid. From these ambiguities—particularly the retreat from the language of individualism to the language of providence—the Boone legend suggests weaknesses, even failures, in the terms of remembrance used for the frontier myths and heroes. Like the legend of Billy the Kid, however, the legend of Daniel Boone places the hero in an easily recognizable symbolic system (this time, that of providence) and so inscribes upon him narrow limits framing any possibility of creative agency.

Perhaps these recognizable frames of interpretation help familiarize—and so popularize—the frontier hero. In any case, Billy the Kid, Daniel Boone, and other Western figures—often mountain men, outlaws, or quick shooters—had captured the interest of a vast majority of reading Americans by the mid-nineteenth century. Later frontier biographies, struggling to satisfy the continuing public appetite for epic adventure, would openly warn readers of the inadequacy of language in any form to capture the grandeur of their subject. For example, Kit Carson's story, as told (apparently) "to a literate friend" around 1856, but not published until 1926, begins with a "final caution to the reader": "Carson was so modest and undemonstrative, and the exploits of his everyday life were frequently so remarkable, that the reader must supplement his simple narration with the resources of his own imagination if he is to appreciate the true nature of the things Carson relates."[20] Through such open appeals to an anxious cultural imagination, a tradition of western iconography grew quickly from the stories of a relatively small number of individual figures.

Despite the innumerable variations within each of the stories of these heroes and despite the many differences among them as individual historical figures, there is something remarkable—and remarkably similar—in the patterns of their narrative life. History—its senses of time, process, and change in the material conditions of existence—is utterly absent in the life stories of these American frontier heroes. Experience is removed from the historical plane onto an epic plane; no legends account for the development of innocence into violence, or violence into civilization; what each tale notes is their odd coexistence. The symbolic strategy of western folklore works by dramatic juxtaposition of irreconcilable oppositions, the framing of everyday action with a recognizable paradigm that lifts these figures out of material existence. While this strategy permits—even promotes—the coexistence of hero and villain legends for the same person, it more significantly eclipses any possibility of representation beyond the bounds of a fixed opposition and enforces a static iconography outside of the realm of experience and history.

EVOLVING WESTERN HEROES

By the turn of the century, writers interested in reanimating the West as a powerful force in national life seemed inclined to start anew—to build a mythology not framed by the familiar symbolic polarities (innocence and violence; the civilized and the wild). Instead, this important second stage in the symbolic life of the West was an attempt to account for exactly those categories ignored and excluded from the form of old western folklore— categories of experience rather than symbol, temporal process rather than frozen iconography. Indeed, many popular representations of the West— in newspapers, periodicals, and fiction—began to distinguish clearly between two different mythic Wests. The old myth had its heroes in figures such as Billy the Kid; the new myth rejected the drama of the outlaw for the steady improvements left by the hard worker.[21]

Although this shift from an iconic to a cumulative view of the meaning of the West shifts America's attention from tall tales of a wild country to well-reasoned stories of a welcoming, tamed frontier, it proves to be a no less controlling style of narrative representation. While the first method dealt with hopes and fears by using the most exaggerated of them to establish a frame of possibility, the second method responded to the same anxiety—what might happen on this field of possibility—by inscribing western life and lore within the paradigm of beneficent development or, more precisely, social evolution.[22]

For a second-stage myth, the theme of "lost possibilities" might have been an alternative standard refrain. One circumstance encouraging this was the inheritance of civil war, transplanted to the west. Despite the fact that many classic nineteenth-century histories of the West do not address these issues, Eugene Berwanger has shown that topics of both nationalism and reconstruction after the Civil War were of extraordinary interest in the West.[23] Union success during the Civil War could not dismantle the entrenched resistance of southern culture, and far less could it prevent the reemergence of such sympathies in the western regions. Late in the century, in fact, the West was home to draft dodgers from both sides, particularly from the South, and there was a strong presence of both Union and Confederate veterans as well.[24]

A number of popular legends were dominated by figures like Jesse James, a transplanted southerner who had belonged to a Confederate guerilla squad. From every angle, his lawless ways seemed quintessentially antinationalistic; he represented a multitude of impediments to an establishment of a regulated system of justice. James was well loved as America's Robin Hood by some popular audiences. He and his cohorts had a degree of romance cast around them, maybe because they seemed to be rooted in the obsolete threat of "the Lost Cause" of the Confederacy.[25] Perhaps in that context, somehow their danger seemed remote, only legendary. This type of tale exemplifies the way that the West had become a perfect setting for tales of anachronism, bound to appeal to a nation seeking immediate healing from the traumas of civil war.[26]

But even if the Civil War had been revived as a symbol of loss and recast in legend in a second stage of mythology, the Wild West was unlamented, its tales left intact, and stories simply began again. At the turn of the century, eastern and western periodicals were flooded with surprising news from the west. In 1903 *Harper's Weekly* explained how a late-nineteenth-century population glut in some western cities had produced first a brief crisis of unemployment: "The towns, swollen with excess of people who had assembled with no definite intentions for the future, nor even clear conception of the present, were left . . . with twice as many inhabitants as could find employment."[27] People caught between mythic Wests, without an earlier generation's "definite intentions for the future" or a subsequent generation's "clear conception of the present," drained western towns of economic prosperity and resources, at least for the moment.

Then, with no concerted effort, the situation seemed to cure itself as a new age began. This newly reassessed West by all accounts had one fundamental quality that would ensure its survival—that is, a deep restlessness, born perhaps of a sense of having missed the great days of old, but also with some innate defense against the retreat to nostalgia. Almost inexplicably, *Harper's* reports, the population of many major cities and towns in the West declined sharply from 1890 to 1900, yet there appeared no alarm. By 1903 those people who had found themselves superfluous to yesterday's promise and who had become invisible—to census takers as well as to much of the settled population of the United States—reemerged to demonstrate a developing balance of urban and rural populations; they suddenly found their places within a newly imagined western society. According to this and many other such reports, the shift was an unspoken national self-corrective: "[I]t marked the beginning of a sounder life, a restoration of equilibrium for America."[28]

Equilibrium in the New West would be a constantly shifting dynamic, but its shifts would be regular and directed, and it would have little use for the volatility of Old Western experience. Writers conceded (with relief) that "the wild, free West of yesterday" was over and that "pioneering [and] experiment" were yielding to lives of greater "permanency."[29] However, they emphasized too that this New West demanded as much active energy as before; the difference now was prescribed direction: "The evolution of the West does not mean that it has come to a position of assured affluence . . . but that it has come to a better understanding of its possibilities, that it is gaining steadily in population and wealth, that it has conquered some of the erroneous ideas of the days of new settlement and is on the substantial way toward business independence. This is not everything, but it is enough to mark a new and important era in the development of the level lands." These writers shared a common purpose: to quell the "exaggerated ideas" left from the pioneer days, to leave them in the sealed trunk of wild western lore, and to overwrite such notions with an understanding of "the real underlying basis of progress" at work on the newly closed frontier.[30]

More elusive than the bold iconography of the Old West, a symbolic vocabulary for the New West became nonetheless recognizable. As the west shifted in identity from being a region of anomaly to being the primary representative of a nation's accomplishments, the United States underwent some of the most divisive decades in its history. Between the Civil War era and the turn of the century, the story of the West changed rapidly from that collection of tall tales to a narrative about the virtues of (characteristically eastern) industriousness and progress.

Despite these changes, though, and despite the major cultural shifts of the late nineteenth century, the old hero tales of the West were never rejected or overturned, nor was there any effort to expand the bounds of their claims. The legend of Billy the Kid, for example, remained important and popular although it continued to fluctuate between its long familiar hero and villain versions. Perhaps most striking culturally is that such a rich and cohesive tale—one well woven enough to be stored for generations—continued to be virtually universally accepted within the bounds of its established parameters, as predictable, inflexible, and outmoded as those parameters quickly became. Calling this tale an example of "the origin of epic subject matter," Alfred Adler has persuasively argued that the main clue left by this and other legends is one about the needs of the culture in time of crisis:

> As a narrative pattern, [the legend of Billy the Kid] could have arisen out of a different set of events. However, it is a common human denomina-tor, a nucleus of basic, extramoral agreement among people who did not seem to agree on anything; it is a piece of evidence that they were able to agree on very important things, where, in the windy regions of social strife literal agreements seemed impossible, they united to descend to the springs of folklore. . . . The case of Billy the Kid leads us to formulate an hypothesis: created at a certain time, a legend is not a reflection of that time, but an indication that the time needed a legend.[31]

No time "needs" a legend as much as the visibly receding past; thus the New West, its new stories and myths, revered the Old West from an odd critical distance. Proclaiming themselves happy to be beyond that danger-ous moment, this generation of westerners expressed in their new sketches of the West (in a wide range of magazines and pamphlets) at once feelings of moral superiority and almost religious dedication to the world framed by the old polarities of hope and fear, innocence and violence. New claims required new stories; new stories required newly imagined symbolic frames. The established western lore would have its due influence; it was, after all, the record of a startling imaginative consensus in the midst of tur-moil. From there, however, the direction turned toward a focused but unframed narrative, one without a defined horizon of ideal hope. By 1900 the teleology of the story of the West—and so the story of America—was dangerously open ended.[32]

In this second stage of mythmaking—the making of narratives inclu-sive of time and change out of the materials of fixed iconography—famil-iar notes of progressive historiography and current terms of evolutionary science offered a known vocabulary and so perhaps a safe start. Countless voices throughout turn-of-the-century United States culture echoed vari-ations on those timeworn themes: "Another kind of opening lies before the settler, in many respects a better one, and its promise is of exceeding brightness. . . . The settler of the early days had to grapple with nature unadorned. . . . The settler of today goes into very different circumstances. . . . The greater lessons have been learned. The age of experiment, with its expensive tutelage, is past. . . . [There has never been] so little probability of failure."[33]

Great opportunities were not to be squandered on careless men, and whatever one's opinion of the Wild West's heroes, they clearly failed to embody stability and commitment, those newly desired qualities for the bright days to come. Nationwide, magazine essays and promotional tracts were particularly careful to say that the West was no longer a land only for hearty, independent souls. Scores of essays were devoted to advertising the safety of emigration for women and children.[34]

What made the New West safe for families was, ironically, the residual roughness of the Old West. Vigilante justice, controversial from the start, gained much wider acceptance and support particularly as vigilantes banded together into "committees." Though in practice, the workings of these watch groups may not have remedied the haste and bias of individual vengeance that characterized vigilante justice, still the appearance of a governing board of moral standards seemed to encourage families to come west, promising a community opposed to feared vices such as prostitution and thievery.[35]

With no sense of controversy or uncertainty, popular magazines announced that "bad men and women always go in the early trains to a new country; but when the country is worthwhile, the men of character and achievement go after them and send the others to their holes."[36] Thus appealing not only to hope but also to the vanity of the successful merchant and the sense of moral duty in the law-abiding easterner, these invitations to the second stage of the American West at once promised peace and invoked activist support: "Though a red shade now and then flutters in the wind of the main street, the second lot of Americans have been received, and these are the real builders of empire. These decent Americans do not care to dwell and to bring up their children in the midst of an immorality which is so prevailing as to make the social atmosphere of the community, and therefore the tough and his companions are moved off quickly by a vigilance committee."[37]

By the turn of the century, the "toughs" of the first wave of emigration were thus divided between law keepers and lawbreakers, for these early pioneers made up the vigilance committees as well as the bands of rogues.[38] That first generation indeed had great chance for moral triumph, but it faced temptations that would be mercifully hidden from subsequent generations.[39] According to this new logic of western heroism, those who overcame temptation and those who came to follow in their respectable footsteps were to be the agents of the new story of national experience; from them the West of the closed frontier would draw the strength of its mythic base.

The cowboy is the figure linking the Old West with the new. Though often referred to as a sort of relic of the past, the cowboy as an icon in the Old West had an equal chance to mature into a ranch owner or a cattle thief.[40] At issue was only "the problem of his own nature."[41] The cowboy who followed the path of virtue and morality was not only the new foundation for the western empire; he was also clear evidence of the importance of will and character in an environment virtually defined by temptation. Most likely he had come west with a sense of reckless adventure; he arrived as a child on an endless playground. But the cowboy who grew to be the "builder of empire" stayed to cultivate, conserve, and protect the land that had seemed so wild to him on his first arrival. He had learned that the most ferocious dangers of the environment were human. He sought conquest no longer of the land but of the most menacing aspects of human nature; he saw these on the range among his associates and, increasingly, in himself.

According to the mythology of the Old West, every cowboy, moral or immoral, promising or corrupt, embodied a spirit of restlessness. Whatever brought him to the prairies eluded precise definition but had something to do with his need for action, growth, and motion. So if the West needed law and order by late in the nineteenth century, it would be an order infused with restlessness, the cowboy's form of order. Because this land continued to be characterized by an atmosphere where "the air is full of the stimulus and the mystery of chance," no static legal system could be effective while still respecting that dynamic quality that drew emigrants west in the first place.[42] In this atmosphere of danger and possibility entwined, survival required quick thinking and improvisational action. The cowboy was the figure that history seemed to designate to carry these traits into the following generations.

Perhaps in the early decades of western emigration, everyone from the lone vagrant to the head of the regional stock growers' association was presumed to share that spirit of restlessness. By the turn-of-the-century, however, that broad spirit had been divided into more specialized qualities. Looking back at the early West, turn-of-the-century American writers made a point of distinguishing between the admirable restlessness of the cowboy and the purely escapist restlessness of others, often called "floaters." Eastern travelers, it was feared, might confuse the two: "One of the most fascinating characters of the West, at least from a picturesque point of view, is the Floater. Somehow he always affords unbounded satisfaction to the Eastern visitor, for he is one of the Western types the stranger fully expects to see. . . . [But in fact] the Floater is one of the most evident signs, himself somewhat a failure, of the invading army of civilization. He is the spume which the inundating wave of humanity throws up; the wave itself will soon lie deep and lasting over all the West."[43]

Western writers had been insisting on exactly this distinction for a long time. As early as 1867 the heroism that saved one from being classed a floater was the act of introducing the institutions of social order, particularly schools and churches. Whereas the floater was an empty seeker, the Western hero was on a mission: "Having followed the 'Star of Empire' in her Westward course, [some emigrants] appeared to have a purpose to perform far more worthy, and with that heroism peculiar to the true pioneer, who *comes* West rather than *floats* West. This [is the] brave band of nature's noblemen."[44] Writers assured the eastern public that "the controlling portion of the population" was made up of this more focused type of emigrant, not robber or outlaw but the "true and loyal American."[45]

THE VIRGINIAN'S WEST

At odds with each paradoxical angle of the symbolic West he had inherited, Wister's West represents neither the lost possibilities of the period of exploration nor the fulfilled achievement of statehood. Everything about the novel's setting defies traditional romantic interpretation. Turning back to the West long after its innate mysteries of geography and indigenous life have been dispelled, Wister focuses our attention on a peculiarly late stage in frontier history, from 1874 to 1890. These years cover some of Wyoming's darkest history. This is a troubled West, no longer the garden of opportunity nor yet the fulfillment of American promise; the Virginian's Wyoming is in transition from territory to state and simultaneously suffering some of the most notorious disasters of the white settlers' experience of frontier history.[46] In the territorial disputes of the Wyoming cattle wars of 1892, large livestock corporations and independent owners of small ranches provided news accounts with material to illustrate the graphic lawlessness of anger, which remained even as native tribes posed an ever-weakening threat.[47] Violence between outlaw rustlers and the often corrupt cattle owners reigned through the end of this period, when northern-tier territories were gaining admission as states.

The Johnson County War, or the War on Powder River, is the direct historical backdrop of the novel.[48] This war first received widespread publicity through the conflicted voice of Asa Shinn Mercer, whose *Northwestern Livestock Journal* in Cheyenne had been "a mouthpiece" for the cattle industry. Apparently under some duress, Mercer's position changed radically, and he denounced the same cattlemen in his 1894 publication, *The Banditti of the Plains, or the Cattlemen's Invasion of Wyoming in 1892.*[49] Not surprisingly, Mercer suffered retaliation for his change in position, but one way or another, most reports were equally partisan. John Clay

Jr.—in support of the industry—simply omits mention of the numerous laws and blacklists designed to drive small ranch owners out of business, while Jack Flagg uses his eleven serial installments in *The Buffalo Wyoming Bulletin* to denounce the kings of the industry by—in his own terms—"all means—fair or foul."[50]

The disputes covered at least a decade of cattle business but focused on an attack by the forces of big business on two alleged cattle rustlers on April 9, 1892. During this, the second year of Wyoming's statehood, vigilante justice was already out of favor, and in this case few would be able to deny the open exploitation of power that was involved. Tensions were high all around due to an extraordinarily bad winter in 1886 and 1887, during which shocking numbers of cattle died of starvation and cold. The April 1892 incident pitted "fifty armed men," surrounding a cabin, against two alleged rustlers who had taken shelter there against a blizzard. Ambushed by gunshots and arson, the two purported criminals were killed. Authorities had not expected the response they received, however: "[T]he people rose, but in such a wave of fury as the West has never seen before or since. Thirty hours after their guilty victory on Powder River, the invaders were besieged in their turn" by cowboys and owners of small ranches. The angry retaliation was so powerful that President Harrison was persuaded to send troops to restore order to the county.[51]

The cowboys and independent ranchers did not see the rustlers as criminals but as rebels, fighting in the true and independent spirit of the Old West. They were tired of what they saw as the abuse of power by large stock associations and their connections to "the law"—laws consistently drawn to protect corporate interests.[52] Powder River would not surrender easily to the interests of land holders; it had been the proud center of many Wild West confrontations between legendary "cowboys and Indians" in the 1860s.[53] By 1880 "Powder River [had been] subjected to the last Indian raid in her history."[54] Between 1884 and 1886, many small ranchers lost half of their stock or more.[55] It was a region and a time later remembered for both confusion and possibility.

Yet even with this notoriously difficult history, Powder River was considered among the richest districts. Up until the Johnson County War, particular circumstances kept Wyoming in a sort of Old West time warp. Political historian Lewis Gould notes that, in the years before oil and coal were of great interest, Wyoming lagged behind its neighboring states in its rate of economic and social development. From the 1870s through the middle of the 1880s, Wyoming seemed a relatively tranquil refuge for the cowboy. The sparse population impeded centralized government, and so, very late into the nineteenth century, Wyoming continued to embody a mythic American west.[56] Promotional publications flooded the market by 1885 to advertise Wyoming, and even after the disastrous winter of 1886–1887, easterners knew little if anything of the harsh realities that settlers had suffered there.[57]

At least until the Johnson County War, virtually all reports emphasized Wyoming's limitless potential, particularly for mining and raising stock. One such promotional text came from J. H. Triggs and focused on the "Gold Fields of the Black Hills, Powder River, and Big Horn Countries." In general, any "hard work, honest endeavor, and capital backed by brains" could be promised "a wide field" and almost "guarantee[d] a sure reward." These were typical terms of praise for western lands: They emphasized familiarity rather than difference and were directed toward eastern audiences. Writers celebrated the "civilizing" influence of the railroad, reporting that "upon acquaintance with her citizens we feel that we can truthfully say that no city in the United States of the same population can boast of more of this true Yankee Spirit than can this 'Magic City' of Cheyenne." As legend told it, ten years after the first sermon was preached there, the city was born "full fledged . . . in a single night." It was peopled by those "with that heroism peculiar to the true pioneer," that late-coming but "brave band of nature's noblemen."[58]

Set in between the days of Wyoming as rich resource and Wyoming as a place of dangerous, nationally feared uprisings, *The Virginian* records a time when both state and nation sought greater organization and control of the population. This transitional time, furthermore, was by no means definitive; versions of chaos reigned long after statehood was established.[59] Apart from the Johnson County War, other acts of infamy in the region included the lynching of "Cattle Kate"—a reputed prostitute who traded with independent ranchers. Once the disputes among cattle owners subsided, violent disputes raged for years between the cattlemen and sheep ranchers.[60] National attention toward the west only increased with the advent of the Roosevelt administration.[61]

By that time the language of the West was focused on telling an irrefutable story of democracy. With only brief histories as states, most territories were openly nationalistic in their political agendas. Ignatius Donnelly, a Populist politician from Minnesota, spoke in terms representative of a broad spectrum of approaches when he explained the western embrace of nationalism over states' rights: "[W]e who come . . . from the far West have not that deep ingrained veneration for state power which is to be found among the inhabitants of some of the older states. . . . We feel ourselves to be offshoots of the nation. . . . We are willing to trust the nation."[62] They trusted the nation precisely because the established East

had made clear that the West represented the living history of its successful policies.

Particularly as expansion became a higher priority in the Roosevelt
administration, the West was promoted as the material issue of American
triumph. Roosevelt spoke of this direct connection as he addressed an
audience at an exposition honoring the anniversary of the Louisiana Purchase in St. Louis on April 30, 1903: "Our triumph in this process of
expansion was indissolubly bound up with the success of our peculiar kind
of federal government."[63] The story of the West and the story of America
were presented throughout turn-of-the-century culture as fundamentally
similar stories. Dominant voices from the East linked the two stories on
democratic terms. The West was everything America should be—a land of
liberty and opportunity.[64]

Whatever dangers expansion held, neither side could afford to reject
its tempting potential as a laboratory for the evolution of social ideals to
mark the identity of the United States. Enough of the West's destiny and
experience remained undefined, and so all sides could turn toward it for
justification and representation of particular ideals, even if those acts were
defenses against considering the realistic fears that made up a core of the
West's identity in eastern minds. One way or another, the West, argues
Rush Welter, was a significant force reconciling mid-nineteenth-century
conservatives to American democracy; "the promise of western development apparently helped reconcile them to the [national form of] democracy."[65]

However, amid this atmosphere of consent, several direct challenges to
American nationalism emerged in the few years immediately preceding
the publication of *The Virginian:* the announced, and quickly accepted, fact
of a "closed frontier"; the centennial anxieties at the advent of a new century; finally, an event less directly tied to Wister's project but certainly a
definitive moment for his generation, the assassination of William
McKinley.

From the start, and particularly in retrospect, the assassination of Lincoln was a symbol of the unspeakable cost of civil war; he became a martyr to the Union cause. When McKinley died, however, explanations were
scarce, and symbolic readings were virtually nonexistent. Instead, McKinley's assassination appeared as a product of the very modernity that should
have protected him. The shooting was read less clearly as a political statement than as an expression of a population beyond control, beyond consensus, and above all, beyond law.

In the many memorials published after McKinley's death, citizens
mourned not only the loss of a president, but also the timing of the action.

From Boston responses came that highlighted the tragic irony: Arthur W. Dolan wrote, "McKinley was assassinated in the twentieth century, in the days of the greatest enlightenment and progress which this country has ever seen." A second city official, Thomas D. Roberts, searched in vain for cause or explanation, finally concluding that the problem "lies, then, largely in the law. We have no law that is equal to this occasion."[66] This "occasion" clearly was not simply murder, not even the murder of a head of state. As an event it seemed to announce the existence of a newly random, unprovoked, and inexplicable violence, with deep national and international implications: It was the nightmare of the newly expanded country, the fulfillment of every fear.

Adding these events to the context of Wister's novel, it is clear that the prevalent themes of conflict and disorder would have resonance not only for easterners moving or traveling west, but much more importantly, also for a culture now deep in national, rather than sectional, turmoil. If a conservative faction felt deceived in having accepted the rapid growth of American democracy after the Civil War, surely they found those fears reanimated by the turn of the century. Moreover, if the settlement of the West had been the great democratic experiment, the Old West—now representing a new myth of American origins—demanded reinterpretation. Whether one believed in the region as an emblem of success or failure, turn-of-the-century America was filled with mandates for the reinscription of the closed frontier within a new national story, and that story, it was clear, could use nostalgia only in the service of a forward-looking vision. A new romance of American history, then, would acknowledge the passing of time in a celebration of what that past time had built, facilitated, or foreshadowed.

11

STORYTELLING AND EVOLUTION'S LOSSES IN *THE VIRGINIAN*

I N *The Will to Believe*, William James separates human experience and its symbols by arguing, "there is a zone of insecurity in human affairs in which all the dramatic interest lies. The rest belongs to the dead machinery of the stage."[1] James's image of that "dead machinery" neatly describes the American West at the close of the nineteenth century.[2] In the eyes of the literary East, the massive symbolic promise that the West once offered had been subsumed—whether literally or figuratively—by a variety of machineries, including developing systems of national iconography no less than industrial technology.[3] These machineries share the qualities (or at least the ideal principles) of efficient systemic operations, focused on the orderly transformation of raw material into products with well-defined particular capacities.[4]

In his hero's evolution and adaptation, Wister illustrates the success of these processes, and yet at another level, the story clearly implies an interest in that which is left out in the case of such development. As a cultural icon of the turn of the century in America, *The Virginian* as plot, character, and text wavers between a desire for, and a fear of, the "zone of insecurity" that lies beyond the stage machinery, no matter how efficient and comprehensive. The text poses major questions regarding the location and function of that zone in a society where virtually all levels of human experience, from industry to popular literature, are considered to be increasingly predictable, even knowable, because mechanized.

When Wister makes clear that he considers his work to be historical romance while setting *The Virginian* very late in the nineteenth century, only about a decade before its publication, the effect is that his text then represents a moment of the condensation of memory into a transmissible textual form, that is, the reentrance of history into the larger, ongoing, narratives of culture. In concrete terms, for Wister, the ongoing cultural narrative most visible is that of America's story of growth, a national story framed by the promises and restrictions of modern democracy. *The Virginian*, in turn, encodes challenges to that reigning model of democratic change.

The vacillation between celebration and fear of the West in the eyes of Wister's young eastern narrator comes as no surprise among the confusion of regional and local divisions that the novel makes present through its historical setting. When the narrator steps off of the train at the town of Medicine Bow, he expects that his westward journey is nearly done and that he will sleep that night at his destination, Judge Henry's ranch. However, this is not the house-to-house travel that an easterner expects. Instead the narrator finds himself "marooned in a foreign ocean," surrounded by "unfeatured wilderness" (6) and with several days' worth of travel remaining between this closest railroad station and the home of his friends. In this key scene the tenderfoot is not initiated into a new world but rather fully disoriented, severed from all that he had known and imagined and left in that state of confusion. He had some ideas of what he expected to see in "the great cattle land" (2); the wild ponies, the cowboys, even the expanse of the countryside fit into his vaguely preconceived notions of the West. However, as quickly as the train leaves him behind, standing bewildered on the platform, the narrator finds himself abruptly transformed from tourist to exile.

The experience of the narrator in these early scenes works neatly as a telescopic romance of the history of intrigue and danger that the Old West held for the traveler and the emigrant throughout much of the nineteenth century. A series of rapidly shifting impressions, resting alternately on horror and wonder (but rarely in between) frame this scene as a paradigm of the mythic identity of the West before the "closing of the frontier." The narrator first looks on in awe when a "wild pony," escaping all efforts to corral him, is suddenly tamed by the mere appearance of the Virginian; the transformation of the pony clearly stands as an emblem of a markedly romantic and entirely nonviolent movement from the raw savagery of nature to a pinnacle of civilization: The pony responds to the Virginian by "walk[ing] in with a sweet, church-door expression" (2). And the Virginian himself, before his identity is revealed to the narrator, appears at once to move "with the undulations of a tiger, smooth and easy, as if his muscles flowed beneath his skin" (2), while also resembling "a slim young giant, more beautiful than pictures" (3). The landscape too alternately resembles "a world of crystal light, a land without end, a space across which Noah and Adam might come straight from Genesis" (10) and "a planet of treeless dust" covered with "empty bottles and garbage . . . more forlorn than stale bones" (9).

The haunting contrast between a world filled only by divine light and a world cluttered with waste and death is a striking image, particularly so early in the romance. In the narration of this scene there is something other than awe; there is an implied contempt for those lurking (invisibly, to the narrator's eye) in the area who must bear responsibility for the gross misuse of the land and its spirit of promise.[5] Here Wister not only reminds us of his belated inheritance of the West, but he also hints at some discomfort with the vaguely menacing world around him. The tenderfoot, already bereft of the deceptive images he carried from the East and not yet armed with any new frame of reference, perceives the distinct threat of an indistinct mystery. As long as the ignorant traveler fails to make the necessary distinctions on sight, he will remain at the mercy of whomever he meets. In that sense—from the easterner's inadequate perspective—western power and authority appear to be totally up in the air through the end of the nineteenth century.

One of the dramas enacted in Wister's novel is the narrator's growing sense of judgment. At one level this is a story of the narrator's changing beliefs about the American West, as seen through his eastern eyes. On another level, however, this is a story of the narrator's search to connect with the Virginian, and as such it is a story that demonstrates over and over the inadequacy of their mutual understanding. In a sense the narrator is a figure for the American reader, along for the ride, to worship the West. This is far from a guidebook on how to judge western characters; the narrator watches and worships for only as long as he can fail to understand what he sees, and by the end of the novel, even that hopelessly optimistic narrator no longer believes in his ability to tell a tale of order from the fragments of what he eventually finds to be a broken world.

After his initial exile into the inscrutability of the "voiceless land" (44) of the West, the easterner quickly perceives the excitement and anxiety of standing in a place where the unsettled scores of national identity may (and will) be fought. With the Virginian's southern ancestry, Wister clearly invokes parallels to George Washington and to some spirit associated with the rebel South.[6] To the narrator, however, this Southern influence serves simply as one more layer of alienation. The Virginian is his only companion, his guide, and his interpreter, yet he speaks a language that is either too western or too southern for the narrator to understand readily. For a young, eastern, self-proclaimed gentleman to be paired with a southern cowboy as he is led deeper into the mysteries of the West disrupts any frontier myths that may have been circulating in his home city of Philadelphia. Instead he quickly learns that this is a land of castaways, misfits, and exiles. Most discomforting of all, the narrator finds that he himself is one among them.

If he had been greeted instead by scenes of the widely proclaimed Americanism of the West—by "western settlers . . . abundantly supplied with slogans and democratic formulas"—the tenderfoot might be seen heading down a familiar path of the reaffirmation of patriotism, even if its tone might be rougher and rawer than that which Wister or his narrator might find immediately appealing.[7] As Donald Worster has shown, one could certainly find in the West—"from the days of the first wagon trains down to the twentieth century"—Fourth of July celebrations, as well as other "overt demonstrations of patriotism."[8] As it is, however, the narrator is marooned within the deep heart of America, far from his familiar Americanism of language and spirit, and left as an inept interpreter of an unfamiliar, at times carnivalesque and even dangerous world.

If he, like Wister himself, traveled west for the curative effects of Medicine Bow and its surroundings, it quickly becomes clear that there is no cure for his burden of uncertainty.[9] Though he will adapt in particular ways, the experience will be more alienating than curative. Never will he be able to overturn his early impressions that he "possessed the secret of estranging people at sight" (13); in one of the very few certainties he can express, he laments, "Clearly, this wild country spoke a language other than mine" (19).

In *The Virginian,* Wister, his narrator, and his hero each depend upon a dream of order, a chart to overlay and so to explain cultural self-expression in the story of the American West. All three perspectives sit comfortably within Turner's story of the frontier. As systems of cultural analysis, these dreams of order bear striking similarities to the terms of late-nineteenth-century science, specifically of theories of evolution. Despite scientific and religious arguments, the broad tenets of evolutionary theories—a balance between continuity and change, a teleological shape to historical development (not new ideas to historiography)—were newly contextualized within analyses of environmental influences on social forms. Both Turner and Wister placed their romantic visions of frontier progress distinctly within these contexts. As a result, these were—in their different forms—familiar romances with just enough metaphor and mystery to generate new stories, new interest.

The acknowledged importance of environmental influences opened inherited models of progressive historiography to a new degree of unpredictability; that unpredictability would come to bear too in relation to the surprising fragments of history, ever emergent and in need of reinscription.

As the Darwinian forces of American culture worked to define the West, so too lives, histories, symbols, and materials from the West worked reciprocally, shaping America's stories about itself. It is this dynamic atmosphere into which the narrator enters at Medicine Bow.

The reciprocities involved here are sketched within those dreams of order shaping Wister's romance. The narrator, as a tenderfoot overwhelmed by the power and mystery of what he sees, attempts to present a world glorified by its distance and inscrutability. For a long time, the hero, the Virginian, controls the world that the narrator sees and that the other characters experience by demonstrating capabilities in language, thought, and action that no others possess. Wister manipulates the relationship between these two characters to control his romance of the West. His book is carefully structured as the easterner's dream vision of Western power and intrigue. The changes manifest in the narrator, the Virginian, and Wister's relation to both of them, suggest a strongly imposed evolutionary myth; yet there is an extent to which those changes resist explanation and narrative control, and that points to the central weaknesses of the myth.

After the opening scenes discussed earlier, the eastern narrator all but disappears as a character. From time to time, he disappears as an observer as well. Wister suggests that we read this disappearance as, on one level at least, the success of assimilation. The narrator's assimilation, in turn, becomes a figure for the reconciliation of the West as America, rather than as its dark and wild secret; that myth works to annex a borderland, a previously contested area, to the known and planned; further, it operates beyond the realm of present time into the realms of memory and cultural foundation. The borderland thus opens to acquire not only a new present meaning, but also a new past, in which it might come to signify the latent potential of present meaning.

THE VIRGINIAN AS STORYTELLER

To both the narrator and the reader, the Virginian should be familiar in many ways. For his identity he draws from the powerful symbolic resources of both old and new Western mythology. Wister is remembered in literary history for "liberat[ing] the cowboy hero from the Dime Novels and provid[ing] a synthetic tradition for a new century."[10] It took decades of writing before he developed a character with this capacity: Wister's earlier short stories are filled with sketches of provisional cowboy heroes, perhaps most notably Specimen Jones in *Red Men and White* (1895), who is an "American wanderer" with a "reserved and whimsical nature," respected by rough men and yet still respectable according to fundamental social virtues.[11]

The Virginian offers the most enduring image of the American cowboy by fusing the mysteries of this cowboy with the mysteries of language on the frontier. Underscoring the grand-scale intentions behind the Virginian, Wister objected strongly to the identification of his nameless cowboy with any historical individual. Frances Stokes, Wister's daughter, later wrote, "dozens of claims have been made by people saying that they were the Virginian, knew the Virginian, or had seen the Virginian. This is not true. The Virginian is a composite character drawn from several different men my father had either seen briefly or known well."[12] In his capacity as a "composite character," the Virginian has evident ties to other imagined figures, including the western outlaws of legend such as Billy the Kid and Daniel Boone, and literary precursors, such as Cooper's Leather-Stocking and perhaps even "Huckleberry Finn, a Huck come to manhood in the Wyoming Territory."[13]

All of these resemblances, however, depend on the mutual mysteries of the characters rather than on any manifest parallels. The violent innocence of Billy the Kid, the isolation of Daniel Boone, Leatherstocking's inscrutability, the impossible condition of "a Huck come to manhood": Mystery—a sense of historical secrets known but untold—is the fundamental attribute that separates the Virginian from the western outlaws and links him to a literary tradition of nineteenth-century American historical romance.[14] Just before publication of his novel, Wister wrote to Oliver Wendell Holmes Jr. that in the character of the Virginian, he had "set out to draw a man of something like genius, the American genius."[15] Later that year he elaborated in a letter to Richard Harding Davis: "[The Virginian] was meant by me to be just my whole American creed in flesh and blood. . . . It was by design he continued nameless because I desired to draw a sort of heroic circle about him, almost a legendary circle and thus if possible create an illusion of remoteness."[16]

If Wister sought to convey mystery, ambiguity, and the capacity to resist definition, early reviews of the novel are a chorus of his success. *The Virginian*, critics claimed, "sharply blazed the way to that quite possible impossibility, the American novel." It captured "the essential spirit" of the frontier and expressed "what precious little other American fiction tries to express—Americanism." That is, the novel was proclaimed to be "characteristic of our life and genius" and "near to the heart of essential Americanism."[17] The reviews were emphatic in their abstract and universalizing claims. Wister's construction of that remote "legendary circle" had clearly left audiences without the means to name and so to limit the hero's character.

Though it was impossible to define the Virginian's character, early reviewers agreed that he clearly was an *individual*. His cultural function seemed indefinably broad, but his personality somehow appealed to readers on an immediate and human scale. "I hardly know a more engaging hero," one reviewer wrote; "he is one of the most distinct personalities that have appeared in American fiction," said another.[18] The *Atlantic Monthly* summarized the paradox of this uniquely drawn character with the broadest possible function in the cultural imagination: "The Virginian is a figure of splendor, and of splendor all the more irresistible because our recognition of it does not depend upon what the author says about him."[19] Hamblen Sears defined the character's "historical importance" in an October 1902 review for the *Book Buyer:*

> It is the Virginian himself who carries your attention; and until you have finished with him, when you sit down and begin to wonder where he is now, what he is doing, what are his views on this or that question . . . this particular American author has done his task. . . .
>
> The Virginian himself is a real man. . . . [It is] as if we had known him in the flesh. . . . That is historical fiction of the sort we want. It tells us of the real man of America in such a human, such an accurate way that we keep on saying "I've seen that a dozen times," when not one of us would ever know he had seen it unless Wister had set it down on paper to come before his eyes.[20]

"The real man of America": From the start of *The Virginian*, Wister's narrative perspective clearly defines the central interest of this novel to be the elusive yet distinct hero, a nameless but specific cowboy surrounded by mystery. This character quickly emerges as the key to a remarkable romance of American unity, woven boldly from some of the strongest known threads of discord—sectional differences, vigilante justice, conflicts of gender and class. Built as a bundle of contradictions—neither eastern nor western, neither establishment nor outlaw—the Virginian mediates successfully among levels of society in conflict. Through his agency, both as designer and participant, intersectional romance culminates in marriage; he, once a frontier loner, evolves into an industrial-age capitalist; and a truce becomes possible between the settled world of (feminine) domestic tranquility and the dangerous (masculine) world of enforced justice and social order. Then too, however, these changes are not simply evidence of agency; they also signify what the powers of agency have purchased. By the novel's end and the hero's full evolution, there has been an exchange, and the reader may decide whether (and for whom) the trade of subjective power for communal closure has been a successful bargain.

As an agent of cultural change, the Virginian directs and stars in a drama of American incorporation, but this drama is strangely devoid of action. Critics have noted that Wister's nameless cowboy demonstrates more rhetorical skill than physical prowess.[21] At all levels of the plot, in fact, stories stand in for action. This becomes especially noticeable in episodes of struggle between outlaws and honest cowboys. The violence expected in these encounters either does not occur or is set well beyond the narrative eye. Here on this newly constructed frontier, agency is already removed from action and derived instead from the mysterious powers of language. *The Virginian* relentlessly focuses on the constitution, interpretation, and eventual destruction of a knowable pattern behind cultural change, and at every level of expression, Wister insists that that pattern is the product of the culture's capacity to control the link between agency and language.

No longer is this the Wild West, shaped by acts of individual heroism and violence. In fact, by nature so fully contradictory, the Virginian becomes less an agent within his historical world than an embodied theory of cultural storytelling. When the Virginian most intrigues his love interest, Molly Wood, and when he brings the local cattlemen most efficiently under his control, he does so primarily through well-chosen stories and silences. The cowboy hero has his claim to cultural agency in the ways in which he controls language with skills greater than those of any other character in the book.

He is, in this sense, Wister's figure of an American cultural storyteller, the figure of isolation who spends his life working to shape the story of his world. In this tradition Cooper's Spy embodies—but cannot tell—a story of America's foundations in the distress of internal division rather than in the documents of independence, and the paradoxical qualities of the scarlet *A* persist in the tale Hawthorne's narrator tells of the divided secret and communal lives of Hester Prynne. The central conflict in Wister's historical romance is not between the Virginian and Molly, West and East, wild and domestic, or male and female. The struggle Wister presents is between fragments of history and a world that does not know what to make of them.

Like the Spy or Hester Prynne, the Virginian begins as a character closely associated with the mysteries of his culture; in all three cases, narrative perspective immediately situates these mysteries not in opposition to, but rather at the very heart of, the historical romance, thus placing extraordinary power on the private, even secret, knowledge of the central character. In this tradition, the secrets known by only one isolated character become—in the eyes of the narrator, and so in the form of the book—so richly evocative that they may function, archetypally, as powerful collective and undefined mysteries confronting their culture. For a time the Virginian is guardian of some such secret world, which we know only in fragments. He at once protects his knowable world from this unknown one and infuses the power of the latter world's mystery back into the culture. Like the Spy or Hester, the Virginian begins as an American storyteller rendered silent by the overwhelming power of his vision.

The paradox here, however, involves the fact that even the Virginian, the dark, mysterious, and forever nameless figure that he remains, faces deeply inscribed limits on his capacities to control the language of the American West. In fact, as he gains economic and social status—that is, as he comes to life in the world of plot—he loses the power that had set him apart, the power of agency, which remains in the realm of language of the story. In this way the Virginian loses the interpretive capacity, the link between agency and language that made him the hero he was, the hero who could mediate between worlds because he had a place in none of them.

The costs of heroism in this fictional world are devastating. Early in the novel, as if sustained by some lingering wild energies from his days as an outlaw rustler, the Virginian works as a ranch hand, and in everything he does, he is a model of capable action. Over the course of the plot, however, he faces a series of challenges, and time after time, the aftermath of the challenge distances agency from language in his character, leaving him closer to the world of patterned order than to that of volatile agency. This pattern makes the central problem of *The Virginian* manifestly one of language: The more the Virginian enters into the realm of the romance, the more the language of the West runs rampant, seemingly divorced from any direct human agency. As a result, the real story of the romance of this world—the one that drew readers in from the beginning—slips beyond the boundaries of the romance of the West into an unspoken reservoir of histories made into secrets.

The mastery of these stories had made the Virginian compelling; when he loses this mastery, what remains compelling are the stories he has lost, rather than the Virginian himself.[22] The Virginian's successful assimilation into American economic and social structures ironically bears an inverse relation to the level of power he has to direct and alter the progress of his culture. The cowboy hero, who begins as a model of American agency, a culmination of Wister's experimental frontier themes and heroes from more than a decade of writing, ends as a model of American constraint, a figure who has not dispelled mystery but simply lost access to it.

The active power he had once exhibited may be easily translated to the world of American enterprise, but in that translation the story he seemed to carry with him—the mystery and intrigue of his character—is gone. By the end of the novel, the Virginian's story is anyone's but his own. He is, as Wister repeatedly insists, a new George Washington, a new breed of businessman, a reformed outlaw; he is anything but a mysterious loner out on the frontier. Certainly with the cowboy matured and married, some disorders of Western history have been resolved, and some dangerous energies have been redirected, contained within a new iconography for the American frontier.

Nevertheless, when *The Virginian*'s plot extends (somewhat awkwardly) beyond the final showdown between hero and villain, to the fairytale domestication and modernization of the cowboy, romance has done its job at only one fragile level. In its narrative energy *The Virginian* has seemed to be consistently directed toward fusing American nationalism and social Darwinism, and yet in the end the novel proves utterly resistant. A romantic design, much like Turner's, actually closes in on the Virginian. In one sense it may be said to preserve him for future generations, but in another sense it recoils on him, trapping and disempowering him, draining him of all interest and intrigue.

Wister's novel sorts through American iconography by first taking stock of available cultural symbolism and then layering materials that have been gathered during the nineteenth century. It evaluates several familiar historiographical models of American identity: Like the dime novels that Wister's audience would have read, *The Virginian* invokes powerful myths of American communal identity through stock images of the outlaw West as well as from two other primary symbolic histories—the mythologies of colonial independence and civil war. This romance of the West moves toward reconciling a conflict deeper than any of those that provide the machinery of the plot; the conflicts of plot, in fact, are directly staged toward a larger effort at reconciling discontinuous, even radically incoherent, models of cultural change.

THE VIRGINIAN AS ROMANCE

In the character of Molly Wood, Wister evaluates the potential strength of the strongest of these traditional symbolic histories, that of the American revolution. As the heroine, Molly is a strong player in the struggle to preserve and transmit an American story for the West. Her family history, the American story as written in the East, represents the traditions and institutions of civilization, the iconography of America's founding ideals. Molly carries with her a miniature portrait of her great-grandmother Stark, a heroine of the revolutionary era to whom Molly bears a visible family resemblance (70). The miniature, Wister clearly suggests, signifies a whole revolutionary story in itself. Molly takes this portrait with her all the way across the continent, and those whom she meets invariably stare, as if waiting for its significance to become clear. There is something remote, however, in this icon that forbids anyone but Molly to understand it; in the end it means something only to her, and she never shares the story with anyone.

Though Molly may carry a significant story, then, she is limited in her capacity to transmit it. In Wister's model, the familiar myths of communal identity—such as the revolutionary story—have come down to the present day in strangely remote and fragile forms. Like all of these dated myths, Molly's story has not survived well over time. In direct contrast to the dime-novel tradition, *The Virginian* invokes such myths only to develop a symbolic method designed around the limits of these histories. Even in New England, Molly's gentility now has no market value; the family mills have failed. Economic hardship serves as a form of material proof of the fragile condition of the revolutionary myth. Its strongest legacy is ironic; economic failure by necessity frees Molly from life as a replica of her great-grandmother, prompting her to set out for the West.

In the West Molly meets the Virginian, who is no descendent of prominent heroes, but—better yet—he is, as Wister repeatedly suggests, a new George Washington, fit for a new age. And the story of this West, accordingly, will not be an encyclopedic incorporation of America's myth-ologies; it is potentially a new mythology, a volatile ground where stories grow unpredictably because of their genesis in language, a force with mys-terious power on the frontier. The tenderfoot narrator notes with aston-ishment "the contagious powers of Rumor. Here through this voiceless land," he says, rumors "spread like a change of weather" (44). Back East, rumors about the West saturate communities. In Molly's hometown of Bennington, Vermont, for example, "a vague and dreadful word—one of those words that cannot be traced to its source," came in "from the mali-cious outside air. . . . Somebody said that Miss Molly Wood was engaged to marry a rustler" (203–4).

These Western stories evolve, Wister shows, into almost living forms. Intriguing enough to demand retelling and accessible enough to be elabo-rated by each of those retellings, the Western story travels across America like a tumbleweed, picking up materials as it goes. To residents of Molly's small Vermont town, there is nothing more frightening in the rumor of her fate than the fact that the word *rustler* "was not in any dictionary, and current translations of it were inconsistent. A man at Hoosic Falls said that he had passed through Cheyenne, and heard the term applied in a complimentary way to people who where alive and pushing. Another man had always supposed it meant some kind of horse. But the most alarming version of all was that a rustler was a cattle thief" (204). In this quiet New England setting, Molly's family and friends are not comforted by discovering that "the truth is that all these meanings were right. The word ran a sort of progress in the cattle country, gathering many meanings as it went." In fact, even in Bennington, Wister writes, the word gathered more meanings: "In a very few days, gossip had it that Molly was engaged to a gambler, a gold miner, an escaped stage robber, and a Mexican bandit; while Mrs. Flynt feared she had married a Mormon" (204).

Mirroring the confused mystery of the scrambled stories and indecipherable news reaching East from the unknown regions of the West, the structure of Wister's narrative is a story as yet without a script. In fact, the culture he represents proves itself to be inexplicable in the familiar terms of nostalgia and progress. Contrary to all expectations of the romance, on the final page of the novel Wister's patriotic narrator explains the safety of this newly imagined American identity by invoking an image so bleak that it shatters the romance to its very foundations. Internal and sectional threats have ceased, this narrator claims, simply because the country is destroyed and bereft of value.

With that haunting conclusion, the novel compels a reassessment of its narrative design. Three stylized plots have concluded happily: The Virginian has won the gunfight against his nemesis, Trampas; he has won the affections of his beloved, Molly Wood; and he has adapted to the massive cultural shift from frontier to industrial identity. These plots have been carefully woven to be complementary, and yet something has gone wrong, and the characters are left to live in "a broken world" (392). Among those three shifting planes of romance, some volatile force of traumatic history has maintained its power to disrupt. That force, stronger than (and yet often hidden by) the romance, is a competing model of cultural change, standing in direct opposition to the more predictable patterns of social and cultural evolution.

Written into *The Virginian's* narrative design and its failures are the nationalist struggle to revive social Darwinism and the nagging reminders of its inadequacy as a story of communal identity. Those voices of dissent are part of social Darwinism's primary challenge in America, the more volatile, less patterned accounts of history and process given by William James, among others. At the level of the romance, Wister's Virginian synthesizes these views—and in doing so, punctures the radical implications of James's critique.

Ideally perhaps, this character and his life story would illustrate the link between the safe and predictable patterns of cultural evolution and the surprising powers of individual will and agency. As the novel begins, it is exactly this link that Wister successfully highlights. By the end of the story, however, the experimental relations between individual agency and cultural pattern that began in the style of a great defense of evolution in culture finally end in fragments that neither convey their message nor disappear from view. These fragments of history and knowledge instead hint of a story of the inadequacy of the vision from which they originate, suggesting a failure of synthesis and a reiteration of pragmatism's historiographical challenge.

TRACES OF A BROKEN WORLD

Nowhere are the Virginian's heroic limits so evident as they are in the episode where his strength is most vigorously tested. Immediately following two frustrating encounters in which the Virginian attempts to exact justice for the growing lawlessness of his fellow cowboys, he sets out to ride alone and collect his thoughts.[23] Absent from the narrative only briefly, the Virginian, it turns out, quickly falls prey to an attack, possibly by roving Indians, but also possibly by former friends, now outlaws.[24] In any case, the narrator gives no access to this scene: He does not witness it, nor does Wister allow the Virginian to remember it. However, the unnarrated event is clearly a key scene in the novel's critique of its hero: The lone frontiersman enters a patch of unsettled wilderness and emerges not as conqueror but as one nearly vanquished by unseen, unnamed forces: "One of his arms hung up to its elbow in the pool, the other was crooked beside his head, but his face was sunk downward against the shelving rock. . . . A patch of blood at his shoulder behind stained the soft flannel shirt, spreading down beneath his belt, and the man's whole strong body lay slack and pitifully helpless" (255).

Molly comes upon her injured lover and tends to him, bringing him back to her cabin. As a figure of absolute weakness in this sequence of scenes, the Virginian experiences a symbolic rebirth at the cost of his distinguishing voice of experiential and historical knowledge. In spite of this he feels not destroyed but at peace. As he first wakes, he looks at Molly "as if the present did not touch his senses. 'I knew hands were touching me. I reckon I was not dead. I knew about them as soon as they began, only I could not interfere. . . . It's mighty strange where I have been. No. Mighty natural' " (257). The devastations of his vision and his strength are here naturalized to be necessary, evolutionary adaptations to a forcibly domesticated world.

During the fevers following his injury, the Virginian slips in and out of consciousness. He lies in a bed surrounded by the familiar artifacts of the identity of the American West—"a Crow Indian war bonnet," "a bow with arrows," "the skin of a silver fox," "the antlers of a black-tail deer," "a bearskin," "a Navajo blanket," his "spurs and pistol and bold leather chaps" (249, 261)—and he sleeps under Molly's prized miniature, the etching of her Grandmother Stark. While the narrator eagerly agrees with the town's hopeful prognosis that "the man's deep untainted strength would reassert its control" (266), the Virginian's consciousness is slow to focus.

He wakes to share with Molly not any revelation of his dream-state, but rather his inability to interpret the story laid out in his surroundings: " 'My haid has been mighty crazy; and that little grandmother of yours yondeh— she—but I can't just quite catch a-hold of these things'—he passed a hand over his forehead—'so many—or else one right along—well, it's all foolishness!' he concluded, with something almost savage in his tone. And after she had gone from the cabin he lay very still, looking at the miniature on the wall" (269). Assimilated now, dismissive of doubt and compelled to bury in silence the visionary qualities that had set him apart, the Virginian has access to the American story only in the material traces that return of their own accord to haunt his memory and challenge his understanding; the "miniature," which catches his eye, is only a mocking reminder that, for him, a coherent national story belongs to a remote generation.

The Old West had persisted in Frederick Jackson Turner's model as a new modern spirit. In *The Virginian,* in a different, more fragmented way, so too traces of a lost ideal remain in a reservoir of history. This reservoir, however, is only latent in present consciousness, unreconciled to present time. This is a vanished world in (paradoxically) its most immediate form; it is the part of Wister's West that still exists, running along concurrent with, but absolutely separate from, the life of the modernized cowboy.

As the Virginian's abilities to adapt to his new world displace the particular powers of his character, those powers are shifted into a realm we may mistakenly stumble upon, a warehouse of leftover history from the American West. Wister's text reminds us that sometimes, inexplicably, stories, rumors, or secrets may escape the bounds of that uncharted place and enter our world. To experience this other world of stories becomes thus random and frightening; in fact, though, that world is not mysterious but simply the heir to cultural memory. While a clear pattern of social evolution orders the knowable world, this world beyond character and plot is kept utterly apart, and it represents a very different agency, one that maintains the power to carry America's story over the plains.

A vivid material trace of this agency is the final note that a rustler named Steve leaves for the Virginian (329).[25] Facing vigilante justice—execution as a cattle thief—Steve scrawls a few quick words of good-bye to the Virginian, once his closest friend, now his executioner. This is an image of brother turned against brother and the resulting blood on the land; in this way it offers one of the text's many oblique references to the Civil War. Steve's words are not (nor can they be, within the operating codes of honor) conveyed at the scene; the Virginian comes upon the note later, quite accidentally. It has been crumpled up as fire kindling at a campsite some distance away; its reappearance is uncanny, startling, and symbolically devastating to the literary pattern of individual control and heroic strength that had been developing in the romance. The note works metonymically to reveal a powerful undercurrent to the romance, a cultural form of language with the power to subsume static iconography and prototypical action.

The romance may transmit topics in retrospect or in prospect; the hidden story, on the other hand, promises to transmit that which is still ongoing. The story that slips beyond the boundaries of Wister's romance of the West depends for its development upon a narrative form that fosters and protects the most powerful lost secrets, the archetypal imaginings of the culture. In the American historical romance, these archetypal imaginings are shaped by patterns of narrative silence, the failures of language. They represent moments of cultural transition, and those transitions are indicated, metonymically, in formal patterns of expression that reveal the limits of the existing symbolic vocabulary. In a state prior to that of an established narrative of events, Wister's tale of the frontier draws its strength from a method riskier than that of the standard structural romance of the West: It necessarily privileges language over action, sustained mystery over known experience.

In Wister's novel, the narrative silences that indicate these power struggles between language and action, secrecy and experience, mark imminent shifts in an American symbolic vocabulary; these narrative silences are associated particularly with the novel's hero, the nameless cowboy. Cooper's Spy, Hawthorne's Hester, and the Virginian all begin as characters closely associated with an elusive cultural story that lies somehow at the heart of their romance; the Spy and Hester remain isolated visionaries. But as the Virginian joins with the social world of his book, he loses access to both the strength and the peril that belong to the American storyteller; the narrative gaps, in turn, begin to work against the comforts of his settled identity. By the end of the book, the Virginian as he once was, the frontier cowboy, is rendered obsolete by the resolution he himself orchestrates.

Yuri Lotman has shown that the texts generated around such moments of cultural restructuration are marked by a pattern of language alternating between silence and noise, corresponding to the reception and transmission of story.[26] At times of reception, cultural stories are received in forms not immediately decipherable; they may be seen as historical traces—fragments of past experience more resistant to present understanding than they first appear. In exile from a context that would supply ready meaning to them, the fragments—like the fragments of history for which Wister's world has no place—find their way into romantic designs that might more comfortably exclude them. The nature of their displaced condition demands that these traces be released in some form of transmission; in that process they come to exist as stories. Wister's historical romance enacts exactly this symbolic incorporation of history. It newly transmits—deeply layered within the form of romance—historical moments of the reception of knowledge. These transmissions may be divided into two different stories of the West, the evolution of the cowboy hero and the struggle for communal justice. Ideally these parallel struggles of the individual and the nation are projected to synthesize in the romance, but through the narrator's eyes Wister's novel eventually concedes this to be an impossibility.

Even so, both stories indicate shifts in cultural forms preceding expression; they define—rather than are defined by—categories of the culture's symbolic vocabulary. Early in the novel, the plot shifts from being a historical romance to an allegory of evolution.[27] In fact, Wister's account of the world emergent through this (still romantic) drama—that is, the product of the forces of narrative design—is nothing less than shocking.

As the novel ends, readers are left with a summary of the Virginian's life from his ascension to ranch partner: Judge Henry, the Virginian's old boss, has succeeded so well in the western economy that "his presence" is needed "in many places distant from his ranch." That success enables him to solidify the Virginian's domesticated status. As a "wedding present," Judge Henry makes "the Virginian his partner." In this position, however, the Virginian is preoccupied with "forestall[ing]" economic disasters visited upon Wyoming by "the thieves" who were "prevail[ing] at length," and when even he can forestall disaster no more, he removes himself in order to allow "the thieves [to bring] ruin on themselves" (392). At this point *The Virginian's* narrator says of the West, with a combination of sadness and relief, that "there [was] nothing left to steal" (392). If the Virginian's social ascent has gone according to evolutionary plan, it has been ironically shadowed by the simultaneous decline of his world. Rather than proving to be a vindication of the true power of social Darwinism to explain cultural change, then, the scope of Wister's romance becomes instead an enactment of the problem that William James had termed "the dilemma of determinism."

Access to knowledge beyond determinism is systematically shut down in the course of Wister's romance plot. The powerlessness of the hero to preserve and transmit the world, which he alone was the last to know, is a tragedy unfolding beyond the limits of his individual strength. The outlines of this separate narrative of loss may be sketched between those two key episodes, representing the highest and lowest points of the hero's physical strength. The Virginian ironically is equally powerless during the climactic vigilante execution of his old friend Steve and in the scene of his own near death in the forest, the result of that unnarrated attack presumably made by Indians.

Wister described his earlier cowboy hero, Specimen Jones, as a figure of powerful self-deception, a figure suggesting the personified frontier West at the turn of the century: "Perfect health and strength kept him from discovering that he was a saddened, drifting man."[28] The Virginian's character development proves him to be nothing like a composite or successor to heroes of the Old West, but rather to be a figure for Specimen Jones, now come to consciousness and tragically aware of his displacement. He is the living embodiment of a late stage in America's use of the frontier myth. From a nostalgic point of view, he is an elegy to the closed possibilities of the last century, while within his own world he loses the agency that made him the hero he seemed to be. He can face only a tragic fate because that late-structured identity is no more than a simple epitaph. In that late myth of the West, there would be no hero, only the correction of the easterner's mistaken vision of the West as curative symbol.

Like his culture, Wister looked to be—but could not be—"cured" by his visions of the West. As a young patient in 1885—afflicted with anxiety and despair—Wister would look outside for cures only to be left with a lifelong battle within himself; so too, the easterner's America would look west for renewal, only to be turned back upon itself in recognition of the costs of nationalism. If Wister's novel expresses the suspicion that William James was right, that human history was more volatile and less patterned than social Darwinists and Spencerians believed, it is also clear in its visionary fear.[29] If agency were to be restored at random, rather than slowly harnessed to the progress of history, the novel argues, not only the West but indeed America would end as "a broken country" with "nothing left to steal" (392).

CONCLUSION
The Storyteller's Legacy from Quentin
Compson to Oedipa Maas

If the myth is the a priori story of history, it cannot be a mere
product of imagination, or even of millenniums-long selection.
The Romantic revival of the "original revelation," this highly visible reversal of the schema of progress, becomes inevitable. While
its content is not something that had withdrawn, once and for all,
from any experience, it clearly is something that could not always
be experiencible, because it only constitutes philosophy's late
experience of history.
> —Hans Blumenberg, *Work on Myth*

Stories are told in order to "kill" something. In the most harm-
less, but not least important case: to kill time. In another and
more serious case: to kill fear.
> —Hans Blumenberg, *Work on Myth*

F O R purposes of suggesting how the legacy of the storyteller—from
Cooper's Spy through Hester Prynne to the Virginian—may have
shaped possibilities for varieties of historical fiction in the twentieth century, I wish to close with brief considerations of one quintessentially modern text—William Faulkner's *Absalom, Absalom!* (1936)—and one
quintessentially postmodern text—Thomas Pynchon's *Crying of Lot 49*
(1965). Though significantly deviating from any generic definition of the
classic historical romance, both of these extraordinary novels address questions familiar to that genre and prove themselves to be deeply rooted in
similarly complex relations among history, language, and nation building.
To see the legacy of the narrative model discussed in the previous chapters
within these later fictions, the defining terms of *narrative design* and *secret
history* might be broadened a bit to allow for the span of years, techniques,

and ideas that separate Faulkner and Pynchon. Narrative design in this context may include any attempt to order the received world through a totalizing imaginative vision, and secret histories may include whatever events of lived history influence the present day by yet standing in need of definition. These secret histories may be considered to be equally strong whether manifest as an emergent topic of preoccupation or a more fully elusive topic, falling outside of the present consciousness of the text.

In the introduction to this book, I noted that in the examples of Cooper, Hawthorne, and Wister, my argument offers sites primarily of depth, not breadth. Yet, as I also note at other times, there is a teleology implied in my argument.[1] Particularly in the study of *The Virginian* as a text marking a shift away from formal and historical patterns linking profound cultural knowledge with silent marginality, this book implies changes unfolding throughout the nineteenth-century American historical romance. My argument positions the Virginian as a character enacting a shift from storyteller to ideologue, and in this I see a paradigm for the cultural institutionalization of literature that occurred between the ages of Cooper and Wister.

To see the Virginian—as he exists at the end of the novel—outside of the model of the storyteller is to see his silence as a space mapped not by raw conflicting energies of consent and discord but by a crude form of ideology, close to what we might term propaganda. By this I mean that in *The Virginian*, the central character's mysteries are absorbed into a story whose ideology is monologic, a force of stabilization and transmission, while the force I imagine in the process of cultural storytelling—reflective of the condition of the Spy, Hester Prynne, the Virginian in his early episodes, and, as I argue below, later characters from Faulkner and Pynchon—certainly is still ideological but is a force of *de*-stabilization and transmission, demonstrative of a cultural condition in which the story to be told necessitates a disruption in historical consciousness.

Of course, this argument implies the lesser cultural (as well as aesthetic) elasticity of *The Virginian* when compared with *The Spy* or *The Scarlet Letter*, but that is not to say that such elasticity would never again be a part of narrative silence in romances of American national identity. It is to emphatically correct any such implications that I choose here the examples of *Absalom, Absalom!* and *The Crying of Lot 49*, both of which provide us with images of silence and secrecy that have not been made safe by the ideological forces of their world; these are dynamic, even culturally risky, historical fictions.

Both *Absalom, Absalom!* and *The Crying of Lot 49* play upon the precisely wrought expectations of American culture's reception of the historical romance, and both do so in similar ways. Both novels—though each differently—return their audiences to the predicament of the reader of the nineteenth-century American historical romance. In order to enter into the fictional world presented, readers are compelled to believe in the powers of narrative design while at the same time remaining open to the radical challenges of historical experience that resonate just below the surface of the plot. Both fictional worlds lock character and reader perception within a specifically, self-consciously, American world, one now distinctive not for its neutral grounds awaiting definition, but rather overdetermined by history.

Here in this new America, language is superfluous, at least insofar as it carries none of the traditional powers (or burdens) of creating or shaping cultural experience. In both novels experience has long since eluded the containment that language has traditionally enforced. For Faulkner, the idea of containing history within narrative remains a compulsion, but one doomed to fail; his various narrators provide an array of different avenues to the same end, the degeneracy of language and the (haunting) persistence of the history beyond its bounds. Here history is the force that, in its inevitable reemergence, shatters the false coherence offered by narrative or even language in general. The relationship between history and language in *Absalom, Absalom!* is fundamentally a struggle for sole dominance that must leave one category decimated, and despite the best efforts of many of the narrative voices, history—again, in the sense of lived experience—will prove the stronger.

For Pynchon, all forms of history, personal and cultural, are deeply buried beneath an outer shell, a shell covered all too profusely with apparently symbolic designs that seem to hold experience together as an abstract coherence. But those designs—collectively, as the apparent coherence they suggest—in turn point only to their own emptiness. In this way, designs in Pynchon's text indicate that something has gone wrong in the text's fictional world: The intricacy of these designs asks that we assume foundational creative and interpretive energies in this narrative world, only then to insist upon the meaninglessness of what they create and interpret.

No less than Faulkner's world, this too is a trap, simply one of a different order. For Pynchon history itself is a puzzle, for which language—like all other vehicles of potential order, such as time—is simply one reservoir of clues. The entrapment within these clues in *The Crying of Lot 49* threatens not the decimation of history or language, but its less violent twin, utter confusion. Here, if history and language could negotiate one another's demands, a fundamental epistemological reality would emerge as a puzzle solved, but the very possibility of such negotiations, Oedipa's

fruitless search will show, is illusory. This trap—this mad collection of
clues in pursuit of a truth that may no longer exist, if it ever did—is dangerous not only because of the decidedly indistinct relation between clue
and puzzle but also because of the manic proliferation of such clues, which
creates an aura of expectation and hope by means of which the journey is
extended indefinitely.

In the nineteenth-century texts studied in the previous chapters, secret
histories within narrative designs function as expressions of extraordinary
anxiety. In the twentieth-century texts discussed here, that anxiety has
risen to the point of madness. In Faulkner's novel, madness takes the form
of terror, while in Pynchon's novel it reaches beyond terror to a space in
consciousness where only paranoia offers a comparatively safe refuge.

"A MEAGER AND FRAGILE THREAD"

Absalom, Absalom! draws attention to the shift in narrative balance that distinguishes the modern and postmodern variations of the model of cultural
storytelling from the nineteenth-century studies in this book. Despite the
extraordinary efforts of each of Faulkner's narrators and despite their formidable set of defenses including an almost impenetrable southern gentility, history and not romance takes the upper hand in his novel. As we have
seen, the nineteenth-century historical romance in America characteristically employs narrative designs to frame the culture's mysteries. Even the
most challenging of these mysteries, secrets, or silences—challenging to
the stasis represented by plot—are perhaps haunted, but not dominated, by
history. Those earlier romances suggest an awareness that narrative designs
cannot dispel the ambiguities of experience, but what they can do, apparently, is encode them. Here in Faulkner's text, though, history will not
remain buried, whether dispelled or encoded. Instead the form of the novel
enacts a battle that results in a shift in power from the romance vision to
history; with this shift, we can see in twentieth-century American fiction
a trend toward historical consciousness tinged with a madness brought on
by an inability not only to master but even to frame its own memories.

The narrative designs of Faulkner's central characters—Thomas Sutpen, Quentin Compson, and Rosa Coldfield—offer three variations on the
modern limits that restrict the power of narrative to quiet the discord of
history. Faulkner shows us that each of these characters is animated by a
dream of making sense of a disordered world. Each narrator must confront
the implicit promise of language that encourages the attempt to tell a full,
whole, story, and yet each finds that—when mapped onto lived history—

such a narrative is no more than a "meager and fragile thread ... by which the little surface corners of men's secret and solitary lives may be joined for an instant now and then before sinking back into the darkness" (313). For Cooper, "darkness" lurked "beyond" all "visible space" of the narrated world; for Faulkner, darkness is the normative state, against which small fragments of reason may cast their vain hopes for the light of order.

Thomas Sutpen's vision of his dynasty represents the blindest of all dreams in the novel, but as Rosa says of him, *"If he was mad, it was only his compelling dream which was insane and not his methods"* (207). With obsessive logic, Sutpen plots his design onto the course of his broken life. Yet his task is impossible, as even he knows. Nothing more clearly signals the futility of Sutpen's demands to control history completely and to live in a world of separateness and fixity than the fact that this design has been conceived in a moment of history's most brutal intrusion into his consciousness, his realization of his class status, which has determined and will continue to determine his social identity.

At the age of fourteen, Sutpen's "innocence" is shattered (or his social identity is confirmed) by a black servant who, in turning him away from entry at a front door, calls attention to the boy's evident poverty and low social standing. The event reveals to Sutpen his relation to the social world, which he, as a young man, is about to enter. In order to make this necessary transition—that is, literally to live in time and history, he must make sense of this new (and unwelcome) consciousness of his own place in this culture. Sutpen's task, that is, is to accommodate the loss of innocence through which knowledge comes; however, he finds himself unable to translate this moment.

Instead, Faulkner narrates the flowering of madness through every word and action of denial. Sutpen responds with a vision of his conscious self as if suddenly separate from the world. He cannot, will not, understand himself as he must exist in the world of experience, and so—within his own fantasy—he wills himself back out of time and history. There, in a realm where a fixed and simplified vision of the past denies the existence of the present, Sutpen will live out the rest of his life, denying any human truth that he sees shaded with the taint of time or historical experience.

Echoing the process of early nation building in colonial and nineteenth-century America, Sutpen spins his romance by entering upon a project of world making. He responds to his trauma by going to a new land and learning a new language. Upon arriving in Haiti, Sutpen feels the necessity to master the French language, or else, Faulkner writes, "that design to which he had dedicated himself would die stillborn" (309). If we consider Sutpen's relation to the French language to be emblematic of the powers of narrative over lived experience, we can see the devastating irony of Faulkner's vision of narrative design. As Sutpen willfully begins his dynasty, he chooses the name "Bon" as the French surname for his son, in effect naming him "Charles [the] Good" (331).

Ironically, that act of naming is not just the first but also the final exertion of control that Sutpen has over this son; Charles Bon is raised to be, and indeed fulfills the role of, "the dynamite which destroys the house and the family and maybe even the whole community" (382). In fact, the haunting trace of this particular effort toward mastery is the final defeat of Sutpen's line—the narrative survival of the invented name and the historical survival of the family become one in Jim Bond, "the scion, the last of his race" (468). Bond's altered name and distant mind represent the degeneration of Sutpen's ideals into a different form of madness, one well beyond the control of language.

The designs imposed over history in *Absalom, Absalom!* thus implode upon themselves. With this disintegration, there is a parallel and ironic intensification of the terror of historical consciousness. This terror is located in the book's secret histories, those stories that language neither fully reveals nor fully conceals; they emerge with a power most threatening to Quentin Compson, the designated heir to the narrative. Like Sutpen ninety years before him, Quentin is the young and unwilling recipient of particular knowledge fundamental to the social and political workings of the world he is about to enter. Like Sutpen, too, Quentin wants nothing more than to escape to a new life, free of the entanglements of history, culture, and the determinism imposed, in his case, by family. Toward the close of the novel, when narrative responsibility is completely suspended and without personal voice, Quentin's impulse to avoid the impending knowledge is clear; so too is his impulse to sustain the narrative gap—the buffer between his own knowledge and the realities of history. He approaches Sutpen's old home "telling himself, recovering himself in that same breath: 'I am not afraid. I just dont want to be here. I just dont want to know ...'" (456):

> He could not help it. He was twenty years old; he was not afraid, because what he had seen out there could not harm him, yet he ran; even inside the dark familiar house, his shoes in his hand, he still ran, up the stairs and into his room and began to undress, fast, sweating, breathing fast. "I ought to bathe," he thought: then he was lying on the bed ... he said "I have been asleep" it was all the same, there was no difference ... waking or sleeping it was the same and would be the same forever as long as he lived. (464)

Quentin can run, try to sleep or bathe, but there is no escape. History will be his grave, and language will be his winding sheet: History has come for him through the very language with which he had tried so hard to keep it at bay.

History's forces, furthermore, do not end with the reception of the emergent story, because they insist on regeneration by insisting on finding their storyteller. The story of the house is transmitted to Quentin, and what becomes even more devastating is that it is up to him, on the last page of the novel, to provide an answer to Shreve, his Canadian roommate, who asks (again): "Why do you hate the South?" (471) Quentin is the chosen recipient of what remains of that narrative design's power over his world, but simultaneously, he is also a sacrificial martyr to the powerful persistence of history's unremitting challenges to that design. For Quentin as for Sutpen, the more the story is told and retold, the more the secrets of history rise up, closing in on the shattering of narrative design.

By the time Quentin and Shreve have finished their storytelling marathon, power has shifted so completely away from language and toward history that Quentin's voice itself fails him. In the last words of the book, Faulkner indicates the shift away from Quentin's capacity for speech. Referring to the South, its history, and his family's entanglements within it, Quentin fights his own self-consciousness: " 'I dont hate it,' [he] said, quickly, at once, immediately; 'I dont hate it,' he said. *I dont hate it* he thought, panting in the cold air, the iron New England dark; *I dont. I dont! I dont hate it! I dont hate it!*" (471). The narrative defenses of the book have been exhausted, and this scream of denial, at a pitch beyond human speech, reflects a final tragic conflation between the degeneration of language and its ironic parallel, the revelation of an experiential knowledge that cannot, even must not, be brought into the shared narrative of culture.

Here, the monologic narrative of design has been stripped away to its essential element, denial, but it is in fact a recognizable reworking of the same design that began in Sutpen's Hundred, this time showing forcefully that the historical consciousness of an individual, a family, or a culture remains potent—indeed, perhaps intensifies—even when the means for the expression of it do not. For both Sutpen and Quentin, stories not only prove to be an inadequate buffer against history, but they also become the actual conduits through which time and experience shatter imaginative order. Although there is a difference in their respective madnesses—Sutpen's so cruel and exploitative, Quentin's so filled with fear—Faulkner dooms them equally, dooms us all equally, to the inevitable resurgence of the tide of history within our words.[2]

Narrative designs are not enough to allow Rosa Coldfield to make sense of the outrages of history, either, but because she fatalistically understands the limits of language—its tragic association with romantic design—her manipulation of it provides her with a form of vengeance against Sutpen, who had mortally offended her many years before. With all of her own designs broken, Rosa is not destroyed but instead has a peculiarly rich sense of the catastrophic; within this, she may see the tragic futility of language. Rosa's acceptance of the inherent limits of communication comes clear through the very abundance of her words:

> I will tell you what he did and let you be the judge. (Or try to tell you, because there are some things for which three words are three too many, and three thousand words that many words too less, and this is one of them. It can be told; I could take that many sentences, repeat the bold blank naked outrageous words just as he spoke them, and bequeath you only that same aghast and outraged unbelief I knew when I comprehended what he meant; or take three thousand sentences and leave you only that Why? Why? and Why? that I have asked and listened to for almost fifty years.) But I will let you be the judge and let you tell me if I was not right. (208)

Rosa's narrative is told with the strong presence of her latent knowledge that she is participating in the inevitable disintegration of all narratives of design, and I think it is not too much to see in her storytelling some measure of vengeance for Sutpen's willing subjugation of all that is human to his impossible design. She tells her story not to preserve history, which is only humiliation to her. But in recalling Sutpen's barbaric assaults on her very existence and that of others, perhaps she chooses to participate in the further unraveling of Sutpen's story. Rosa passes her version of the story on because she wants it told and retold within that insufficient medium—language—so that she can *fail* as a storyteller and further doom others to the same failure. Her failure, I would argue, is the means by which she can do the most damage to Sutpen; it is the means to the absolute contamination of his master design through the repeated contact of the world of life and time that is necessary for the manifestation of the storyteller's voice. The force of Rosa's vengeance is not her condemnation of Sutpen's actions, nor any intentional distortion of his history. It is the perpetual regeneration of a story that, with every thought, word, and action of the teller or listener, necessarily moves farther away from the purity of design to which Sutpen had dedicated his life.

Rosa and Clytie, Sutpen's daughter born of his slave, ensure that Sutpen's

design will be broken beyond repair, and that—in ever more distorted fragments—it will endure well into the unknown expanse of future generations, a haunting mockery of the denial of time and history at the center
of his vision. Clytie sees to it that what remains of the design is finally the
sole property of a madman—Jim Bond—who, as Faulkner's appendix tells
us, "disappeared from Sutpen's Hundred" in 1910, living still, "whereabouts
unknown" (477). She awaits the discovery of the wasted Henry Sutpen by
Rosa and Quentin, for they would breathe life into the story again and
again, their lives thus becoming reenactments of the failure of Sutpen's
design just as she had allowed Jim Bond to escape the burning house, to
go running through the wilderness moaning and bellowing. Her
vengeance is not so much the burning of the house as it is the perpetua-
tion of the dynasty in a form that parodies every one of Sutpen's original
ideals—from his racist desires for "purity" in his lineage through all of his
other dreams of order. Faulkner writes:

> . . . and then for a moment maybe Clytie appeared in that window from
> which she must have been watching the gates constantly day and night
> for three months—the tragic gnome's face beneath the clean headrag,
> against a red background of fire, seen for a moment between two swirls
> of smoke, looking down at them, perhaps not even now of triumph and
> no more of despair than it had ever worn, possibly even serene above the
> melting clapboards before the smoke swirled across it again—and he, Jim
> Bond, the scion, the last of his race, seeing it too now and howling with
> human reason now since even he could have known what he was howl-
> ing about. But they couldn't catch him. They could hear him; he didn't
> seem to ever get any further away but they couldn't get any nearer and
> maybe in time they could not even locate the direction of the howling.
> (468)

No dramatic annihilation in flames can redeem this story of the south
because it exists to be told and retold in so many distorted and fragmented
voices. Jim Bond's cries provide a telling example of one of those configu-
rations of that story; in a dialogic sense, his voice simply responds to every
past failure of narrative design by merging the madness of the dream of
order with the madness of the method of telling; along with Quentin's
inability to speak as the novel closes, Bond's words, the novel suggests,
stand as one of the most efficient accounts of the history surrounding
Thomas Sutpen; it is thus fitting that when Shreve asks Quentin, "you've
got [Bond] there still. You still hear him at night sometimes. Dont you?,"
Quentin says only, "Yes" (471).

"SHALL I PROJECT A WORLD?"

To return to the terms of my analysis: the narrative form created by the interactions of romantic designs and historical secrets first may suggest repression or the failures of memory, but as Faulkner's novel emphatically shows, that form also provides avenues through which—for better or worse—the residual life of history may reenter present experience. History is never gone, and language is never bankrupt, because their limits and failures together form a space apart, where secret histories may gain the strength to become the most vital forces in, or symbols of, culture. Once fixed or appropriated, symbols lose their dynamic potential, their capacity to transform the communities they serve; they become possessions of culture rather than creative agents of it. But outside of the security (and corresponding restrictions) of known cultural patterns, these symbols generated by historical secrecy may work instead in regions of limitless possibility and undirected energy. In these gaps of definition, rather than in known or named functions, cultural symbols gain their power and sustain their life.

The dual legacy of the function of narrative silence within romantic design—its capacity to solicit both fear and reverence—provides the framework also for the issues of language and history in Pynchon's *The Crying of Lot 49*. Oedipa Maas, Pynchon's central character, quite accidentally falls into a pursuit of history fueled through an exploration of the powers and limits of language, and it is a search destined to end in a form of exile. *The Crying of Lot 49* is a novel about the possibilities of language, about what it can bring to life and what it cannot; it is a story built around a quest to find some interior meaning and to identify the avenues or impediments to that meaning. The immediate problem in Pynchon's America is a sense that all historical knowledge has been lost and that there are no known avenues to its recovery; thus the novel explores the opposite terror from Faulkner's, where history is all too close. In Oedipa's world, those characters who devote themselves to an understanding of the past—even simply of one very limited event or symbol of the past—are pushed outside of the workings of everyday life. To be a working part of Pynchon's America, one must accept that in this already too crowded present, there surely is no room for the past. This point is made vividly within the text, when Metzger, the former child-actor, now lawyer, is questioned about the fact that innumerable graves were plowed up in order to build a new freeway: he explains simply that the dead "had no right to be there, anyway" (61).

Oedipa wants to know why America has tended toward dissipation even as it has grown more crowded, seemingly more fully labeled, more easily defined. It is as if the culture's surface has become so completely covered by names, freeways, buildings, and billboards, that it is hard to tell what—if anything—is underneath, holding it all together. Maybe, the novel implicitly muses, this surface of America is just a flat plane of dispersed atoms, with nothing underneath it but what is already dead. In fact, maybe even the dead have been broken apart, as they were under the San Narcisso Freeway. But even if this is true, even if the legacy or history that Oedipa pursues is *this* image of America, she has dedicated herself to making sense of it: "So began, for Oedipa, the languid, sinister blooming of The Tristero. Or rather, her attendance at some unique performance, prolonged as if it were the last of the night, something a little extra for whoever'd stayed this late. . . . [It seemed] as if a plunge toward dawn indefinite black hours long would indeed be necessary before The Tristero could be revealed in its terrible nakedness" (54). Pynchon places us in a world where there is a double danger to language. It is dangerous if we give up, if we say that the clues given by words and symbols are enough, that they don't have to signify something more. The danger there is clear: the world would be left devoid of any imaginative structure. But it is dangerous too if we try to follow meaning to its end. Maybe those secrets to be revealed would be less fulfilling than terrifying. This double danger to language in Pynchon's novel is a legacy of American self-definition in the tradition of the nineteenth-century historical romance. It leaves his hero trapped, afraid to stop searching for what she still fantasizes might be "the Word," but afraid, too, of what that and other words might say.

Oedipa is faced with the overabundance of clues and the inaccessibility of sure knowledge. Unlike Thomas Sutpen, she cannot respond by blindly projecting a new design, a new language, or a new symbol system over her world; there is, literally, no room left for that. There may not even be enough room to discover—or recover—what has been done and said already. When Randy Driblette, the director of the revenge tragedy staged in the novel, says to Oedipa, "you could waste your life assembling clues and never touch the truth" (80), he is undoubtedly right, but that is only half of the problem to which Pynchon draws our attention. He also wants us to ask where the world would be left if no one made the effort to assemble clues anymore. Melville's Ahab,[3] too, may have wasted his life by assembling clues about the white whale, and certainly he crossed over into madness. But judged by other standards—specifically by romantic or visionary standards—both Ahab and Oedipa might be said to maintain a different kind of responsibility, the responsibility to assert the power of imagination in a world that will never confirm their vision. In the Tristero, Oedipa senses that there is "a secret richness, a concealed density of dream"

(170). For her, its great draw is not only its mystery but also its specific offer of possible communication. Perhaps this secret system might provide an entire network of communication, which would compensate for the failures of the mainstream culture. This speculation is the closest that anyone in Oedipa's world can come to the formulation of a romantic design; it is the interpretation of the barren spirit of modern America as a shell that must be enclosing a dynamic system. Somewhere, the seeker then believes, is a prize—so alive as to seem to bear its own agency, and thus eagerly awaiting the arrival of its own discoverer.

But the Tristero system, the secret that propels Oedipa's journey, is a *subversive* system of language, a communication system thought to be a threatening alternative to the U.S. Mail. Oedipa is not a naturally subversive character. It seems unlikely that she would want to see the government postal system overthrown; she is, after all, a suburban housewife whose past refuges have included Tupperware parties, television, and the Young Republicans; Oedipa cannot think about the possibility of discovery without some elements of dread and shock. The best qualities of the Tristero as she imagines it are also those that make it most frightening: it provides an image of a separate world, an undefined alternative to the emptiness she knows. It also helps her to explain the emptiness she knows: maybe, she thinks, the Tristero system damaged America, caused the lack of connection and general dissipation of the world she knows. But if so, then that once-subversive system is now more appealing: it may be a storehouse of energy and communication that she can access in order to retrieve those powers for her own world.

Caged in this world of paradox, Oedipa needs nothing short of a miracle to achieve what she imagines. An anarchist from Mexico whom Oedipa meets on her journey explains to her that a miracle is "another world's intrusion into this one. Most of the time we coexist peacefully, but when we do touch there's cataclysm" (120). Miracles are hard to come by in Pynchon's world, and it is not entirely clear what might be gained when those two narrative worlds—the worlds of order and of secrecy—do meet. In fact, it is surely significant that the Tristero, which stands for the world of revelation—is, if it exists at all, by definition a counterfeit and a fraud. But what Pynchon's book shows is that both of these worlds are necessary to the imagination, even if the world of design is weak and easily contradicted, and even if the world of historical knowledge is just another fantasy.

Just another fantasy—not the revelation of history but a deeper layer of fiction: this postmodern dilemma makes this novel at once more and less terrifying than *Absalom, Absalom!*. Faulkner frightens us with the vision that all imaginative forms lead back to an unspeakable nightmare of history; Pynchon reminds us that that nightmare is our own, relived as it is re-imagined. Oedipa's decision in the face of all of this is a decision in favor of the intrusion of historical consciousness, whatever it might bring, into an otherwise weak, depleted, and altogether inadequate present consciousness. She chooses paranoia over emptiness: "For there either was some Tristero beyond the appearance of the legacy America, or there was just America and if there was just America then it seemed the only way she could continue, and manage to be at all relevant to it, was as an alien, unfurrowed, assumed full circle into some paranoia" (182). Oedipa's paranoia might be her chosen form of madness, her assertion of a design narrative that, she hopes, may remain vulnerable to contradiction, to the infusion of miracle, while also helping her to appropriate a sense of order into her life. More so than most narratives of design, Oedipa's paranoia is particularly powerful because it provides a complex means of acknowledging greater depths of experience than are accessible otherwise, while simultaneously transforming whatever might lurk in these depths within a controlled structure of the imagination. But for whatever liberation it provides, paranoia surely is a trap as well; like a fun-house mirror, it is a trap of infinite self-referentiality.

The compensations that these twentieth-century American narratives offer for the recognition of the limits of language in the face of history are small but not insignificant—Quentin's speechless denials, Oedipa's consuming paranoia. Although these texts suggest that one form of madness or another is the fate of these storytellers who are doomed by the brittleness of language, still in that madness they imagine a site of consciousness beyond the recognition of the limits of language. With these final scenes of silent creativity conflated with historical consciousness, these characters remind us of what the martyrdoms of the Spy and Hester Prynne, as well as the losses of the Virginian, deferred from their own times. When both language and history seem to fail in perhaps such different ways from one another, then particularly there is much work for the resonant silences of culture to do, drawing together the fragments of each into a new, if still residual, language.

None of the narratives studied here fully enacts that language, and their attendant secrets change form as they move through history. As Georg Simmel has written, "the secret is a form which constantly receives and releases contents: what originally was manifest becomes secret, and what once was hidden later sheds its concealment."[4] Even if it were possible, then, to uncover what is hidden in each of the studied narratives, that process would not make the narrative form studied here redundant. Just as we come to see some of what destroyed Thomas Sutpen, for example—

that is, precisely during the very moments in which we have been figuring that out—new matters have accumulated. Returning to Borges's Funes: just as we come face to face with some matters of memory, personal and collective alike, we push others aside. However, as Pynchon's novel so brilliantly demonstrates, that process makes the quest to understand the past look futile only until we consider the alternative, the utter loss of history and memory, a willing submersion in the business of the everyday (such as the world from which Oedipa has come, the world of "Tupperware part[ies]," "the greenish dead eye of the TV tube," "Muzak," and "supermarket booze" [9–10, 13]). And so to look for what history has to say, to listen to the resonant silences of culture, may be forever to await revelation, even at times to be caught looking at the banalities of the everyday as if they were indeed revelation. Or, it may be to find revelation not in the transcendent but in layers, in histories, in fragments embedded in our world. But even in the high parodic form of this condition of desire—as it is imagined in the final scene of *The Crying of Lot 49*—Oedipa, as she waits and listens, has come a long way. Eager for the auction cry of "Loren Passerine, the finest auctioneer in the West," Oedipa waits in a deeply resonant narrative silence of her own; and there, just as in the secret histories within the American narratives studied throughout this book, that silence continues to entice her imagination and ours, while still resisting cultural definition. The parody is evident, but still, with Oedipa, readers feel in this silence—as in others within the romances studied in this book—the continued encoding of both the promises and the dangers of what history might have to tell. Pynchon writes all of this into his extraordinary closing scene:

> Loren Passerine, on his podium, hovered like a puppet-master, his eyes bright, his smile practiced and relentless. He stared at [Oedipa], smiling, as if saying, I'm surprised you actually came. Oedipa sat alone, toward the back of the room, looking at the napes of necks, trying to guess which one was her target, her enemy, perhaps her proof. An assistant closed the heavy door on the lobby windows and the sun. She heard a lock snap shut; the sound echoed a moment. Passerine spread his arms in a gesture that seemed to belong to the priesthood of some remote culture; perhaps to a descending angel. The auctioneer cleared his throat. Oedipa settled back, to await the crying of lot 49. (183).

Perhaps the passivity of expectation is Oedipa's one mistake: the silences of these narrative worlds do not seem prone to speaking to us; they offer instead a call to interpretation. It may never be fully clear what historical forces drive the creation of narrative silences, but it must be clear that—aesthetically and historically—it is imperative that we notice these silences, and further that we do what we can to excavate them, to read what they have to tell us about history and art, cultural process and aesthetic form.

NOTES

Notes to Introduction

1. Among others, Michael Kammen's *Season of Youth: The American Revolution and the Historical Imagination* provides ample evidence for this claim.

2. I refer in particular to the work of Sacvan Bercovitch (*The Office of the Scarlet Letter*) and of Jonathan Arac, "The Politics of The Scarlet Letter."

3. See Yuri M. Lotman, *Universe of the Mind: A Semiotic Theory of Culture.*

4. My interest in secrecy in American literature is part of a tradition, including Gordon Hutner's *Secrets and Sympathy: Forms of Disclosure in Hawthorne's Novels;* Robert S. Levine's *Conspiracy and Romance: Studies in Brockden Brown, Cooper, Hawthorne, and Melville;* and most recently, Paul Downes's *Democracy, Revolution, and Monarchism in Early American Literature.*

5. This "cultural consciousness" might be imagined as much like Fredric Jameson's notion of "The Political Unconscious" (Jameson, *The Political Unconscious: Narrative as a Socially Symbolic Act*).

Northrop Frye defines the "archetypal symbol" generally to be "a natural object with a human meaning, and it forms part of the critical view of art as a civilized product, a vision of the goals of human work" (*Anatomy of Criticism: Four Essays,* 113). Within the context I am developing here, my working definition for the archetype both borrows from and modifies Frye's definition. A parallel definition that I posit here provisionally is "a human story with a cultural meaning, forming part of the critical view of art as a national product, a vision of the goals of social order."

6. The answers to which I refer here are those offered by the popular legends in each section of the book; these are answers only emergent to the contemporary audience but now familiar, that is, imagining the revolution as a force destructive to domestic tranquility.

7. Specifically, I would like to distinguish my narrative model from two familiar alternatives—the tropes of "the past surpassed" and "the past recuperated." (See these "master tropes" in Stephen A. Tyler, "On Being Out of Words," 1.) My sense of what is happening in the reemergence of history through narrative is neither overwriting nor recovery, but one more level of *re*-presentation, in which the audience is left with neither the "lies" of narrative nor the "truth" of history, but with an epistemological imperative for reinterpretation.

8. This aspect of my argument has been inspired by Benedict Anderson's foundational work, *Imagined Communities: Reflections on the Origin and Spread of Nationalism*, and by the debates that followed from that landmark text. See for example the essays in *Nationalism*, ed. John Hutchinson and Anthony D. Smith.

9. "Secrecy," as Elias Canetti argues, "lies at the very core of power" (*Crowds and Power*, 290).

10. Jorge Luis Borges, *Labyrinths: Selected Stories and Other Writings*, 59–66.

11. Blumenberg, *Work on Myth*, 597.

12. We might connect this level of language to Whitman's story of the American language in *An American Primer*. "These States," he writes, "are rapidly supplying themselves with new words, called for by new occasions, new facts, new politics, new combinations. . . . [W]ords continually used among the people are, in numberless cases, not the words used in writing, or recorded in the dictionaries by authority." And while representing something elusive or even defiant of authority, these new American words, Whitman notes, "are the body of the whole of the past." Though Whitman's tone does not suggest the dark repository of memory I would like to invoke here, his terms—especially the interdependence of history and language—are worth noting (*An American Primer*, 5, 7).

13. Benjamin writes: "His gift is the ability to relate his life; his distinction, to be able to tell his entire life. The storyteller: he is the man who could let the wick of his life be consumed completely by the gentle flame of his story" ("The Storyteller: Reflections on Nikolai Leskov," in *Illuminations: Essays and Reflections*, 108–9).

14. These framing narratives might more recognizably be termed narratives of containment, but I hope to challenge this more predictable argument in the readings that follow.

15. "Secrecy itself," argues Michael Taussig, may be seen "as the primordial act of presencing" (*Defacement: Public Secrecy and the Labor of the Negative*, 3). For Taussig, the effect of the unmasking of secrecy is something like the infinite unfolding of possible meanings ("Yet is the mystery dissipated by unmasking? It does not seem so. It merely changes and, perhaps, becomes even deeper, certainly more complex, on account of its revelation" [190]), while for earlier theorists of secrecy including Elias Canetti, the effects of unmasking cause the world to shrink (223). My sense of secrecy in this book is closer to Taussig's, though certain distinctions are made along the way.

16. Scott is absolutely an influence on each of the authors studied here; we may see, for instance, echoes of *Rob Roy* (1817) in *The Spy*, and the Puritan regicide, whose legend is of central concern in part 2 of this book, makes one of his mysterious appearances in *Peveril of the Peak* (1823). In fact it was both flattering and annoying to Cooper to be commonly known throughout the literary circles of his day as "The American Scott" (see George Dekker, *James Fenimore Cooper: The American Scott*, 20).

17. Brander Matthews argues that the form is so difficult as to be impossible; see *The Historical Novel and Other Essays*, 20.

18. Elisabeth Wesseling lists many of the genealogical arguments in *Writing History as a Prophet: Postmodernist Innovations of the Historical Novel*, 32; she offers origins that range from the ancient Greeks (see Helen Hughes, *The Historical Romance*, who cites the influence of Longinus's romances, 3), to Scottish philosophical histories; see also Dekker, *The American Historical Romance*, 11ff.

19. Georg Lukács, *The Historical Novel*, 35.

20. See ibid., 36ff. Ina Ferris provides a synthesis of a large critical consensus (and in terms particularly applicable to my argument) on the *Waverly*-hero: "Like [Scott] himself, his historical heroes found themselves living in unsympathetic ages; in the battles in which they fell, they had been able to sow the corn for future ages to harvest" (*The Achievement of Literary Authority: Gender, History, and the Waverly Novels*, 112).

21. One matter of interest in the interaction of character and context was, and is, the degree of determinism that may be inferred from one to the other. Lukács makes this one of his recurring questions, as have many who followed him, including Harry B. Henderson III (*Versions of the Past: The Historical Imagination in American Fiction*, 14–15, 52) and David Brown (*Walter Scott and the Historical Imagination*, esp. pp. 200–201).

22. See, for example, Harold Orel, *The Historical Novel from Scott to Sabatini: Changing Attitudes toward a Literary Genre, 1814–1920*, 20.

23. Lukács, *The Historical Novel*, 19.

24. Ibid., 25.

25. This subculture might be the American equivalent of Lukács's "mass" culture; to formulate the matter differently but to a similar end, we might say that the American historical romance works in the service of mass culture insofar as mass culture is ideologically reframed as the American republic.

26. While the great international traditions of this genre are not the focus of my argument, the evolution of the form of the historical romance in these traditions is a point of critical consensus with which I too agree. The strong presence of this tradition—whether one imagines it to start abruptly in 1814, with *Waverly*, or gradually, through the experiments with narrative romance over centuries—does not preclude the probability that local forces too are major components of each national incarnation of the form.

27. See Hughes, *Historical Romance*, 2.

28. Dekker, *The American Historical Romance*, see especially 15–16, 23–24, 26, 28, 220. Dekker is careful (as I too hope to be) to use his terminology precisely when referring to specific generic functions of the romance or the novel but argues that in other sections of his discussion, one term is as good as the next. In addition, like Lukács, Dekker gives an analysis of this hybridity of form that also takes into account the epic functions of historical romance/fiction. Dekker draws on Fredric Jameson, *The Political Unconscious: Narrative as a Socially Symbolic Act*, for some of this argument.

29. Alessandro Manzoni, *On the Historical Novel (1850)*.

30. Writing about Scott, Balzac, and Dreiser, Fredric Jameson argues that "the first great realisms are characterized by a fundamental and exhilarating heterogeneity in their raw materials and by a corresponding versatility in their narrative apparatus. In such moments, a generic confinement to the existent has a paradoxically liberating effect on the registers of the text, and release[s] a set of heterogeneous historical perspectives . . . normally felt to be inconsistent with a focus on the historical present" (*The Political Unconscious*, 104).

31. A rich and complex reassessment of this legacy is Ann Rigney's *Imperfect Histories: The Elusive Past and the Legacy of Romantic Historicism*.

32. Doris Sommer's analysis of Latin American romance is of interest here: "[T]he coherence [of these romances] comes from their common project to build through

reconciliations and amalgamations of national constituencies cast as lovers destined to desire each other." Sommer makes a compelling argument that, "in the national romance, one level represents the other and also fuels it, which is to say that both are unstable. The unrequited passion of the love story produces a surplus of energy . . . that can hope to overcome the political interference between the lovers" (*Foundational Fictions: The National Romances of Latin America*, 24, 47).

33. This frame is one manifestation of the category of order and design introduced earlier.

34. The image of the attic is conveniently spatial as well as suggestively temporal, but my larger point is that there are places (in the abstract sense) within narrative that harbor such possible articulations of the past. In the case of Hawthorne's novel, these "places" shift from the attic to the *A* to the consciousness of the narrator of the Custom House and finally to the consciousness of Hester Prynne herself, as she is reanimated.

35. Gordon Hutner, *Secrets and Sympathy: Forms of Disclosure in Hawthorne's Novels*, 6.

36. Here and throughout, my interests have an evolving context in new approaches to American studies. For example, in "Representative/Democracy: The Political Work of Countersymbolic Representation," Dana D. Nelson addresses "questions about where political practice overlaps with and is reshaped or limited or enabled by particular aesthetic modes of representation" (218). In this essay Nelson shows through the model of the countersymbolic the ways in which democracy and its cultural forms are not "reducible to containment of symbolic representation" and, further, that such models are not oppositional but instead "open up the spaces closed by the demands of unity" (240).

37. Whitman, *An American Primer*, 17.

38. Webster, preface to *An American Dictionary of the English Language*, reprinted in *The American Literary Revolution, 1783–1837*, 337. On the evolution of Webster's thought, see Spiller's headnotes to both of the selections in this collection, from *Dissertations* and the *Dictionary*, 59, 335, and Larry E. Tise, *The American Counterrevolution, 1783–1800*, 358–67.

39. In my emphasis on the peculiarly rich subjective consciousness of the "hero" in these historical romances, I depart from traditional critical analysis that attributes the decline of historical fiction to the lack of psychological development of the central character. Such arguments (Lukács, Dekker, et al.) contend that the psychological realism that follows the great ages of historical fiction bears witness to this lack within the central characters of the earlier genre; I concede the very different—indeed more open, knowable—representation of character consciousness in psychological realism, but I do not agree that the central figure of the historical fictions discussed here lacks internal complexity.

40. Victor Turner calls "articulation" the "presence of the past." See *Dramas, Fields, and Metaphors: Symbolic Action in Human Society*, 298.

41. Thus narrative may be identified with a specifically utopian cultural design. As Hans Blumenberg has written, "In its intensified instances utopia is the result of a sum of negations, when it is focused solely on avoiding contamination by what currently exists and when it culminates in a prohibition against saying anything positively imag-

ined and graphically descriptive about the new land as it will be after the bursting open of all delusion systems. . . . The utopian prohibition of images demands submission, by refusing to provide stories" (*Work on Myth*, 221).

42. Pynchon, *The Crying of Lot 49*, 59.

43. For fascinating discussions of the ironic and perhaps dangerous strength of social authority vested in those who insist on, or are trapped within, silence, see Mary Douglas's *Purity and Danger: An Analysis of the Concepts of Pollution and Taboo* and Michel de Certeau's *The Writing of History*.

44. In *Constituting Americans: Cultural Anxiety and Narrative Form*, Priscilla Wald compellingly addresses similar issues of known and hidden stories in American texts, arguing that "official stories are narratives that surface in the rhetoric of nationalist movements and initiatives. . . . They change in response to competing narratives of the nation that must be engaged, absorbed, and retold: the fashioning and endless refashioning of 'a people' " (2). For Wald, "disruptions in literary narratives caused by unexpected words, awkward grammatical constructions, rhetorical or thematic dissonances . . . mark the pressure of untold stories" (1), while my argument situates such stories among the layers of historical discourse.

45. Here again, Benjamin's terms are enlightening: "[N]ot only a man's knowledge or wisdom, but above all his real life—and this is the stuff that stories are made of— first assumes transmissible form at the moment of his death" ("The Storyteller," in *Illuminations*, 94).

46. This struggle among competing meanings layered in the text and in the consciousness of its readers has been discussed in many contexts; Fredric Jameson's definition is central to the concept as I use it in my argument: "Interpretation is not an isolated act, but takes place within a Homeric battlefield, on which a host of interpretive options are either openly or implicitly in conflict" (*The Political Unconscious*, 13).

47. See Taussig, *Defacement*, especially p. 2. Taussig's book focuses on a specific kind of secret—"the public secret," which he defines as "knowing what not to know" and characterizes as being a "mix of impenetrability and everydayness" (2, 162).

48. My first chapter clarifies this use of Cooper's sense of "visible space." It is a concept complemented by the extraordinary dangers Cooper hides in his wilderness; on these dangers, to characters and readers alike, see Philip Fisher's "Killing a Man: The Historical Novel and the Closing Down of Pre-History," in *Hard Facts: Setting and Form in the American Novel*.

49. Some indication of the distance between the agent and the story that I imagine here is described in helpful terms in the introduction to *Culture/Power/History: A Reader in Contemporary Social Theory*, ed. Nicholas B. Dirks, Geoff Eley, and Sherry B. Ortner: "If the cultural construction of the subject as an active agent must be concerned, at least in part, with the question of resisting or at least eluding that subjection . . . [f]rom a theoretical point of view we need a subject who is at once culturally and historically constructed, yet from a political perspective we would wish this subject to be capable of acting in some sense 'autonomously,' not simply in conformity to dominant cultural norms and rules. . . . But this autonomous actor may not be defined as acting from some hidden well of innate 'will' or consciousness that has somehow escaped cultural shaping and ordering. . . . 'Identities' may be seen as . . . *attempts* to create and maintain coherence out of inconsistent cultural stuff and inconsistent life experience,

but every actor always carries around enough disparate and contradictory strands of knowledge and passion so as always to be in a potentially critical position. Thus the practices of everyday life may be seen as replete with petty rebellions and inchoate discontent" (18).

50. We might say that he suffers the "sort of ontological freeze" that occurs when the "secret" becomes "the public secret"; Taussig argues that "the inherent capacity of beings to transform ceases" at this point (*Defacement*, 113).

51. Taussig, ibid., 6. As Taussig studies the transformation of the "secret," which he sees as "sealed and pure," into the "public secret," he argues that this latter form of secrecy acquires a " 'skin' or 'outer edge,' a "membrane pulsing with an inner, hidden, and presumably magnificent life"; in this way, he argues, "not-knowing" thus becomes "haunted by a secret history and by what seems . . . like a revolution in the very basis of identity and of relationship, a revolution in mimetic facility" (111).

52. William Faulkner, *Absalom, Absalom!* 124, 313.

53. It is important to note that the narrative secrets suggested throughout this manuscript are *not* being theorized exclusively or even particularly as trauma. In contrast to Cathy Caruth's *Unclaimed Experience: Trauma, Narrative, and History,* my interest lies in the fact that not only the deeply traumatic but often also the everyday are oddly, systematically, eclipsed at certain moments in narrative representation.

54. Jameson, *The Political Unconscious*, 85.

Notes to Chapter 1

1. Anon., "American Poetry," *Southern Quarterly Review* 1 (1842): 495.

2. See Robert A. Ferguson, "'We Hold These Truths': Strategies of Control in the Literature of the Founders," in *Reconstructing American Literary History*, 1–28.

3. Warner, *The Letters of the Republic: Publication and the Public Sphere in Eighteenth-Century America*; Looby, *Voicing America: Language, Literary Form, and the Origins of the United States*, 2; Fleigelman, *Declaring Independence: Jefferson, Natural Language, and the Culture of Performance.*

4. Josiah Quincy (1812) quoted in Richard Buel Jr., *Securing the Revolution: Ideology in American Politics, 1789–1815*, 282.

5. As Paul Downes argues, "To suggest that the American Revolution found its heroes outside of the visible circles of economic and political exchange is to suggest, of course, that secrecy was necessary to, and thus belongs to the formation of, the democratic United States" (*Democracy, Revolution, and Monarchism in Early American Literature*, 168).

6. Thomas Jefferson, letter to Albert Gallatin (Dec. 26, 1820), in *Writings*, 1448.

7. Caleb Cushing, *Eulogy* (Newburyport, Mass.), given for John Adams and Thomas Jefferson, in *A Selection of Eulogies . . . in Honor of . . . John Adams and Thomas Jefferson*, 48.

8. Trumbull, *Autobiography, Reminiscences and Letters of John Trumbull from 1756 to 1841*, 284, 286.

9. See for example the *United States Literary Gazette* 9 (3), Aug. 1, 1825, 239.

10. George Bancroft, in *Memorial of James Fenimore Cooper* (New York: G. P. Putnam, 1852), 76.

11. W. H. Gardiner, "Review," 7.

12. Cynthia Jordan also has written about the improvisational qualities of the new American story that emerges in the postrevolutionary years: These self-consciously national tales each offer "much needed, though still experimental, behavioral models to meet the unprecedented challenges to social stability and personal identity ushered in by the American Revolution. . . . [The story they tell is] of a society that has to make itself up as it goes along and of representative Americans who have to name and rename reality as new circumstances continue to arise." For Jordan these stories are driven by the cultural need to "repress self-striving" and to "defuse any . . . story that threatens the desired narrative—or sociopolitical—order," and they are characterized by strategies of language that "suppress the truth" (*Second Stories: The Politics of Language, Form, and Gender in Early American Fictions*, 1, 26).

My notion of the new American story focuses instead on the evolution of particular narrative strategies that addressed a cultural need to *include* matters of historical knowledge in stories of cultural identity.

13. Hawthorne, "The Custom House," in *The Scarlet Letter*, 38. Hawthorne's uses of romance are the subject of part 2 of this book.

14. Cooper, letter to Andrew Thompson Goodrich (July 12, 1820), in *The Letters and Journals of James Fenimore Cooper*, vol. 1, 49.

15. Compare, for example, John Neal's *1776* (1823). Neal explicitly contrasts his own "concept of realism" to Cooper's vision, which he finds limited. Donald Rindge writes: "Neal complains that Cooper's great fault is his lack of 'courage to describe what he sees; to record that, as it is—that, which he has power enough to see, as it is'" ("The American Revolution in American Romance," 353; citing Neal, from *Blackwood's*, 18 [1825], 317).

16. W. H. Gardiner, "Review," 66; Sarah Hale, "Review," *Port Folio*, 4th ser., vol. 13 (1822), 90.

17. W. H. Gardiner, "Review," 59, 61.

18. As Emily Miller Budick writes, "Cooper's neutral ground *is* history"; "this is the history of a nation coming into being on a neutral ground that does not stand between history and the imagination but is reality, a reality of conflicts, poses, and irreconcilable alternatives" (*Fiction and Historical Consciousness: The American Romance Tradition*, 6, 17). For a discussion focusing on the particularly significant *landscape* of the neutral ground, see H. Daniel Peck, *A World by Itself: The Pastoral Moment in Cooper's Fiction*, 96–100.

19. Shirley Samuels calls this "familiar scenario [in which] marital choices . . . are identical to political choices" "the congruence model" (*Romances of the Republic: Women, the Family, and Violence in the Literature of the Early American Republic*, 65). The Spy, as character and symbol, works outside of that model and thus accounts for the irresolution of an otherwise "congruent" romance.

20. It is worth noting that the interplay of these two plots creates early moments fraught with irony, which should alert readers that there is something more going on. For example, the polite social discourse of the parlor romance is here replaced with talk of killing (54), and the playful competition between sisters foreshadows the madness and destruction of the weaker of the two (51).

21. On the relation of various characters to this structure of deception, see Donald A. Ringe, *James Fenimore Cooper*, 15.

22. James Fenimore Cooper, *The Spy, A Tale of the Neutral Ground*, 294. All subsequent quotations are noted by page number parenthetically the text.

23. "[M]an is by nature a political animal. Any one who by his nature and not simply ill-luck has no state is either too bad or too good, either subhuman or superhuman. . . . [H]e who is such by nature is mad on war: he is a non-cooperator like an isolated piece in a game of draughts" (Aristotle, *The Politics*, vol. 1, ii, 59–60).

24. My understanding of such systems is indebted to Sacvan Bercovitch's discussion of "cultural symbology" in *The Rites of Assent*, 14–18.

Notes to Chapter 2

1. Adams to Jefferson, July 30, 1815, and Jefferson to Adams, August 10, 1815, in *The Adams-Jefferson Letters*, ed. Lester J. Cappon, 451–52.

2. Alexander Moultrie, "Oration on the Fourth of July," 5.

3. James Davis Knowles, "Oration on the Fourth of July," 8.

4. See for example, Adams, *Works*, vol. 10, 282. Looby argues that "Adams did not trust that words would call into being their adequate objects" (*Voicing America*, 26).

5. Joseph Sprague, "Eulogy" (Aug. 10, 1826), in *A Selection of Eulogies*, 259.

6. Paine, *Common Sense*, in *Common Sense and Other Political Writings*, 51.

7. McWilliams, *Hawthorne, Melville, and the American Character*, 26.

8. The quotations are from Fourth of July Orations by Charles Sprague, 20–21; Barnum Field, 13; Simeon H. Calhoun, 4.

9. Thomas Jefferson, letter to Major John Cartwright (June 5, 1824), in *Writings*, 1491.

10. Clifford Geertz, *The Interpretation of Cultures*, 311.

11. As David Simpson notes, such moments are useful in distinguishing "the most traditional speech habits" of a culture, but simultaneously, the "linguistic differences" evident at these times often work to impede "mutual comprehension" at the very moment when it "is most necessary and might make the greatest possible contribution"; thus the tendency, which I explain later, for stories of America to be most peculiarly revealing in their strategies of opacity and even silence (*The Politics of American English, 1776–1850*, 160).

12. Gordon S. Wood, "Introduction" to *The Rising Glory of America, 1760–1820*, 8, 3; emphasis added.

13. Virgil, *The Eclogues*, vol. 4, pp. 5, 57. As Michael Warner notes, the language of nationalism that emerges early in America "can be sharply distinguished from the kind of literary nationalism that would become powerful in the 1830"—and so provides the context to my next chapter, on Hawthorne—"because republican trade nationalism did not entail a liberal ideology of the literary" (*Letters of the Republic*, 121–22).

14. Here and throughout this section of the book I use the term "nation" to denote the modern form of the American community. But as Eric Hobsbawm notes, much of the rhetoric of the early United States "preferred to speak of 'the people,' 'the union,' 'the confederation,' 'our common land,' 'the public,' 'public welfare,' or 'the community' in order to avoid the centralizing and unitary implications of the term 'nation' against the rights of the federated states" (*Nations and Nationalism since 1780*, 18).

15. Benedict Anderson, *Imagined Communities: Reflections on the Origin and Spread of Nationalism*, 40, 20.

16. Foundational analyses of the ways in which the early republic emerged out of the Federalist years are provided by J. G. A. Pocock, *The Machiavellian Moment: Florentine Political Thought and the Atlantic Republican Tradition*, and Gordon S. Wood, *The Creation of the American Republic, 1776–1787* (Chapel Hill: University of North Carolina Press, 1969).

17. We might imagine this as Pocock's "language of republicanism," which Michael Warner defines as "a conceptual vocabulary that made the whole range of republican political arguments possible" (*Letters of the Republic*, 63). Part of the strength of this language comes from the fact that it is fortified by a strong cultural continuity. Recent criticism is divided on the role of the language of the American revolution within the larger narrative of American culture. Lester Cohen's study of the revolutionary historians, for example, argues that "a radical transformation of assumptions and ideas about nature and the meaning of history" set writings about the Revolution clearly apart from earlier expressions of American identity (*The Revolutionary Histories: Contemporary Narratives of the American Revolution*, 15), while Sacvan Bercovitch's work on George Bancroft argues for the force in American symbology of "continuing revolution"—a myth of American identity that draws its power by casting the war for independence as a "sacred movement" in the encompassing "symbolic drama of American nationhood" that began in the great migration (*The Rites of Assent: Transformations in American Symbology*, 173–75). As I hope to show, finding ways to encode history was the central concern of the cultural imagination at this time; though the illusion of the rhetoric suggested a break from past forms, every imaginative strategy both depended upon and fortified cultural continuity.

18. "[T]he post revolutionary period of American history is one overwhelmingly marked by dire political contention and exigent popular disunity, as well as by a powerful countervailing aspiration to national solidarity—that is, by the unresolved *problem* of national unity" (Looby, *Voicing America*, 5).

19. David Ramsay, *The History of the American Revolution*, vol. 1, 53, 58.

20. Mercy Otis Warren, *History of the Rise, Progress, and Termination of the American Revolution*, vol. 1, 54.

21. For the politics behind these shifting cultural tastes in the first decades of national history in the United States, see Gordon S. Wood, *The Creation of the American Republic, 1776–1787*, and Larry E. Tise, *The American Counterrevolution: A Retreat from Liberty, 1783–1800*.

22. Paul K. Longmore, *The Invention of George Washington*, 171; George B. Forgie, *Patricide in the House Divided: A Psychological Interpretation of Lincoln and His Age*, 89. For an account of the appeal of heroic biography generally in the early republic, see Theodore P. Greene, *America's Heroes: The Changing Models of Success in American Magazines*, 38–39.

23. Warren, *History*, vol. 1, 122, and Ramsay, *History*, vol. 1, 190. Cultural images of heroes in Cooper's own time were no less complicated. In *Notions of the Americans*, the Traveling Bachelor writes of "the lingering of ancient prejudices" evident in the controversial Society of Cincinnati and looks forward to its disbanding: "The Society is daily getting of less importance though possibly of more interest, and there is no

doubt but it will disappear entirely with the individuals who were personal actors in the scenes" (Cooper, *Notions of the Americans: Picked up by a Traveling Bachelor*, 302–3).

24. For a full and fascinating discussion of the André affair as background to *The Spy*, see Bruce A. Rosenberg, *The Neutral Ground: The André Affair and the Background of Cooper's The Spy*. The relationship between the André legend and Cooper's text is overt, and André's situation is mentioned a number of times throughout the text. The relationship between the McCrea legend and Cooper's text is not overt, and as I discuss later, the only near mention of the event is an ironic moment of incomprehension. Here my concern is not with the textual echoes themselves but rather with the analogical function that both legends serve as we encounter Cooper's experiment with making cultural secrets into narrative form.

25. As Michel de Certeau writes, "it might seem that an entire society expresses what it is in the process of fabricating through representations of what it is in the process of losing." See his *Writing of History*, 135.

26. Letter from George Washington, read at the trial proceedings, printed in the Appendix to William Dunlap, *André: A Tragedy in Five Acts* (1798), ed. Brander Matthews (New York: Dunlap Society, 1887), 110. André's arrest actually took place on the "neutral ground," outside of either British or colonial encampments.

27. See for example, a letter from Alexander Hamilton to Elizabeth Schuyler, written on the day of André's execution: "When André's tale comes to be told, and present resentment is over," Hamilton fears, the mandate to hang André as a spy "will be branded with too much obduracy" (*Papers of Alexander Hamilton*, vol. 2, 448); Irving, *The Life of George Washington*, vol. 4, 108.

28. G. R. Gleig [Elizabeth L. Foster Cushing], *Saratoga: A Tale of the Revolution*, vol. 2, 108.

29. Dwight, *A Discourse on Some Events of the Last Century* (Jan. 7, 1801), 23, 19, 11, 42, 45.

30. Ernst Bloch, *The Utopian Function of Art and Literature: Selected Essays*, 126.

31. Greenough to Bryant, May 7, 1851, in *Letters of Horatio Greenough, American Sculptor*, 390.

32. Washington, letter to Schuyler (July 22, 1777), in *George Washington: A Collection*, 89–90.

33. Letter to the *Mohawk Herald* (New York), Dec. 27, 1823, quoted in James Austin Holden, "The Influence of the Death of Jane McCrea on the Burgoyne Campaign," 273.

34. David Wilson, *The Life of Jane McCrea, with an Account of Burgoyne's Expedition in 1777*, 13, 113–14.

35. See Lewis Leary's Introduction to Hilliard's *Miss McCrea: A Novel of the American Revolution*, 5.

36. Gates to Burgoyne, September 2, 1777, cited in *The Pictorial History of the American Revolution*, 252.

37. *London Annual Register* (1777), 2d ed. (London, 1781), 156, quoted in Holden, "Influence of the Death of Jane McCrea," 291.

38. John Marshal, *The Life of George Washington*, vol. 1, 200.

39. Lippard, *Washington and His Generals, or Legends of the Revolution*, 176.

40. Washington Irving, *Life of George Washington*, vol. 3, 152.

41. Burgoyne, quoted in David Wilson, *Life of Jane McCrea*, 115. Even patriot

historians seemed disinclined to take Gates literally at his word. In his 1822 *History* Paul Allen writes, "There is little doubt that General Gates purposely exaggerated the circumstances which attended the melancholy fate of this young lady—sufficiently melancholy, indeed, without the aid of fancy," vol. 2, 6).

42. See two articles from the Pennsylvania *Evening Post,* Aug. 12, 1777, printed in *Diary of the American Revolution, from Newspapers and Original Sources,* vol. 1, 475–76.

43. Sources for this version of the legend include W. H. Bartlett and B. B. Woodward, *The History of the United States of North America,* vol. 1, 440 (relying on the authority of Benjamin J. Lossing's *Field Book of the American Revolution*), and A. S. Barnes, *Centenary History: One Hundred Years of American Independence,* 211.

44. Elizabeth Barnes's provocative book about early American tales of seduction and incest argues that "Far from subverting the goals of national union, however, incest and seduction represent the logical outcome of American culture's most cherished ideals. . . . [S]eduction, while ostensibly representing a breach in legitimate union, actually serves as a model for the ways in which political union is effected after the Revolutionary War. . . . Rather than challenging national values, incest and seduction become the unspoken champions of a sentimental politics designed to make familial feeling the precondition for inclusion in the public community" (*States of Sympathy: Seduction and Democracy in the American Novel,* 3). While the tale of Jane McCrea does not quite fit Barnes's paradigm for a variety of reasons, the reading of seduction as peculiarly community-affirming translates well to my analysis of this tale.

45. Lydia Maria Child, *The Rebels; Or, Boston before the Revolution,* 95.

46. Anon., *Amelia; or the Faithless Briton,* 1, 7.

47. Hilliard, *Miss McCrea,* 49–50.

48. For example, compare "Jane McCrea," in William Allen, *An American Biographical and Historical Dictionary,* with Benjamin J. Lossing, *The Field Book of the American Revolution,* vol. 1, 48, 96–99, 101, and cited in Bartlett and Woodward, *History,* vol. 1, 440.

49. Jared Sparks, *American Biography: Benedict Arnold,* 107.

50. In comparison, the British writer Richard Lamb called "the melancholy transaction" of Jane's death the tragic exception to an otherwise untroubled relation between Burgoyne and his employed Indians (*An Original and Authentic Journal of Occurrences during the Late American War,* 145).

51. David Wilson, citing Burgoyne, *Life of Jane McCrea,* 40.

52. Thacher (Sept. 2, 1777), *Military Journal of the American Revolution,* 95.

53. R. M. Devens, *Our First Century,* 73. For one of the most moderate American accounts of the event and of Burgoyne's culpability, see Mercy Otis Warren, *History,* vol. 1, 223–34.

54. See Burgoyne's letters in the appendix of *A State of the Expedition from Canada.* There he writes on July 29, 1777, of the necessity of strong posts at Ticonderoga, Fort George, and Fort Edward, to prevent "a breach into my communication [that] must either ruin my army entirely, or oblige me to return in force to restore, which might be the loss of the campaign," lxxiv).

55. Washington Irving, *Life of Washington,* vol. 3, 154.

56. James Austin Holden, "Influence of the Death of Jane McCrea," 294.

57. David Wilson, *The Life of Jane McCrea,* 117.

58. Irving, *Life of Washington*, vol. 3, 154.

59. Ibid.

60. Mason Locke Weems, *Life of Washington*, 69.

61. Dr. Andrews, *History of the Late War* (London, 1786), quoted in Holden, "Influence of the Death of Jane McCrea," 292.

62. Ramsay, *History of the American Revolution*, vol. 2, 371.

63. Holden, "Influence of the Death of Jane McCrea," 249.

64. "It is the magic of nationalism to turn chance into destiny" (Benedict Anderson, *Imagined Communities*, 19).

65. Robert B. Roberts, *New York's Forts in the Revolution*, 200.

66. Hilliard, *Miss McCrea: A Novel of the American Revolution*, 41.

67. Congressional Report (1777), cited in Holden, "Influence of the Death of Jane McCrea," 274.

68. "An Act more effectually to prevent the mischiefs arising from the example and influence of persons of equivocal and suspected characters in this State" (June 30, 1778; revised from March 7, 1777) in *Laws of the State of New York*, vol. 1, 87–88; reprinted in *The American Revolution: New York as a Case Study*, ed. Larry R. Gerlach, 113–15. See generally, *Minutes of the Committee and of the First Commission for Detecting and Defeating Conspiracies in the State of New York*.

69. "An Eyewitness Account," cited in Bartlett and Woodward, *History of the United States*, vol. 1, 490.

70. Livingston, letter to William Duer, June 12, 1777, in Robert R. Livingston papers, in the New York Historical Society, quoted from Edward Countryman, *A People in Revolution: The American Revolution and Political Society in New York, 1760–1790*, 165.

71. Thacher, Nov. 24, 1780, *Military Journal*, 237–38.

72. Ibid., 255.

73. *Rivington's Gazette* (July 4, 1781), printed in *Diary of the American Revolution, from Newspapers and Original Documents*, ed. Frank Moore, vol. 2, 448–49.

74. André, letter to George Washington (Oct. 1, 1780), in *Proceedings of a Board of General Officers . . . Respecting Major John André, September 29, 1780*, 16.

75. André, quoted in the appendix to William Dunlap's *André*, 111–12.

76. Thacher, *Military Journal*, 216.

77. Two articles from the *Pennsylvania Packet*, October 10, 1780, printed in *Diary of the American Revolution*, ed. Frank Moore, vol. 2, 323, 332.

Caleb Crain notes that Arnold and André "wrote each other letters disguised in the vocabulary of commerce and encrypted in a numerical code keyed to various editions of "Blackstone's Commentaries" (*American Sympathy: Men, Friendship, and Literature in the New Nation*, 6).

78. Wright, *Views of Society*, 87.

79. Lamb, *An Original and Authentic Journal of Occurrences during the Late American War*, 327.

80. R. M. Devens, *Our First Century*, 100.

81. J. W. Barber, *Incidents in American History*, 167.

82. André, letter to Washington, Oct. 1, 1780, in *Proceedings*, 16.

83. Ramsay, *History*, vol. 2, 518.

84. *The Case of Major John André . . . who was put to Death by the Rebels . . .* , 21.

85. In a recent study of friendship among men in early America, Caleb Crain includes a fascinating account of André's place in the culture of his time. As Crain puts it, André stood for "an ideal to which America as a nation aspired—the disinterested fraternity of men" (*American Sympathy*, 2).

86. James Thacher, *Military Journal*, 229.

87. Mason Locke Weems, *The Life of Washington*, 103.

88. Longing for visible evidence of the sorrow and desperation they imputed to Washington as he condemned André to hang as a spy, Patriot writers penned stories with varying amounts of historical plausibility to illustrate a crisis of widespread treachery. See especially the tale of John Champe, first published in Henry Lee, *Memoirs of the War in the Southern Department of the United States*, vol. 2, 159–87.

89. David Ramsay, *History*, vol. 2, 524.

90. Richard Snowden, *A History of the American Revolution, in Scripture Style*, 179.

91. Hamilton to E. Schuyler, Oct. 2, 1780, in *Papers*, vol. 2, 449.

92. Ramsay, *History*, vol. 2, 518.

93. Snowden, *History*, 179.

94. Ibid., 180.

95. Wright, *Views of Society and Manners*, 84.

96. Washington Irving, *Life of Washington*, vol. 4, 115.

97. Ramsay, *History*, ed. Cohen, vol. 2, 523.

98. Dunlap, *André*, 4, 3; subsequent references are noted parenthetically as WD, followed by a page number.

99. Examples of Federalist fears of secrecy and conspiracy are given in Fisher Ames, "Laocoön," and Jedidiah Morse, "The Present Dangers and Consequent Duties of the Citizens." The Connecticut Wits brought similar themes into literature (see *The Anarchiad*, for example). Republicans too used similar language to express their fears (for example, Abraham Bishop, "A Republican View of Federalist Conspiracy"). Thus I argue that secrecy is less an issue of party politics than an emergent language of national narrative at the dawn of the nineteenth century.

100. [John Frost], *The Heroes and Battles of the American Revolution*, 201.

101. Bunce, *The Romance of the Revolution: Being a History of the Personal Adventures, Romantic Incidents, and Exploits Incidental to the War of Independence*, 179.

102. [Anon.], *The Literary Magazine, or Journal of Criticism, Science, and the Arts*, vol. 1 (7), 3.

103. Adams, quoted in Morse, *Annals of the American Revolution*, 261.

104. Rosenberg, *The André Affair*, 67.

Notes to Chapter 3

1. This is not to relegate all historical romances outside of the tradition elaborated here to the role of cultural conciliation exclusively, but in broad terms this seems to have been the function of the genre throughout the nineteenth century. In identifying challenges to this tradition, I work with specific circumstances and contexts; variations elsewhere would have their own rich contexts, which would necessitate careful excavation of their own. A contrast to my argument is Philip Gould's greater emphasis on the dissenting qualities of the romance as genre: "In the absence of a

school of revisionist historiography, historical romance provided one outlet for cultural dissent" (*Covenant and Republic: Historical Romance and the Politics of Puritanism*, 13).

2. Woodworth, *The Champions of Freedom, or The Mysterious Chief,* vol. 1, v; subsequent references are indicated by SW, followed with volume and page number.

3. Cumings, *A Sermon Preached before Thomas Cushing,* 34, 54.

4. See Cathy N. Davidson, *Revolution and the Word: The Rise of the Novel in America.* The early novel, Davidson argues, "constituted a definition of America different from the official one being worked out after the end of the Revolutionary war" (vii). Accordingly, it met the resistance of the establishment: "For men of power and prestige, too, it was a chaotic new world, and the novel, more than any other literary genre, was seen as the sign of a time when their authority was being called into question" (39).

5. Jefferson, letter to Nathaniel Burwell (March 14, 1818), in *Writings,* 1411.

6. Choate, "The Importance of Illustrating New-England History by a Series of Romances like the Waverly Novels" (Salem, 1833), in *Works,* vol. 1, 321, 323, 338.

7. Review of Cooper's writings from *The Southern Literary Messenger,* vol. 4, quoted in the introduction to *Fenimore Cooper: The Critical Heritage,* ed. George Dekker and John P. McWilliams, 7.

8. Belknap (1794), quoted in Daniel J. Boorstin, *The Americans: The National Experience,* 363–64.

9. Delia Bacon, *The Bride of Fort Edward, founded on an incident of the Revolution,* 34.

10. James Monroe, second annual message (Nov. 17, 1818), seventh annual message (Dec. 2, 1823), fourth annual message (Nov. 14, 1820), all in *The Statesman's Manual: The Addresses and Messages of the Presidents of the United States . . . from 1789 to 1846,* 410, 452–53, 460, 420, 410.

This is, of course, just one in a long series of appropriative policies toward Native American lands, but in the context of the evolving cultural imagination it signified a public expression of a broader anxiety as well: The land would never openly reveal all of its secrets; stories of America would be more nourished by that resistance than by any newly drawn maps or acquired territories.

11. Hilliard, *Miss McCrea: A Novel of the American Revolution,* 24.

12. Wheeler Case, "The Tragical Death of Miss Jane McCrea . . . ," in *Poems on Several Occurrences, in the Present Grand Struggle for American Liberty,* 17.

13. Mason Locke Weems literalizes this figural bond between Washington and the American land when he writes that, as a young child, Washington went out to the family garden to find that the cabbage plants had sprouted to spell his name clearly in the earth. Inspired by this message, Weems's Washington later realizes that his own father had planted the seeds "to introduce [Washington] to [his] true father," a divine voice speaking through the prenational land. Other artists and historians too promoted such images, all efforts to naturalize Washington's character, to identify him as an indigenous product of America (Weems, *Life of Washington,* 13–14).

14. My argument is that the primary function of this identification is, as I explain later, a mythic consecration of Washington. Certainly, however, like Monroe's political policies, this is another stage in the appropriation of the figure of the Native American for the United States.

15. The notion of Washington as divinely chosen—the moral of this legend—has its roots as early as 1755. On August 17 of that year Reverend Samuel Davies preached

a sermon titled "Religion and Patriotism: The Constituents of Good Soldiers" to an independent company of volunteer forces in Hanover County, Virginia. He argued that God was "pleased to diffuse some sparks of this martial fire through our country" and cited "as a remarkable instance of this," "that heroic youth, Colonel Washington, whom I cannot but hope Providence has hitherto preserved in so signal a manner, for some important service to his country" (*Sermons,* vol. 3, 101). William Alfred Bryan calls this "a famous mention of Washington which was often quoted" in the Federalist and early republican years (*George Washington in American Literature, 1775–1865,* 52).

16. Custis, *Recollections and Private Memoirs of Washington, by his adopted son,* 303–4; first published in the *United States Gazette,* May 27, 1826.

17. Josiah Quincy, quoted in a review of Fourth of July orations (given in Boston in 1826) by Quincy, David Child, Edward Everett, Henry Colman, and George Bancroft, in *The United States Literary Gazette,* vol. 3 (11–12), Sept., 1826, 423.

18. The configuration of Washington as a skilled negotiator of the land and its people became a stock image in American romance. A particularly rich example of this is given in Woodworth's *Champions of Freedom,* a romance of the War of 1812. In this tale the ghost of Washington appears as a "mysterious chief" whose easy transcendence of time and place allows him to resolve multiple precarious public and private conflicts.

19. Cooper's departure from the safely patterned imaginings of his culture drew him criticism in his own time; see for example William Gilmore Simms, "The Writings of Cooper," 218–19. Reviewers of his later work, too, from Edgar Allan Poe to Francis Bowen, argued that Cooper's entire career showed him to be "altogether irregardless, or incapable" of the "construction of plot" (Poe, review of *Wyandotté,* in *Graham's Magazine,* vol. 24 [1843], and Bowen, review of *Gleanings in Europe,* in *North American Review,* vol. 46 [1838], both in *Critical Heritage,* eds. Dekker and McWilliams, 207, 10). Cooper himself confessed that "no plot was fix'd on until the last volume was half done"; "the *denouement* of the story is crowded and hurried" (*Letters and Journals,* vol. 1, 676 [1820], and vol. 4, 341 [1843]).

Nonetheless, as I hope to show, there are many reasons—including Cooper's ties to the De Lancey family and their complicated history in the Revolution—that make it little surprise that he would investigate disorder rather than order in the war.

20. J. G. A. Pocock, *Politics, Language, and Time: Essays on Political Thought and History,* 243–44. In this regard, Peter Brooks's comment on "narrative as a form of thinking" is relevant to the cultural function of *The Spy:* Certain tales function in response to problems for which "explanation, in the logical and discursive sense, seems impossible or impertinent"; these stories can work to transmit not knowledge in the familiar sense, but "a kind of wisdom that itself concerns transmission: how we pass on what we know about how life goes forward" (*Reading for the Plot: Design and Intention in Narrative,* 9).

21. Channing, 1830, in Robert E. Spiller, ed., *The American Literary Revolution, 1783–1837,* 359.

22. This was by request of the British government. Bruce A. Rosenberg writes: "In August 1821 a British detachment from the frigate *Phaeton,* which had sailed to America for that purpose, led by His Majesty's consul in New York, James Buchanan, removed André's bones from his unadorned grave in Tappan." "When he was reinterred, the peach tree which had subsequently grown over André's grave was carefully

removed as well, for planting in one of the king's gardens. The major's remains were reburied in the south aisle of Westminster Abbey, and a monument erected there to his honor and remembrance" (*The Neutral Ground*, 59, 108).

23. Hilliard, *Miss McCrea*, 56.

24. Elizabeth Foster Cushing, *Saratoga; A Tale of the Revolution*, vol. 1, 35–37.

25. Specifically, Cooper's readers would have seen the contrast between Frances and the "camp followers" often depicted in romance as women of dubious morals who could come to no good end. See for example Adeline in [Giles Gazer], *Frederick de Algeroy; A Hero of Camden Plains*, esp. 83–108.

26. Antidotes to Jane's story were common in the early republic. See for example "Lady Harriet Ackland's passage through the enemy's army, to attend her wounded husband, then their prisoner," a tale that, in its various circulated forms, regularly announces the virtues it celebrates: It is written as "an interesting picture of the spirit, the enterprize, and the distress of romance, realized and regulated upon the chaste and sober principles of rational love and connubial duty" ("Analecta," in *The General Repository and Review*, Oct. 12, 1812, vol. 2, 320–24).

27. Betty's bar, with its sign promising "entertainment for man and beast," is interestingly located at Four Corners, which James Pickering has noted is the site of the home of one of André's captors, Isaac Van Wort.

28. The important exception to this is Frances's inadvertent discovery of the Spy's affiliation with the colonial army, though his exact role remains vague in her mind. Nevertheless, true to the program of social stability that Frances represents, she never reveals this story. Instead, she considers herself "mistress of [the Spy's] secret" (385).

29. The comparison is reiterated throughout—see pp. 63, 72, 83, 87–88, 96–97, 112, 323, 326–42—but never does Henry's character begin to do the cultural work that the symbolic André could do.

30. In the opening scene, when Washington appears in the guise of a mysterious stranger approaching the area to look for rest, it might well be expected that this would be the title character. Further, during the confusion surrounding Henry's trial, the two function explicitly as doubles, both on the landscape and in their actions (see for example p. 382).

31. William Alfred Bryan, *George Washington in American Literature*, 197. And in *The New World of James Fenimore Cooper*, Wayne Franklin suggests that the "real attraction" of the Spy as a character "comes from his ability to survive history rather than from his immovable principles" (174–75).

32. George Lippard, among others, represents David Jones's absence from the scene of Jane's murder as a reprehensible failure (*Washington and His Generals*, 176).

33. James P. Collins, *The Autobiography of a Revolutionary Soldier*, 11.

34. Wirt, *The Letters of the British Spy*, 29–30, 49, 133, 208–09.

35. [Gazer], *Frederick de Algeroy*, 9–11. This hermit's social isolation, his ability to negotiate otherwise impenetrable terrain, and his finally revealed attachment to the American cause all mark him as a clear echo of Cooper's Spy.

36. Henderson, *Versions of the Past: The Historical Imagination in American Fiction*, 57, 60.

37. Hannah Arendt, *On Revolution*, 204.

38. W. H. Gardiner, "Review," 59, 61.

Notes to Chapter 4

1. Bushnell, "The Doctrine of Loyalty," in *Work and Play; or Literary Varieties*, 351.

2. Anderson, *Imagined Communities*, 17.

3. Lewis, *The American Adam: Innocence, Tragedy, and Tradition in the Nineteenth Century*, 91, 89, 5, 128, 123.

4. When the Spy does speak—as for example in his chance meeting with the disguised George Washington at the Wharton's home—he does so not to communicate directly but to reveal information covertly. As T. Hugh Crawford writes, the Spy's "every word and gesture betray a hidden meaning that only a few can decipher" ("Cooper's *Spy* and the Theater of Honor," 410).

5. In *Notions of the Americans*, Cooper's Cadwallader is also associated with a powerfully silent way of communicating. The Bachelor observes, "I never before associated with one, who was at the same time so communicative and so reserved"; "Cadwallader . . . has a silent, significant manner of conveying truths" (*Notions of the Americans: Picked up by a Traveling Bachelor*, 14, 128). During the Revolution, though, silence—regardless of its intent—was considered subversive to the cause of independence. The *Connecticut Courant*, Cathy Davidson writes, denounced the silence of the Jacobins, saying "it was 'ominous of evil. The murder listens to see if all is quiet, and then he begins. So it is with the Jacobins'" (*Revolution and the Word: The Rise of the Novel in America*, 162).

6. Cooper, *Wyandotté, or the Hutted Knoll: A Tale*, 3.

7. John McWilliams has argued that the neutral ground itself, without definition or precise borders, "make[s] heroic deeds difficult to achieve and impossible to memorialize" (*Political Justice in a Republic: James Fenimore Cooper's America*, 53).

8. Often his words have an air of prophecy to the other characters. James H. Pickering notes that one of the Spy's messages is apparently anachronistic—or, I might argue, prophetic—by at least a couple of weeks; this occurs when the Spy announces the battle of Blackstock's Hill (Tiger River) on p. 61. For a slightly different example, see p. 59, where Katy, with "no opportunity of listening . . . ever neglected," still fails to determine virtually anything about the Spy's life and identity.

9. It may be that the Spy's apparent love of money is part of his mask, but some descriptions suggest otherwise. For example, "Harvey's eyes twinkled as he contemplated the reward; and . . . [he] coolly stretched forth his hand, into which the dollars fell with a most agreeable sound; but not satisfied with the transient music of their fall, the peddler gave each piece in succession a ring on the stepping-stone to the piazza" (78).

10. The "ritual function" of the Spy has been well established. See for example James Franklin Beard, "Cooper and the Revolutionary Mythos," 89, and Marius Bewley, *The Eccentric Design: Form in the Classic American Novel*, 79. For Bewley it is the Spy's success in his ritual role that makes him "a channel of communication." In this context it is interesting to note a comparison between the Spy and the "mediocre hero" that Georg Lukács found in Walter Scott's historical novels: "Scott always chooses as his principle figures such as may, through character and fortune, enter into human contact with both camps. The appropriate fortunes of such a mediocre hero, who sides passionately with neither of the warring camps in the great crisis of his time can provide a link of this kind without forcing the composition" (*The Historical Novel*, 36–37).

Cooper adds the complications of double agency and patriotic mission, and—I would argue—thwarts the Spy's ritual function precisely to the effect of "forcing the composition" of his narrative frame.

11. Victor Turner, *The Forest of Symbols: Aspects of Ndembu Ritual*, 95, and see also his *Dramas, Fields, and Metaphors: Symbolic Action in Human Society*, 232–33, 237.

12. See Renato Rosaldo's discussion of the "cultural borderland," which emphasizes the dynamic potential of ritual, transitional, and border states, in *Culture and Truth: The Remaking of Social Analysis*, esp. 17, 26–30, 45, 96.

13. Benjamin, "The Storyteller: Reflections on the Works of Nikolai Leskov," in *Illuminations: Essays and Reflections*, 108–9.

14. Hans Blumenberg, *The Legitimacy of the Modern Age*, 138.

15. The sound that startles Katy is in fact one of Mr. Birch's dying groans; this detail suggests yet another level to the series of symbolic misreadings that prevent the revelation of historical knowledge.

16. "My life," the Spy says to Washington, "was nothing to me, compared to your secrets." Cooper leaves it to his audience to determine whether this is a report of the effect or intent (or both) of the Spy's service.

17. Here she refers not to Washington's perhaps excessive adherence to decorum, but on the contrary, to his interactions with ordinary characters and particularly to his engaging in disguise.

18. [Hale], review, *Port Folio*, 90.

19. Victor Turner, *The Forest of Symbols*, 102. The way that this knowledge is both concealed and revealed makes for its sustained cultural power as a story. Taussig argues that "we take refuge in an unmasking that all the more effectively masks through continuous deferral" *(Defacement*, 166).

20. In contrast to my reading, Paul Downes argues that "Washington's note, and in particular his signature, appears here as the Revolution's last word. His signature brings the last (and first) patriot back into the fold of national recognition" *(Democracy, Revolution, and Monarchism in Early American Literature*, 173).

21. Benjamin, "The Storyteller," in *Illuminations*, 94.

22. Perhaps the sacrifice is ineffectual, without higher meaning, but even if it *is* sacrifice in the most genuine way, "sacrifice," as Susan Mizruchi has shown, "is associated with spiritual loss" (*The Science of Sacrifice: American Literature and Modern Social Theory*, 26).

23. As Michael Walzer writes, one way that a culture may "assert a political obligation to die" is to "describe the reason or the obligation . . . as a function of the state's foundation" (*Obligations: Essays on Disobedience, War, and Citizenship*, 77). In this sense the Spy's untold story is a function of his nation's origins, which is to say, the Spy's obligation to the state is to ensure the silence of his story, before and after his death.

24. I agree here with Downes's argument that the Spy represents the necessary "inheritance of an irreducible secrecy" as part of the movement forward of the culture, yet I also see this secrecy is paramount to the Spy as (limited) agent, and so I read the novel as seeking to convey and encode that secrecy rather than, as Downes does, as "seek[ing] . . . to dispel secrecy" (*Democracy, Revolution, and Monarchism*, 177).

25. Michel de Certeau discusses the possibilities for the disturbance from within an established interpretive frame—and, specifically, the powers for resistance that the sub-

ject may acquire while apparently trapped there, in "Discourse Disturbed: The Sorcerer's Speech," *The Writing of History*, 244–68.

26. In Delia Bacon's version of the legend of Jane McCrea, *The Bride of Fort Edward*, the heroine announces in her last moments that she trusts in "that strange future on whose threshold I am lying here" (161). Cooper's scene both invokes and undercuts this sort of martyr's faith.

27. See Walzer, *Obligations*, 7. Further, despite the exile preventing the Spy's death from becoming a martyrdom, an entanglement with the culture equally prevents his life and death from becoming evidence of self-assertion. The sociocultural and subjective goals in the Spy's world are misaligned, inaccessible to one another, and so although the culture would like to claim the Spy as a martyr, and although his service to the cause qualifies his final end as (in Durkheim's terms) something like an altruistic suicide, these interpretive frames remain radically separate, and neither adequately explains the function of his story within the American community (see Émile Durkheim, *Suicide*).

28. Most critics have accepted the Spy's death as a form of narrative resolution; I join Charles Hanford Adams in his sense of the Spy's "enduring alienation" after death (*"The Guardian of the Law": Authority and Identity in James Fenimore Cooper*, 41).

29. [Hale], review, *Port Folio*, 96, 94, 95.

Notes to Chapter 5

1. Hawthorne, *The Scarlet Letter*, 38. All subsequent quotations from the romance are identified parenthetically by page number as taken from this edition.

2. As Evan Carton puts it, this is "the charged, shifting, perilous, and anything but 'neutral territory' of romance" (*The Rhetoric of American Romance*, 151).

3. My understanding of the powers and dangers of language within particular cultural formations is informed by Mary Douglas's *Purity and Danger: An Analysis of the Concepts of Pollution and Taboo*, 94–113. For a detailed account of what Dennis E. Baron calls "Federal English, an American language independent of its origins (though not necessarily cut off from them), a language that could be planned to reflect the peculiar American political, social, and cultural genius, a language in which the laws and literature of the new nation could be inscribed," see his *Grammar and Good taste: Reforming the American Language*, 7–67, passim. See also Michael P. Kramer, *Imagining Language in America: From the Revolution to the Civil War*, and David Simpson, *The Politics of American English, 1776–1850*.

4. E. P. Whipple, review of *The House of the Seven Gables*, in *Graham's Magazine* 38 (May 1851), in *Hawthorne: The Critical Heritage*, ed. J. Donald Crowley, 201.

5. Reynolds, *European Revolutions and the American Literary Renaissance*, 89.

6. Arac, "The Politics of *The Scarlet Letter*," 258.

7. Reynolds, *European Revolutions and the American Literary Renaissance*, 96.

8. Arac, "The Politics of *The Scarlet Letter*," 258, 259.

9. Ibid., 253. As Bercovitch points out, though, this is not just a play on words: "It is no accident that Hawthorne would have connected the revolutions abroad with his loss of tenure at the Salem Custom House," as many Democrats—suddenly and with great surprise put out of power by Polk's loss in 1848—saw in the insurgent powers abroad figures for their native opposition (*The Office of the Scarlet Letter*, 75).

10. Bercovitch, *The Office of the Scarlet Letter*, 87.

11. Here and throughout, my use of Bancroft is not intended as a parallel to Hawthorne, but rather as an example of a notable and dominant cultural voice; Bancroft and Hawthorne share some broad interests in the American past, but their politics are different. As John P. McWilliams has written, "Superficially, Hawthorne may resemble Bancroft in portraying the Revolution as an expression of the Puritan temper, but where Bancroft detects progress, Hawthorne detects only restoration." In Hawthorne's work, as opposed to Bancroft's, "acts of king resisting can be valid types of the Revolution only if one acknowledges the underside of Puritan character" (*Hawthorne, Melville, and the American Character*, 77–78). For more on the complicated similarities between these men of different political temperaments, see Brook Thomas, "Citizen Hester: *The Scarlet Letter* as Civic Myth," 182–83, and Sacvan Bercovitch, *The Office of the Scarlet Letter*.

12. Bercovitch, *The Office of the Scarlet Letter*, 86.

13. As Reginald Horsman has shown, a central difference between the prehistory of Cooper's novel and the context of Hawthorne's is one of political mood. Horsman demonstrates that the American chauvinism of the revolutionary era is inherently "optimistic," while America in 1850 was infused with a sense that its own "idealistic mission had been corrupted" (*Race and Manifest Destiny*, 300, 297).

14. Hutner, *Secrets and Sympathy: Forms of Disclosure in Hawthorne's Novels*, 4.

15. Thomas, "Citizen Hester: *The Scarlet Letter* as Civic Myth," 181–211. In terms helpful to illuminating what I mean by revising national language, Thomas argues, "*The Scarlet Letter* does not so much reject civic notions of good citizenship as question empty platitudes about them while expanding our sense of what they can entail." Further, Thomas notes the troubling limits of the efficacy of Hawthorne's experiments with language: "That expanded sense of good citizenship is by no means sufficient to solve issues of racial inequality" (201).

16. Benjamin, "The Storyteller," in *Illuminations*, 89.

17. In fact, such rhetoric of the new is shown to be perhaps one of the most burdensome of Hawthorne's inheritances. These quotations, from Henry F. Chorley's review of *The Blithedale Romance* in the *Athenaeum* (July 10, 1852), in *Hawthorne: The Critical Heritage*, ed. Crowley, 245, are representative of so many reviews of nineteenth-century fiction and of that perceived inheritance that, I argue, shapes Hawthorne's historical consciousness.

18. As Larry Reynolds has shown, "Hester's ventures into new areas of thought link her, significantly, with the overthrow of governments" (*European Revolutions and the American Literary Renaissance*, 931).

19. The popularity of this legend (from the 1820s through the 1850s especially, but also even further into the nineteenth century) is noteworthy and is not restricted to the United States. Certainly, as George Dekker points out, the legend is a mythic type, recurrent in world literatures ("the ancient *topos* of the national champion *redivivus*," like "Charlemagne, Frederick Barbarossa, and especially King Arthur" [*The American Historical Romance*, 137]). Whether—as Dekker further argues (*The American Historical Romance*, 135)—the American popularity of this tale stems from the legend's appearance in Walter Scott's *Peveril of the Peak* (1822), or whether it comes about from an increased interest in native accounts of the early Puritan era (I would argue that both

forces are at work, though my immediate concern is more with the latter), it is true that the regicide tale became one of the most popular historical source legends for American fiction, poetry, and drama during Hawthorne's era. See for example James Nelson Barker's *Superstition* (1824), Cooper's *Wept of Wish-Ton-Wish* (1829), and James McHenry's *Specter of the Forest* (1823).

20. With Richard H. Millington, I would argue that these recurrences are "returns with a difference" and, further, that such a pattern leaves open certain radical possibilities. Millington argues, "freedom is achieved not by acts of transcendence but by acts of revision" (*Practicing Romance: Narrative Form and Cultural Engagement in Hawthorne's Fiction*, 59, 65).

The problem of assimilating recurrences is expanded later with reference to Yuri M. Lotman's *Universe of the Mind: A Semiotic Theory of Culture.*

21. Blumenberg, *Work on Myth*, 221.

22. As Brook Thomas argues, "Hester dramatizes how important it is for the state to promote spaces in which the capacity for sympathy can be cultivated while simultaneously guarding against the dangers of natural liberty. Thus, even though Hester has no space within the civic sphere, she, unlike Dimmesdale, helps to bring about a possible structural realignment of Puritan society by having it include what we can call the nascent formation of an independent civil society" ("Citizen Hester: *The Scarlet Letter* as Civic Myth," 197).

23. We might think of this dynamic as something like the inverse of Marcel Mauss's theory of the gift. Here, in accordance with Mauss's theory, the "gift" may be given in order to indebt the recipient to the giver. In tension with this function, however, is the function that eludes the giver's control and turns the recipient from the object of action into potential subject.

24. Hawthorne, "Main Street," *Tales and Sketches*, 1047.

25. The parallels work reciprocally, too. Puritanism here signifies foundation, of course, but also disruption, by reference to Cromwell's England. The American revolution similarly has a primary symbolic quality of the disruptive, but within American history has long been marked as a continuity of independent spirit.

26. The dangers Hester poses are interestingly analogous to those associated in her culture with witchcraft (cf. Michel de Certeau, *The Writing of History*, 244–68).

27. Whitman, *An American Primer*, 2, 8.

Notes to Chapter 6

1. Bell, *Hawthorne and the Historical Romance of New England*, ix.

2. McWilliams, *Hawthorne, Melville, and the American Character*, 21.

3. See for example, Michael Davitt Bell, *Hawthorne and the Historical Romance of New England*, and Larry Reynolds, *European Revolutions and the American Literary Renaissance.* For purposes of this argument, a particularly interesting point that Reynolds makes is the temporal parallel between the deaths of Dimmesdale and Charles I (see p. 86); his analysis provides a further possible connection between the two in the common imagery he sees in Dimmesdale's late surrender to the powers around him and Andrew Marvell's imagery of the deposed King's beheading in his "Horatian Ode"; see Reynolds, p. 84.

4. The legend's fundamentally conservative function, discussed later, is evident from the interesting fact that some of the most politically and morally unyielding attacks on Hawthorne's subject—the condemnations of its "labyrinth of moral horrors" (anon., "American Literature: Poe, Hawthorne," in *Tait's Edinburgh Magazine* 22 (January 1855), in *Hawthorne: The Critical Heritage*, ed. Crowley, 308)—actually mention the regicide as a topic preferable to the life of Hester Prynne for fiction: "Why, amid all the suggestive incidents of life in a wilderness . . . amid the historical connections of our history with Jesuit adventure, savage invasion, regicide outlawry, and French aggression, should the taste of Mr. Hawthorne have preferred as the proper material for romance, the nauseous amour of a Puritan pastor, with a frail creature of his charge, whose mind is represented as far more debauched than her body?" (Arthur Cleveland Coxe, "The Writings of Hawthorne," *Church Review* 3 (January 1851), in ibid., 182).

That regicide could make for good romance but Hester's revival of the same theme would not clearly points to what feminist critics of the novel have long known— the story's foregrounding of the female body is one of the most powerfully revolutionary aspects of Hester's literary existence. See, for example, Shari Benstock, "*The Scarlet Letter* (a)dorée, or the Female Body Embroidered," 288–303.

5. In fact, Cooper's figure of the regicide in *The Wept of Wish-Ton-Wish* is referred to simply as "Submission."

6. This phrase is from *Mercurius Publicus, Kingdom's Intelligencer*, quoted in *The Trial of King Charles the First*, ed. J. G. Muddiman, 188–89. *Eikon Basilike: The Pourtracture of His Sacred Majestie in His Solitudes and Sufferings* (London, 1649) is a religious diary presented as the deposed king's own record of his time in prison. It becomes a particular locus for sympathy because it is filled with conciliatory rather than aggressive rhetoric (e.g., "As our sins have turned our Antidotes into Poyson, so let thy Grace turn our Poysons into Antidotes" [4]). The text is now believed to have been put together by John Gauden, based on notes made by Charles I.

7. Alden Bradford, *The History of Massachusetts for Two Hundred Years, from the Year 1620–1820*, 64. See also W. H. Carpenter, *The History of Massachusetts, from its earliest settlement to the present time:* "During the progress of the Civil War in England, Massachusetts preserved a prudent neutrality. When the attempt was made by parliament in 1646 to assert its jurisdiction over the colonies, the authorities of Massachusetts firmly protested against the innovation as an infringement of their charter" (112–13).

8. "Petition to the Parliament in 1651," reprinted in *The History of the Colony and Province of Massachusetts-Bay*, by Thomas Hutchinson, 428.

9. "An Address to Oliver Cromwell" by the General Court of Massachusetts, August 24, 1654, reprinted in Hutchinson, *History*, ed. Mayo, 434.

10. This is noted in Sacvan Bercovitch, *The Office of the Scarlet Letter*, 34–37.

11. Ralph Waldo Emerson, Blotting Book (1831), in *Journals and Miscellaneous Notebooks*, 277.

12. Hypocrisy is perhaps the most common charge made against Cromwell by historians with an anti-Puritan perspective, and it is the trait most adamantly denied by most supporters. Ezra Stiles, for instance, addresses the issue directly in his celebratory portrait, insisting that Cromwell's central virtues were his sincerity, his resistance to hypocrisy, and overall, his "unabashed . . . undissembled and undisguised religion" (Stiles, *A History of Three of the Judges of King Charles I*, 244–46).

13. Bancroft, *History of the United States*, 334–35. Hawthorne, in his Rome note-book (January 1858) expresses a similar concern with the image of drastic change embodied by Cromwell: "I used to try to imagine how splendidly the English Cathe-drals must have looked in their primeval glory, before the Reformation, and before the whitewash of Cromwell's time had overlaid their marble pillars" (*French and Italian Notebooks*, 48).

14. John Stetson Barry, *The History of Massachusetts, The Colonial Period*, 324.

15. In this view, however, Cromwell still shines in comparison to the treacherous Charles I because his crimes are only immediate whereas the King's are timeless: "The murderer . . . destroys what time will repair, and, deep as is his guilt, society suffers but transiently from the transgression. But the king who conspires against the liberty of the nation, conspires to subvert the most precious bequest of past ages, the dearest hope of future time. . . . His crime would not only enslave a present race of men, but forge chains for unborn generations" (Bancroft, *History*, vol. 2, 1–2, 15).

16. Bancroft, ibid., 21.

17. Bancroft, ibid., vol. 1, 339. Similar distinctions are common in nineteenth-century American views. Cf. Emerson: "[T]he fact is Society is fluid: there are no such roots and centers but any monad there may instantly become the center of the whole movement and compel the whole to gyrate around him as every man of strong will, like Cromwell or Pitt, does for a time and every man of truth, like Plato or Paul, does for-ever" ("Politics," in *Early Lectures*, 240).

18. Richard Hildreth's *Theory of Politics: An Inquiry into the Foundations of Govern-ments and the Causes and Progress of Political Revolutions* presents Cromwell as an exem-plum of the "primary elements of power" embodied. He defines these elements as muscular strength, skill, dexterity or art, sagacity, force of will, knowledge, eloquence, and virtue (31–48), and then elsewhere in his text offers a portrait of Cromwell that fulfills each requirement: "Cromwell, by means of his superior sagacity, activity, courage, temper, and warlike and political skill, largely aided by his mystical influence over the Independents . . . raised himself to supreme power" (188).

19. Bancroft, *History*, vol. 2, 12, 27.

20. The original appeared in *The New England Historical and Genealogical Register* for 1866; it was reprinted as a pamphlet in Boston later that year.

21. There are many references to the rumor on which this pamphlet is based, but it remains unsubstantiated. Cotton Mather reports the story as fact in *Magnalia Christi Americana*, vol. 1, 79. It seems that by the nineteenth century, the rumor was looked upon with general skepticism. Even Bancroft, rarely one to turn down material for a good tale, denies the story, suggesting that Cromwell is a man of such fixed purpose that emigration would not have been a suitable alternative to revolution for him. Full and lively discussions of the story, however, are still common in nineteenth-century American histories, and the quoted passage (as reprinted in Dean) is taken from one such source, Edward Rodolphus Lambert, *History of the Colony of New Haven*, 16–17.

22. Carlyle's Cromwell is sketched as a mythic hero, and this image is strongly influential on later American portraits. See Carlyle's introduction and notes to *Oliver Cromwell's Letters and Speeches*, in two volumes.

23. This comparison is made in other American accounts as well. See, for example, Frederic Harrison's *Washington and Other American Addresses*. And, from France,

Guizot writes in 1826, "Three men, Cromwell, Washington, and William III, remain in history as the chiefs and representatives of those sovereign crises which have decided the destiny of two great nations. In extent and energy of natural talent, Cromwell is perhaps the most eminent of the three" (*History of the English Revolution*, 76).

24. Sherman B. Canfield, *A Lecture on the Life and Character of Oliver Cromwell*, January 28, 1847, 8, 12, 14, 35–36, 121, 155.

25. Harrison, *Washington and Other Addresses*, 147.

26. Lemuel A. Welles, *The History of the Regicides in New England*, 25.

27. Numerous sources report this, from the seventeenth century through recent accounts. See for example Isabel MacBeath Calder, *The New Haven Colony*, 221.

28. Anon., *A Declaration concerning . . . judges on the life of our late martyr'd soveraign*, 1–2.

29. Heneage Finch, Earl of Nottingham, *An Exact and Most Impartial account of the indictment, arraignment, trial and judgment . . . of twenty-nine regicides*, 20.

30. Anon., *Rebels No Saints, or A Collection of the speeches, private passage, letters, and prayers of those persons lately executed*, 3, 15.

31. Finch, *Exact and Impartial Account*, 15.

32. See for example William Assheton, *The cry of royal innocent blood heard and answered*, or George Bate, who curses the escaped regicides to "wander about the world as Vagabonds, like *Cain*, with the cry of blood at their heels . . . [until they are] found out by the All searching hand of divine Justice" (*The Lives, actions, and execution of the prime actors . . . of that horrid murder of . . . King Charles the First*, 95). To Bate this is a particularly appropriate fate for the escapees, guilty of the crime of having hunted Charles "like a *Partridge* upon the top of the Mountaines" (n.p.).

33. Throughout the eighteenth and nineteenth centuries, most—though not all—histories only bitterly recall both the Revolution and its leaders; much of this tradition stems from Edward Hyde Clarendon's *History of the Rebellion and Civil Wars in England*, where Clarendon's devotion to Charles is clear throughout, and the only positive mentions of any aspect of the Revolution are moments of grudging admiration for Cromwell, who, in Clarendon's summary judgment, was "a brave wicked man" (vol. 3, 990). Both Gilbert Burnet's *History of His Own Time* and David Hume's *History of Great Britain* are comparatively complimentary toward Cromwell (pardoning him, that is, through their use of rhetorical ambiguity), yet both still refuse to endorse other aspects of the Revolution.

34. Hutchinson claims to base his account of the regicides on diaries and papers that had come into his possession, presumably from the Mather family after Cotton Mather's son Samuel married Hutchinson's sister. What papers Hutchinson might have had, however, were lost in the mob fire on his home in 1765 (see Ezra Stiles, *History of Three of the Judges of King Charles I*, 29). The remaining letters and papers relating to the regicides are among the Mather papers at the Massachusetts Historical Society and are published in the *Collections of the Massachusetts Historical Society*, 4th ser., vol. 8, 122–225.

35. The only exception that I found is in Timothy Dwight's *Travels in New England and New York*. There he reports that the regicides arrived in Hadley, Massachusetts in 1654. This must be a typesetter's error for 1664, when most sources report that they traveled from New Haven to Hadley. Of course, it would significantly change the

context of the regicides' choice to live in New England if they had indeed arrived this early, but there is no other evidence of arrival before the restoration. In fact, there are accounts of Whalley and Goffe active in the government of the Protectorate in the mid- and late-1650s. The arrival date and place of John Dixwell is not known, but it also postdates the restoration, and historical accounts agree that he spent some time in Germany before coming to New England.

36. The dates used in this summary are drawn from many sources and seem generally undisputed. See, for example, Hutchinson, *The History of the Colony and Province of Massachusetts Bay*, 183–37, and Lemuel A. Welles, *The History of the Regicides in New England*, 1927. For interesting details on New England's reception of the news of the restoration, see, for example, John Endicott's letter to British authorities in the Hutchinson papers, *Collections of the Massachusetts Historical Society*, 51–52; accounts of Puritan fears of "evil" coming from the restoration in *The History of the City of New Haven*, ed. Edward E. Atwater, 6; and Francis Bremer's article, "In Defense of Regicide: John Cotton on the Execution of Charles I," 103.

37. *The Letters, Speeches, and Proclamations of King Charles I*, ed. Sir Charles Petrie, 239 (letter dated Nov. 29, 1648).

38. The offer of pardon, conditional on the regicides' surrender, was made several weeks after the arrest order, in June of 1660.

39. This act, revoking the offer of pardon for those who had not appeared, was issued on Aug. 29, 1660 (Calder, *New Haven Colony*, 222).

40. Davenport, *The Saints Anchor-Hold, in All Stormes and Tempests*, 197–99. It is interesting to note that in this same sermon Davenport argues that God is angry with the Puritans because "[they trusted] too much in the arm of flesh, in the Parliament, in the Army, or in the Protector; and thereupon became carnally secure and wanton. . . . The Lord awaken and humble his people for it, and cause their eyes, for the future, to be towards him alone" (221).

41. George Chalmers, *Political Annals of the Present United Colonies, from Their Settlement to the Peace of 1763*. The image of the regicide as "angel," referenced in Davenport's echo of the biblical passage (from Heb. 11:37–38 and 13:2) dominates virtually every future retelling.

42. Later American historians proudly suggest that the search was deliberately delayed by New England officials, allowing the escape of Whalley and Goffe to New Haven; see Alden Bradford, *The History of Massachusetts for Two Hundred Years, from 1620–1820*, 66: "Endicot and Bellingham were in office at the time; and neither, probably, made greater efforts to apprehend the regicides than their stations as magistrates required of them."

43. This order is dated March 5, 1661, and reprinted in *The Collections of the Massachusetts Historical Society*, 3rd ser., vol. 7, 123.

44. Welles, *History of the Regicides*, 34.

45. The Massachusetts Court's consent to the search was written by Thomas Danforth and dated June 10, 1661: "We further judge, that the warrant and letter from the King's majesty for the apprehending of Colonell Whalley and Colonell Goffe, ought to be diligently and faithfully executed by the authority of this court. And also that the generall court may doe safely to declare, that in case, for the future, any [person] legally obnoxious and flying from the civil justice of the state of England, shall come over to

these parts, they may not here expect shelter" (reprinted in Hutchinson, *History*, 439–40.

46. Quotation taken from Welles, *History of the Regicides*, 41.

47. This period of the judges' lives is marked by a famous anecdote, the tone of which confirms both colonial confusion about the Puritan revolution and later historians' devotion to the legendary memory of its participants: "They were secreted by Mr. Tomkins, in the basement story of a shop standing near his dwelling. . . . It is related that Tomkins's daughters often spun in the shop, and would sometimes sing some poetry, which was composed about that time, concerning the martyrdom of Charles I (in which [Whalley and Goffe] were mentioned), which much amused the judges. The girls were unacquainted with their concealment" (Lambert, *History of New Haven*, 144). Ezra Stiles adds to this legend that the girls "little thought that they were serenading angels" (*A History of Three of the Judges of King Charles I*, 90).

48. Welles writes: "May it not have been because Charles II and his advisers, who were well posted on what had happened at New Haven, meant to obliterate the colony, as a punishment for concealing Whalley and Goffe?" (*History of the Regicides*, 63).

49. Goffe, quoted in Hutchinson, *History*, 442.

50. John Lisle, another regicide judge, had been killed in Switzerland in August of 1664.

51. John Russell was apparently a contact of Davenport's, who seems to have arranged the lodging.

52. William Hooke to Goffe (June 24, 1663), in *The Massachusetts Historical Society Collections*, 4th ser., vol. 8, 124.

53. Goffe, quoted in Stiles, *History of the Three Judges*, 116.

54. Hutchinson, *History*, 186n.

55. Davenport to Goodwin, letter (1665), in *The Massachusetts Historical Society Collections*, 4th ser., vol. 8, 127. Goffe's writings have a similar tone. In 1671 he writes to an unknown recipient of the "e[v]ill consequences to the churches, both in O: & N: E." (129). Some of this rhetoric, of course, is simply typical of second-generation New England, and in that sense such evidence is noteworthy in its conventionality, demonstrating the remarkable assimilation into the life and language of New England that would transform the judges, for later generations, into distinctly New World heroes.

56. Goffe to his wife (July 5, 1672), *Massachusetts Historical Society Collections*, ibid., 136.

57. Unnamed correspondent to Goffe (Oct. 18, 1661), ibid., 166.

58. Peter Tilton to Goffe (July 30, 1679). *Massachusetts Historical Society Collections*, ibid., 225.

59. Mrs. Goffe to her husband (Oct. 13, 1671), *Massachusetts Historical Society Collections*, ibid., 133–34. Goffe's answer to her offer confirms this: "[T]he aire of this countrey in the winter is exceeding pearcing, that a sickely person must not dare to venture out of Dores" (letter dated July 5, 1672, *Massachusetts Historical Society Collections*, ibid., 142).

60. Welles reports skeptically on rumors of Goffe's departure for a southern colony (*History of the Regicides*, 106); most sources seem to believe that he lived out his life in New England. Goffe was still alive at the end of July in 1679, but beyond that date nothing is known of his whereabouts.

61. Histories are not consistent in assigning the precise identity to Goffe, but Hutchinson does, and Hutchinson is the earliest known written source for the legend. Of course, the individual identity of the one at the center of this legend is quickly eclipsed by myth in any case, and there is nothing specific to Goffe's known character or person that is evident from the legend.

62. Hutchinson, *History*, 187n.

63. Edward Rodolphus Lambert, *History of the Colony of New Haven*, 61.

64. Welles, *History of the Regicides*, 94.

65. Increase Mather, *History of King Philip's War, with a History of the Same War by Cotton Mather*, 62, and Russell, quoted in Mather, 82.

66. Ibid., 84–85. Even with a large-scale win by the colonists that followed later in the month, Mather recalls these times as "black and fateful," with haunting images of women and children left alone and "above sixty Persons buried in one dreadful Grave" (86).

67. Welles details this interpretation in his *History of the Regicides*, 95ff. Along with Mather's history of the war, another account considered generally reliable is Hubbard's *Narrative of the Trouble with the Indians* (1677). Like Mather, Hubbard includes no mention of the alleged episode at Hadley.

68. These phrases, as well as the headnote to this portion of the chapter, are taken from a letter from Charles I to his son, reprinted as an appendix to *Eikon Basilike*, 153–54.

69. Stiles, *A History of Three of the Judges of King Charles I*, 30.

70. Ibid., 8, 338, 8.

71. Stiles recalls that as late as December 1684, when Edward Randolph had become a primary (and certainly belated) pursuant of the judges, Endicott wrote to Randolph with assurances that he had had no knowledge of their whereabouts for more than twenty years.

Davenport is one of the clear heroes of Stiles's book. He writes, "What staggered Governor Endicott, a man of heroic fortitude, and other Hearts of Oak at Boston, never staggered Mr. Davenport. He alone was firm, unshaken, unawed. . . . Davenport's enlightened greatness, fidelity and intrepidity, saved the judges" (95).

72. Stiles, *History*, 34, 110–11, 28, 27.

73. Ibid., 282, 252, 208, 207.

74. George Sheldon, "Introduction" to Sylvester Judd's *History of Hadley*, ix.

75. George Bancroft, *History of the United States*, 14th ed., vol. 2, 32.

76. Ibid., 34.

77. This somewhat morbid fetishism is not unique to Huntington's address. As the previous chapter mentions, the early republic celebrated many exhumations of revolutionary figures, including both John André and Jane McCrea. Both the *New Haven Palladium* and the *New Haven Register* record that John Dixwell was exhumed for honored reburial on November 22, 1849. The relic that Huntington displays, though, is supposedly from Whalley, whose grave, according to Huntington, was originally in the basement of John Russell's home and opened in 1795 (40).

78. Huntington, "Address for the Celebration of the 200th Anniversary of the Settlement at Hadley, June 8, 1859," 12, 6–7, 49, 36, 40–41.

79. This chapter offers a representative rather than an exhaustive discussion of the legends associated with the regicides. For other tales not mentioned here, see Stiles's

History of Three of the Judges and John Warner Barber's *Connecticut Historical Collections
. . . relating to the History and Antiquities of Every Town in Connecticut*, 18–21. For a fascinating lecture on the regicides that furthers many of the themes discussed here—but
falls a bit outside of the time period of my concern—see Chandler Robbins, *The Regicides Sheltered in New England: A Lecture . . . Delivered before the Lowell Institute, February 5, 1869*.

80. Lambert, *History of New Haven*, 60; see also Stiles. Hollister notes the irony of
having the animal intruder appear so "terrible to men who had proved themselves to
possess true courage when man meets man on the battle-field," and along with lessen-
ing the ferocity of the judges' images, another overall effect of this particular legend
seems to be the effective highlighting of New England's success in saving the judges
from every kind of savagery—a world where one's predators are everywhere, watching
as the potential victim sleeps. (G. H. Hollister, *The History of Connecticut from the First
Settlement of the Colony*, vol. 1, 243). Leonard Bacon reports that "a modern hand" later
inscribed above the entry to that cave, " 'Opposition to tyrants is obedience to God' "
(*Thirteen Historical Discourses*, 134).

Notes to Chapter 7

1. This is, of course, not to say that there were no more materials to be uncovered,
but only that enough official remembrances had been instituted to encourage new
questions about how such remembrances fit together into a coherent story of national
emergence.

2. Rufus Choate, "The Importance of Illustrating New England History by a
Series of Romances like the Waverly Novels" (delivered at Salem, 1833), in *Addresses
and Orations of Rufus Choate*, 2, 8.

3. Choate, ibid., 23.

4. These ideas are familiar in the works of mid-century American romantics. Consider for example Emerson in "The American Scholar"—"I embrace the common, I
explore and sit at the feet of the familiar, the low"—or Whitman's "Song of Myself,"
celebrating "what is commonest, cheapest, nearest, easiest" (*Selections from Ralph Waldo
Emerson*, 78; *Complete Poetry and Selected Prose by Walt Whitman*, 33).

5. Choate, "The Eloquence of Revolutionary Periods" (a lecture delivered before
the Mechanic Apprentices' Library Association, February 19, 1857), in *Addresses and
Orations*, 167, 173.

6. Choate, "The Importance of Illustrating New England History," in ibid., 14, 16.

7. See for instance Hawthorne's description of the Cathedral of Amiens in 1858
(*French and Italian Notebooks*, 9–10).

8. Hawthorne, "My Kinsman, Major Molineux," in *Tales and Sketches*, 86.

9. Hawthorne, "Alice Doane's Appeal" and "The Gray Champion," in ibid., 206, 240.

10. Hawthorne, *True Stories from History and Biography*, 158.

11. For perhaps the most promising resonances of this legend, see the *American
Claimant Manuscripts*. Of particular interest are passages from "Etherege," 108, 126,
180, 200–5, 222, 262–63, 334, and "Dr. Grimshawe's Secret," 420–21.

12. My understanding of the rich ambiguity inhering in American Puritan uses of
language is based on the early works of Sacvan Bercovitch, *The Puritan Origins of the
American Self* and *The American Jeremiad*.

13. Amy Schrager Lang and Joel Pfister are among the critics who find radicalism in Hester Prynne. See Lang, *Prophetic Woman: Anne Hutchinson and the Problem of Dissent in the Literature of New England* (Berkeley: University of California Press, 1987), and Pfister, *The Production of Personal Life: Class, Gender, and the Psychological in Hawthorne's Fiction.* The potentially revolutionary nature of Hawthorne's writing is resisted at even the most basic levels in mid-century reviews: Andrew Preston Peabody writes that although some "fictions . . . usurp the realm of fact, and change its order into anarchy . . . [and so] disturb and displace the fabric of things as they are, and build up their ideal world in the very same space, which the actual world occupies," Hawthorne's works are to be praised for "leav[ing] things as they are; but breath[ing] into them a vital glow" (from Peabody's review of *Twice-Told Tales,* in *The Christian Examiner,* vol. 25 [Nov., 1838] and reprinted in *Hawthorne: The Critical Heritage,* ed. J. Donald Crowley, 64).

14. Larry Reynolds has noted that "It is Pearl, of course, who anticipates what Hester will become—a revolutionary—and reveals the combative streak her mother possesses" (*European Revolutions and the American Literary Renaissance,* 91). As Reynolds demonstrates, much of the "combative" language of the text is used in reference to Pearl's actions and attitudes.

15. Hawthorne, preface to *The Blithedale Romance* and preface to *The House of the Seven Gables,* in *Novels,* 633, 351.

16. In fact, his romances obliquely point to the regicides' stories, not only in the character of Hester Prynne, but throughout *The House of the Seven Gables* (a house with "secrets to keep, and an eventful history to moralize upon" [27]) as well. The introduction to Hawthorne, *Letters 1853–56,* vol. 17 of *Works,* 61, notes the relation of Matthew Maule to the regicides, and see Hawthorne, *The House of the Seven Gables,* 77, for mention that the Pyncheons are descendants of the regicides' major sponsor, John Davenport.

The location of more remotely historical influences on Hawthorne's fictional character development should not obscure the fact that, as David S. Reynolds has shown, Hawthorne's characters may also be seen as developments of stock characters, particularly from sensational and reform literatures of his day. See Reynolds, *Beneath the American Renaissance: The Subversive Imagination in the Age of Emerson and Melville,* 123, 263.

17. Hawthorne, in "The Gray Champion," in *Tales and Sketches,* 240–41.

18. Hawthorne, letter to Sophia (Sept. 14, 1841), in *Letters, 1813–43,* vol. 15 of *Works,* 571.

19. The description of the tombstone (*On a Field, Sable, The Letter A, Gules*) is a line taken from Marvell's poem, "The Unfortunate Lover."

20. If indeed this echo of "The Garden" (*The Poems and Letters of Andrew Marvell,* 48–49; lines 16, 47–48) resonates for Hawthorne, surely it does so with the full complications of the pastoral tradition; to emphasize Hester's capacity for prophecy born of solitude is not to deny the otherwise stifling capacities of such isolation.

Notes to Chapter 8

1. In terms helpful to an understanding of this change in the culture's code of self-definition, Victor Turner has distinguished between the functions of the "liminal" and the "liminoid"—the change in the relation of the transitional (or transgressing)

character to the status quo. While in traditional cultures (in Turner's terminology), the liminal condition is "demanding" and "compulsory," the "liminoid" (modern cultures' version of the liminal) is a condition of will and choice in which "great public stress is laid on the individual innovator, the unique person who dares and opts to create." Furthermore, Turner argues, liminality in traditional cultures "secretes the seed of the liminoid, waiting only for major changes in the sociocultural context to set it agrowing." In this model, to the fictional Puritans of Boston, Hester is clearly and simply liminal. Her status as an outsider is an enforced punishment. In Hawthorne's representation of Hester's personal history, however—in the course of her life and in her entrance into the United States of 1850—Hester more and more resembles the "liminoid"; she is the harbinger of a modernity fusing new cultural contexts to the seeds that allow them to grow (Turner, "Liminal to Liminoid, in Play, Flow, and Ritual: An Essay in Comparative Symbology," *Rice University Studies* 60 [1974], 53–92).

2. Colacurcio, *The Province of Piety: Moral History in Hawthorne's Early Tales*, 457.

3. Anne W. Abbott finds Hawthorne's "favorite metaphor of the guillotine" to be one of the undesirable and "unpoetical" aspects of the romance.

4. Hester herself envisions such a future—albeit a future from which she excludes herself—as she instructs Pearl in the celebration of Governor's Day: "[T]o-day, a new man is beginning to rule over [the colony]; and so—as has been the custom of mankind ever since a nation first gathered—they make merry and rejoice; as if a good and golden year were at length to pass over the poor old world!" (228).

5. Benjamin, "The Task of the Translator," in *Illuminations*, 74–75.

6. Hawthorne, "Endicott and the Red Cross," in *Twice-Told Tales*, 436. The "grim beadle" in *The Scarlet Letter* echoes this sentiment: "'A blessing on the righteous Colony of the Massachusetts, where iniquity is dragged out into the sunshine'" (54).

7. Benjamin, "The Task of the Translator," in *Illuminations*, 80.

8. [Anne W. Abbott], 147.

9. In terms helpful to understanding the magistrates' sincere but inadequate use of language, Mary Douglas describes the evolution of cultural roles: "All the attribution of dangers and powers is part of this effort to communicate and thus to create social forms" (*Purity and Danger*, 101).

10. For Hawthorne, of course, purely rational language would be as insufficient as the purely transcendental. For a discussion of this conflict, see Philip Gura, *The Wisdom of Words: Language, Theology, and Literature in the New England Renaissance*.

11. Here again, the imagery is specifically revolutionary: See p. 163, in "Another View of Hester":

It was an age in which the human intellect, newly emancipated, had taken a more active and wider range than for many centuries before. Men of the sword had overthrown nobles and kings. Men bolder than these had overthrown and rearranged—not actually, but within the sphere of theory, which was their most real abode—the whole system of ancient prejudice, wherewith was linked much of ancient principle. Hester Prynne imbibed this spirit. She assumed a freedom of speculation, then common enough on the other side of the Atlantic, but which our forefathers, had they known of it, would have held to be a deadlier crime than that stigmatized by the scarlet letter. In her lonesome cottage, by the sea-shore, thoughts visited her, such as dared to enter no other dwelling in New

England; shadowy guests, that would have been as perilous as demons to their entertainer, could they have been seen so much as knocking at her door.

12. Charles Feidelson Jr., *Symbolism and American Literature*.

13. On the religious and educational importance of language to the New England Puritans, see Baron, *Grammar and Good Taste*, esp. 119–39.

14. Hawthorne, "Endicott," in *Twice-Told Tales*, 435.

15. For evidence of this dominant tone, we need look no further than John Winthrop's famous sermon—"A Model of Christian Charity" (1630)—on board the *Arbella*, as it sailed toward the soon-to-be-established Massachusetts Bay Colony.

16. For the implications of deviance specifically within Puritan culture, see Kai T. Erikson, *Wayward Puritans: A Study in the Sociology of Deviance*.

17. Douglas, *Purity and Danger*, 38. This is the moment at which emergent, involuntary, cultural memory has the greatest potency. Taussig argues that the appearance of involuntary memory "fus[es] the real with the imaginary" (*Defacement*, 142).

18. In Hawthorne's model this glittering letter might be compared to Endicott's reflective and unlettered breastplate in "Endicott and the Red Cross" because of its power to reflect the symbolic sum total of the Puritan colony—past, present, and future. See Sacvan Bercovitch's "Endicott's Breastplate: Symbolism and Typology in 'Endicott and the Red Cross,'" *Studies in Short Fiction*.

19. Here again we might contrast the contained power of the regicides within New England legend. While retaining some substantial claim to secrecy, these men do not carry with them a story that cannot be predicted or controlled. Their revolution has been defeated; they are thus images of lost possibility and the hopes that such memory can foster, rather than images of radical futurity. The social turmoil suggested by the magistrates' lack of control comes from the particular quality of "social pollution" that enables Hester to be both sinner and saint to her community. She embodies the type of deviance that Douglas calls "danger from internal contradiction, when some of the basic postulates [of a society] are denied by other basic postulates." Douglas says that such a case is characteristic of a social "system [that] seems to be at war with itself" (*Purity and Danger*, 122).

20. Hawthorne makes the connection between Hester and the Puritan sermon as explicit as that between Dimmesdale and the sermons: "If she entered a church, trusting to share the Sabbath smile of the Universal Father, it was often her mishap to find herself the text of the discourse" (85).

21. As I have suggested throughout this chapter, I believe that Hawthorne's world of historical symbolism mirrors the ideology of northern liberalism in 1850 in that both worlds delegate the (democratic) epistemological burden to society, though by noting the reflection it is not my purpose to present Hawthorne's tone as didactic.

22. Following Taussig, we might say that because Pearl, as a child, cannot "keep" a secret in the same way that adults can, so she also cannot "be kept by it" (*Defacement*, 121).

23. As Michael Taussig notes, there is "something so strange emanat[ing] from the wound of sacrilege wrought by desecration" that the exile that comes with defilement becomes a form of magic, and that "desecration [is] the closest many of us are going to get to the sacred in this modern world" (*Defacement: Public Secrecy and the Labor of the Negative*, 1).

24. Hester is, at the start, a peculiar figure of the Virgin Mary; not only does she obscure the paternity of her child, resulting in social exile, but the tale ultimately also makes clear that she carries the child of the resident Man of God. However resonant these plot lines are, though, the parallels decidedly do not result for Hester in any of the experiences of transcendence familiar to the New Testament story.

25. Douglas defines this "double play on inarticulateness" that invests Chillingworth with a potential power and makes his refusal to tell his story all the more damaging to the social order: "First there is a venture into the disordered regions of the mind. Second there is the venture beyond the confines of society. The man who comes back from these inaccessible regions brings with him a power not available to those who have stayed in control of themselves and of society" (*Purity and Danger*, 95).

26. [Abbott], 141.

27. That is to say, the language seems to me characteristic enough of Hawthorne that it may not carry any intentional irony, but in combination with the details elaborated in this chapter, an ironic reading seems merited by the overall tone of the passage.

28. What interests me here is the double abstraction, which renders the analogy only more difficult to imagine than either of its component parts and clearly undoes the primary function of analogy, which is to render the abstract more accessible to a world resistant to such language.

29. Benjamin, "The Storyteller," in *Illuminations*, 108–9.

30. Larry Reynolds makes a fascinating point when he connects the image of the scaffold to the European revolutions of 1848. Reynolds demonstrates that to attribute the scaffold to the Puritans is a "historical inaccuracy"; instead, he argues, Hawthorne must be using the term as a synecdoche for the guillotine. See *European Revolutions and the American Literary Renaissance*, 84.

31. See Bushnell, *The Fathers of New England*, 7, 12–13, 30–31.

32. Hester's bond to Dimmesdale is clear, and so too should be her bond to Chillingworth, when we posit the powers of secrecy within the novel. As Brook Thomas argues, "Chillingworth's 'new secrets' [as learned among the Indians] might be associated with a 'primitive' realm that Hester's vision of an enlightened future hopes to overcome, but the 'promise of secrecy' that once again binds husband and wife suggests a possible connection between the two" ("Citizen Hester," 191).

33. Benjamin, "The Storyteller," in *Illuminations*, 89, 91–92.

34. Hawthorne, 1855 entry in *The English Notebooks*, 225.

35. Noah Webster, *Dissertations on the English Language*, 18; as quoted in Baron, *Grammar and Good Taste*, 45.

36. David S. Reynolds is among the critics who sees the end of *The Scarlet Letter* differently, arguing that it provides evidence that "Hawthorne explore[d] the subversive and then recoil[ed] to the pious." In this ending Reynolds sees what he argues is a frequent strategy in Hawthorne's work, the "strategy of tacking a benign moral conclusion onto a deeply disturbing tale" (*Beneath the American Renaissance*, 121–22).

Notes to Chapter 9

1. Wister (July 6, 1885), in *Owen Wister Out West: His Journals and Letters*, 31.

2. Wister (July 10, 1885), ibid., 33.

3. Fussell, *Frontier: American Literature and the American West.*

4. These popular impressions of the West have received extensive critical attention from many different perspectives. See for example Ray Allen Billington, *Land of Savagery, Land of Promise: The European Image of the American Frontier,* and Richard Slotkin, *Regeneration through Violence: The Mythology of the American Frontier 1600–1860.*

5. Castle Freeman Jr., "Owen Wister: Brief Life of a Western Mythmaker: 1860–1938," 42.

6. There are, of course, different varieties of Western heroes, and as Henry Nash Smith and subsequent critics have shown, these figures vary generationally as well (*Virgin Land: The American West as Symbol and Myth*). The broad commonalities mentioned here are very widely applicable and are broken down later in the chapter.

7. The quotation in this sentence is from John G. Cawelti, *Adventure, Mystery and Romance: Formula Stories as Art and Popular Culture,* 224. John A. Barsness discusses the images of Jackson and Roosevelt in "Theodore Roosevelt as Cowboy: *The Virginian* as Jacksonian Man," 609–19, and see Richard W. Etulian, *Owen Wister,* 11. Gary Scharnhorst's article "*The Virginian* as Founding Father" directly contests the more common, earlier associations with Roosevelt and Jackson emphasizing instead the imagery of Washington and Jefferson. Even the earliest reviews make claims for the Virginian's rich heritage among founding American figures; a review of the novel in the October 23, 1902, issue of *The Nation* compares Wister's hero's identifying traits with those of George Washington (331).

8. This idea of Wister's romanticized version of the West works well in relation to the novel. But it is also true that over the course of Wister's life *after* the publication of *The Virginian,* his feelings about the West ran much more toward disillusionment; for example as Castle Freeman Jr. has written recently, "[Wister] had believed a new kind of American would be produced by the simplicity and rigor of life there: an honorable, chivalrous, high-minded natural aristocrat not unlike the Virginian. Instead he found his beloved Wyoming increasingly overrun with what he disdainfully regarded as the rabble of an excessive democracy: populist politicians, traveling salesmen, rebellious workers, unassimilated immigrants, and tourists" ("Owen Wister," 42).

9. The quotation is from Theodore Roosevelt, *Address . . . upon the Occasion of the Opening of the Louisiana Purchase Exposition,* 14.

10. "Books New and Old: Summer Fiction," 277; William Morton Payne, "Review," 242.

11. I take the term *living option* from William James's *Will to Believe* (1896). There, a "living option" is defined as "one in which both hypotheses are live ones," each appealing in some sense, and neither easily disqualified.

12. Wister, 1928 preface to *The Virginian,* ed. John Seelye, xli.

13. James, cited from John Seelye's introduction to the Penguin edition of the novel, xix. Seelye takes the quotation from Edwin H. Cady's *Virginian: The Light of Common Day.*

14. All quotations of Wister's text are hereafter made parenthetically and taken from *The Virginian: A Horseman of the Plains.*

15. Here we might see echoes of the highly influential theories of Humboldt, which suggest that historical process grew not so much out of the past or cultural traditions,

but out of the process of man's "biological adjustment to his milieu" (see Smith, *Virgin Land*, 40–41).

16. Buffalo Bill's "Wild West Show" had opened in St. Louis in 1883; by 1887 the troupe had been to England, and by 1889 they had toured Paris, Spain, Italy, Germany, and Belgium. Buffalo Bill novels came out in great numbers beginning around 1887. Ray Allen Billington argues that "the Buffalo Bill fad, coinciding as it did with the vogue of the dime novel in America and Europe, basically altered Europe's image of the West," resulting in the plainsman/cowboy replacing the frontier hunter as the recognizable hero of the American West (*Land of Savagery, Land of Promise: The European Image of the American Frontier in the Nineteenth Century*, 48–50).

17. For the ways in which the ideology of expansionism is intertwined with that of a complex and far-reaching racism, see Reginald Horsman, *Race and Manifest Destiny: Origins of American Racial Anglo-Saxonism*. See also Ernest Lee Tuveson, *Redeemer Nation: The Idea of America's Millennial Role*, and T. J. Jackson Lears, *No Place of Grace: Antimodernism and the Transformation of American Culture, 1880–1920*.

18. Tompkins writes: "Semiconsciously, in the novel, Wister tells a double story, the surface one of glamour and success and an understory of unhappiness hidden deep within" (*West of Everything: The Inner Life of Westerns*, 138).

19. Wister attended the Columbian exposition in Chicago at which Turner delivered his famous speech, but there is no account of his attendance at the lecture.

20. Turner to William E. Dodd (Oct. 7, 1919), box 29 of the Frederick Jackson Turner papers at the Henry E. Huntington Library. Cited in Ray Allen Billington, *Frederick Jackson Turner: Historian, Scholar, Teacher*, 112.

21. On the "telos of closure" of Turner's thesis, see Alan Trachtenberg, *The Incorporation of America: Culture and Society in the Gilded Age*, 13.

Notes to Chapter 10

1. Lighton, "Where Is the West?" p. 702.

2. Ibid., 703.

3. On the traits and types of traditional Western heroes, see Steckmesser, *The Western Hero*, esp. 241, 252.

4. [Don Jenardo, pseud.], "The True Life of Billy the Kid," 2, 15. This is the first known narrative of Billy the Kid's life. He had been dead only about six weeks when this was published.

5. *New Southwest and Grant County Herald*, Silver City, New Mexico, July 23, 1881; quoted in Kent Ladd Steckmesser, *The Western Hero in History and Legend*, 2.

6. Trachtenberg notes the prevalence of this phenomenon, calling it a "proto-populist image of opposition" (*The Incorporation of America*, 24)

7. The Lincoln County War has been remembered as "the historical prototype for the 'range wars' of Western fiction and films" (Steckmesser, *The Western Hero*, 59).

8. See ibid., 84–85. Pat Garrett was not only the sheriff who executed Billy, but he was also the biographer who memorialized him in print. His text, *The Authentic Life of Billy, the Kid*, deeply influenced the tales that followed. Examples of the most vivid sentimentalization of the tale include Walter Woods's *Billy the Kid* (1903) and Walter Noble Burns, considered to have formally "established" this active legend in 1926 with

The Saga of Billy the Kid.

9. [Jenardo, pseud.], "The True Life of Billy the Kid," 3, 5, 14.

10. It is interesting that it is Billy's death, and not his existence, that comes into question. Cunningham, *Famous in the West*, cited in Ramon F. Adams, *Six-Guns and Saddle Leather: A Bibliography*, 161.

11. The earlier narrative is written in the first person but acknowledged to be ghost written; the second is by Boone's nephew (Daniel Bryan). Both texts, as Henry Nash Smith points out, are "emphatic concerning [Boone's] devotion to social progress" (*Virgin Land*, 53).

12. [Daniel Boon, Levi Todd, James Harrrod], preface to John Filson, *The Discovery, Settlement And Present State of Kentucke . . . To which is added An Appendix, Containing the Adventures of Col. Daniel Boon. . . .*

13. Ibid., 6.

14. Steckmesser, *The Western Hero*, 4.

15. Filson, *Discovery*, 8–10.

16. Ibid., 21.

17. Ibid., 49–50.

18. Ibid., 81. This emphasis on the ambiguities of revolutionary experience is prevalent in many of the writings of J. Hector St. John Crèvecoeur. See, for example, "The American Belisarius," one of his *Sketches of Eighteenth-Century America*—essays omitted for one reason or another from the 1782 publication of *Letters from an American Farmer* and later collected and edited for publication in 1923. Like many of these essays, "Belisarius" is mournful in tone and records the private tragedies among the national victories of the American revolution.

19. As Roosevelt wrote, Boone "will always occupy a unique place in our history as the archetype of the hunter and wilderness wanderer. . . . [He was] self-reliant, fearless, and possessed of great bodily strength and hardihood" ("Daniel Boone and the Founding of Kentucky," in Henry Cabot Lodge and Theodore Roosevelt, *Hero Tales from American History*, 12–13).

20. *Kit Carson's Autobiography*, ed. Milo Milton Quaife, xxxv.

21. The classic term for this second-stage myth is Henry Nash Smith's "Garden of the World" (*Virgin Land*), though my analysis configures this garden somewhat differently from the way Smith does.

22. As early as 1839, well before social Darwinism could make a claim on America's definition of the West, one New York periodical described the region and its possibilities in terms so deeply charged by the end of the century that their appearance here seems almost uncanny: "[The West is] the region where those principles [that] have always marked the Anglo-Saxon race, should be most perfectly developed in action. [Its] fertility, its commercial advantages, its manufacturing capabilities, and its climate, all these promise a dense, wealthy, and working population: and when we consider the parentage of the people that will fill it . . . we cannot but feel that the prospects of what we call 'the West' are wonderful beyond all precedent" (Anon., "Western Literature," *New York Review* (1839), as cited in Welter, *Mind of America*, 322.)

23. Berwanger, *The West and Reconstruction*, 5. On p. 255 Berwanger refers specifically to Hubert Howe Bancroft's lack of attention to the issue.

24. Ibid., 18.

25. See Richard Slotkin, *Gunfighter Nation: The Myth of the Frontier in Twentieth-Century America,* 134.

26. Many critics have noted the parallels between the western and medieval chivalric romance. Several other legends are discussed later in this chapter as textual constructions of a western cast of characters. Jesse James stands alone here as a primary example of the anachronism of southern hopes in western history; in terms of the folklore of the American west, James is a rare figure whose romance grows largely out of the history he represents. As I will show later in the chapter, the usual western hero is distinctly devoid of history and defined precisely by his or her immediate actions.

27. "The Problem of the Prairies," *Harper's Weekly,* 1204–5.

28. Ibid., 1205.

29. Frederick R. Bechdolt, "The Field Agent of Settlement: The Cowboy's Contribution to American Civilization," *The Outlook,* 19.

30. "The Evolution of the West" (editorial), 295–97.

31. Adler, "Billy the Kid: A Case Study in Epic Origins," 152. Adler's interpretation of myth in this article is largely ahistorical and thus differs from my own view, but I find his claim that the time of legend is a time that "needs a legend" to be absolutely persuasive; in fact, that particularly rooted historical and cultural analysis of "need" is what I hope to offer here.

32. Here we might recall the pleasure Wister's audience took in the much safer teleology of his romance.

33. Charles Moreau Harger, "To-Day's Chance for the Western Settler," 981–82.

34. See for example Charles Moreau Harger, "The Prairie Woman: Yesterday and To-Day." Harger argues that the West is nearly equal to the East as a place to have a rich and civilized social life; adding to this, he claims that the West is alone in offering women—as well as men—greater opportunities.

35. In "The Vigilantes of the West," Charles Michelson writes of the prevalent fears that, over the past half-century, "criminals of all nations swarmed into the golden land without a law" (200). Far from denying their existence, however, Michelson is one of many to defend the vigilantes at the turn of the century: "There was nothing mob like about the vigilance committees, though they had to override the law. Their sessions were orderly, regular, and deliberate" (202). As early as 1851 one membership certificate from the San Francisco vigilance committee read that the organization was created "for the mutual protection of life and property rendered insecure by the general insufficiency of the law and its maladministration" (cited in Michelson, 206).

36. Henry Loomis Nelson, "The Spirit of the West," 203. Nelson concludes: "This is what is happening in the West" (ibid.).

37. Ibid., 199.

38. That is, whereas early frontier heroes were identified by their simultaneous abilities to embody the best and the worst of humanity, the change that occurred split this paradox, isolating virtue from vice in a way that would have made the legends of Billy the Kid impossible.

39. Nelson explains further: "Unrestrained freedom is bad all around, and socially bad . . . [T]he young man who seeks liberty . . . how he is to come out is the problem of his own nature. He may become a cattle thief or a steady 'puncher'; he may take to liquor and gambling or he may become a 'leading citizen.' . . . [H]e may graduate as a

typical cowboy nuisance, wearing queer clothes, shoot[ing] off pistols and strange oaths, or he may become a real ranchman—a 'builder-up of empire,' to use one of our newest phrases, with a strong hankering after churches [and] schools" (ibid., 200).

40. Emerson Hough makes a classic statement of this view in his interesting but notoriously unreliable and romanticized book of 1897, *The Story of the Cowboy*. The theme is reiterated throughout the book, but see especially v, viii, 33, 322–35 passim.

41. Nelson, 200

42. Ibid., 199.

43. Ray Stannard Baker, "The Western Spirit of Restlessness," 467–69.

44. Triggs, *History of Cheyenne*, 22.

45. Ibid., 117.

46. Wyoming was organized as a territory with a delegate and a legislature elected in the fall of 1869. The first governor was John A. Campbell, whose service in the Union Army garnered him the appointment from (then President) Ulysses Grant. Wyoming became a state in 1890, under the presidency of Benjamin Harrison. Between 1889 and 1890, amid disastrous years for the cattle industry, the country continued to expand; the Dakotas, Montana, Idaho, Washington, and Wyoming were each admitted to the union as states.

47. The Red Cloud War against Plains Indians in the Powder River area (1866–1868) and the Great Sioux War (1876) had devastated the native population in this area. See Harry Sinclair Drago, *The Great Range Wars: Violence on the Grasslands*,

48. Narratives of this war tell of independent ranchers fearing the powers of the cattle industry, while on the other side, industry leaders argued that the ranchers were increasingly willing to associate with rustlers (looked upon as wandering thieves) in their effort to band together into groups powerful enough to break the growing monopolies.

A good source for the particular setting of Wister's novel is Helena Huntington Smith, *The War on Powder River*. Lewis L. Gould's *Wyoming: A Political History, 1868–1896* provides a broad and deep investigation into the larger context of the novel's action.

49. Helena Huntington Smith reports that the first written attention given to the war was by Sam Clover in the *Chicago Herald*. Mercer was the second, but far more influential, reporter. In fact, his text of the *Banditti* caused such a stir that the printing plant was seized and most copies were picked up and destroyed by members of the cattle industry who felt he had betrayed them.

50. H. H. Smith, foreword to *The War on Powder River*, viii.

51. Ibid., xii. According to Wyoming political historian Lewis Gould, Harrison's actions did not reflect his overt support of either side; without knowing the precise details of the situation, Harrison was responding to the general problem of civil disorder (Gould, *Wyoming*, 137ff.)

52. Especially controversial was the 1884 Maverick Law, which essentially denied the independent rancher one of his main avenues for increasing his herd. This law prohibited the branding of unclaimed roaming cattle by small ranchers. Similar laws hit cowboys who did not own ranches even harder. They were denied rights to own or purchase cattle without owning a ranch. Under the Maverick Law all roaming cattle—"mavericks"—were claimed on behalf of the Wyoming Stock Growers' Association.

53. See James W. Forsyth and F. D. Grant, *The War Department's Report of an Expedition up the Yellowstone River, Made in 1875*, 16; and H. E. Palmer, *The Powder River Indian Expedition, 1865: A Paper Read . . . February 2, 1887*. Palmer refers to the Forsyth and Grant text in terms that underscore the mythic dimensions of both that text and his own: "The report of this 'Yellowstone Expedition' reads like a romance. . . . They met with a daily repetition of thrilling experiences, hair-breadth escapes and, for many of the party, no escape except in death" (58).

54. Moreton Frewen, *Melton Mowbray and Other Memories*, 205.

55. Ibid., 223. Some reports claim that between 65 and 90 percent of cattle perished during that time (cf. Drago, *The Great Range Wars*, 251ff.)

56. Gould, *Wyoming*, 9, 13, 267, 158. By the end of the nineteenth century, issues such as land conservation and national parks were already active concerns in the region. See John K. Rollinson, *Wyoming Cattle Trails*, 296.

57. See Drago, *The Great Range Wars*, 254: "Throughout the terrible winter no word of disaster appeared in the newspapers controlled by Secretary Sturgis [secretary of the Wyoming Stock Growers' Association]. Instead they published fantastic tales about how cozy things were in Wyoming. Such tales were for the moneyed east, not for home consumption."

58. Triggs, *History of Cheyenne*, 46, 53, 55, 67, 10, 18, 14, 22.

59. There are numerous first-person accounts of Wyoming life near the end of the nineteenth century that bear this out; a representative selection may be found in John K. Rollinson, *Wyoming Cattle Trails*.

60. Cf. Drago, *Great Range Wars*, 259.

61. President William McKinley, first elected in 1896, had been reelected in 1900. Vice President Hobart, McKinley's original running mate, had died in 1899, and McKinley chose Theodore Roosevelt for his new running mate, partly in the hope that Roosevelt's more radical views on expansionism would help the ticket gain reelection. McKinley was shot by an assassin at the Buffalo Exposition on Sept. 6, 1901; at this time Roosevelt became acting president. McKinley died from his wounds on Sept. 14, 1901.

62. Donnelly quoted in Eugene Berwanger, *The West and Reconstruction*, 214.

63. Roosevelt, *Address . . . at St. Louis, April 30, 1903*, 6. The version of the address cited here is part of the Ayer Collection at the Newberry Library.

64. See Rush Welter, *The Mind of America, 1820–1860*, especially pp. 298–306. Welter cites numerous government publications, such as the *Congressional Globe* and influential periodicals from the east, such as the *Democratic Review*, in drawing this conclusion.

65. Ibid., 318.

66. Both quotations are taken from *Memorial of William McKinley from the City of Boston*, ed. John F. Dever, 11, 13.

Notes to Chapter 11

1. This quotation is taken from the essay "The Importance of Individuals," which James wrote in response to Grant Allen and John Fiske in 1890, as part of their ongoing debate in print regarding notions of "Great Men." It is reprinted in James, *The Will to Believe and Other Essays in Popular Philosophy*, 257–58.

2. The "dead machinery" may be considered to include not only the worn symbols

of the Old West, but also the extraordinary machinations of romance—absolutely out-moded by 1900—which Wister invokes to end his hero's story without tragedy.

3. At the end of Wister's romance, the radical dismantling of the hero and his world must be considered in relation to that promise and its obscurity behind the machinery of national progress.

4. For the violence inherent in this mode of progress, see Trachtenberg's *Incorpo-ration of America*, especially Chapter 2, "Mechanization Takes Command," 38–69.

5. The tone of this contrast, so completely at odds with the notion of a pure and undiscovered world, sounds more like Thomas Pynchon's West than any nineteenth-century version. In *The Crying of Lot 49*, the landscape is scattered with similar debris—debris made sinister by its association with the dust of human bones, found in everything from cigarette filters to pool patio mosaics.

6. It is also certain that the Virginian's Southern ancestry is used to facilitate the theme of intersectional romance: Here the hero, a Southerner-turned-Westerner will marry the Northerner-Easterner, Molly Wood. According to Ernest E. Leisy, this pat-tern inverts the predictable intersectional romance of the late nineteenth century; he notes that Northern heroes and Southern belles were the more familiar couples to audi-ences (*The American Historical Novel*, 183).

7. Patricia Nelson Limerick, *The Legacy of Conquest: The Unbroken Past of the American West*, 83. Limerick goes on to explain that this stereotype, though dominant, is unreliable.

8. Worster, *Under Western Skies: Nature and History in the American West*, 227. Such celebrations, Worster writes, "were performed with the fervor of . . . nationalism" in the West; in fact, they were performed in a competitive spirit, designed "to put their east-ern fellows to shame" (ibid.).

9. Even the name of the town tempts travelers to seek health there.

10. David B. Davis, "Ten-Gallon Hero," 19.

11. Wister, *Red Men and White*, 49.

12. Stokes, *My Father, Owen Wister*, 16.

13. Seelye, "Introduction" to *The Virginian*, xi.

14. This makes clear what has been implicit throughout the chapter: The early tales of the Wild West, with their containing iconographic structure, serve the same cultural function as does the romance—the function of closure, fostering the twin beliefs in nostalgia and progress.

15. Wister, cited in John L. Cobbs, *Owen Wister*, 22.

16. Wister to Davis (Nov. 11, 1902), cited in ibid., 81.

17. Anon., "Mr. Owen Wister's Stories of Americanism," *The World's Work*, 2794.
Charles W. Kent, "Marks of Distinction," in "The Most American Books," 787 (this long article has a total of ten contributing authors, including Wister himself).
Anon., *The Dial* (June 1, 1902), 32, 392.

18. Anon., *The Forum* (1902) 34, 223; Payne, 242.

19. Anon., "Books New and Old: Summer Fiction," 277.

20. Sears, "The Historical Importance of *The Virginian*," 250–51.

21. See for example, Lee Clark Mitchell, " 'When you call me that. . . .' Tall Talk and Male Hegemony in *The Virginian.* "

22. That is to say, that while Hamblen Sears (above) imagined readers "sit[ting]

down and begin[ning] to wonder where [the Virginian] is now, what he is doing, what are his views on this or that question," the Virginian's life and his politics are all too well imagined by the end of the novel. (Sears, "The Historical Importance of *The Virginian*," 250–51).

23. The most important of these frustrating encounters, described below, is the execution of Steve, the horse thief who was once the Virginian's closest friend. The second episode is the one originally written as a separate short story, "Balaam and Pedro," in which the Virginian attempts to retaliate against Balaam (his neighbor and incidentally the husband of the woman who invited Molly Wood to the West) for the gross mistreatment of a horse. The graphic violence of this scene was much discussed among Wister's critics, and even Theodore Roosevelt believed it to be excessive.

24. The community suspects Indians, but given Wister's knowledge of the limited Native American presence in the area at that time, as well as the hints provided by the preceding action, it seems likely that the reader is expected at least to entertain the notion of an encounter with (white) outlaws.

25. Tompkins argues that "[t]he Virginian's relation to Steve is the most charged relation in the novel" and that "[t]he death of Steve is the price the hero pays for becoming successful, being foreman, getting money for a ranch, acquiring authenticity. His own legitimation and Steve's death are inseparable" (*West of Everything*, 150–51); on both points I fully agree.

26. Lotman, *Universe of the Mind: A Semiotic Theory of Culture*.

27. Michael Denning's comments on the functions of allegory in manipulating a plot for public consumption are helpful here. Citing Alfred Habegger, he notes that " 'Allegory is one of many human artifacts expressing a sense of human powerlessness.' So if allegorical modes of reading are in one sense traditionalist resistance to the novel's individualism, they are also a sign of the powerlessness of working class readers. The dime novels that elicit allegorical readings in order to make sense of them as novels of disguise . . . [a]ll depend on magical transformations to compensate for the impossibility of imagining 'realistic' actions by powerful agents" (*Mechanic Accents: Dime Novels and Working-Class Culture in America*, 74). I am arguing in a different context, but I find Denning's explanation of allegory as a defense—ironically not against, but as evidence of—some hidden agency beyond, below, or within the structure itself, and yet fully veiled by the familiar allegorical mode, to be most compelling.

28. Wister, *Red Men and White*, 56.

29. For present purposes, these groups are essentially similar in their notions of evolution as applied to society, but as T. J. Jackson Lears shows, there are important differences. Spencer, Lears argues, "was no 'social Darwinist.' . . . He had a great deal of trouble fitting Darwinian notions of struggle and arbitrary brutality into his orderly, progressive scheme. Instead of systematically appropriating Darwin, Spencer drew eclectically on a variety of evolutionary ideas to buttress his essential vision: a lawful cosmos evolving inexorably toward something better" (*No Place of Grace*, 21).

Notes to Conclusion

1. Once again, though, I maintain that this teleological dimension should not obscure the fact that I do not wish to represent my account as totalizing, but rather

as limited and conditional, shaped by the complex forces elaborated through the argument.

2. Faulkner's famous statement in his Nobel Prize acceptance speech—"I believe that man will not merely endure: he will prevail"—seems to me necessarily ironic in this light. With the endurance of Sutpen's line figured solely in the character of Jim Bond, Faulkner's optimism in the speech seems in conflict with the literary evidence, particularly—but not exclusively—of *Absalom, Absalom!* (*The Faulkner Reader*, 4).

3. At one point in her journey, Oedipa's notebook entry makes clear her connection to the monomaniacal Ahab: "she wrote *Shall I project a world?* If not project then at least flash some arrow on the dome to skitter among constellations and trace out your Dragon, Whale, Southern Cross. Anything might help" (82).

4. Simmel, *The Sociology of Georg Simmel*, 335.

BIBLIOGRAPHY

[Abbott, Anne W.]. "Review." *North American Review* 71 (July 1850): 135–48.

Adams, Charles Hansford. *The Guardian of the Law: Authority and Identity in James Fenimore Cooper.* University Park: Pennsylvania State University Press, 1990.

Adams, John. "Dissertation on the Feudal and the Canon Law," in *The Rising Glory of America, 1760–1820,* ed. Gordon S. Wood. Rev. ed. Boston: Northeastern University Press, 1990.

———. *Works.* Charles Francis Adams, ed. Boston: Little, Brown, and Company, 1856.

Adams, Ramon F. *Six-Guns and Saddle Leather: A Bibliography.* Rev. ed. Norman: University of Oklahoma Press, 1969.

Adler, Alfred. "Billy the Kid: A Case Study in Epic Origins." *Western Folklore* 10 (April 1951).

Allen, Paul. *A History of the American Revolution.* Baltimore, Md.: Franklin Betts, 1822.

Allen, William. *An American Biographical and Historical Dictionary.* 2d ed. Boston: William Hyde & Co., 1832.

Ames, Fisher. "Laocoön." In *The Fear of Conspiracy: Images of Un-American Subversion from the Revolution to the Present.* David Brion Davis, ed. Ithaca, N.Y.: Cornell University Press, 1971 [1799].

Anderson, Benedict. *Imagined Communities: Reflections on the Origin and Spread of Nationalism.* New York: Verso, 1983.

Anon. *Amelia; or the Faithless Briton.* Boston: W. Spotswood and C. P. Wayne, 1798.

Anon. "American Poetry." *Southern Quarterly Review* 1 (1842).

Anon. "Books New and Old: Summer Fiction." *Atlantic Monthly* 90 (1902).

Anon. *A Declaration concerning . . . judges on the life of our late martyr'd soveraign.* London: Printed for George Horton, 1660.

Anon. "The Evolution of the West." *The Independent* (January 30, 1902).

Anon. "Mr. Owen Wister's Stories of Americanism." *The World's Work* 5 (1902).

Anon. "The Problem of the Prairies." *Harper's Weekly* 47 (July 18, 1903).

Anon. *Rebels No Saints, or A Collection of the speeches, private passage, letters, and prayers of those persons lately executed.* London: [n.p.], 1661.

Anon. [Review of *The Virginian*]. *The Nation* 75 (October 23, 1902).

Anon. *Stories about Arnold, the Traitor, André, the Spy, and Champe, the Patriot, for the Children of the United States.* 2d ed. New Haven, Conn.: A. H. Maltby, 1831.

Anon. [untitled]. *The Dial* 32 (June 1, 1902): 392.

Anon. [untitled]. *The Forum* 34 (1902): 223.

Anon. [untitled]. *The Literary Magazine, or Journal of Criticism, Science, and the Arts*, 3d series of the *Analectic Magazine* of Philadelphia, vol. 1 (February 17, 1821).

Arac, Jonathan. "The Politics of *The Scarlet Letter.*" In *Ideology and Classic American Literature.* Sacvan Bercovitch and Myra Jehlen, eds. New York: Cambridge University Press, 1986, 247–66.

Arendt, Hannah. *On Revolution.* New York: Viking Penguin, 1987 [1963].

Aristotle. *The Politics.* T. A. Sinclair, trans. Revised by Trevor J. Saunders. New York: Penguin, 1981.

Assheton, William. *The cry of royal innocent blood heard and answered.* London: Daniel Brown, 1683.

Atwater, Edward E., ed. *The History of the City of New Haven.* New York: W. W. Munsell & Co., 1887.

Bacon, Delia. *The Bride of Fort Edward, founded on an incident of the revolution.* New York: S. Colman, 1839.

Bacon, Leonard. *Thirteen Historical Discourses.* New Haven, Conn.: Durbie & Peck, 1839.

Bailyn, Bernard. *The Ideological Origins of the American Revolution.* Cambridge, Mass.: Belknap of Harvard University Press, 1967.

Baker, Ray Stannard. "The Western Spirit of Restlessness." *Century Magazine* 76 (July 1908).

Balseiro, José Augustín. *The Americas Look at Each Other.* Muna Muñoz Lee, trans. Coral Gables, Fla.: University of Miami Press, 1969.

Bancroft, George. *History of the United States,* vol. 1. Boston: Little, Brown, 1882.

———. *History of the United States,* vol. 2., 14th ed. Boston: Little, Brown, 1848.

Barber, John Warner. *Connecticut Historical Collections . . . relating to the History and Antiquities of Every Town in Connecticut.* New Haven, Conn.: Durrie & Peck, 1836.

———. *Incidents in American History.* 3d ed. New York: George F. Coolidge & Brother, 1847.

Barker, James Nelson. *The Tragedy of Superstition.* Philadelphia: A. R. Poole, 1826.

Barnes, A. S. *Centenary History: One Hundred Years of American Independence.* New York: A. S. Barnes & Co., 1876.

Barnes, Elizabeth. *States of Sympathy: Seduction and Democracy in the American Novel.* New York: Columbia University Press, 1997.

Baron, Dennis E. *Grammar and Good Taste: Reforming the American Language.* New Haven, Conn.: Yale University Press, 1982.

Barry, John Stetson. *The History of Massachusetts, The Colonial Period.* Boston: Phillips, Sampson, & Co., 1855.

Barsness, John A. "Theodore Roosevelt as Cowboy: *The Virginian* as Jacksonian Man." *American Quarterly* 21 (Fall 1969): 609–19.

Bartlett, W. H., and B. B. Woodward, *The History of the United States of North America.* New York: George Virtue & Co. [1856].

Bassett, Francis. *An oration, delivered on Monday, the fifth of July, 1824. . . .* Boston: Wells and Lilly, 1824.

Bate, George. *The Lives, actions, and execution of the prime actors . . . of that horrid murder of . . . King Charles the First.* London: Thomas Vere, 1661.

Beard, James Franklin. "Cooper and the Revolutionary Mythos." *Early American Literature* 11 (1976).

Bechdolt, Frederick R. "The Field Agent of Settlement: The Cowboy's Contribution to American Civilization." *The Outlook* 43 (September 18, 1909).

Bell, Michael Davitt. *Hawthorne and the Historical Romance of New England.* Princeton, N.J.: Princeton University Press, 1971.

Benjamin, Walter. *Illuminations: Essays and Reflections.* Hannah Arendt, ed. Harry Zohn, trans. New York: Schocken Books, 1986.

Benstock, Shari. "*The Scarlet Letter* (a)dorée, or the Female Body Embroidered." In *The Scarlet Letter: Case Studies in Contemporary Criticism.* Ross C. Murfin, ed. New York: Bedford Books, 1991.

Bercovitch, Sacvan. *The American Jeremiad.* Madison: University of Wisconsin Press, 1978.

———. "Endicott's Breastplate: Symbolism and Typology in 'Endicott and the Red Cross.'" *Studies in Short Fiction* 4 (1967).

———. *The Office of the Scarlet Letter.* Baltimore, Md.: Johns Hopkins University Press, 1991.

———. *The Puritan Origins of the American Self.* New Haven, Conn.: Yale University Press, 1975.

———, ed. *Reconstructing American Literary History.* Cambridge, Mass.: Harvard University Press, 1986.

———. *The Rites of Assent: Transformations in American Symbology.* New York: Routledge, 1992.

——— and Myra Jehlen, eds. *Ideology and Classic American Literature.* New York: Cambridge University Press, 1986.

Berwanger, Eugene. *The West and Reconstruction.* Champaign: University of Illinois Press, 1981.

Bewley, Marius. *The Eccentric Design: Form in the Classic American Novel.* New York: Columbia University Press, 1959.

Billington, Ray Allen. *Frederick Jackson Turner: Historian, Scholar, Teacher.* New York: Oxford University Press, 1973.

———. *Land of Savagery, Land of Promise: The European Image of the American Frontier.* New York: W. W. Norton, 1981.

Bishop, Abraham. "A Republican View of Federalist Conspiracy." In *The Fear of Conspiracy: Images of Un-American Subversion from the Revolution to the Present.* David Brion Davis, ed. Ithaca, N.Y.: Cornell University Press, 1971 [1802].

Bloch, Ernst. *The Utopian Function of Art and Literature: Selected Essays.* Jack Zipes and Frank Mecklenburg, trans. Cambridge, Mass.: MIT Press, 1988.

Blumenberg, Hans. *The Legitimacy of the Modern Age.* Robert M. Wallace, trans. Cambridge, Mass.: MIT Press, 1985.

———. *Work on Myth.* Robert Wallace, trans. Cambridge, Mass.: MIT Press, 1985.

Boorstin, Daniel. *The Americans: The National Experience.* New York: Vintage, 1965.

Borges, Jorge Luis. *Labyrinths: Selected Stories and Other Writings.* Donald A. Yates and James E. Irby, eds. Preface by André Maurois. New York: New Directions, 1964.

Bourdieu, Pierre, and Jean-Claude Passeron. *The Inheritors: French Students and Their Relation to Culture.* Richard Nice, trans. Chicago: University of Chicago Press, 1979.

Bradford, Alden. *The History of Massachusetts for Two Hundred Years, from the year 1620 to 1820.* Boston: Hilliard, Gray & Co., 1835.

Bremer, Francis. "In Defense of Regicide: John Cotton on the Execution of Charles I." *William and Mary Quarterly,* 3d series, vol. 37, 1980.

Brodhead, Richard H. *The School of Hawthorne.* New York: Oxford University Press, 1986.

Brooks, Peter. *Reading for the Plot: Design and Intention in Narrative.* New York: Vintage, 1984.

Brown, David. *Walter Scott and the Historical Imagination.* London: Routledge, 1979.

Bryan, William Alfred. *George Washington in American Literature, 1775–1865.* New York: Columbia University Press, 1952.

Budick, Emily Miller. *Fiction and Historical Consciousness: The American Romance Tradition.* New Haven, Conn.: Yale University Press, 1989.

Buel, Richard Jr. *Securing the Revolution: Ideology in American Politics, 1789–1815.* Ithaca, N.Y.: Cornell University Press, 1972.

Bunce, Oliver. *The Romance of the Revolution: Being a History of the Personal Adventures, Romantic Incidents, and Exploits Incidental to the War of Independence.* New York: Bunce and Brother, 1856.

Burgoyne, John. *A State of the Expedition from Canada.* 2d ed. New York: Arno Press Reprint, 1969 [1780].

Burnet, Gilbert. *Bishop Burnet's History of His Own Time.* London: Thomas Ward, 1724 (written before 1715; published posthumously in 1724 and 1734).

Burns, Walter Noble. *The Saga of Billy the Kid.* Garden City, N.Y.: Garden City Publishing Co., 1926.

Bushnell, Horace. *The Fathers of New England.* New York: Charles Scribner, 1850.

———. *Work and Play; or, Literary Varieties.* New York: Charles Scribner, 1864.

Butler, Frederick. *A Complete History of the United States of America.* Hartford, Conn.: Roberts and Burr, 1821.

Bynack, V. P. "Noah Webster's Linguistic Thought and the Idea of an American National Culture." *Journal of the History of Ideas* 45 (1984).

Cady, Edwin H. *The Virginian: The Light of Common Day.* Bloomington: Indiana University Press, 1971.

Calder, Isabel MacBeath. *The New Haven Colony.* New Haven, Conn.: Yale University Press, 1934.

Calhoun, Simeon H. "Oration on the Fourth of July." Williamstown, Mass.: Ridley Bannister, 1829.

Calvert, George. *Arnold and André: An Historical Drama.* Boston: Lee & Shepard, 1876.

Canetti, Elias. *Crowds and Power.* Carol Stewart, trans. New York: Farrar, Straus & Giroux, 1984.

Canfield, Sherman B. *A Lecture on the Life and Character of Oliver Cromwell.* Cleveland, Ohio: Younglove's Steam Press, 1847.

Cappon, Lester J., ed. *The Adams-Jefferson Letters.* Chapel Hill: University of North Carolina Press, 1959.

Carlyle, Thomas. *Oliver Cromwell's Letters and Speeches,* 2 vols. New York: Harper and

Brothers, 1859.

Carpenter, W. H. *The History of Massachusetts, from its earliest settlement to the present time.* Philadelphia: Lippincott, Grambo, & Co., 1854.

Carton, Evan. *The Rhetoric of American Romance.* Baltimore, Md.: Johns Hopkins University Press, 1985.

Caruth, Cathy. *Unclaimed Experience: Trauma, Narrative, and History.* Baltimore, Md.: Johns Hopkins University Press, 1996.

The Case of Major John André . . . who was put to Death by the Rebels. New York: James Rivington, 1780.

Case, Wheeler. *Poems on Several Occurrences, in the Present Grand Struggle for American Liberty.* 4th ed. Trenton, N.J.: Isaac Collins, 1779.

Castronovo, Russ, and Dana D. Nelson, eds. *Materializing Democracy: Toward a Revitalized Cultural Politics.* Durham, N.C.: Duke University Press, 2002.

Caughey, John W. *Their Majesties the Mob.* Chicago: University of Chicago Press, 1960.

Cawelti, John G. *Adventure, Mystery, and Romance: Formula Stories as Art and Popular Culture.* Chicago: University of Chicago Press, 1976.

Certeau, Michel de. *The Writing of History.* Tom Conley, trans. New York: Columbia University Press, 1988.

Chalmers, George. *Political Annals of the Present United Colonies, from their Settlement to the Peace of 1763.* London, 1780.

Child, Lydia Maria. *The Rebels; Or, Boston before the Revolution.* Boston: Phillips, Sampson, & Co., 1850 [1825].

Choate, Rufus. *Addresses and Orations of Rufus Choate.* Boston: Little, Brown, and Co., 1891.

———. *Works.* Samuel Gilman Brown, ed. Boston: Little, Brown, 1862.

Clarendon, Edward Hyde. *History of the Rebellion and Civil Wars in England.* Oxford: Clarendon Press, 1807 [1702–1704].

Cobbs, John L. *Owen Wister.* Boston: Twayne Publishers, 1984.

Cohen, Lester. *The Revolutionary Histories: Contemporary Narratives of the American Revolution.* Ithaca, N.Y.: Cornell University Press, 1980.

Colacurcio, Micahel. *The Province of Piety: Moral History in Hawthorne's Early Tales.* Cambridge, Mass.: Harvard University Press, 1984.

Collections of the Massachusetts Historical Society, 3d series, vol. 7, 1838, and 4th series, vol. 8, 1868.

Collins, James P. *The Autobiography of a Revolutionary Soldier.* John M. Roberts, ed. Clinton, La.: Feliciana Democrat, 1859.

Cooper, James Fenimore. *The Letters and Journals of James Fenimore Cooper.* James Franklin Beard, ed. Cambridge, Mass.: Belknap of Harvard University Press, 1960–1968.

———. *Notions of the Americans: Picked up by a Traveling Bachelor.* Gary Williams, ed. Albany, N.Y.: SUNY Press, 1991.

———. *The Spy, A Tale of the Neutral Ground.* James H. Pickering, ed. Schenectady, N.Y.: New College and University Press, 1971.

———. *The Wept of Wish-Ton-Wish.* Philadelphia: Carey, Lea & Blanchard, 1836.

———. *Wyandotté, or the Hutted Knoll: A Tale.* Thomas Philbrick and Marianne Philbrick, eds. Albany, N.Y.: SUNY Press, 1982.

Countryman, Edward. *A People in Revolution: The American Revolution and Political Society in New York, 1760–1790.* New York: W. W. Norton, 1989.

Crain, Caleb. *American Sympathy: Men, Friendship, and Literature in the New Nation.* New Haven, Conn.: Yale University Press, 2001.

Crawford, T. Hugh. "Cooper's *Spy* and the Theater of Honor." *American Literature* 62 (1990).

Crèvecoeur, J. Hector St. John. *Letters from an American Farmer and Sketches of Eighteenth-Century America.* Albert E. Stone, ed. New York: Viking Penguin, 1981.

Crews, Frederick. *The Sins of the Fathers: Hawthorne's Psychological Themes.* Berkeley: University of California Press, 1989.

Crowley, J. Donald, ed. *Hawthorne: The Critical Heritage.* New York: Barnes & Noble, 1970.

Cumings, Henry. *A Sermon Preached before Thomas Cushing.* Boston: T. & J. Fleet, 1783.

Cushing, Caleb. *Eulogy* [Newburyport, Mass.]. In anon. *A Selection of Eulogies . . . in Honor of . . . John Adams and Thomas Jefferson.* Hartford, Conn.: Norton and Russell, 1826.

Cushing, Elizabeth Foster. *Saratoga; A Tale of the Revolution.* Boston: Cummings, Hilliard, & Co., 1824.

Custis, George Washington Parke. *Recollections and Private memoirs of Washington, by his adopted son.* Benson J. Lossing, ed. New York: Derby & Jackson, 1860.

Davenport, John. *The Saints Anchor-Hold, in All Stormes and Tempests.* London: W. L. for George Hurlock, 1661.

Davidson, Cathy N. *Revolution and the Word: The Rise of the Novel in America.* New York: Oxford University Press, 1986.

Davies, Samuel. *Sermons.* William B. Sprague, ed. Philadelphia: Presbyterian Board of Publication, 1864.

Davis, David Brion *The Fear of Conspiracy: Images of Un-American Subversion from the Revolution to the Present.* Ithaca, N.Y.: Cornell University Press, 1971.

———. "Ten-Gallon Hero." In *The Western: A Collection of Critical Essays.* James K. Folsom, ed. Englewood Cliffs, N.J.: Prentice Hall, 1979.

Dean, John. "The Story of the Embarkation of Cromwell and his friends for New England." In *The New England Historical and Genealogical Register,* 1866.

Dekker, George. *The American Historical Romance.* New York: Cambridge University Press, 1987.

———. *James Fenimore Cooper: The American Scott.* New York: Barnes and Noble, 1967.

———, and John P. McWilliams, eds. *Fenimore Cooper: The Critical Heritage.* Boston: Routledge & Kegan Paul, 1973.

Denning, Michael. *Mechanic Accents: Dime Novels and Working-Class Culture in America.* New York: Verso, 1987.

Devens, R. M. *Our First Century.* Springfield, Mass.: C. A. Nichols & Co., 1880.

Dever, John F., ed. *Memorial of William McKinley from the City of Boston.* Boston: Municipal Printing Office, 1902.

Dirks, Nicholas B., Geoff Eley, and Sherry B. Orner, eds. *Culture/Power/History: A Reader in Contemporary Social Theory.* Princeton, N.J.: Princeton University Press, 1994.

Douglas, Mary. *Purity and Danger: An Analysis of the Concepts of Pollution and Taboo.*

New York: Ark, 1988.

Downes, Paul. *Democracy, Revolution, and Monarchism in Early American Literature.* New York: Cambridge University Press, 2002.

Drago, Harry Sinclair. *The Great Range Wars: Violence on the Grasslands.* New York: Dodd, Mead & Co., 1970.

Dray, Philip. *At the Hands of Persons Unknown: The Lynching of Black America.* New York: Random House, 2002.

Dunlap, William. *André: A Tragedy in Five Acts.* Brander Matthews, ed. New York: Dunlap Society, 1887 [1798].

Durkheim, Émile. *Émile Durkheim: Selected Writings.* Anthony Giddens, ed. and trans. New York: Cambridge University Press, 1972.

———. *Suicide.* George Simpson, ed. John A. Spaulding and George Simpson, trans. New York: The Free Press, 1951.

Dwight, Timothy. *A Discourse on Some Events of the Last Century.* New Haven, Conn.: Ezra Read, 1801.

———. *Travels in New England and New York.* New York: Timothy Dwight, 1821.

Eikon Basilike: The Pourtracture of His Sacred Majestie in His Solitudes and Sufferings. London, 1649.

Emerson, Andrew L. *An Oration delivered at Portland, July 5, 1824.* Portland, Maine: Adams & Paine, 1824.

Emerson, Ralph Waldo. *Early Lectures,* vol. 3. Stephen E. Whicher and Robert E. Spiller, eds. Cambridge, Mass.: Belknap of Harvard University Press, 1972.

———. *Journals and Miscellaneous Notebooks,* vol. 3. William H. Gilman and Alfred R. Ferguson, eds. Cambridge, Mass.: Harvard University Press, 1960.

———. *Selections from Ralph Waldo Emerson.* Stephen E. Whicher, ed. Boston: Houghton Mifflin, 1960.

Erikson, Kai T. *Wayward Puritans: A Study in the Sociology of Deviance.* New York: Macmillan, 1966.

Etulian, Richard W. *Owen Wister.* Boise, Idaho: Boise State College Press, 1973.

Everett, Edward. "Oration." In *The American Literary Revolution, 1783–1837.* Robert E. Spiller, ed. New York: Doubleday & Co., 1967.

Fairbanks, Gerry. *An Oration, pronounced July 4, 1821.* Boston: True, Green, & Field, 1821.

Faulkner, William. *Absalom, Absalom!* New York: Vintage Random House, 1987 [1936].

———. *The Faulkner Reader: Selections from the Works of William Faulkner.* New York: Random House, 1954.

Feidelson, Charles Jr. *Symbolism and American Literature.* Chicago: University of Chicago Press, 1953.

Ferguson, Robert A. " 'We Hold These Truths': Strategies of Control in the Literature of the Founders." In *Reconstructing American Literary History.* Sacvan Bercovitch, ed., 1–28. Cambridge, Mass.: Harvard University Press, 1986.

Ferris, Ina. *The Achievement of Literary Authority: Gender, History, and the Waverly Novels.* Ithaca, N.Y.: Cornell University Press, 1991.

Field, Barnum. *An Oration, pronounced in commemoration of American Independence.* Dedham, Mass.: H. & W. Mann, 1822.

Filson, John. *The Discovery, Settlement And Present State of Kentucke . . . To which is added*

An Appendix, Containing the Adventures of Col. Daniel Boon . . . Wilmington, Del.: James Adams, 1784.

Finch, Heneage. *An Exact and Most Impartial account of the indictment, arraignment, trial and judgment . . . of twenty-nine regicides.* London: R. Scot, T. Basset, R. Chiswell, & F. Wright, 1679.

Fisher, Philip. *Hard Facts: Setting and Form in the American Novel.* New York: Oxford University Press, 1987.

Fliegelman, Jay. *Declaring Independence: Jefferson, Natural Language, and the Culture of Performance.* Stanford, Calif.: Stanford University Press, 1993.

Forgie, George B. *Patricide in the House Divided: A Psychological Interpretation of Lincoln and His Age.* New York: W. W. Norton, 1979.

Forsyth, James W., and F. D. Grant. *The War Department's Report of an Expedition up the Yellowstone River, made in 1875.* Washington, D.C.: Government Printing Office, 1875.

Franklin, Wayne. *The New World of James Fenimore Cooper.* Chicago: University of Chicago Press, 1982.

Freeman, Castle Jr. "Owen Wister: Brief Life of a Western Mythmaker: 1860–1938." *Harvard Magazine* 104, no. 6 (2002): 42.

Frewen, Moreton. *Melton Mowbray and Other Memories.* London: Herbert Jenkins Ltd., 1924.

[Frost, John.] *The Heroes and Battles of the American Revolution.* Philadelphia: Willis P. Hazard, 1845.

Frye, Northrop. *Anatomy of Criticism: Four Essays.* Princeton, N.J.: Princeton University Press, 1971.

Fussell, Edwin. *American Literature and the American West.* Princeton, N.J.: Princeton University Press, 1966.

Gardiner, W. H. "Review." *North American Review* 15 (July 1822), in *Critical Heritage,* ed. Dekker and McWilliams.

Garrett, Pat. *The Authentic Life of Billy, the Kid.* Santa Fe: New Mexico Printing and Publishing, 1882.

[Gazer, Giles]. *Frederick de Algeroy, The Hero of Camden Plains: A Revolutionary Tale.* New York: J. & J. Harper, 1825.

Geertz, Clifford. *The Interpretation of Cultures.* New York: Basic Books, 1973.

The General Repository and Review 2 (October 12, 1812).

Gerlach, Larry R., ed. *The American Revolution: New York as a Case Study.* Belmont, Calif.: Wadsworth Publishing Co., 1972.

Goodrich, Charles. *A History of the United States of America,* 3d ed. Hartford, Conn.: Barber & Robinson, 1824.

Gould, Lewis L. *Wyoming: A Political History, 1868–1896.* New Haven, Conn.: Yale University Press, 1968.

Gould, Philip. *Covenant and Republic: Historical Romance and the Politics of Puritanism.* New York: Cambridge University Press, 1996.

Greene, Theodore P. *America's Heroes: The Changing Models of Success in American Magazines.* New York: Oxford University Press, 1970.

Greenough, Horatio. *Letters of Horatio Greenough, American Sculptor.* Nathalia Wright, ed. Madison: University of Wisconsin Press, 1972.

Guizot, François. *History of the English Revolution of 1640.* William Hazlitt, trans. London: Bell & Daldy, 1868.

Gunning, Sandra. *Race, Rape, and Lynching: The Red Record of American Literature, 1890–1912.* New York: Oxford University Press, 1996.

Gura, Philip. *The Wisdom of Words: Language, Theology, and Literature in the New England Renaissance.* Middletown, Conn.: Wesleyan University Press, 1981.

Gustafson, Thomas. *Representative Words: Politics, Literature, and the American Language, 1776–1865.* New York: Cambridge University Press, 1992.

[Hale, Sarah]. "Review." *Port Folio*, 4th series, vol. 13, 1822.

Hamilton, Alexander. *Papers of Alexander Hamilton*, vol. 2 (1779–1781). Harold C. Scott, ed. New York: Columbia University Press, 1961.

Handley, William R. *Marriage, Violence, and the Nation in the American Literary West.* New York: Cambridge University Press, 2002.

Harger, Charles Moreau. "The Prairie Woman: Yesterday and To-Day." *The Outlook* 70 (April 26, 1902).

———. "To-Day's Chance for the Western Settler." *The Outlook* 80 (December 17, 1904).

Harrison, Frederic. *George Washington and Other American Addresses.* New York: Macmillan, 1901.

Hawthorne, Nathaniel. *American Claimant Manuscripts*, vol. 12 of *Works.* Edward H. Davidson, Claude M. Simpson, and L. Neal Smith. eds. Columbus: Ohio State University Press, 1977.

———. *The English Notebooks.* Randall Stewart, ed. New York: Modern Language Association, 1941.

———. *French and Italian Notebooks*, vol. 14 of *Works.* Thomas Woodson, ed. Centenary ed. Columbus: Ohio State University Press, 1980.

———. *The House of the Seven Gables.* Seymour L. Gross, ed. New York: Norton, 1967.

———. *Letters, 1813–1843*, vol. 15 of *Works.* Thomas Woodson, L. Neal Smith, and Norman H. Pearson, eds. Columbus: Ohio State University Press, 1984.

———. *Letters, 1853–1856*, volume 17 of *Works.* Thomas Woodson, L. Neal Smith, and Norman H. Pearson, eds. Columbus: Ohio State University Press, 1987.

———. *Novels*, ed. Millicent Bell. New York: Library of America, 1983.

———. *The Scarlet Letter*, ed. Harry Levin. Boston: Houghton Mifflin, 1960.

———. *Tales and Sketches*, ed. Roy Harvey Pearce. New York: Library of America, 1982.

———. *True Stories from History and Biography*, vol. 6 of *Works.* Thomas Woodson and Bill Ellis, eds. Centenary ed. Columbus: Ohio State University Press, 1972.

———. *Twice-Told Tales*, vol. 9 of *Works.* William Charvat, Roy Harvey Pearce, and Claude M. Simpson, eds. Centenary ed. Columbus: Ohio State University Press, 1974.

Henderson, Harry B. III. *Versions of the Past: The Historical Imagination in American Fiction.* New York: Oxford University Press, 1974.

Hildreth, Richard. *Theory of Politics: An Inquiry into the Foundations of Governments and the Causes and Progress of Political Revolutions.* New York: Harper, 1853 [1841].

Hilliard, Michel René. *Miss McCrea: A Novel of the American Revolution.* Lewis Leary, ed. Eric LaGuardia, trans. Gainesville, Fla.: Scholars' Facsimiles and Reprints, 1958 [1784].

Hoadly, Laommi Ives. *An Address, delivered . . . July 5, 1824.* Worcester, Mass.: William Manning, 1824.

Hobsbawm, Eric. *Nations and Nationalism since 1780: Programme, Myth, Reality.* Cambridge: Cambridge University Press, 1990.

Holden, James Austin. "The Influence of the Death of Jane McCrea on the Burgoyne Campaign." *Proceedings of the New York State Historical Association* 12 (1913).

Hollister, G. H. *The History of Connecticut from the First Settlement of the Colony,* 2d ed. Hartford, Conn.: Case, Tiffany, & Co., 1857.

Horsman, Reginald. *Race and Manifest Destiny: The Origins of American Racial Anglo-Saxonism.* Cambridge, Mass.: Harvard University Press, 1981.

Hough, Emerson. *The Story of the Cowboy.* New York: Grosset and Dunlap, 1897.

Hubbard, William. *Narrative of the Trouble with the Indians.* Boston: John Foster, 1677.

Hughes, Helen. *The Historical Romance.* New York: Routledge, 1993.

Hume, David. *History of Great Britain: The Reigns of James I and Charles I.* Duncan Forbes, ed. Harmondsworth, England: Penguin, 1970 [1754–1762].

Humphreys, David, Joel Barlow, John Trumbull, and Lemeul Hopkins. *The Anarchiad: A New England Poem.* William K. Bottorf, ed. Gainesville, Fla.: Scholars' Reprints, 1967.

Huntington, Frederic D. *Address for the Celebration of the 200th Anniversary of the Settlement at Hadley, June 8, 1859.* Northampton, Mass.: Bridgman & Childs, 1859.

Hutchinson, John, and Anthony D. Smith, eds. *Nationalism.* New York: Oxford University Press, 1994.

Hutchinson Papers. *Collections of the Massachusetts Historical Society,* 3rd series, vol. 1, 1846.

Hutchinson, Thomas. *The History of the Colony and Province of Massachusetts-Bay.* Lawrence Shaw Mayo, ed. Cambridge, Mass.: Harvard University Press, 1936.

Hutner, Gordon. *Secrets and Sympathy: Forms of Disclosure in Hawthorne's Novels.* Athens: University of Georgia Press, 1988.

Irving, Washington. *The Life of George Washington.* New York: G. P. Putnam, 1856.

Jacobsen, Joel. *Such Men as Billy the Kid: The Lincoln County War Reconsidered.* Lincoln: University of Nebraska Press, 1994.

James, William. *The Will to Believe and Other Essays in Popular Philosophy.* New York: Dover Publications, 1956.

Jameson, Fredric. *The Political Unconscious: Narrative as a Socially Symbolic Act.* Ithaca, N.Y.: Cornell University Press, 1981.

Jefferson, Thomas. *Writings.* Merrill D. Peterson, ed. New York: Library of America, 1984.

Jehlen, Myra. "The Novel and the Middle-Class in America." *Salmagundi* 36 (1977).

[Jenardo, Don, pseud.]. "The True Life of Billy the Kid," in *The Five Cent Wide Awake Library,* vol. 1, no. 451. Frank Tousey, ed. (n.p.: n.p., August 29, 1881).

Jordan, Cynthia. *Second Stories: The Politics of Language, Form, and Gender in Early American Fictions.* Chapel Hill: University of North Carolina Press, 1989.

Judd, Sylvester. *History of Hadley.* George Sheldon, ed. Springfield, Mass.: H. R. Hunting & Co., 1905.

Kammen, Michael. *A Season of Youth: The American Revolution and the Historical Imagination.* New York: Alfred A. Knopf, 1978.

Kent, Charles W. "Marks of Distinction" (a section of a collaborative article, "The Most American Books"). *The Outlook* 72 (1902): 787.

Knowles, James Davis. "Oration on the Fourth of July." Washington, D.C.: John S. Meehan, 1823.

Kramer, Michael P. *Imagining Language in America: From the Revolution to the Civil War.* Princeton, N.J.: Princeton University Press, 1992.

Lamb, Richard. *An Original and Authentic Journal of Occurrences during the Late American War.* Dublin: Wilkinson & Courtney, 1809.

Lambert, Edward Rodolphus. *History of the Colony of New Haven.* New Haven, Conn.: Hitchcock & Stafford, 1838.

Lears, T. J. Jackson. *No Place of Grace: Antimodernism and the Transformation of American Culture, 1880–1920.* New York: Pantheon, 1981.

Lee, Henry. *Memoirs of the War in the Southern Department of the United States.* Philadelphia: Bradford and Inskeep, 1812.

Leisy, Ernest E. *The American Historical Novel.* Norman: University of Oklahoma Press, 1950.

Levine, Robert S. *Conspiracy and Romance: Studies in Brockden Brown, Cooper, Hawthorne, and Melville.* New York: Cambridge University Press, 1989.

Lewis, R. W. B. *The American Adam: Innocence, Tragedy, and Tradition in the Nineteenth Century.* Chicago: University of Chicago Press, 1955.

Lighton, William R. "Where Is the West?" *The Outlook* 74 (July 18, 1903).

Limerick, Patricia Nelson. *The Legacy of Conquest: The Unbroken Past of the American West.* New York: Norton, 1987.

Lippard, George. *Washington and His Generals, or Legends of the Revolution.* Freeport, N.Y.: American Fiction Reprints, 1971 [1847].

Locke, John. *An Essay concerning Human Understanding.* London: William Tegg and Co., 1879.

Lodge, Henry Cabot, and Theodore Roosevelt. *Hero Tales from American History.* New York: Charles Scribner's Sons, 1926.

Longmore, Paul K. *The Invention of George Washington.* Berkeley: University of California Press, 1988.

Looby, Christopher. *Voicing America: Language, Literary Form, and the Origins of the United States.* Chicago: University of Chicago Press, 1996.

Lossing, Benjamin J. *The Field Book of the American Revolution.* Cottonport, La.: Polyanthos, 1972 [1850–1852].

Lotman, Yuri M. *Universe of the Mind: A Semiotic Theory of Culture.* Umberto Eco, ed. Ann Shukman, trans. Bloomington: Indiana University Press, 1990.

Lukács, Georg. *The Historical Novel.* Fredric Jameson, ed. Hannah Mitchell and Stanley Mitchell, trans. Lincoln: University of Nebraska Press, 1983.

Macherey, Pierre. *A Theory of Literary Production.* Geoffrey Wall, trans. New York: Routledge & Kegan Paul, 1986.

Manzoni, Alessandro. *On the Historical Novel (1850).* Sandra Berman, ed. and trans. Lincoln: University of Nebraska Press, 1984.

Marcus, George E., ed. *Rereading Cultural Anthropology.* Durham, N.C.: Duke University Press, 1992.

Marshal, John. *The Life of George Washington.* 2d ed. Philadelphia: James Crissy, 1832.

Marvell, Andrew. *The Poems and Letters of Andrew Marvell,* vol. 1. H. M. Margoliouth, ed. Oxford: Clarendon Press, 1927.

Mather, Cotton. *Magnalia Christi Americana*. Hartford, Conn.: Silas Andrus & Co., 1855 [1702].

Mather, Increase. *History of King Philip's War, with a History of the Same War by Cotton Mather*. Samuel G. Drake, ed. Albany, N.Y.: J. Munsell, 1862.

Mather Papers. *Collections of the Massachusetts Historical Society*, 4th series, vol. 8, 1868.

Matthews, Brander. *The Historical Novel and Other Essays*. New York: Charles Scribner's Sons, 1901.

Mauss, Marcel. *The Gift: Form and Reason for Exchange in Archaic Societies*. W. D. Halls, trans. Mary Douglas, foreword. New York: W. W. Norton, 1990.

McWilliams, John P. Jr. *The American Epic: Transforming a Genre, 1770–1860*. New York: Cambridge University Press, 1989.

———. *Hawthorne, Melville, and the American Character: A Looking-Glass Business*. New York: Cambridge University Press, 1984.

———. *Political Justice in a Republic: James Fenimore Cooper's America*. Berkeley: University of California Press, 1972.

Michelson, Charles. "The Vigilantes of the West." *Munsey's Magazine* 25 (1901).

Millington, Richard H. *Practicing Romance: Narrative Form and Cultural Engagement in Hawthorne's Fiction*. Princeton, N.J.: Princeton University Press, 1992.

Minutes of the Committee and of the First Commission for Detecting and Defeating Conspiracies in the State of New York. New York: New York Historical Society, 1924.

Mitchell, Lee Clark. *Westerns: Making the Man in Fiction and Film*. Chicago: University of Chicago Press, 1996.

———. " 'When You Call Me That . . .: 'Tall Talk and Male Hegemony in *The Virginian.*' " *PMLA* 102 (January 1987).

Mizruchi, Susan L. *The Power of Historical Knowledge: Narrating the Past in Hawthorne, James, and Dreiser*. Princeton, N.J.: Princeton University Press, 1988.

———. *The Science of Sacrifice: American Literature and Modern Social Theory*. Princeton, N.J.: Princeton University Press, 1998.

Monroe, James. "Fourth Annual Message," in *The Statesman's Manual: The Addresses and Messages of the Presidents of the United States . . . from 1789 to 1846*. Edwin Williams, ed. New York: Edward Walker, 1846.

———. "Second Annual Message," in *The Statesman's Manual: The Addresses and Messages of the Presidents of the United States . . . from 1789 to 1846*. Edwin Williams, ed. New York: Edward Walker, 1846.

———. "Seventh Annual Message," in *The Statesman's Manual: The Addresses and Messages of the Presidents of the United States . . . from 1789 to 1846*. Edwin Williams, ed. New York: Edward Walker, 1846.

Moore, Frank, ed. *Diary of the American Revolution, from Newspapers and Original Sources*. New York: Charles Scribner's Sons, 1860.

Morse, Jedidiah. *Annals of the American Revolution*. Hartford, Conn.: [n.p.], 1824.

———. "The Present Dangers and Consequent Duties of the Citizens," in *The Fear of Conspiracy: Images of Un-American Subversion from the Revolution to the Present*. David Brion Davis, ed. Ithaca, N.Y.: Cornell University Press.

Moses, Norton H., comp. *Lynching and Vigilantism in the United States: An Annotated Bibliography*. Westport, Conn.: Greenwood Press, 1997.

Moultrie, Alexander. "Oration on the Fourth of July." Charleston, S.C.: A. E. Miller, 1822.

Muddiman, J. G., ed. *The Trial of King Charles the First*. New ed. by Alan Dershowitz. Birmingham, Ala.: Notable Trials Library, 1990.

Nelson, Dana D. "Representative/Democracy: The Political Work of Countersymbolic Representation," in *Materializing Democracy: Toward a Revitalized Cultural Politics*. Russ Castronovo and Dana D. Nelson, eds. Durham, N.C.: Duke University Press, 2002.

Nelson, Henry Loomis. "The Spirit of the West." *Harper's Monthly* 109 (July 1904).

Nolan, Frederick. *The Lincoln County War: A Documentary History*. Norman: University of Oklahoma Press, 1992.

Orel, Harold. *The Historical Novel from Scott to Sabatini: Changing Attitudes toward a Literary Genre, 1814–1920*. New York: St. Martin's Press, 1995.

Paine, Thomas. *Common Sense and Other Political Writings*. Nelson F. Adkins, ed. New York: Macmillan, 1953.

Palmer, H. E. *The Powder River Indian Expedition, 1865: A Paper Read . . . February 2, 1887*. Omaha, Nebr.: The Republican Co., 1887.

Payne, William Morton. "Review." *The Dial* 33 (October 16, 1902).

Pearce, Roy Harvey. "Romance and the Study of History," in *Hawthorne Centenary Essays*. Roy Harvey Pearce, ed. Columbus: Ohio State University Press, 1964.

Peck, H. Daniel. *A World by Itself: The Pastoral Moment in Cooper's Fiction*. New Haven, Conn.: Yale University Press, 1977.

Petrie, Charles, ed. *The Letters, Speeches, and Proclamations of King Charles I*. London: Cassell & Co., Ltd., 1935.

Pfister, Joel. *The Production of Personal Life: Class, Gender, and the Psychological in Hawthorne's Fiction*. Stanford, Calif.: Stanford University Press, 1991.

Pictorial History of the American Revolution, The. New York: Robert Sears, 1846.

Pocock, J. G. A. *The Machiavellian Moment: Florentine Political Thought and the Atlantic Republican Tradition*. Princeton, N.J.: Princeton University Press, 1975.

———. *Politics, Language, and Time: Essays on Political Thought and History*. New York: Athenaeum, 1971.

Prats, Armando José. *Invisible Natives: Myth and Identity in the American Western*. Ithaca, N.Y.: Cornell University Press, 2002.

Proceedings of a Board of General Officers . . . Respecting Major John André, September 29, 1780. Providence, R.I.: John Carter, 1780.

Proceedings of the Massachusetts Historical Society, 1st series, vol. 3, 1855–1858.

Pynchon, Thomas. *The Crying of Lot 49*. New York: Harper and Row, 1986.

Quaife, Milo Milton. *Kit Carson's Autobiography*. Chicago: Lakeside Press, 1935.

Ramsay, David. *The History of the American Revolution*. Lester H. Cohen, ed. Indianapolis, Ind.: Liberty Classics, 1990 [1789].

Reynolds, David S. *Beneath the American Renaissance: The Subversive Imagination in the Age of Emerson and Melville*. Cambridge, Mass.: Harvard University Press, 1988.

Reynolds, Larry. *European Revolutions and the American Literary Renaissance*. New Haven, Conn.: Yale University Press, 1988.

Rigney, Ann. *Imperfect Histories: The Elusive Past and the Legacy of Romantic Historicism*. Ithaca, N.Y.: Cornell University Press, 2001.

Ringe, Donald. "The American Revolution in American Romance." *American Literature* 49 (1977).

————. *James Fenimore Cooper.* Updated ed. Boston: Twayne, 1988.

Robbins, Chandler. *The Regicides Sheltered in New England: A Lecture . . . Delivered before the Lowell Institute, February 5, 1869.* Boston: John Wilson and Son, 1869.

Roberts, Robert B. *New York's Forts in the Revolution.* London: Associate University Presses, 1980.

Rollinson, John K. *Wyoming Cattle Trails.* Caldwell, Idaho: Caxton Printers, 1948.

Roosevelt, Theodore. *Address . . . upon the Occasion of the Opening of the Louisiana Purchase Exposition at St. Louis, April 30, 1903.* Ayer Collection, Newberry Library.

Rosaldo, Renato. *Culture and Truth: The Remaking of Social Analysis.* Boston: Beacon Press, 1989.

Rosenberg, Bruce A. *The Neutral Ground: The André Affair and the Background of Cooper's* The Spy. Westport, Conn.: Greenwood Press, 1994.

St. George, Robert Blair, ed. *Possible Pasts: Becoming Colonial in Early America.* Ithaca, N.Y.: Cornell University Press, 2000.

Samuels, Shirley. *Romances of the Republic: Women, the Family, and Violence in the Literature of the Early American Nation.* New York: Oxford University Press, 1996.

Scharnhorst, Gary. "*The Virginian* as Founding Father." *Arizona Quarterly* 40 (1984): 227–41.

Scott, Walter. *Peveril of the Peak.* Edinburgh: Archibald Constable, 1822.

Sears, Hamblen. "The Historical Importance of *The Virginian.*" *Book Buyer* 25 (October 1902).

Seelye, John. "Introduction" to *The Virginian.* New York: Viking Penguin, 1988.

Simmel, Georg. *The Sociology of Georg Simmel.* Kurt H. Wolff, ed. and trans. New York: Free Press, 1950.

Simms, William Gilmore. "The Writings of Cooper," *Magnolia,* n.s., vol. 1 (1842), in *Critical Heritage,* ed. Dekker and McWilliams, 218–19. Boston: Routledge and Kegan Paul, 1973.

Simpson, David. *The Politics of American English, 1776–1850.* New York: Oxford University Press, 1986.

Slotkin, Richard. *Gunfighter Nation: The Myth of the Frontier in Twentieth-Century America.* New York: Athenaeum, 1992.

————. *Regeneration through Violence: The Mythology of the American Frontier, 1600–1860.* Middletown, Conn.: Wesleyan University Press, 1973.

Smith, Helena Huntington. *The War on Powder River.* New York: McGraw Hill, 1966.

Smith, Henry Nash. *Virgin Land: The American West as Symbol and Myth.* Cambridge, Mass.: Harvard University Press, 1978.

Snowden, Richard. *A History of the American Revolution, in Scripture Style.* Frederic Co., Md.: Matthias Bartgis, 1823.

Sommer, Doris. *Foundational Fictions: The National Romances of Latin America.* Berkeley: University of California Press, 1992.

Sparks, Jared. *American Biography: Benedict Arnold.* New York: Harper & Brothers, 1902.

————. *The Life of George Washington.* Boston: Little, Brown, & Co., 1852.

Spiller, Robert E., ed. *The American Literary Revolution, 1783–1837.* New York: Doubleday & Co., 1967.

Sprague, Charles. "Oration on the Fourth of July." Boston: True and Greene, 1825.

Sprague, Joseph. *Eulogy.* In anon. *A Selection of Eulogies . . . in Honor of . . . John Adams and Thomas Jefferson.* Hartford, Conn.: Norton and Russell, 1826.

Steckmesser, Kent Ladd. *The Western Hero in History and Legend.* Norman: University of Oklahoma Press, 1965.

Stiles, Ezra. *A History of Three of the Judges of King Charles I.* Hartford, Conn.: Elisha Babcock, 1794.

Stokes, Frances. See Wister, Fanny Kemble.

Taussig, Michael. *Defacement: Public Secrecy and the Labor of the Negative.* Stanford, Calif.: Stanford University Press, 1999.

Thacher, James. *Military Journal of the American Revolution.* Hartford, Conn.: Hurlbut, Williams & Co., 1862 [1823].

Thomas, Brook. "Citizen Hester: *The Scarlet Letter* as Civic Myth." *American Literary History* 13, no. 2 (2001): 181–211.

Tise, Larry E. *The American Counterrevolution: A Retreat from Liberty, 1783–1800.* Mechanicsburg, Pa.: Stackpole Books, 1998.

Tompkins, Jane. *West of Everything: The Inner Life of Westerns.* New York: Oxford University Press, 1992.

Trachtenberg, Alan. *The Incorporation of America: Culture and Society in the Gilded Age.* New York: Hill and Wang, 1982.

Triggs, J. H. *History of Cheyenne and Northern Wyoming.* Omaha, Neb.: Herald Steam Book and Job Printing House, 1876.

Trumbull, John. *Autobiography, Reminiscences and Letters of John Trumbull from 1756 to 1841.* New York: Wiley & Putnam, 1841. In *The Rising Glory of America, 1760–1820,* rev. ed. Gordon S. Wood, ed. Boston: Northeastern University Press, 1990.

Turner, Victor. *Dramas, Fields, and Metaphors: Symbolic Action in Human Society.* Ithaca, N.Y.: Cornell University Press, 1974.

———. *The Forest of Symbols: Aspects of Ndembu Ritual.* Ithaca, N.Y.: Cornell University Press, 1967.

———. "Liminal to Liminoid, in Play, Flow, and Ritual: An Essay in Comparative Symbology." *Journal of the History of Ideas* 45 (1984): 53–92.

Tuveson, Ernest Lee. *Redeemer Nation: The Idea of America's Millennial Role.* Chicago: University of Chicago Press, 1968.

Tyler, Stephen A. "On Being Out of Words." In *Rereading Cultural Anthropology.* George E. Marcus, ed. Durham, N.C.: Duke University Press, 1992.

United States Literary Gazette 3 (11–12), September 1826.

United States Literary Gazette 9 (3), August 1, 1825.

Virgil. *The Eclogues.* Guy Lee, trans. New York: Penguin, 1984.

Wald, Priscilla. *Constituting Americans: Cultural Anxiety and Narrative Form.* Durham, N.C.: Duke University Press, 1995.

Walzer, Michael. *Obligations: Essays on Disobedience, War, and Citizenship.* Cambridge, Mass.: Harvard University Press, 1970.

Warner, Michael. *The Letters of the Republic: Publication and the Public Sphere in Eighteenth-Century America.* Cambridge, Mass.: Harvard University Press, 1990.

Warren, Mercy Otis. *History of the Rise, Progress, and Termination of the American Revolution.* Lester H. Cohen, ed. Indianapolis, Ind.: Liberty Classics, 1988 [1805].

250 *Bibliography*

Washington, George. *George Washington: A Collection.* W. B. Allen, ed. Indianapolis, Ind.: Liberty Classics, 1988.

Webster, Noah. *Dissertations on the English Language.* Boston: Isaiah Thomas, 1789.

———. 1828. Preface to *An American Dictionary of the English Language.* Reprinted in *The American Literary Revolution, 1783–1837.* Robert E. Spiller, ed. New York: Doubleday & Co., 1967.

Weems, Mason Locke. *Life of George Washington.* Marcus Cunliffe, ed. Cambridge, Mass.: Belknap of Harvard University Press, 1962.

Welles, Lemeul A. *The History of the Regicides in New England.* New York: Grafton Press, 1927.

Welter, Rush. *The Mind of America, 1820–1860.* New York: Columbia University Press, 1975.

Wesseling, Elisabeth. *Writing History as a Prophet: Postmodernist Innovations of the Historical Novel.* Amsterdam: John Benjamins Publishing Co., 1991.

Whitman, Walt. *An American Primer.* Facsimile ed. Horace Traubel, ed. San Francisco: City Lights Books, 1970.

———. *Complete Poetry and Selected Prose by Walt Whitman.* James E. Miller Jr., ed. Boston: Houghton Mifflin, 1955.

Wilson, David. *The Life of Jane McCrea, with an Account of Burgoyne's Expedition in 1777.* New York: Baker, Godwin & Co., 1853.

Wilson, James. *Works.* Philadelphia: Lorenzo Press, 1804.

Wirt, William. *The Letters of the British Spy.* 7th ed. Baltimore, Md.: Fielding Lucas [1820].

Wister, Fanny Kemble. *My Father, Owen Wister.* Laramie, Wyo.: [self-published], 1952.

———, ed. *Owen Wister Out West: His Journals and Letters.* Chicago: University of Chicago Press, 1958.

Wister, Owen. *Red Men and White.* New York: Macmillan, 1928.

———. *The Virginian: A Horseman of the Plains.* John Seelye, ed. New York: Viking Penguin, 1988.

Wood, Gordon S., ed. *The Rising Glory of America, 1760–1820,* rev. ed. Boston: Northeastern University Press, 1990.

Woods, Walter. *Billy the Kid* (1903). In *The Great Diamond Robbery and Other Recent Melodramas.* G. H. Leverton, ed. Princeton, N.J.: Princeton University Press, 1940.

Woodworth, Samuel. *The Champions of Freedom, or the Mysterious Chief.* New York: Charles N. Baldwin, 1816.

Worster, Donald. *Under Western Skies: Nature and History in the American West.* New York: Oxford University Press, 1992.

Wright, Frances. *Views of Society and Manners in America.* Paul R. Baker, ed. Cambridge, Mass.: Belknap of Harvard University Press, 1963.

INDEX